I0714448

WASH DAY

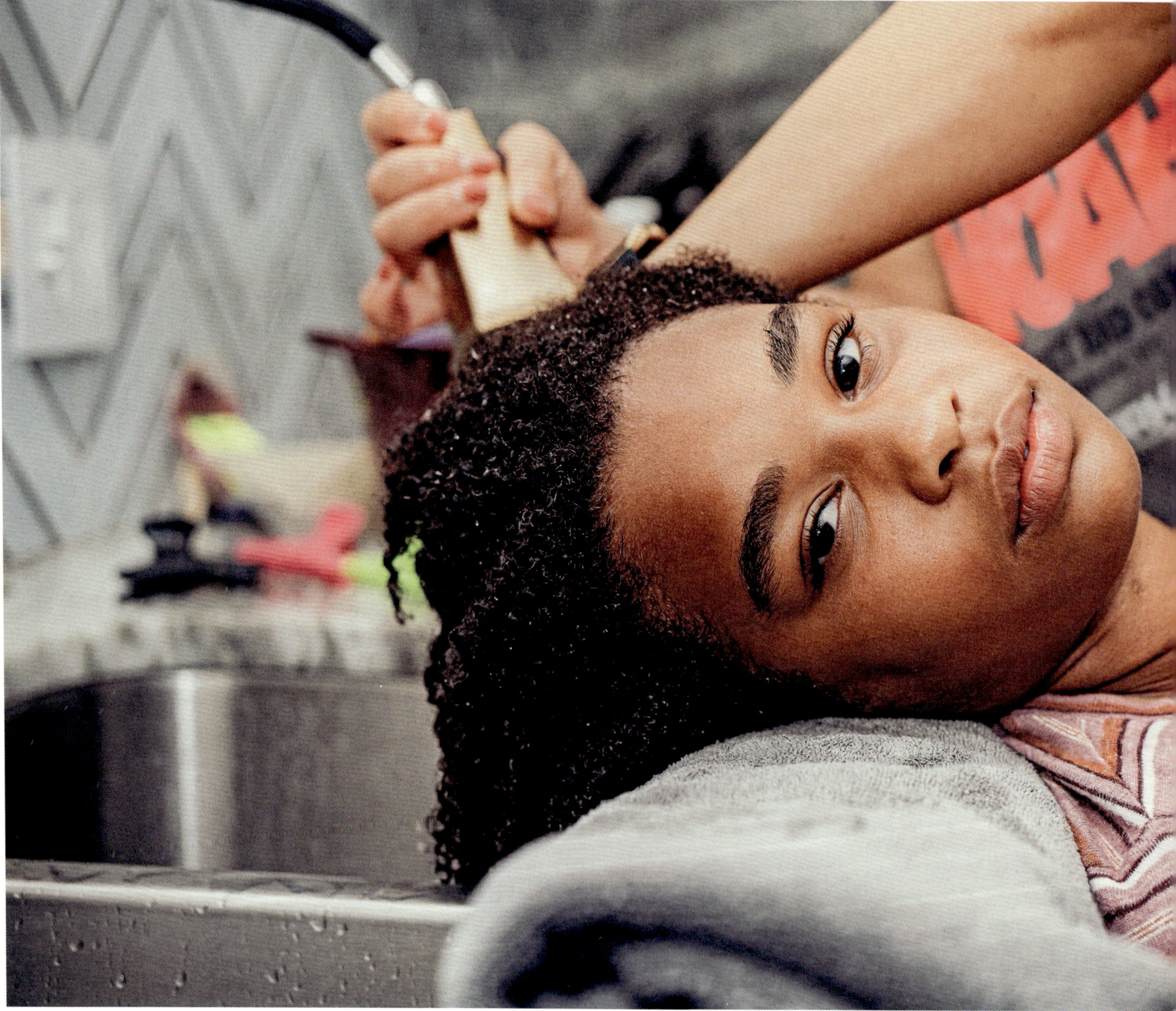

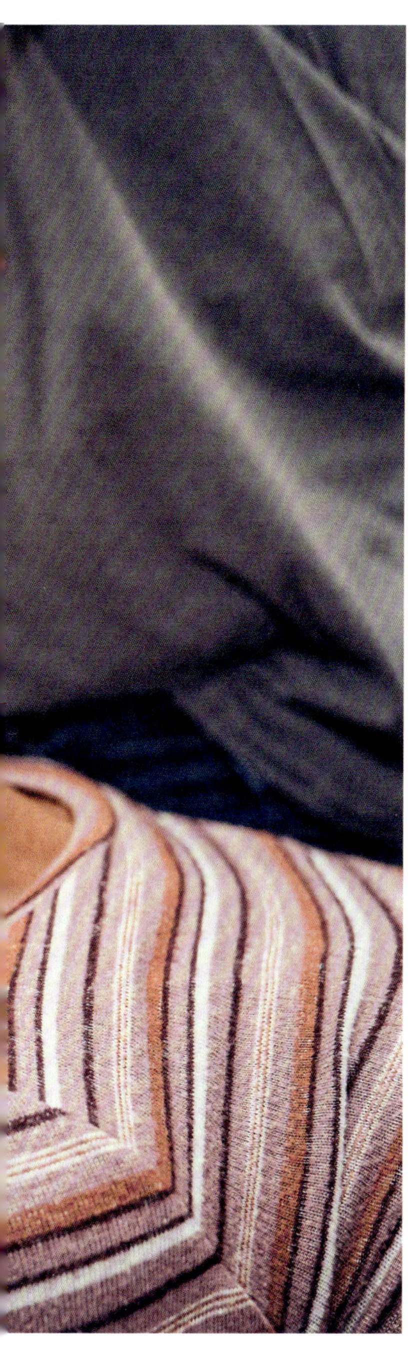

WASH DAY

PASSING THE LEGACY, RITUALS, AND LOVE OF NATURAL HAIR TO THE NEXT GENERATION

Written and Photographed by
TOMESHA FAXIO

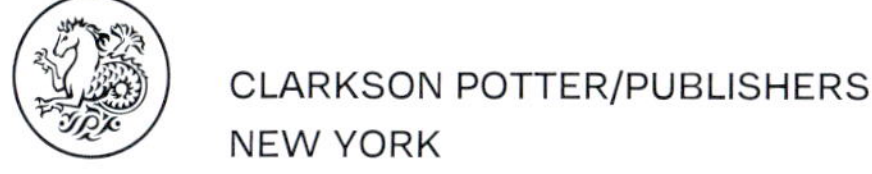

CLARKSON POTTER/PUBLISHERS
NEW YORK

To my loves, Josie and Abri:
when they tell you to shrink—don't.

Contents

Foreword

BY TALIAH WAAJID

WASH DAY is a book that is well overdue. These stories of resilience, strength, beauty, and identity focus on our rich history of natural hair while highlighting experiences that all of us with textured hair have had in our lives. I love the way *Wash Day* also takes us through Tomesha's own hair story and how she shares positivity about natural hair with her daughters. I wish my mother had this book when I was young, back when we struggled through wash days. Fortunately, my wash day stories and experiences, though stressful, have helped shape me into the Queen of Natural Hair.

For me, wash days were painful. I cried, pouted, and was traumatized during the process of preparing my hair to be shampooed and plaited. When my mother finally started washing my hair, I would purposely snatch my head away from the comb and keep moving farther away in the hopes that my mother would become too frustrated and stop trying. Needless to say, it didn't work. After we got through the shampooing, I remember her giving me a little break. Now that I think about it, the break was probably more for her, though we were both stressed out.

As I look back on my hair journey, I remember a time when my mother refused to let me to get a chemical relaxer to straighten my tightly coiled hair. I couldn't believe that she would say, "No." Not only would my hair be straight like my friends', but it would relieve her from those stressful days of washing and combing through my big bushy hair. But she insisted that I keep my hair in its natural state. Looking back, I can see the many ways that decision had a positive, life-changing impact on me and my ability to care for my textured hair.

My mother was never taught how to do hair, but she tried her best and I felt the pain of her efforts. Despite all her frustration, she never said anything negative to me or anyone else about my hair or my texture, even though she struggled to comb and style it. This, along with years of experiencing the way my mother worked with my curls, gave me the patience and confidence to figure my hair out. I watched how it reacted to rain, what happened when it was pressed, how it curled when I perspired, how long my curls would last when I put rollers in, and so on. The more I learned about my hair, the more I loved my hair.

There is a hair story entwined into every curl, kink, coil, and wave, all packed with vivid memories and mixed emotions. Being a master natural hair care specialist and a master cosmetologist, as well as rightfully named, The Queen of Natural Hair, my journey has exposed me to many of those stories. Lots of them are from when I owned a natural hair–care salon and would listen to my clients struggle through their relationships with their hair. Some of those struggles negatively impacted their love lives, family lives, and even their employment. As I listened to their stories, I noticed the terms they used to describe their hair. Terms like "nappy," "bad," "horrible," and "rough."

Words said are powerful, but words unsaid can be just as powerful. Though our hair stories have been (and sometimes still are) overlooked or treated with little importance, they will always be embedded into our lives and memories. They are stories filled with joy, pain, frustration, and happiness, keeping us connected to our heritage and culture. My hair story led me to understand and love my hair, and eventually go on to become an advocate for natural hair and share its beauty with as many people as I could. It also inspired my journey of becoming the first manufacturer of a complete product line formulated specifically for natural hair care, styling, and maintenance. My brand, The Taliah Waajid Brand, was introduced in 1996. Now, I am the producer of the first and largest annual event that celebrates natural hair, The World Natural Hair, Health & Beauty Show. The stories of our curls, kinks, coils, and waves will live forever through our daughters and children, so let's all work to keep the conversations around our hair positive.

My Natural Hair Journey

I DIDN'T KNOW my "naps" were tiny curls until my late twenties. Since I wasn't blessed with "good hair," I don't recall ever hearing the word *curly* being used to describe my tightly coiled texture. Just "nappy," which, back in the 1990s, definitely wasn't a compliment.

I learned early in life that my "bad hair" required a remedy. One such remedy came in the form of heat. I have vivid memories of Saturday night hot comb presses and holding on to my ears to shield them from getting burned. I remember the smell, the anxiety, and the result: straight hair that was deemed presentable for church on Sunday.

The more permanent solution for my "unwanted" texture required chemicals. I don't remember my first hair relaxer, but I know it was applied pretty early in life. So early that I recall little to nothing about the head full of kinky hair that existed prior. After the cycle of regular relaxers began, my only interaction with my textured hair occurred when the troublesome "new growth" appeared and needed to be "touched up" with more relaxer. This routine conditioned me to dislike my hair in its natural state—the way it grew out

of my scalp. I was taught to fix it, to alter it, to make it lay down and behave. I had no concept of any other way to treat my natural hair. I was only made to understand that it was not welcome.

One of my earliest memories of the extent of this conditioning is of a nine-year-old me, looking into the mirror after a full day of swimming. My skin had darkened from hours in the California sun and the edges of my hair were shriveled from exposure to the chlorinated water. I hated my reflection so much that I swore to never swim again.

Similar to many Black women, I was the recipient of generation upon generation of indoctrination about how my hair should look. My mother, grandmother, and mothers before them didn't escape it, so neither did I. My grandmother had to get her hair pressed regularly when she was young because she was told she didn't have "good hair" like her sister. My mother has expressed the desire to embrace her natural hair, but still feels societal pressure to keep her hair straight. This same pressure led her to decide to relax my hair before I was old enough to know the difference.

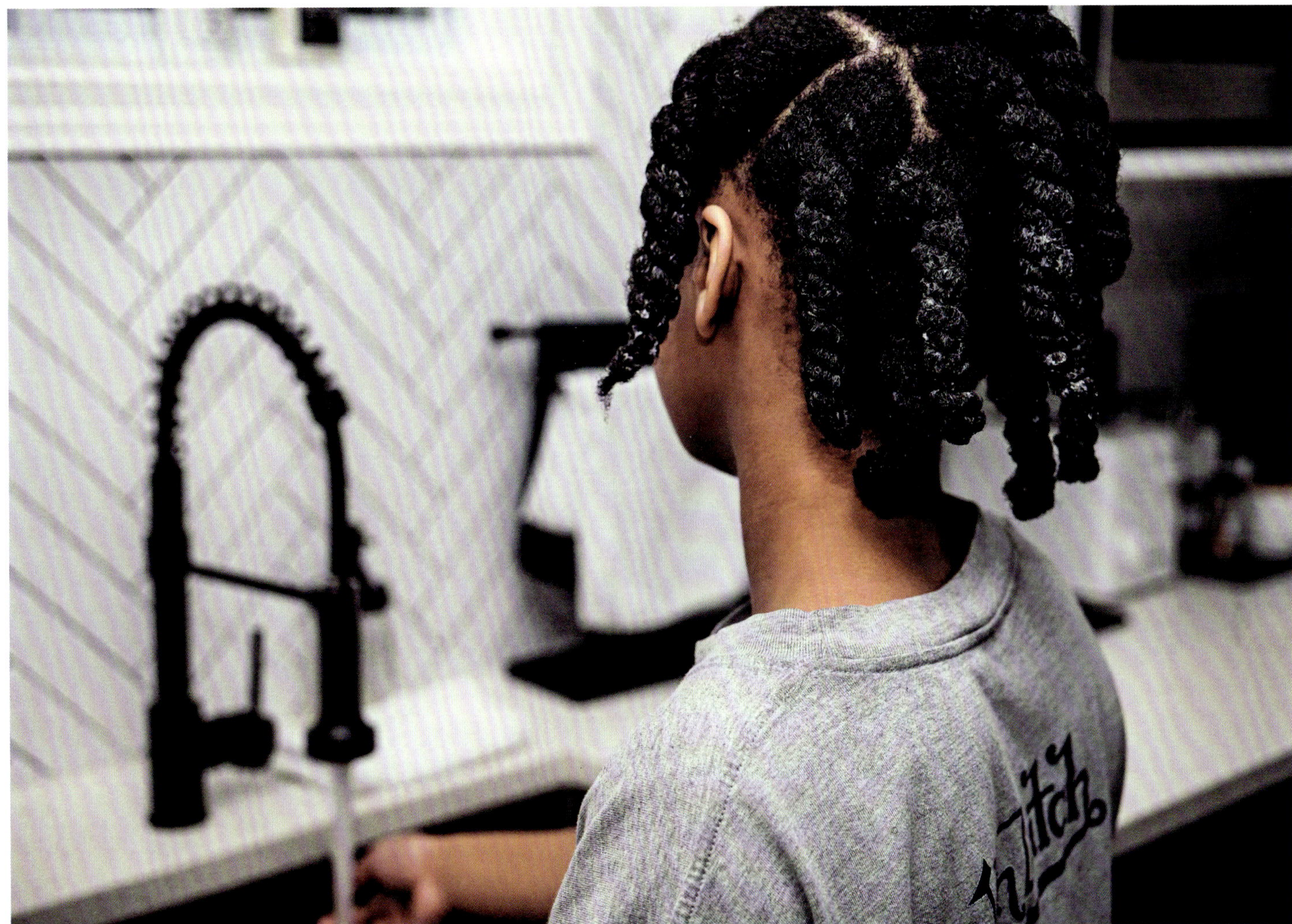

Growing up, I was surrounded by television shows, advertisements, and music videos that reinforced the idea that light skin and long, straight hair equaled beauty. Absent from my youth were mainstream representations of kinky-haired women presented as love interests or women in professional work environments. Years of anti-Black programming opened the door to subconscious self-hate in the form of my reliance upon heat and/or chemicals to keep my hair straight.

It wasn't until the natural hair movement that I began to see my natural hair in a different light. Reminiscent of the "Black Is Beautiful" movement of the 1960s, the natural hair movement of the mid-to-late 2000s opened my eyes to the possibility that natural hair could be normal. While the movement began in the U.S., it spread throughout the diaspora—anti-Blackness and anti-kinky hair is a global issue, not just a U.S. issue. Many Black women started walking away from perms (relaxed hair)—some were motivated by a desire to prioritize the health of their hair, and others were inspired by the freedom that the natural hair movement offered. Either way, those who chose to go natural inevitably had to learn how to tend to their hair, some for the very first time. Thanks to social media, Black women were able to share and watch instructional videos, purchase products made specifically for their textures, read blogs depicting the journeys of fellow naturalistas, and publicly commune with one another about their hair. Thousands of natural hair blogs and vlogs were started in order to usher Black women toward the natural hair lifestyle. Black women no longer had to feel alone if they wanted to try natural hair. They were able to find communities of women online who were doing the same thing. Furthermore, through this virtual community, an entire culture was created where natural hair took center stage and self-acceptance was the goal.

This movement inspired me to question what I had grown up believing about my hair. Is my natural hair *really* unpresentable? Unprofessional? Unacceptable? No. I took a closer look at the prevailing beauty standard and realized it was never meant to include me. I realized that I don't require fixing, alteration, or assimilation. I began to see that nappy has always been beautiful. So, in 2008, I cut off all of my relaxed hair and started my natural hair journey.

My decision to let my coils loose was the first step. The very next one included learning how to care for them. My big chop introduced me to my natural hair for the very first time. This meant I had no idea how to wash, detangle, condition, style . . . nothing. So, I, like many Black women during the early days of the most recent natural hair movement, turned to YouTube, natural hair blogs, and friends who had already made the transition. My community helped me figure out the process that would eventually become my regular ritual of self-care.

My natural hair journey is a continuous one. Having learned to embrace my hair, I am now passing the baton to my daughters. Even though my daughters have only ever seen me with natural hair, attended a predominantly Black pre-school, and had many Black aunties to look up to, White supremacy in the form of the hair texture hierarchy still managed to reach my oldest daughter when she was in kindergarten. I vividly remember the day she told me she wanted "White hair." She asked, "Why doesn't my hair lay down and swing around?" I knew at that moment that I had to be more intentional about ensuring both my girls learned about the value and beauty of their unique hair textures. I have the privilege of doing my part to ensure the "good hair/bad hair" lie surrenders its power. I'm continuously teaching my daughters about the origins of that lie, the current iterations of that lie, and ultimately, how to live free of that lie. I get to break the cycle. Today, both of my girls proudly show off their afros.

I'm certainly not an anomaly. The natural hair movement and the continued normalization of natural hair textures has not only impacted me, but many other Black mothers as well. So many of us have learned to accept ourselves more fully, and, in turn, are able to teach our children to do the same. We are now more informed about why we grew up thinking our hair was ugly. We have a better understanding of where these negative views of ourselves came from. We can see that these views are steeped in racism. We know that anti-Blackness is the culprit, not Blackness itself. In turn, we are equipped to teach our children the roots of racism and texturism, which is the idea that straighter hair is more beautiful or desirable than kinkier hair, so that they hopefully do not internalize the myths that keep these "isms" alive. While our children will likely continue to contend with non-inclusive beauty standards, we are putting them in a better position to understand and eradicate them.

As a photographer, reflecting on my natural hair journey, and likewise, the collective journey Black women have been on with their hair for centuries, I knew I wanted to capture the significance and beauty of this moment in Black hair history. I want to tell the natural hair stories of Black women and show how we are continuing our journeys through our children. I could not think of a better way to illustrate this generational story than through the ritual commonly known as wash day.

What Is Wash Day?

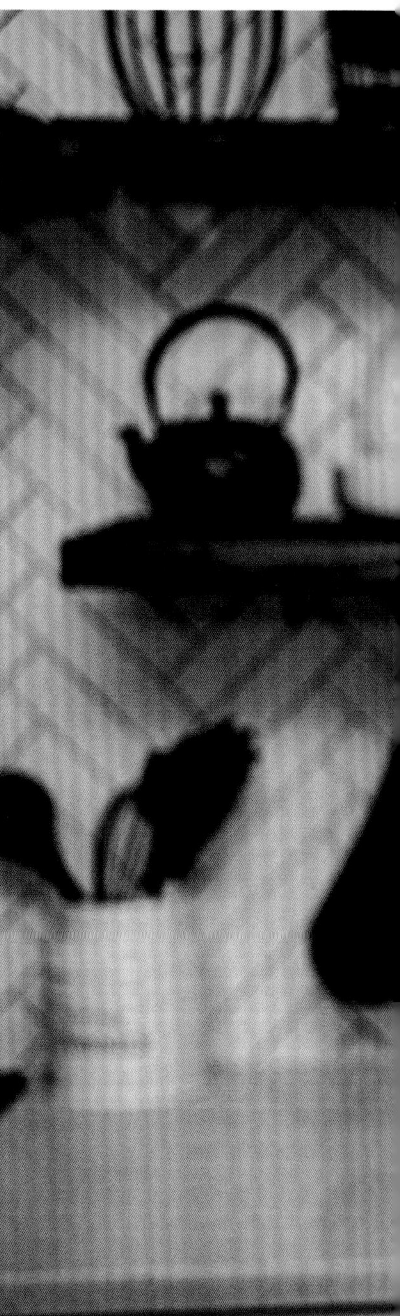

HERE, the term *wash day* is used to refer specifically to the time set aside to wash and care for natural hair textures. Kinkier textures typically require more time to detangle and condition in order to remain healthy. This "day" can last anywhere from a couple of hours to multiple days. Wash day involves detailed product selection, specialized grooming techniques, and, most of all, patience. While particularities may differ greatly, there are some common components to most wash-day routines:

1. Pre-wash, a.k.a. "pre-poo" (which usually includes taking down a previous style, detangling the hair, and potentially pre-conditioning to prepare for shampooing)

2. Washing

3. Deep conditioning

4. Application of a leave-in conditioner and oil

5. Styling

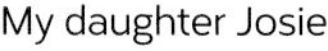

My daughter Josie

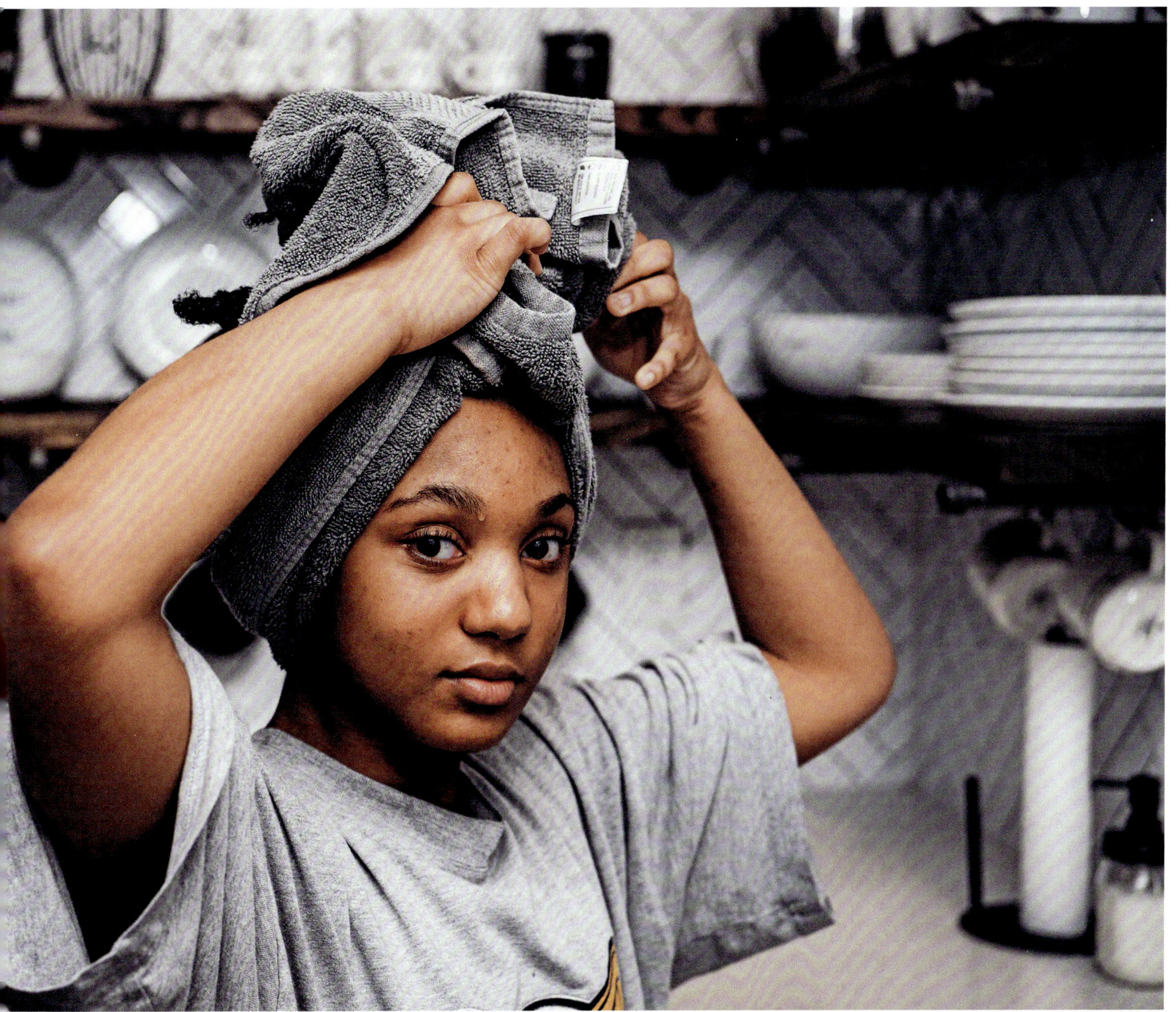

In addition, some commonly used natural hair and/
or wash day–related terms or processes[1] that you will see
throughout this book include:

BIG CHOP—the act of cutting all relaxed/
chemically straightened hair off at one time in
order to more quickly transition to natural hair

BRAID-OUT OR TWIST-OUT—a style created by
braiding or twisting one's hair while it is damp, and
once undone, it reveals a defined pattern

BREAKAGE—the loss of parts of the hair strand
due to damage

BONNET—a hair covering, typically worn at night,
to protect the hair from drying, friction, and tangling

CO-WASH—the process of washing the hair with
conditioner, or a cleansing product meant for co-
washing, instead of shampoo

CREAMY CRACK—a term used to refer to chemical
relaxers. The term is indicative of the addictive
nature of perms.

HAIR TYPES—a system created by hair stylist

Andre Walker to identify different hair textures.
The textures include, ranging from straightest to
curliest, 2A, 2B, 2C, 3A, 3B, 3C, 4A, 4B, and 4C.

HEAT DAMAGE—refers to damage resulting from
excessive heat applied to the hair, which often
alters the original curl pattern of the hair

LOC METHOD—a.k.a. liquid, oil, and cream, and ref-
erences the order in which the products are applied

LOCS—a style in which the hair, over time, becomes
permanently secured into a rope-like appearance

PALM ROLLING—a method of loc maintenance
and tightening where the loc is rolled between the
palms of the hands

PROTECTIVE STYLE—a style that requires little to
no manipulation of the hair and offers protection
from environmental elements

SHRINKAGE—a term used to describe visual
reduction in hair length as a result of the hair
returning to its natural pattern

SILK PRESS—a temporary method of straightening

hair achieved by blow-drying the hair and applying heat with a flat iron

STRETCHING—any styling technique used to visually lengthen the hair by temporarily elongating the curl pattern

TRANSITIONING—a term used to describe the process of "going natural" whereby the natural hair is grown out and the relaxed hair is trimmed off in stages

T.W.A.—teeny weeny afro

WASH AND GO—a style where the hair is worn in its natural curl pattern after washing and applying styling products

The wash-day process is more than just hair care; it is also self-care. This form of self-care is as unique and precious as it is centered in Blackness. Historically speaking, much of what was known about how to care for our textured hair was lost during the slave trade, as enslaved Africans were forced to have their heads shaved.[2] In *Hair Story: Untangling the Roots of Black Hair in America,* Ayana D. Byrd and Lori L. Tharps state, "Given the importance of the hair to an African, having the head shaved was an unspeakable crime," not unlike stripping a person of their identity.[3] This disregard for the significance of their hair was a far cry from the beautiful culture of hair care that existed in their homeland—hair that was once intricately styled to communicate one's marital status, religion, ethnic identity, or geographic origin, among many other things.[4] For the enslaved Africans, taking the time to care for their hair was once an enjoyable part of their culture. But this precious time was stolen from them. As a result, their hair often became matted and broken, and scalp diseases that led to patches of baldness became common.[5] The hair that was once celebrated and revered became a source of disdain and shame. Being forced to live in a world that was built around Whiteness, including the speed with which they can wash and comb their hair, allowed African hair to be dismissed as abnormal. Over time, we have come to believe that caring for our natural hair is difficult and time-consuming. In her contributing essay in *Textures: The History and Art of Black Hair,* Lori. L. Tharps writes, "Black hair is not inherently complicated; it became so in the process of removing it from its original birthplace and placing it in hostile territory where people were unable and unwilling to appreciate its greatness."[6] In many ways, wash day signifies our ability to reclaim our time and our right to care for ourselves. It represents a time to take back what was stolen: self-care and self-love.

The Significance of the Kitchen

AS you will notice, most of the images in this book feature mothers and their children in the kitchen for at least some portion of the wash-day process.

Some of my earliest memories of getting my hair done are of my mom or grandmother doing my hair in the kitchen. The hot comb came right off the kitchen stove to my kinky edges. My grandmother, who is a licensed hairdresser, had a salon connected to her kitchen. Summers with grandma were not complete without waking up to the smell of hair grease and curling irons.

For many (or perhaps most) of us, the kitchen is the location for all or part of our wash-day ritual with our children. Easy access to a sink, space to place multiple supplies and products, in addition to the ability to interact with the rest of the family, watch television, and eat a snack makes this location convenient and comfortable for the long hours of wash day. I'll admit, I was surprised by the handful of Black women in this book who wash their children's hair in the tub or shower. But even for these women, they typically move to the kitchen or living room area for the post-wash portions of the process.

The significance of the kitchen to wash day isn't surprising when we consider the role the kitchen plays in many families. The kitchen is a place of community. We cook meals for and with each other. We eat together. We talk about the highs and lows of the day. In 2020, the kitchen table worked triple duty for some families, being the school desk, office space, and meal location. And with more and more modern homes featuring open floor plans, kitchens have only grown more visible and central to our lives. Indeed, *The Kitchen Table Series* by Carrie Mae Weems speaks volumes as to the important role the kitchen plays in our lives, especially the lives of women.[7] Wash day can be a really long day in many families, so room to spread out and get comfortable is optimal.

Of course, I must also mention the culturally relevant dual meaning: the kitchen and the "kitchen." While the "kitchen" simply refers to the hair in the back of a person's head or nape of the neck (often where the curliest hairs are found), I've always understood this term to mean "nappy," unruly hair, resistant to hot combs and other straightening methods. When someone mentions your "kitchen," it typically is not to tell you how great it looks. There are many explanations of the origins of this term with reference to hair. My mother and grandmother agree that a likely reason for the use of "kitchen" in this way is that in many older

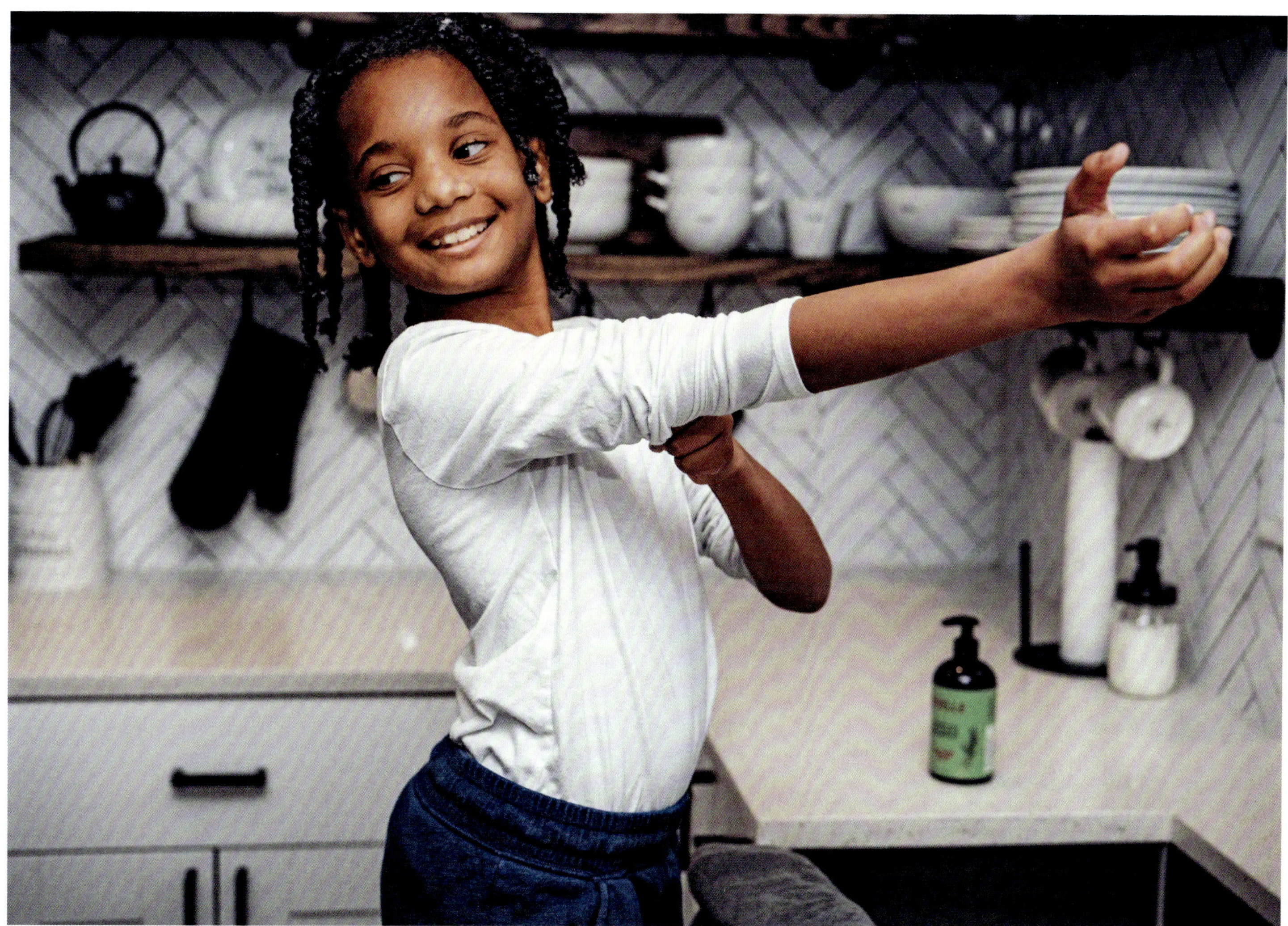

My daughter Abri

homes (and perhaps many homes today) the kitchen was in the back of the house. I've also heard the explanation that the kitchen is where peas are cooked, or where "peasy" hair gets straightened. Another possibility is that it has something to do with hot combs, which were heated on the kitchen stove and used to straighten the "kitchen." So not only has the kitchen long been the location of home salons, it also carries a meaning that is deeply entrenched in Black hair culture.

The "Why" Behind This Book

THIS BOOK celebrates wash day by documenting the unique routines and rituals of twenty-six families. Through photographs of mothers taking the time to wash, detangle, condition, and style their children's natural hair, these stories illustrate the ways in which Black mothers are passing on an inheritance of pride to the next generation. For us, wash day is a time where we can be intentional about reminding our children that their coils are worthy of the extra care and maintenance we give them. Throughout these pages, I aimed to create art that confirms the inherent beauty of each and every nappy strand, as well as the process of caring for them.

While this book focuses on the unique attributes of wash day as it pertains to natural hair, it is in no way intended to devalue hair-care routines that exist outside of the natural hair world. The focus of this book is the specific role that wash day plays in celebrating natural hair, rather than the overall role that hair care plays in the Black community in general. The goal here is to move us closer to hair freedom, not to put additional bondage on Black women with regard to their hair-care choices. The "you're not Black enough" attitude has existed within both the "Black Is Beautiful" and natural hair movements, negatively judging those who did not sport the afro or wear their natural hair.[8] Unfortunately, in our zealous attempts to reclaim lost identity, pride, and freedom, we have actually gotten in our own way at times. There is more than enough policing of Black bodies, and this book shall not add to any of that. Furthermore, even though I grew up with processed hair, I still have warm memories of getting my hair done by my mother and grandmother. I still inherited a legacy from them: an understanding of the importance of taking time for my hair.

Beyond all else, I want this book to serve as a source of empowerment for those with hair textures that Whiteness has told time and time again are unfit. As we know, representation is critical. I want my daughters to be able to look through these images and connect with the beautiful faces looking back at them. I want every Black child who sees these photographs to feel the type of affirmation that was missing from my childhood.

It has been my greatest joy as a photographer to capture and share these wash-day rituals. Perhaps because it's not just my story. It's *our* story. I am humbled to have created images through which so many of us can speak. Each mom in this series has opened her home to allow me to capture her wash-day routine, as well as to hear about her own wash-day story (a.k.a. natural hair journey). As you will see, each process and story are different, but no less unifying. From LaTroya, we hear about how she decided to return to natural after realizing that, as an adult, she had no idea what her real hair looked like. From Coretta, we hear how she continues to struggle with societal pressures regarding "kept" hairstyles, but has given her daughter room to fall in love with her natural hair. Kameron shares how she braids her daughters' hair prior to washing in order to reduce tangling. And detailed photographs illustrate how Leslie gently detangles her daughter's hair by hand, rather than using brushes or combs, to reduce strain on her daughter's sensitive scalp. I've learned so much from these women and have implemented many of their practices into my own routine.

Spending time with these moms, watching them pour love over their children's tresses, has changed me. I now look forward to wash day in a way that I never have before. Rather than a chore, it has become a labor of love. This is not surprising given the amount of time I've spent reflecting on wash day and the role it can play in reinforcing hair love. I hope this book inspires you as well. For the Black mommas, I hope you're inspired to reclaim joy in the wash-day process with your littles. For naturalistas, I hope you're inspired to see your hair and your wash-day routine in a whole new way. For everyone else, I hope you're inspired to learn more about the beauty that is wash day.

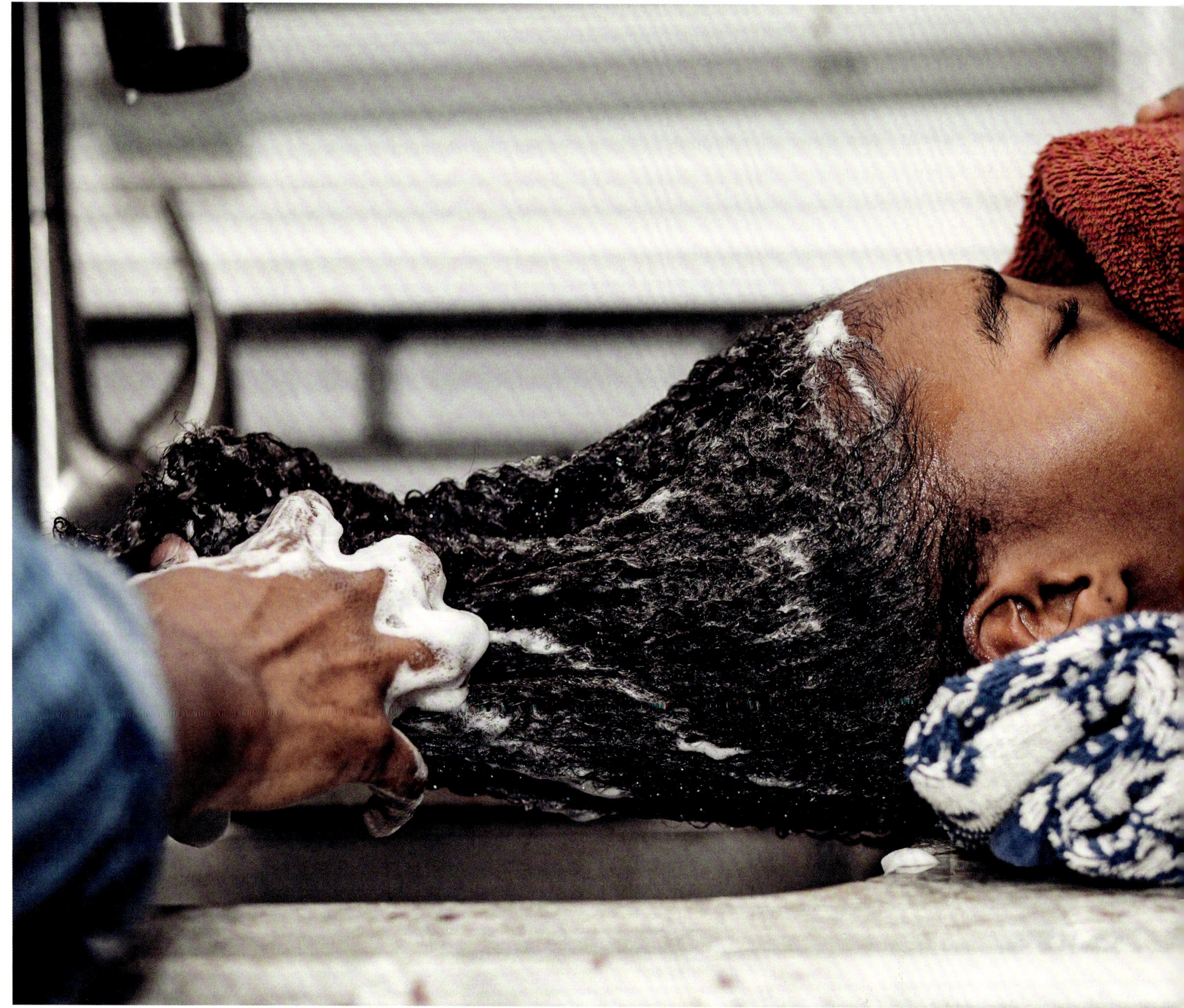

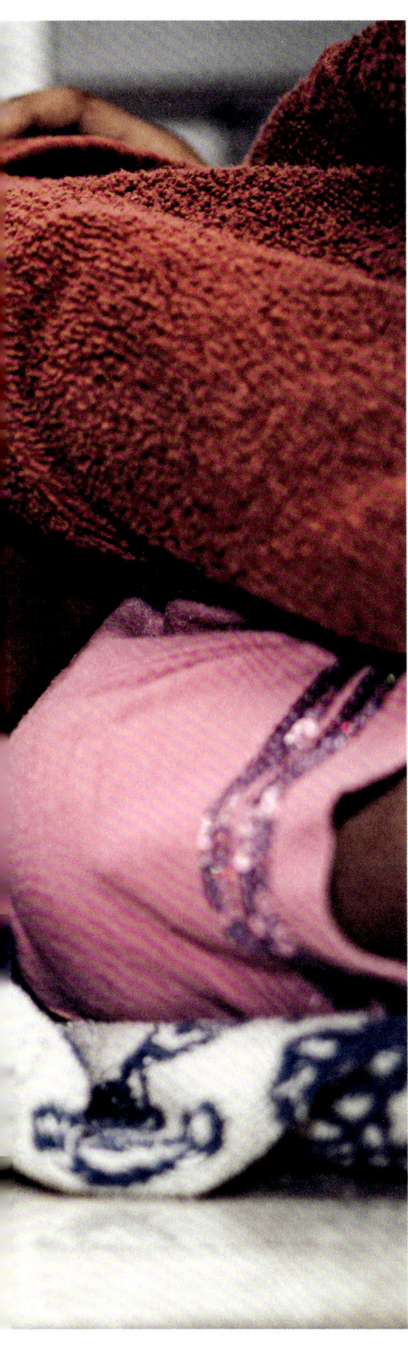

Wash-Day Stories

"Wash day, in my opinion, is one of the best bonding times between mothers and their children. Although those hands in your head don't feel like love initially, the end result always shows, they are."

—CORETTA

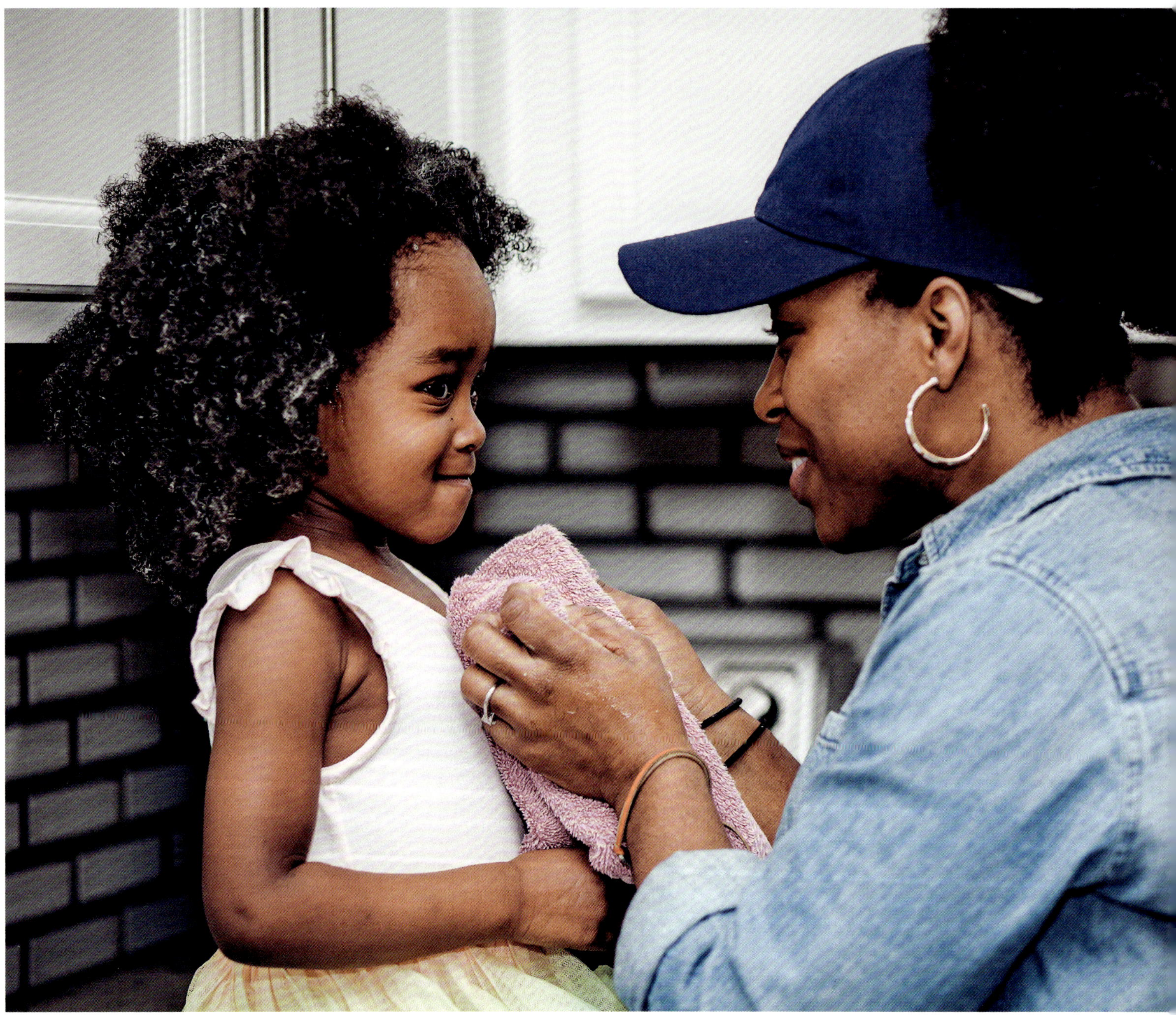

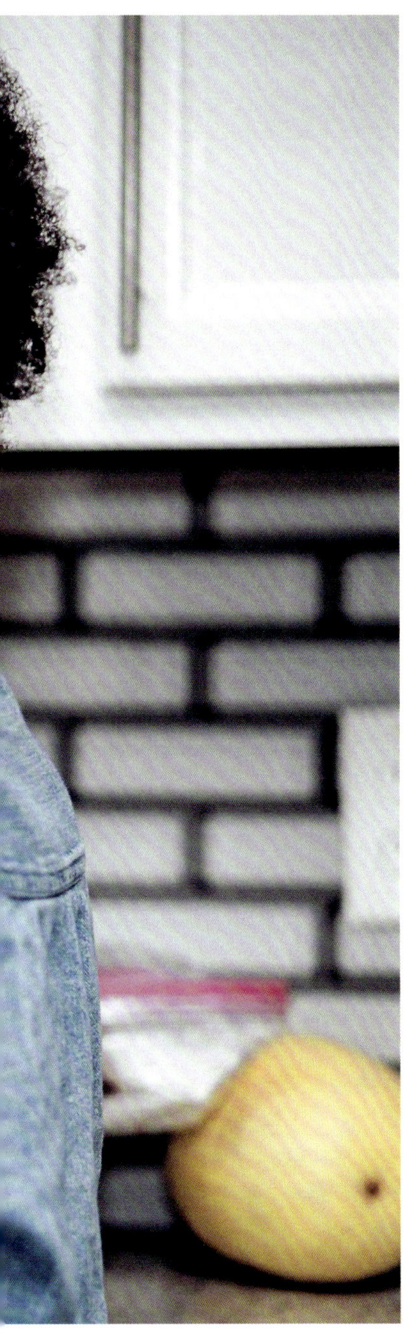

LaTroya, Eliah & Deja

"Some hair is meant to grow downward and be flowy like a river. That's nice. But some hair is meant to grow upward toward the sky like the proud branches of a blossoming tree, big and showy. That's also nice."

LATROYA'S natural hair journey began with an introspective thought. "It dawned on me that I didn't know the feel, texture, or behavior of my real hair, and I determined that it was time I discovered it," LaTroya reflected.

As a child, LaTroya got her hair pressed regularly and began getting relaxers when she turned thirteen. The constant straightening left no opportunity for her to see her natural hair. Inspired by the natural hair movement, LaTroya decided to go natural in 2011. However, the natural hair influencers she was watching at that time all had sleek, shiny curls. They had the kind of hair that mimicked those looser textures she had been trained to believe are ideal. She hoped that her natural hair journey would reveal similar curls on her own head; those curls that hung long and stretched. Such was not the case.

When LaTroya saw that her hair did not automatically resemble what she was seeing on YouTube, she thought she could manipulate it to look that way. But after tons of experimentation with products and techniques to achieve those seemingly effortless curls, she had to accept that her hair was just not going to change. Her hair was not going to hang in loose, shiny curls. She was not going to have the type of hair that she had been socialized to believe is "good." She found herself faced with a familiar question: Am I pretty?

Due to the reality of texturism, many of us have had to sit with this question.

As transformational as the natural hair movement was, and continues to be, the stain of texturism, a term coined by Dr. Tameka N. Ellington, has proven quite difficult to remove. Preference for loose curls and waves versus tight kinks and coils remains evident in many of our styling practices. I don't think there is anything wrong with Bantu knots, twist-outs, and other methods of elongating and stretching natural hair. Not at all. I only point this out to identify that all textures are not yet deemed to be equal.

The roots of texturism run deep, making it extremely difficult to eradicate from our perceptions of beauty. As Ayana D. Byrd and Lori L. Tharps explain in *Hair Story,* in nineteenth-century America, many of the more than one hundred thousand free Black people were the biracial children of the first African arrivals and Europeans.[9] Those living on plantations came to understand that lighter-skinned Black people with looser curl patterns were typically "house slaves" who performed less physically demanding labor and often had access to better clothes, food, and education.[10] This differential treatment had much to do with the fact that many of these light-skinned enslaved people were the result of non-consensual relationships between enslavers and the enslaved.[11] Eventually, a hierarchical system was established within the enslaved community. The term "good hair" became associated with lighter-skinned enslaved people, while "bad hair" became associated with darker-skinned enslaved people.[12] Good hair was closer in appearance to straight hair, while bad hair was the complete opposite. This social structure was reinforced in a number of ways by enslavers; one being that they would pay almost five times more for a "house slave" than a "field slave," literally placing a higher dollar value on light skin and "good hair."[13]

Black people began to internalize the value judgments of enslavers, leading to the false belief that those with dark skin and kinky hair were "less attractive, less intelligent, and worth less . . . "[14] Byrd and Tharps go on to explain in *Hair Story*, "By the time slavery was officially abolished in 1865, 'good' hair and light skin had become the official keys to membership in the Negro elite."[15] It seems silly now, but the "comb test" and "brown paper bag test" were used to determine membership into Black elite schools, social organizations, and churches.[16] Even my alma mater Spelman College, a historically Black college, is suspected of having used similar criteria to ensure early classes were of the "proper" pedigree.

Texturism is just the "good hair/bad hair" lie in new clothes. While you would think that the natural hair movement would have put an end to this foolishness once and for all, such is not the case. As I recall, the goal of many of the products hitting the market early in the movement, as well as popular stretching techniques, was to achieve big, curly hair, rather than tight, shrunken kinks. In her book, *Twisted: The Tangled History of Black Hair Culture,* Emma Dabiri notes, "I look at the images from some of today's natural-hair conventions and I am reminded that not as much has changed between 1919 and 2019 as we might want to imagine."[17]

Unfortunately, it will take a bit more time to dismantle a structure that goes back almost as far as racism itself. Black hair trauma is one of the many wounds of slavery that has yet to be healed.

It is against this backdrop that LaTroya sat with the question of her own beauty. By the time she stood up, she had come to realize that her hair "was its own unique individual with its own temperament and preferences." She now understood the benefits of her unique hair type. She realized that its density was actually a good thing. That the coarseness of her hair helped her retain more length and helped her hair to grow longer than it ever had when it was straight. She genuinely began to see the greatness of *her* texture. She let go of curl chasing and trying to make her hair do things it was not meant to do and learned that she didn't have to rely on the security blanket of straight hair or shiny curls to know that she and her hair were beautiful.

LaTroya has come to a place of true appreciation for her hair and all of its personalities. Her journey toward acceptance and appreciation of her texture has allowed her to gain a treasure trove of wisdom that she now bestows upon her two daughters, Eliah and Deja. She is very intentional in her communication regarding each child's unique hair texture. She aims to ensure they are able to appreciate their curl patterns in a culture that isn't quite there yet. She often tells them that they have magical hair that is capable of wonderful things. It can be curly, then straight. Short, then long. Just like magic.

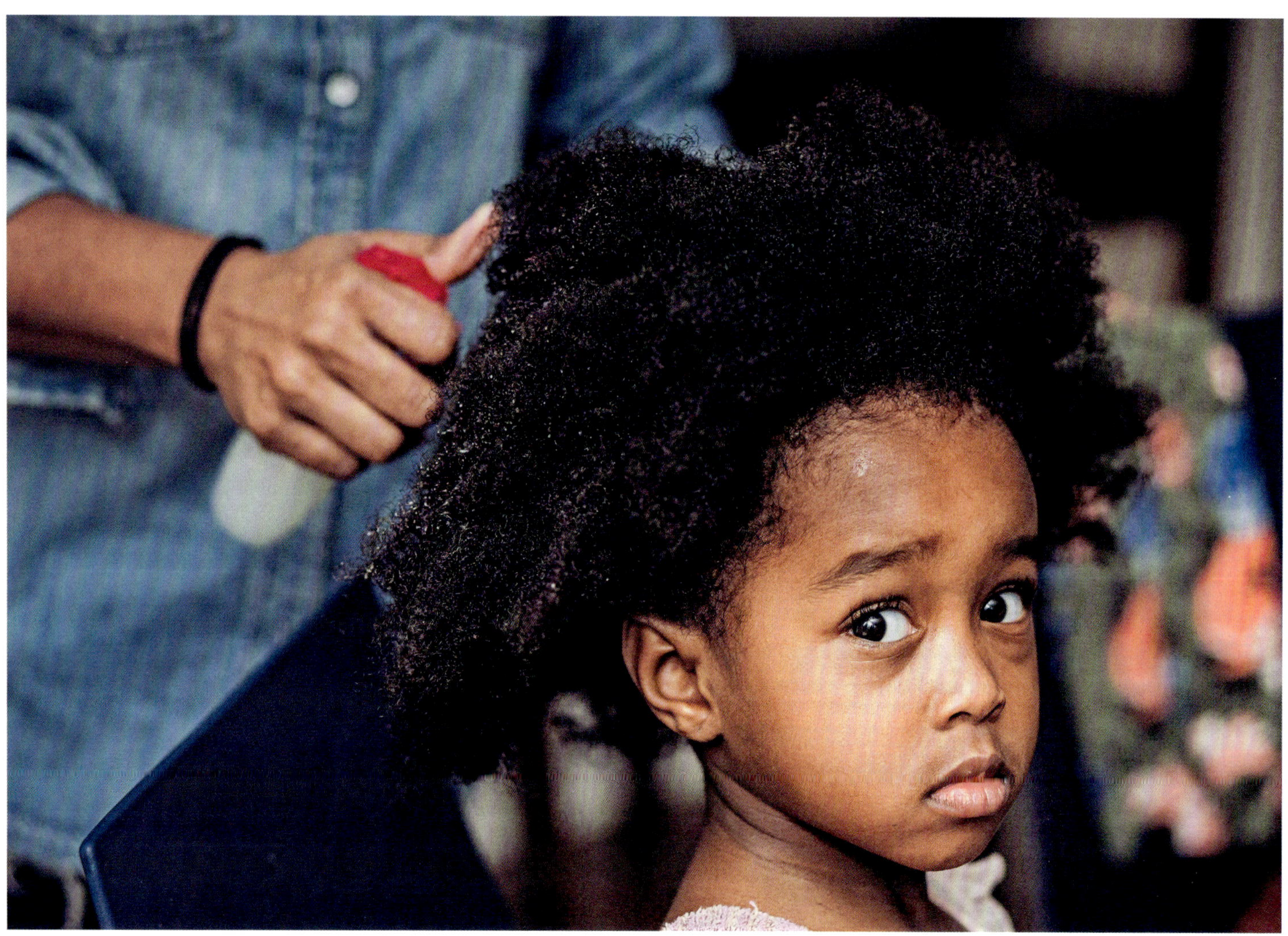

LaTroya's wash day, which occurs every other week, is super efficient. Since she usually skips the deep conditioning and doesn't spend a ton of time detangling, she can finish in under two hours. She occasionally applies a clay mask to the their hair before washing, which adds an additional thirty minutes to an hour.

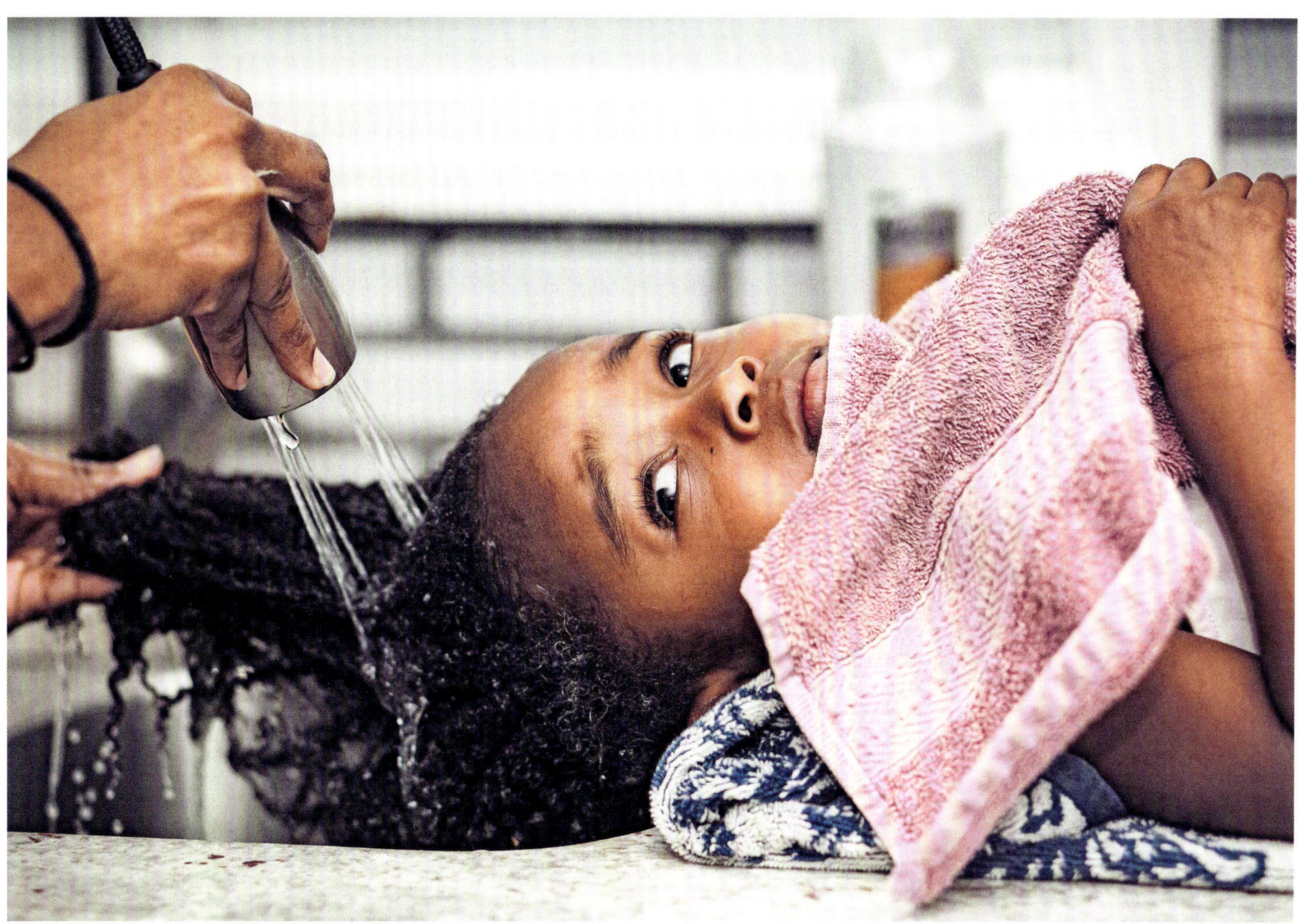

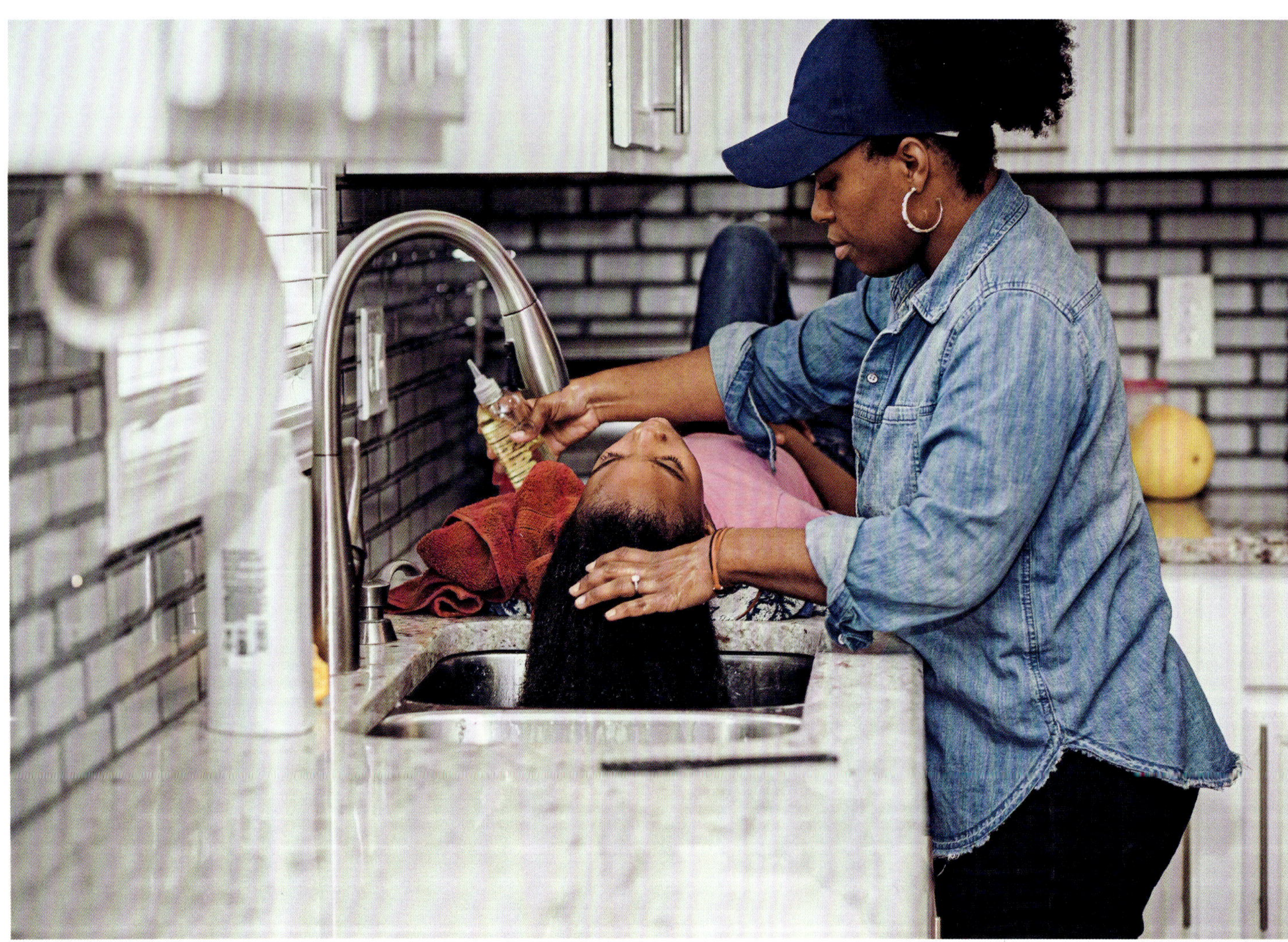

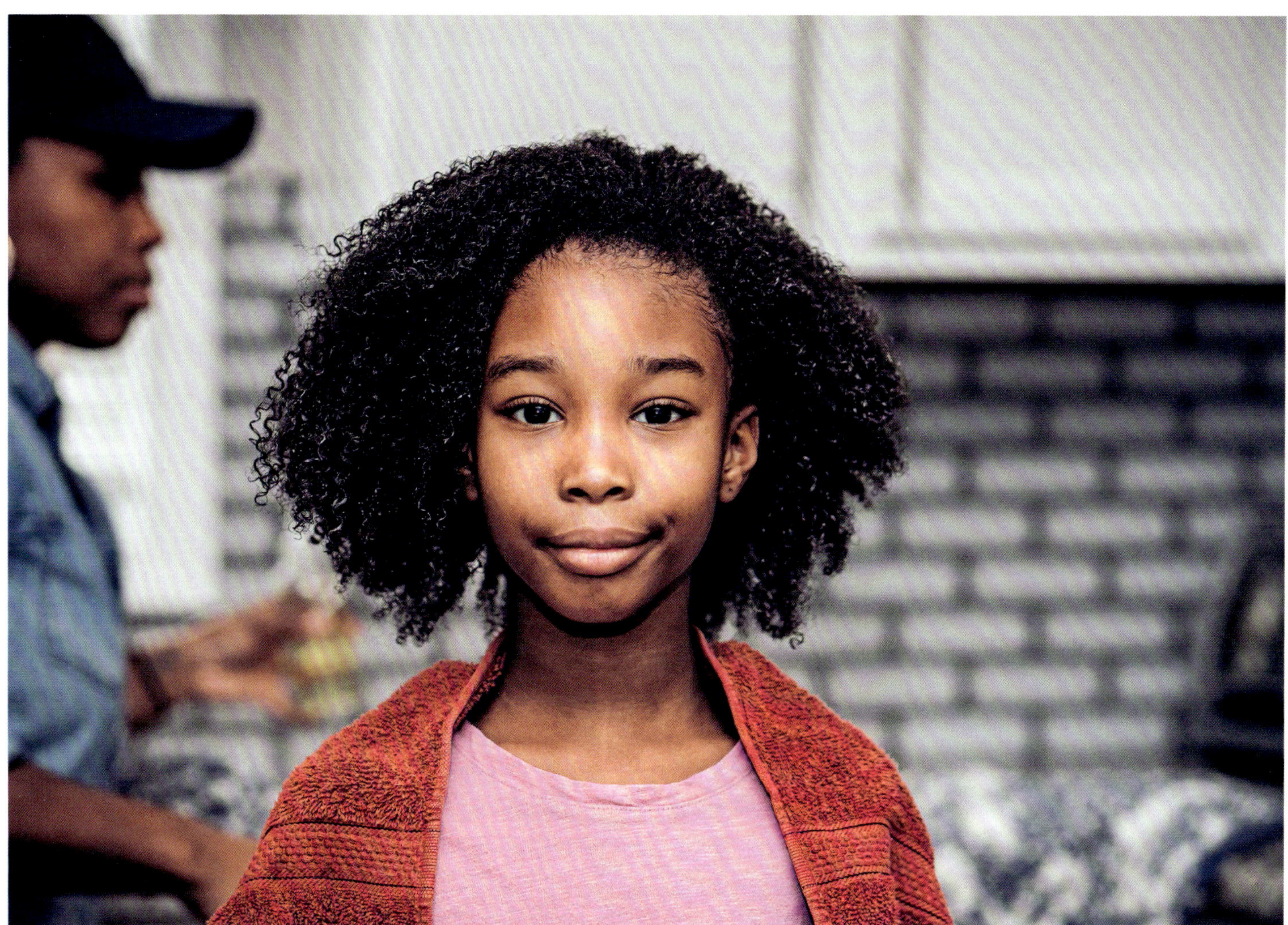

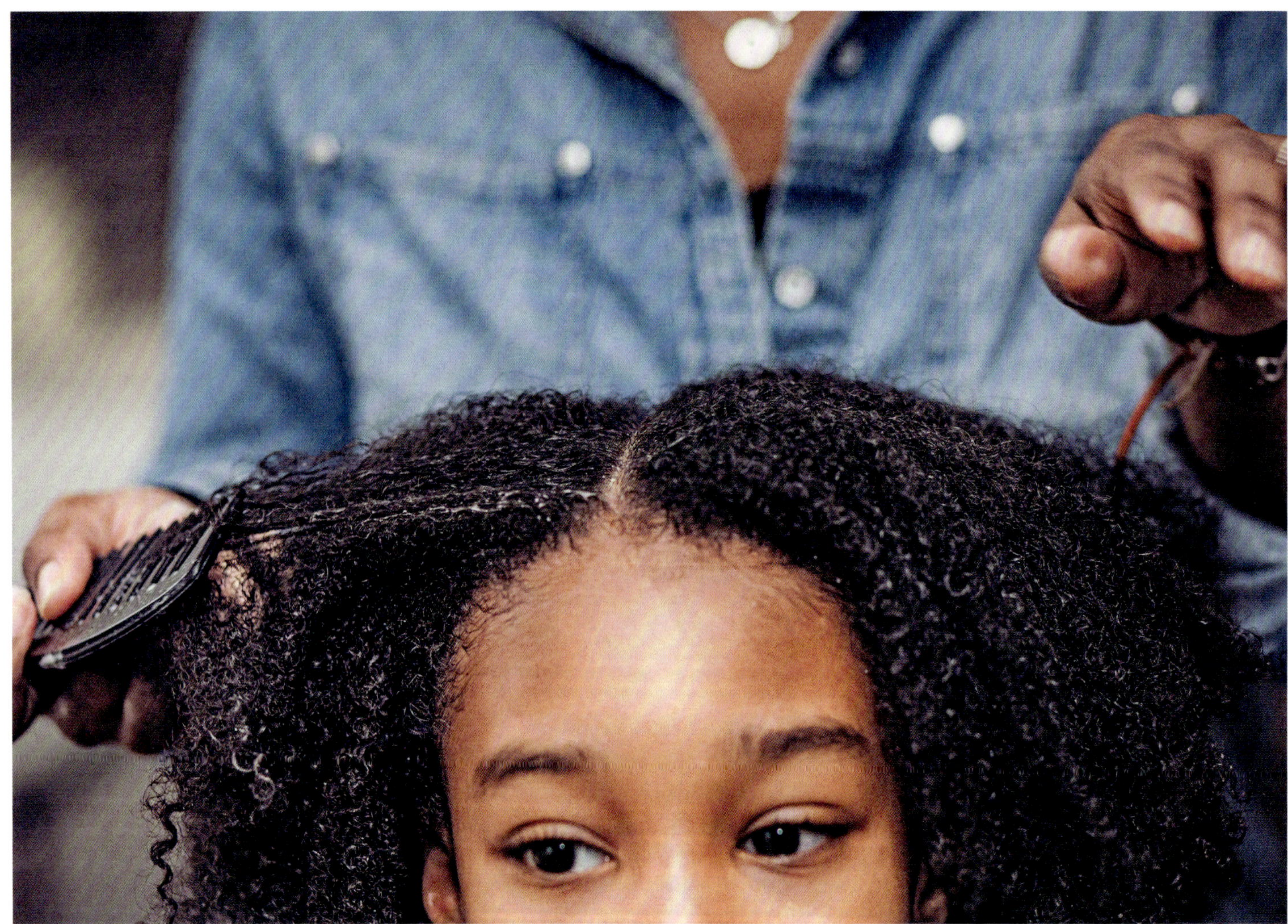

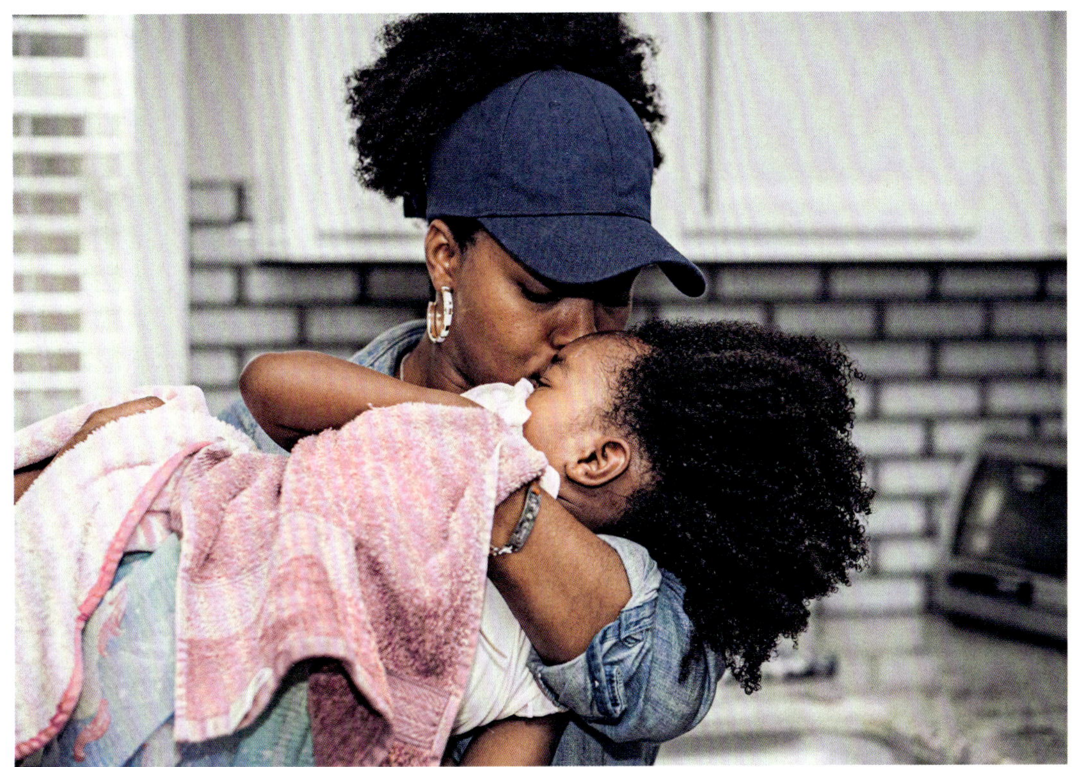

"I also want them to know their hair is not hard to manage. I want them to learn that as long as they are not attempting to force their hair into being something it is not, it will never be hard to manage." —LATROYA

Jamia & Journey

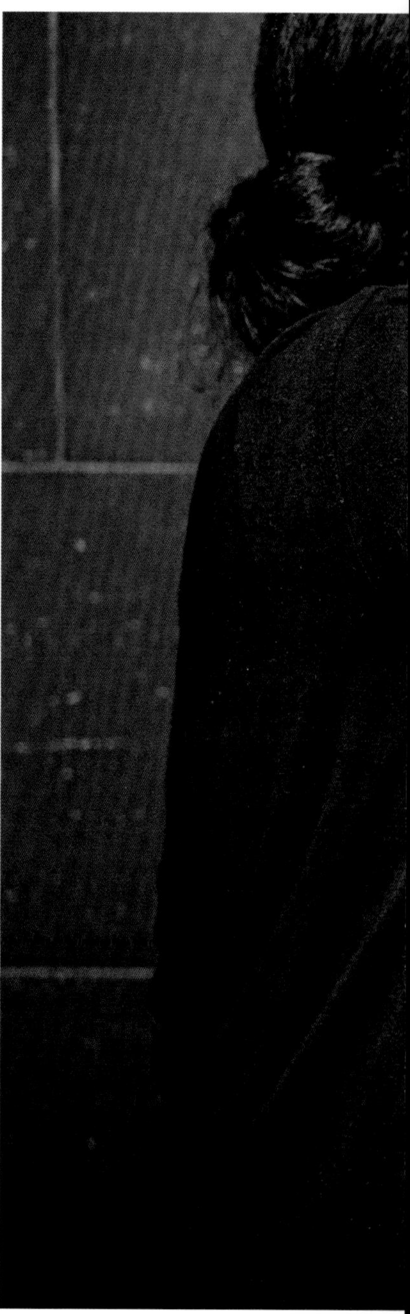

"Leaving the house wasn't an option in the pandemic, and with more time to think about my values and the truest expression of my advocacy and my activism, I wanted to embrace a less Eurocentric, more authentic and unapologetic me."

FOR many of us, the pandemic forced us to amend our beauty routines. We had to go without the help of professionals, and learn how to perform the necessary beautification tasks on our own. This was a time of high anxiety for obvious reasons, and for many Black women, this anxiety included figuring out what to do with their hair. Personally, I was rocking a super short fade before the pandemic, and since I could not go to my barber, I had to learn how to cut my own hair. It was not cute. Not even close. I had to get comfortable with a less-than-perfect cut. At this time, many women found themselves evaluating their priorities,

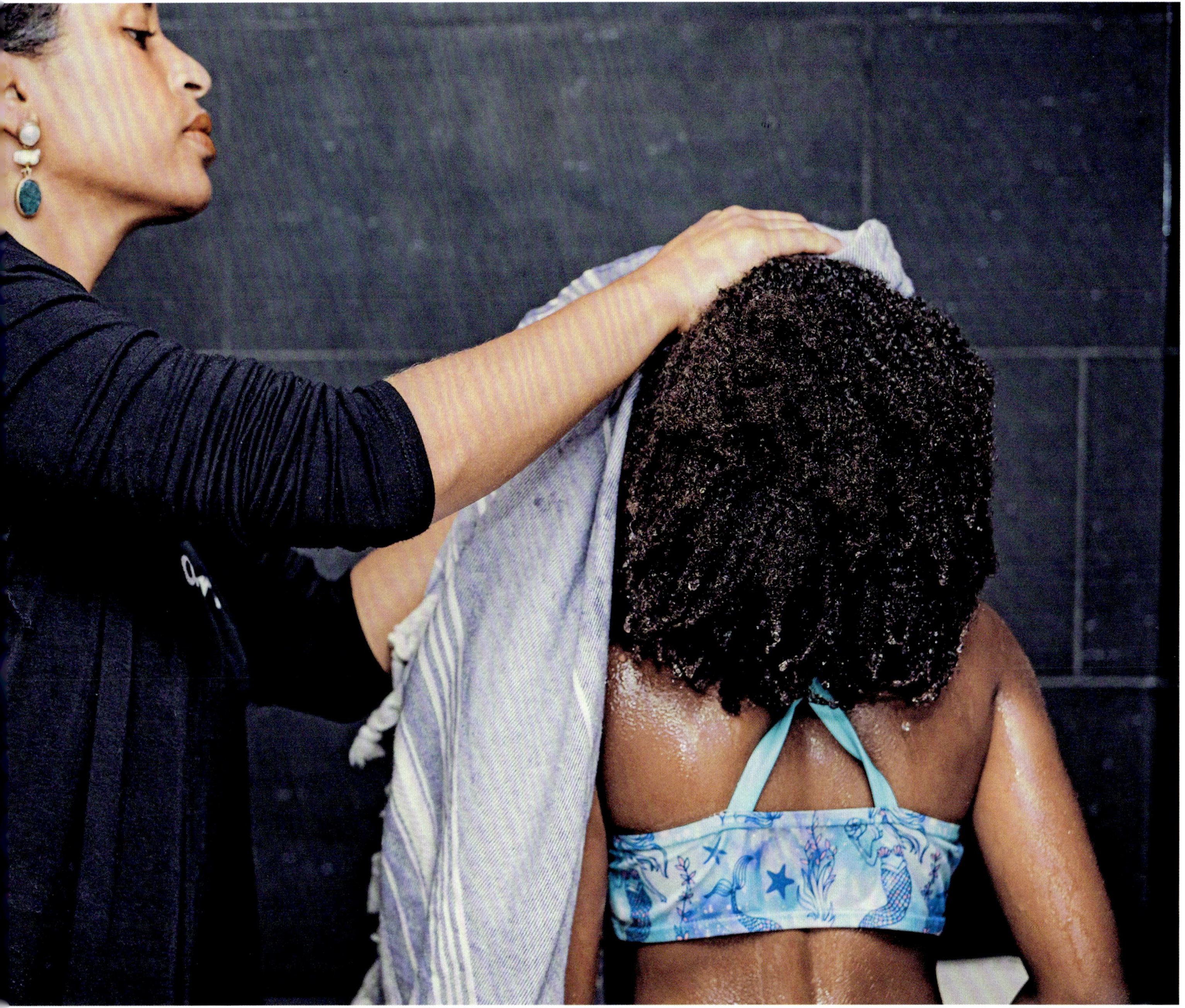

confronting deeply held beliefs, and exploring different approaches to hair care.

As you read through the stories in this book, you will see that, for a number of Black women, the pandemic represented a significant period in their natural hair journey. The recurrence of this theme herein, I believe, speaks to its prevalence beyond what you see in these pages. Some women already had natural hair, but decided to stop pressing their hair, or at least, press it less often. Others decided to try hairstyles believed to be "unprofessional" by others. Some were finally able to invest time into learning how to care for their hair on their own. And many, like Jamia, went natural for the very first time.

This is a reminder that while the natural hair movement was indeed powerful, many Black women continued to relax their hair. Whether this was due to a fear of how they would be perceived, comments from friends and family, internalized racist beliefs that natural hair is unattractive or unprofessional, or even a desire to maintain their existing hair-care routines, natural hair did not seem like a safe or appealing option for many Black women.

I don't have the data, but I believe we will look back and see that 2020 ushered in a new wave of the natural hair movement. So, what *was* it about 2020 that sparked, what I believe we will one day call, a new era in Black hair history?

I'm sure there are a number of reasons, but one I hear most often is that the safety of being at home—away from public spaces, especially Eurocentric work environments—made them feel comfortable enough to finally give natural hair a try. Black women have been wrestling with whether natural hair is appropriate for the workplace for a very long time. The roots can be traced back to racism, respectability, and assimilation. In *Hair Story: Untangling the Roots of Black Hair in America,* Ayana D. Byrd and Lori L. Tharps explain, in the early 1900s, "[f]or White Americans, education and training made little difference if a person looked too 'African.' Kinky hair, wide noses, and full lips translated to 'ignorant,' 'uncivilized,' and 'infantile.'"[18] Thus, Black people hoping to access better opportunities had to mimic European attributes as well as they could. This meant those kinks had to go.

This attitude has withstood the test of time. A 2023 study found that approximately 41 percent of Black women straighten their hair for job interviews and that Black women are 54 percent more likely to feel that they have to wear their hair straight to be successful in an interview.[19] A 2016 study found that Black women experience high levels of anxiety surrounding their hair and *perceive* that there is a social stigma against textured hair.[20] But we aren't wrong to feel this way. Research has shown that White women rate natural hair as less beautiful, less attractive, and less professional than smooth hair.[21]

Jamia grew up believing that "it is unwritten how you should keep your hair in corporate spaces." However, working from home offered her the opportunity to dip her toe in the water without worrying about whether or not her hair texture would be considered inappropriate.

Another reason for this new era is that the Black pride that swept the nation in the summer of 2020 prompted some Black women to finally embrace the hair that signified their tie to the motherland. The killings of Breonna Taylor and George Floyd, among many other murders of unarmed Black men and women by police officers, ushered in what some have called a "summer of racial reckoning." Since pandemic shutdowns removed the distractions we enjoyed prior to COVID-19, people were without excuse when it came time to face the realities of racism, particularly anti-Blackness, in the U.S. and abroad. And while we were sitting with the murder of Ahmaud Arbery (reminiscent of the murder of Trayvon Martin), we were forced to witness a modern-day public lynching as officer Derek Chauvin knelt on George Floyd's neck for what seemed like an eternity.

It was a time of extreme sadness, anger, and frustration. But I think this is why it was also a time of global awakening. I have quite a few White friends who realized they could no longer sit comfortably in their privilege. Some expressed shame to have been so clueless about the continued existence of White supremacy. "Black Lives Matter" marches were taking place all over the world. No one could hide, though many tried, from the truth; anti-Blackness is not only real, but deadly. President Barack Obama's election did not end racism, and Trump didn't reinvent it. Our country was literally built on it, and Black people still suffer because of it.

While 2020 was traumatic for so many of us, it also offered many people a renewed sense of freedom and expression. In fact, I started working on this book in 2020; I had to find a creative space to channel my rage. All I wanted to do was immerse myself in Blackness. To celebrate Blackness. To stand up for Blackness. And honestly, I felt more thankful to be Black than ever before.

No wonder Black women found themselves reconsidering their attitudes toward natural hair. It was as good a time as any to take a closer look at the reasons they believed they needed straight hair to be professional; scrutiny of this belief will always uncover racist roots. Jamia can attest to this. She shared, "For over seven years I had been dressing more culturally in corporate settings and felt comfortable. Why hadn't my hair enjoyed this freedom as well?" In 2020, Jamia decided it was time to fully embrace, in her words, "a less Eurocentric, more authentic and unapologetic" version of herself. Wearing her natural hair for the first time in her life was her way of doing just that.

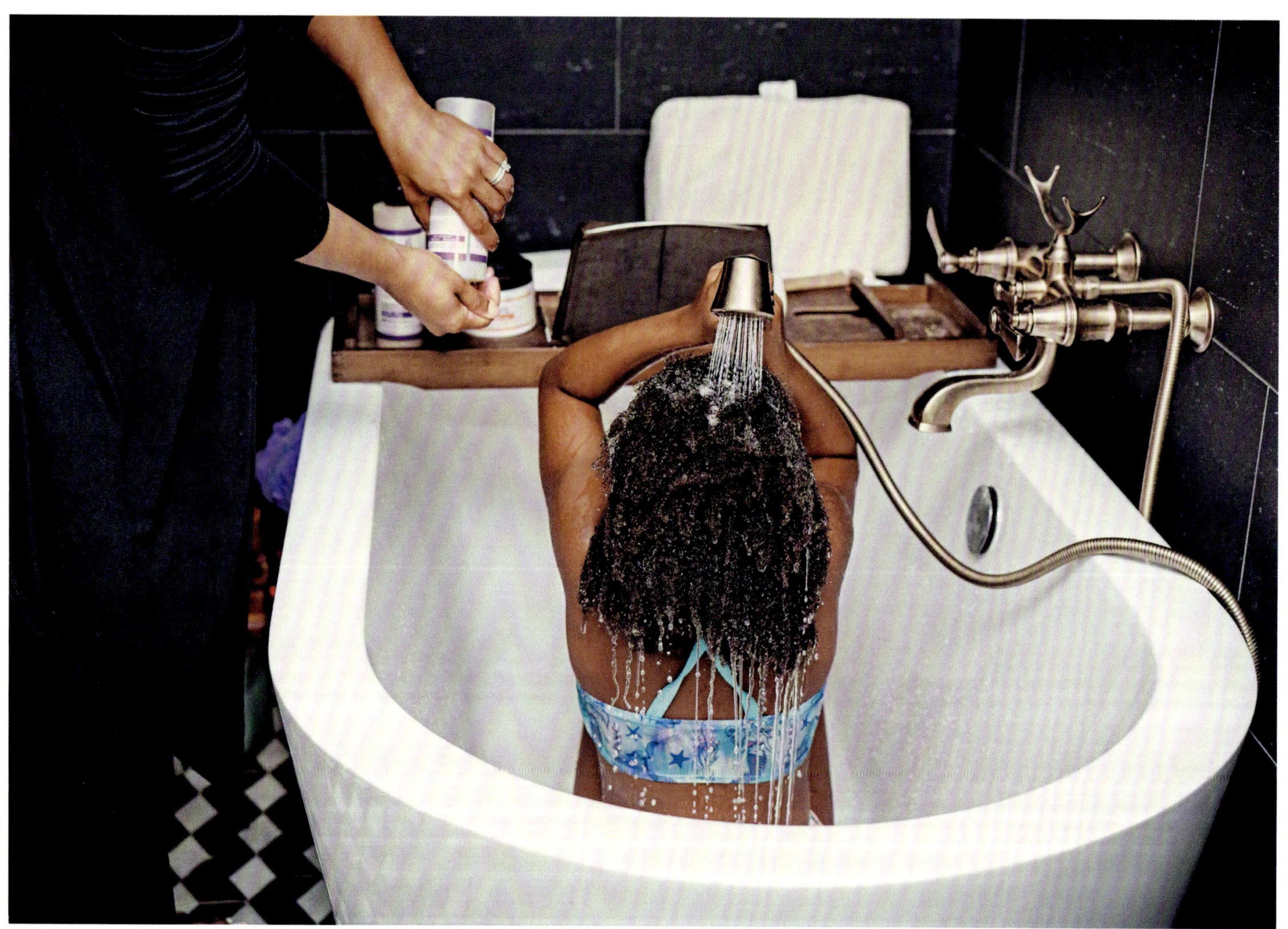

Wash day for Jamia and Journey is governed by the three P's: products, prayer, and patience. Amen. The process lasts about three to four hours, twice a month.

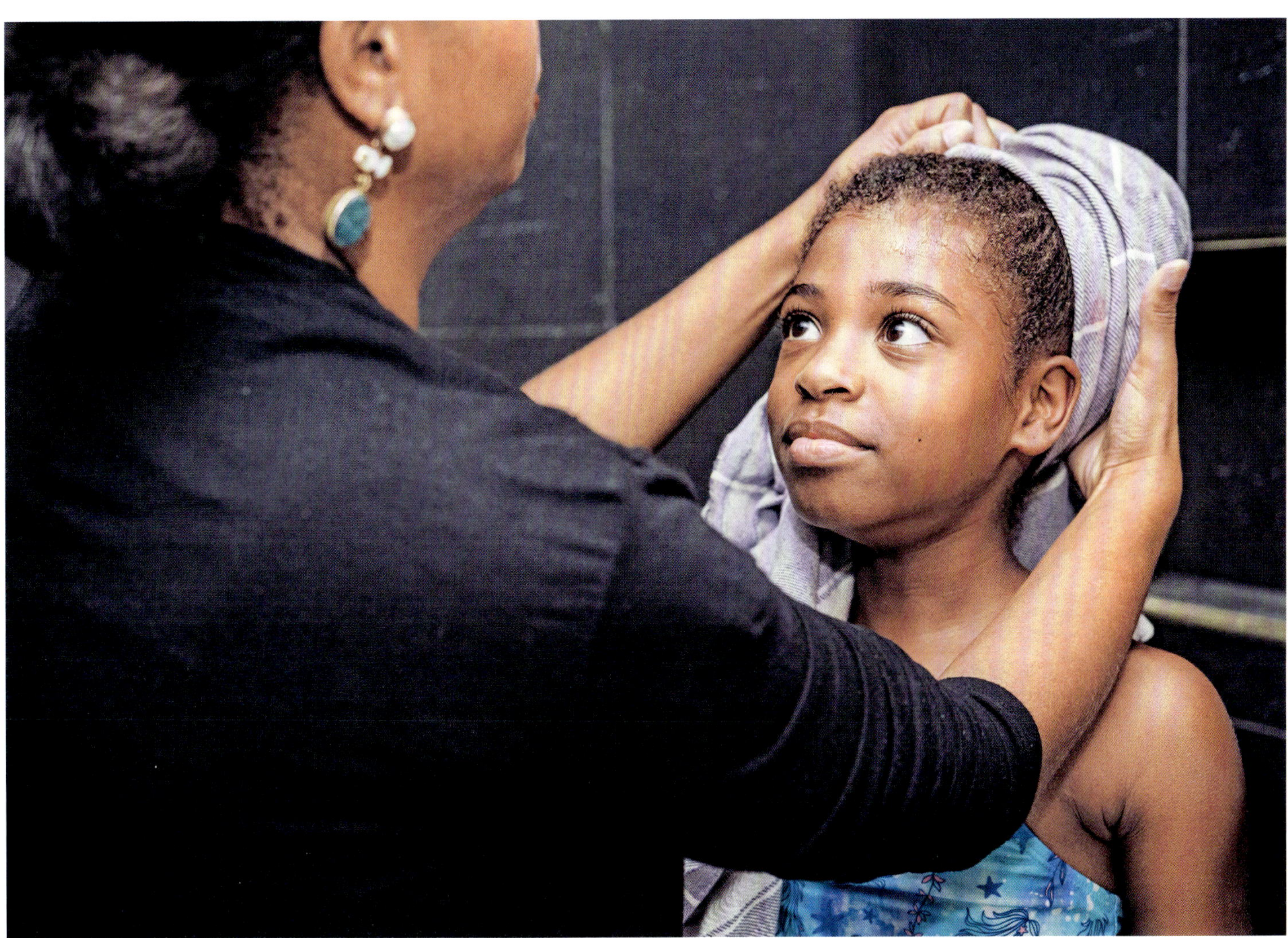

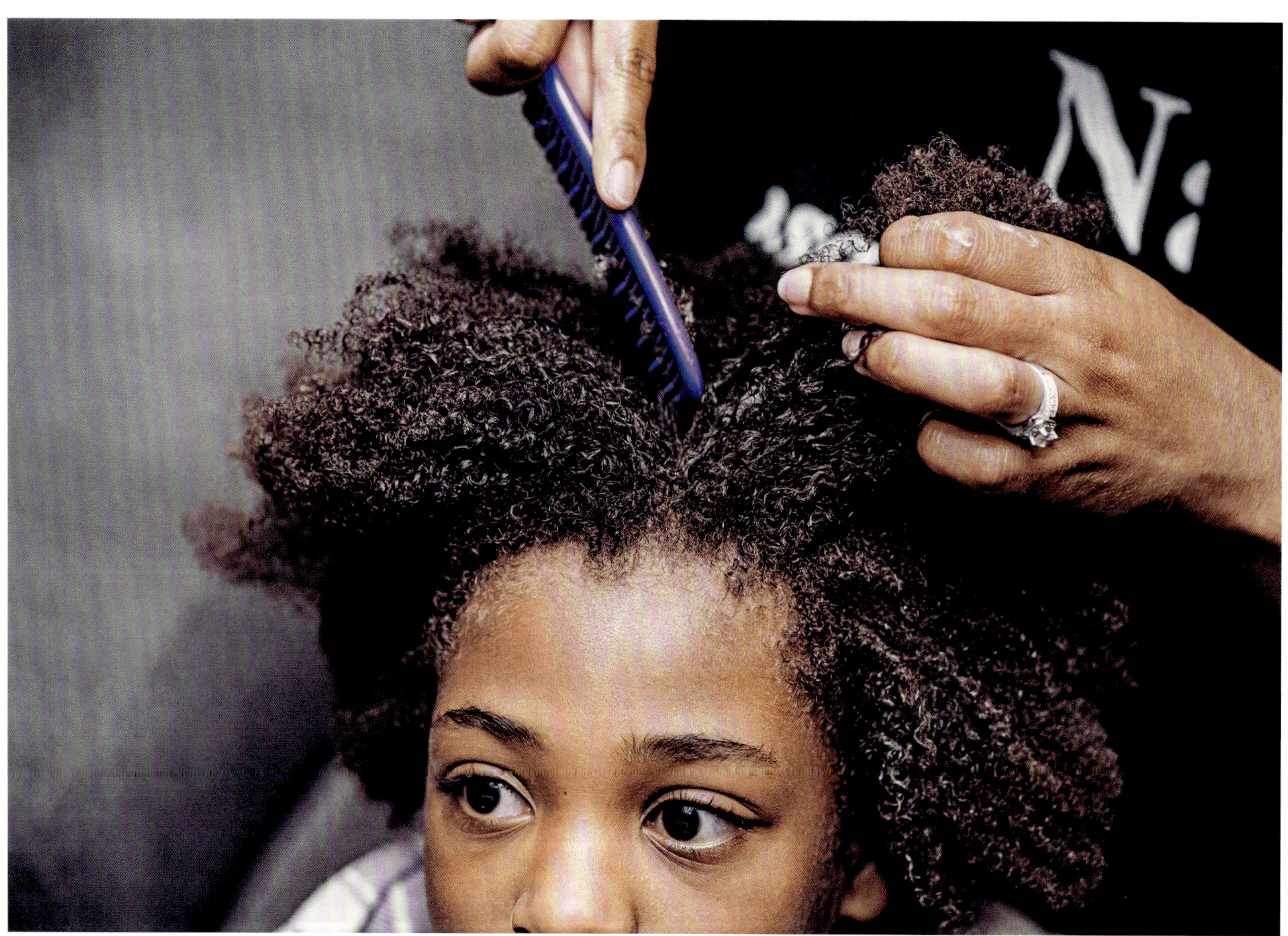

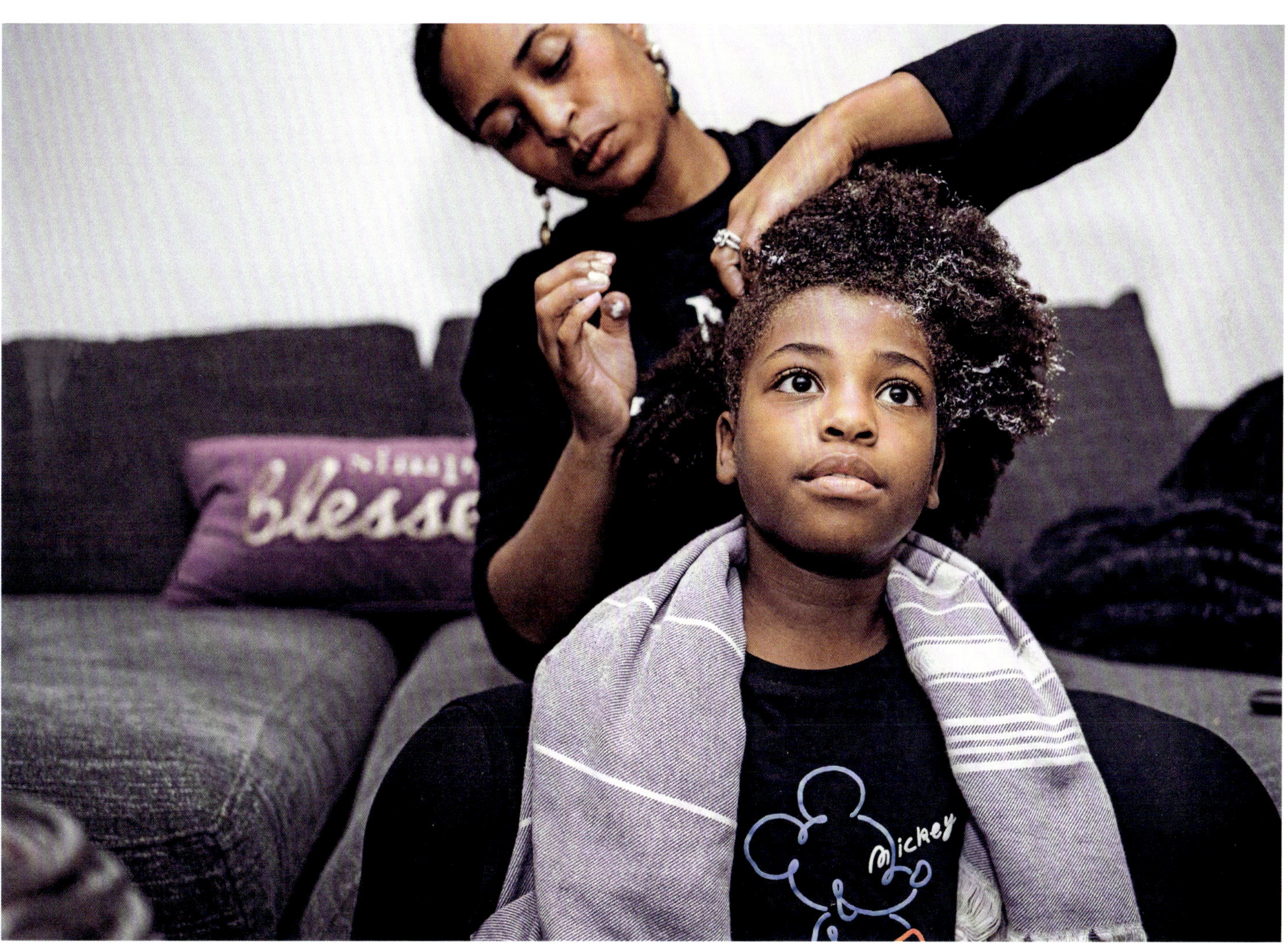
blesse
Mickey

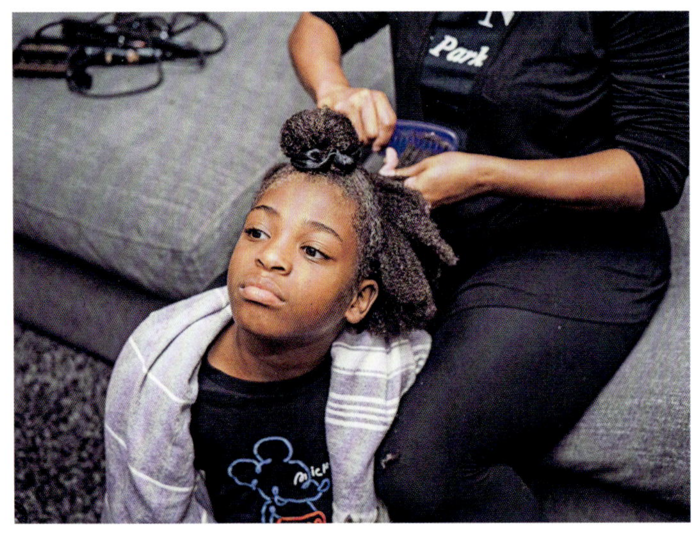
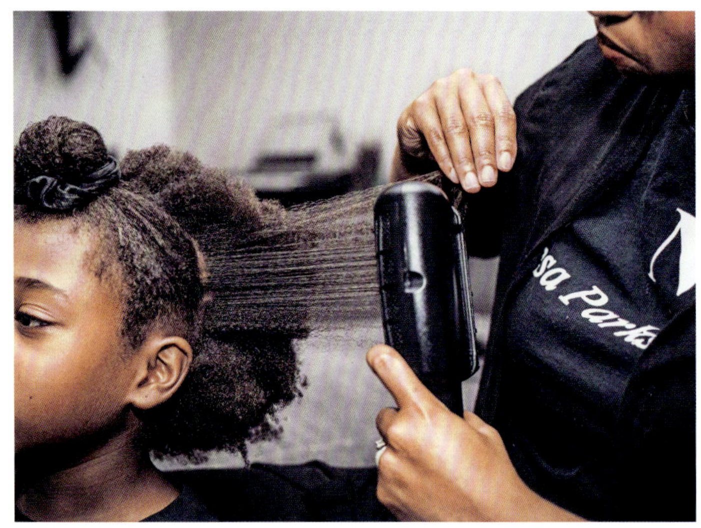
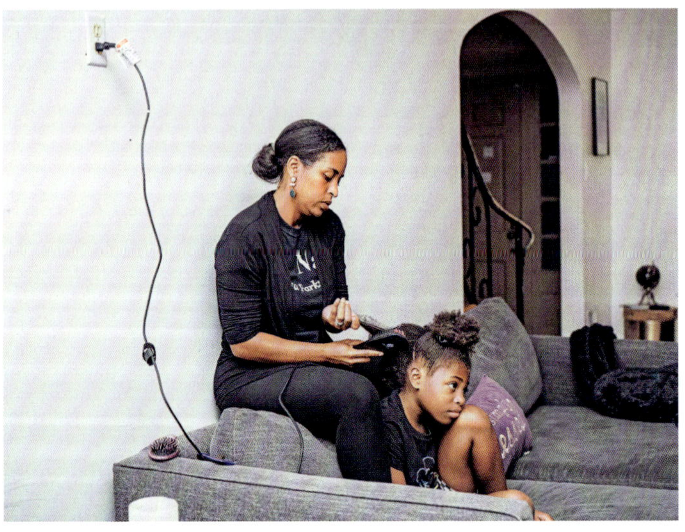
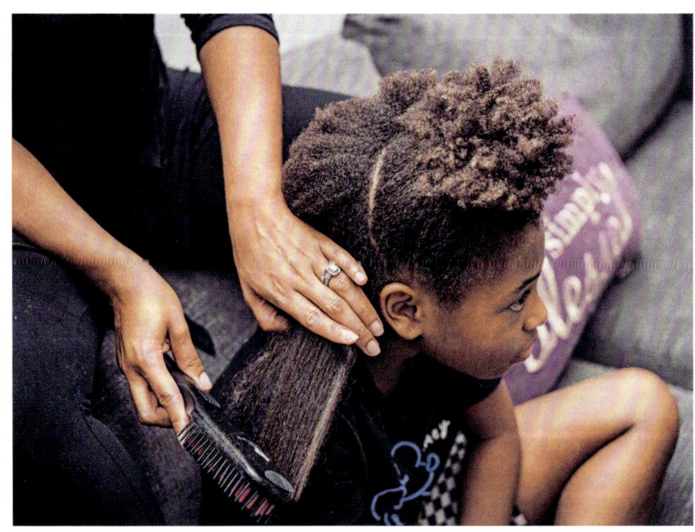

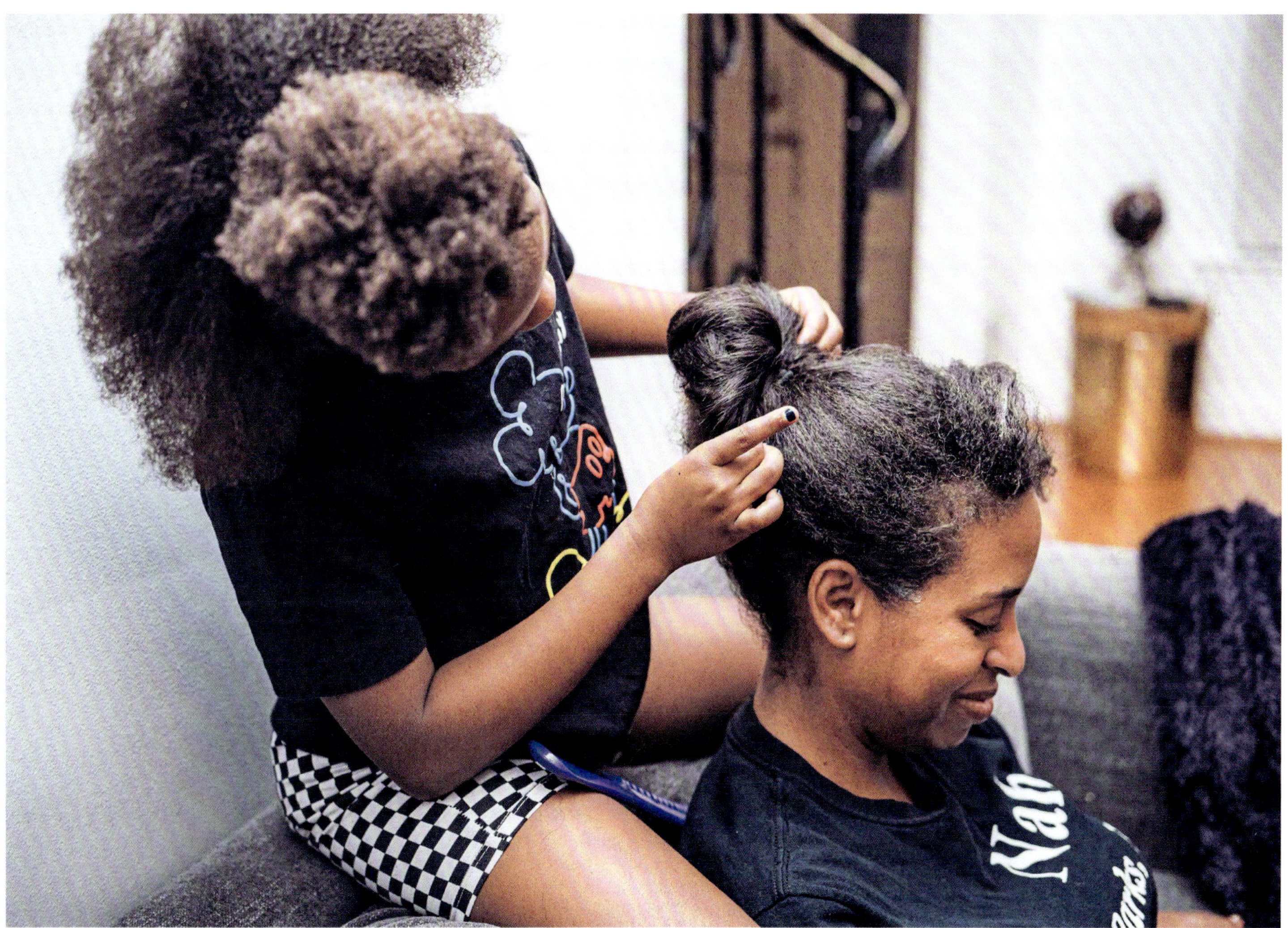

Opposite page, top left and top right: After detangling, Jamia blow dries Journey's hair. *Opposite page, bottom left and bottom right:* The outlet nearest the couch in Jamia's older home sits high up on the wall, so she moves closer to it to use the heated brush to further fluff out Journey's hair. *Above:* Journey enjoys styling her mom's hair when wash day is complete.

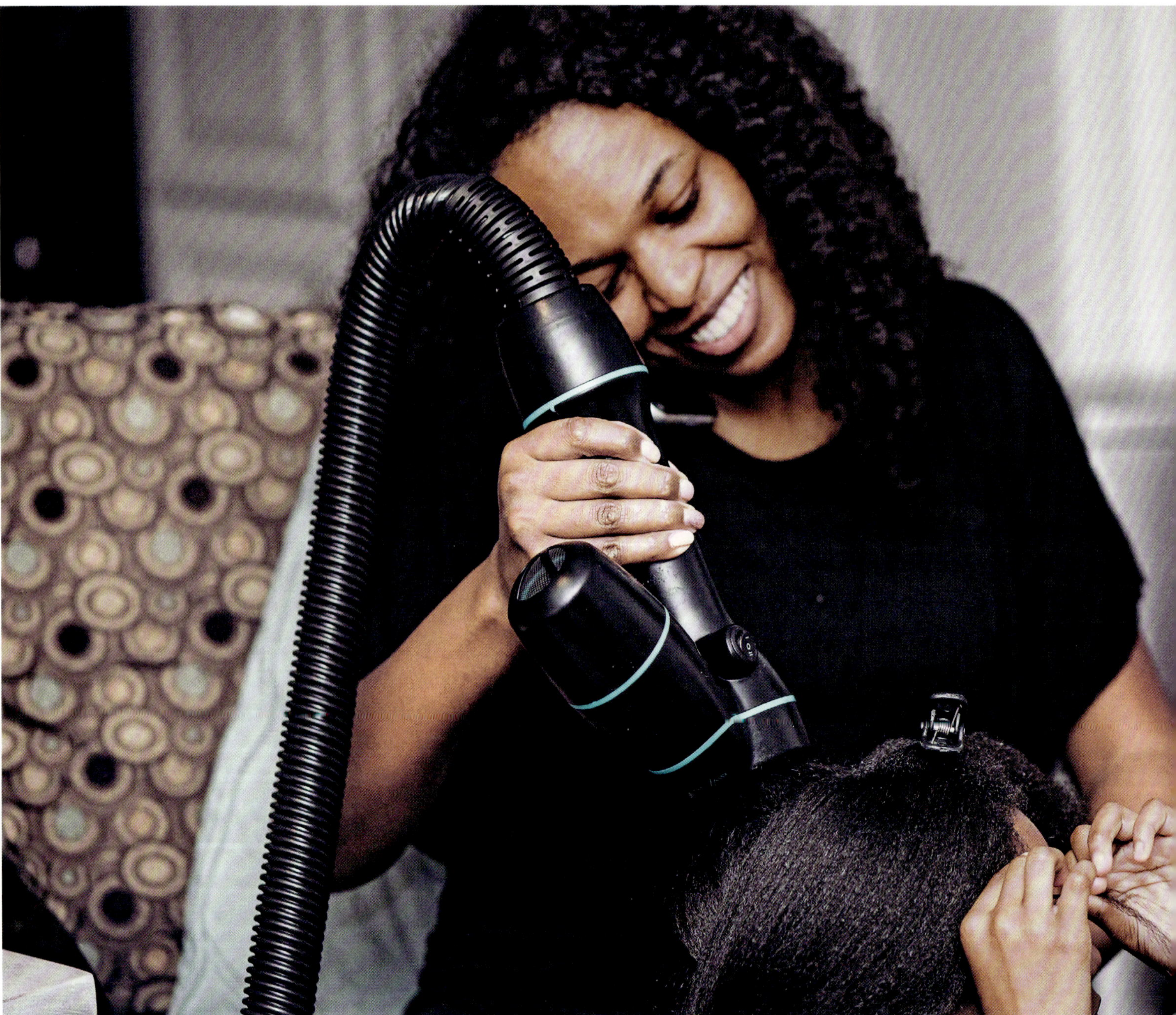

Kameron, Kaylee & NiaGrace

KAMERON was a naturalista long before that word became popular. As she was growing up in the 1980s and '90s,
she was ahead of her time and wise beyond her years. She
maintained her natural hair at a time when there was little
access to products, resources, or knowledge about how
to care for natural hair. No YouTube channels. No blogs or
communities of Black women sharing their stories. None of
that. Nonetheless, she wasn't interested in changing her
hair texture like so many others were doing at the time.
She didn't want to use chemicals because she believed
they would damage her hair. Besides, her hair was long,

thick, and healthy, and she loved it. It was the hair God had given her and she saw no reason to change it. I mean, if "if it ain't broke" was a person . . .

Kameron was the only one in her family with natural hair, and since she didn't have access to natural hair inspiration, she experimented with different ways to style it on her own. Without a relaxer, Kameron wasn't able to rock the trendy hairstyles that ruled the 1990s (hello, finger waves). But for her, the short-term benefit of having a cool hairstyle was not worth the long-term consequence of the damage she believed relaxers would cause to her hair. So, rather than trying to tame her frizzy mane with perms, she religiously wore braids or a bun to avoid unplanned afros. When she wanted a different look, and the weather permitted, she would wear a braid-out ponytail. She took the less-is-more approach, and it worked for her.

To make styling a bit easier, she would get her hair pressed by her "old-school hairdresser," Ms. Margaret. Kameron has fond memories of being the youngest person in the salon and listening to the older women talk about life. She also remembers that hot comb, holding her ears to keep them from getting burned, and the loads of hair grease Ms. Margaret would slather on her head. Once pressed, Ms. Margaret would put her hair in a French braid because she wasn't sure how else to style Kameron's natural hair. This wasn't unusual. Many hair stylists at that time didn't quite know what to do with natural hair other than to keep it pressed and/or braided. Even so, Kameron recalls having healthy hair under the care of Ms. Margaret.

The lack of understanding of Black natural hair among professionals was cemented for Kameron when she, through a modeling agency, was booked for an Aveda hair show. While she was excited to be a model in the show, she was worried about what exactly was going to be done to her hair. It quickly became clear that the White stylist was not used to styling Black natural hair. Kameron sat there, smiling to hide her stress, while the stylist created what she believed to be a masterpiece. The hairstyle was a complete failure. Kameron recalls, "There were no Black stylists there or any other Black hair models. I had no one to talk to, commiserate with, or even exchange glances with to communicate how I really felt about the style."

Kameron has had her share of struggles with Black stylists as well. When she wanted something other than Ms. Margaret's French braid, she would go to more modern Black stylists. Most vocalized their preference for relaxed hair and were unwilling to spend the time and energy required to do her hair, or they charged exorbitant prices for doing natural hair, which was considered a specialty service. Again, this was a time when knowledge about how to care for Black natural hair was not widespread, even among Black cosmetologists. Luckily, education around Black natural hair is slowly becoming a part of the curriculum in cosmetology schools.[22]

In addition to an unsupportive hair-care industry, Kameron's decision to maintain natural hair was met with opposition from her family. She recalls elder family members saying things like, "You aren't leaving the house like that are you?" Her mother, who kept her own hair relaxed or texturized, was proud of Kameron's long, thick hair, but still, she urged her toward a relaxer to make it *more* beautiful. To her mother, leaving her hair natural was only dimming its light.

This eventually led Kameron to relax her hair in the ninth grade. It was long, flowy, and silky, just like her mom told her it would be. However, after about two years of relaxing, she noticed breakage, thinning, and weakening of her once long, thick, and healthy hair. It was damaged, just as she imagined it might be. Her hair's response to the relaxer was the very reason she had avoided chemicals for so long. So, rather than continuing to damage her hair with relaxers, she decided to return to what she knew, and she has been natural ever since.

Kameron's brief experience with relaxers solidified what she had already grown to understand. She is a nonconform-

ist and so is her hair. Trying to be like other people is a fruitless pursuit. Rather than fighting her uniqueness, she found it most rewarding to embrace it, and to be completely and unapologetically herself. While her big hair made others uncomfortable, it made her feel empowered. Negative comments actually made her feel even more defiant and determined to show her crown proudly. Now, her goal is to ensure her girls feel free to proudly rock their natural curls. She hopes to teach her daughters that "being fearfully and wonderfully made also includes their unique hair textures."

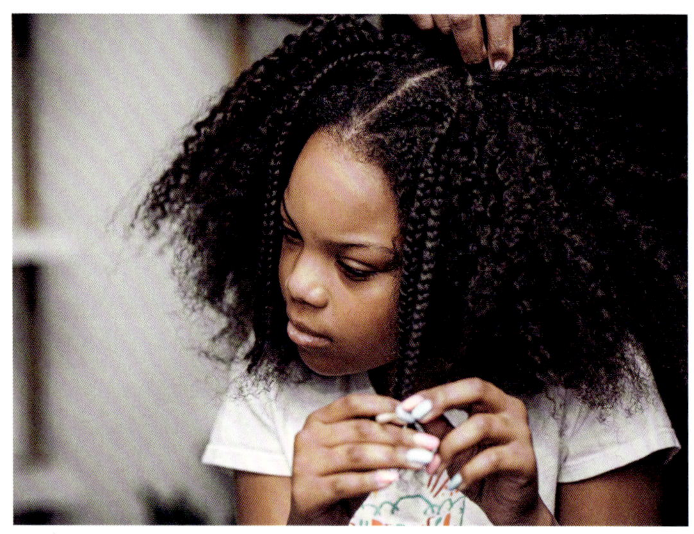
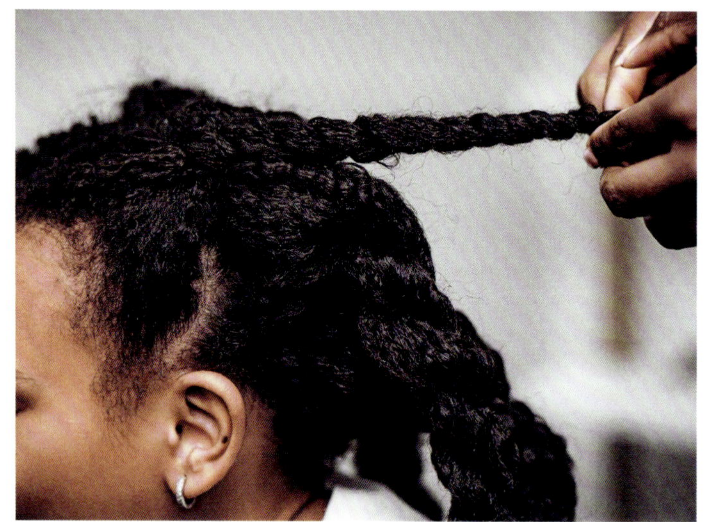
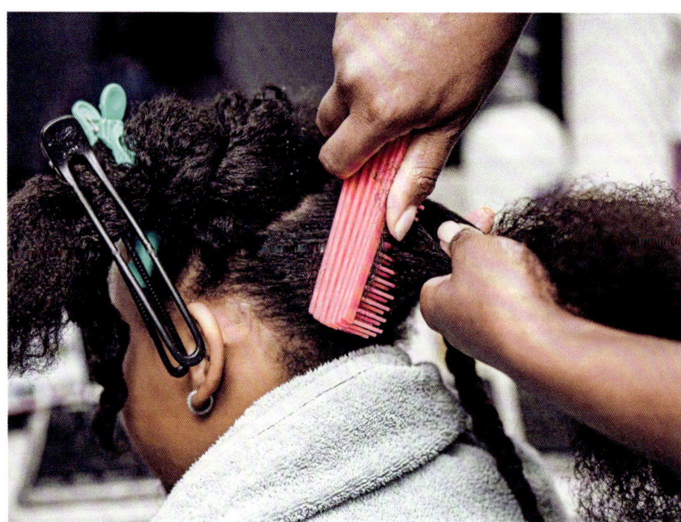
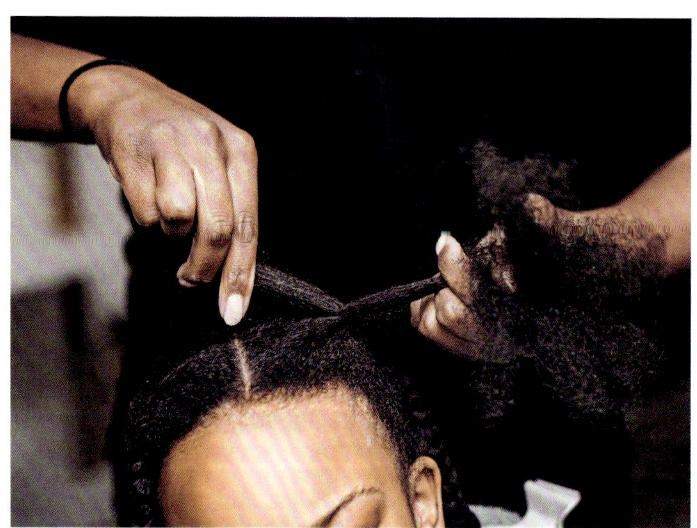

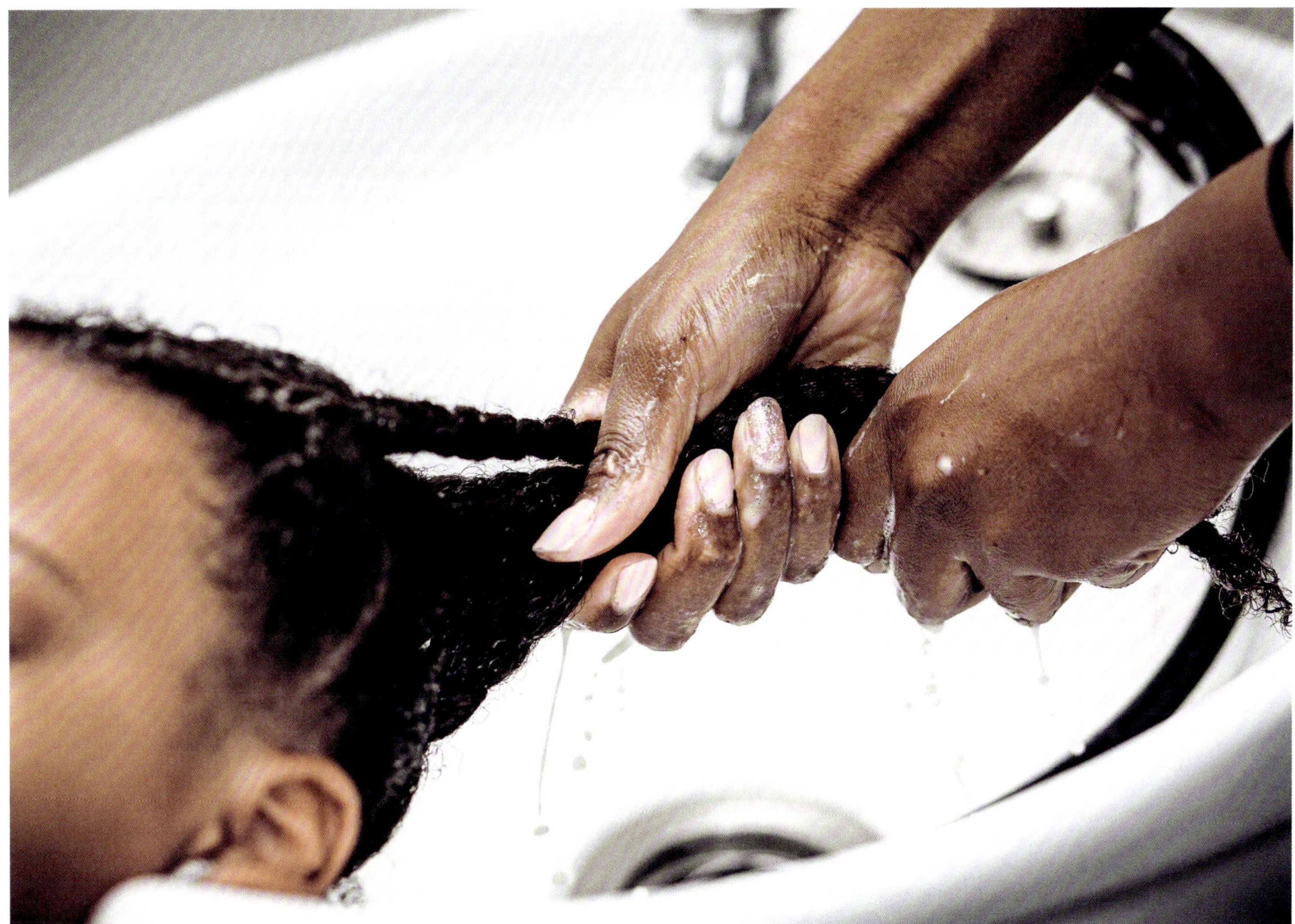

Kameron usually breaks up wash day into three days, but packed as much into one day as possible for my visit. After photographing her near-professional techniques, I was inspired to step up my game. She taught me one of my favorite wash-day hacks—detangling then braiding (or twisting) the hair *before* washing it to reduce tangling. Game changer!

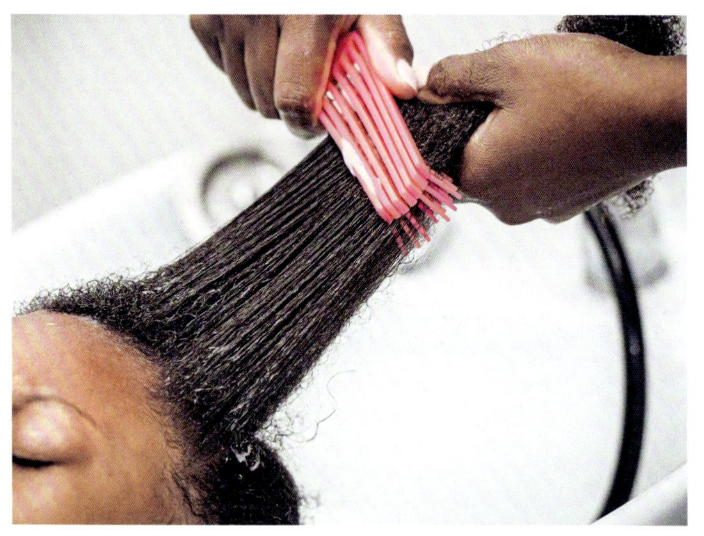
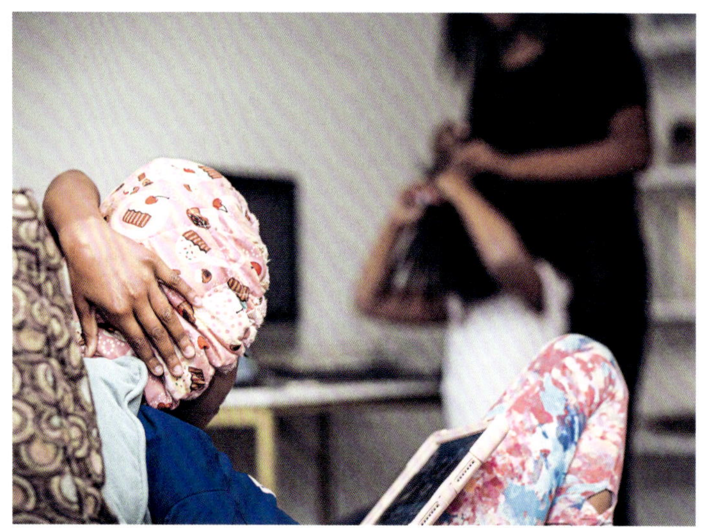
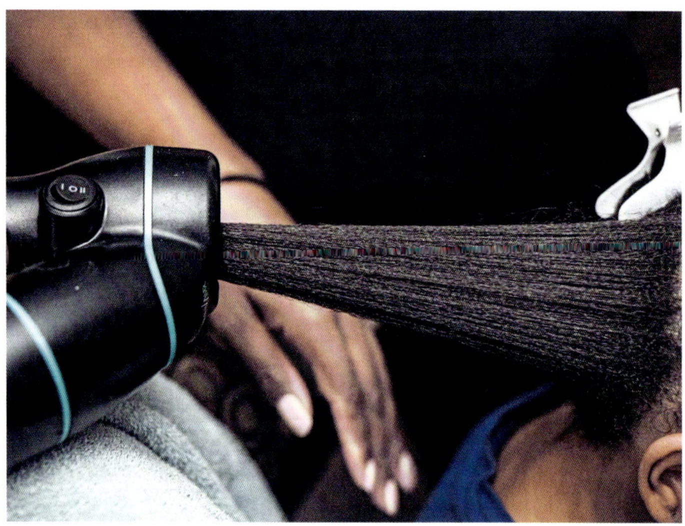
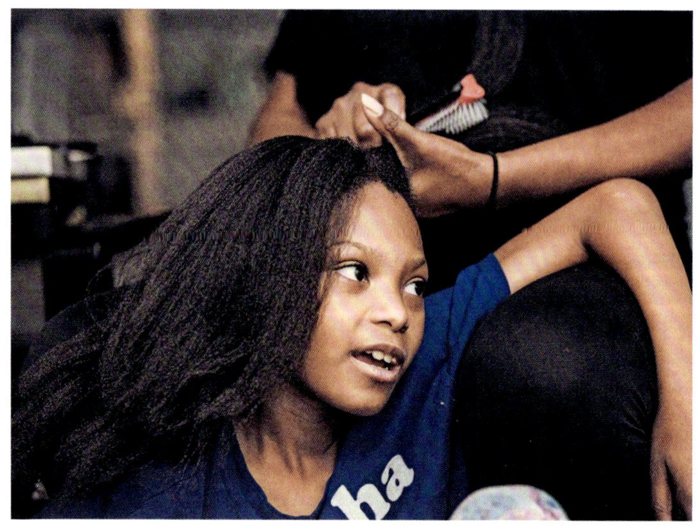

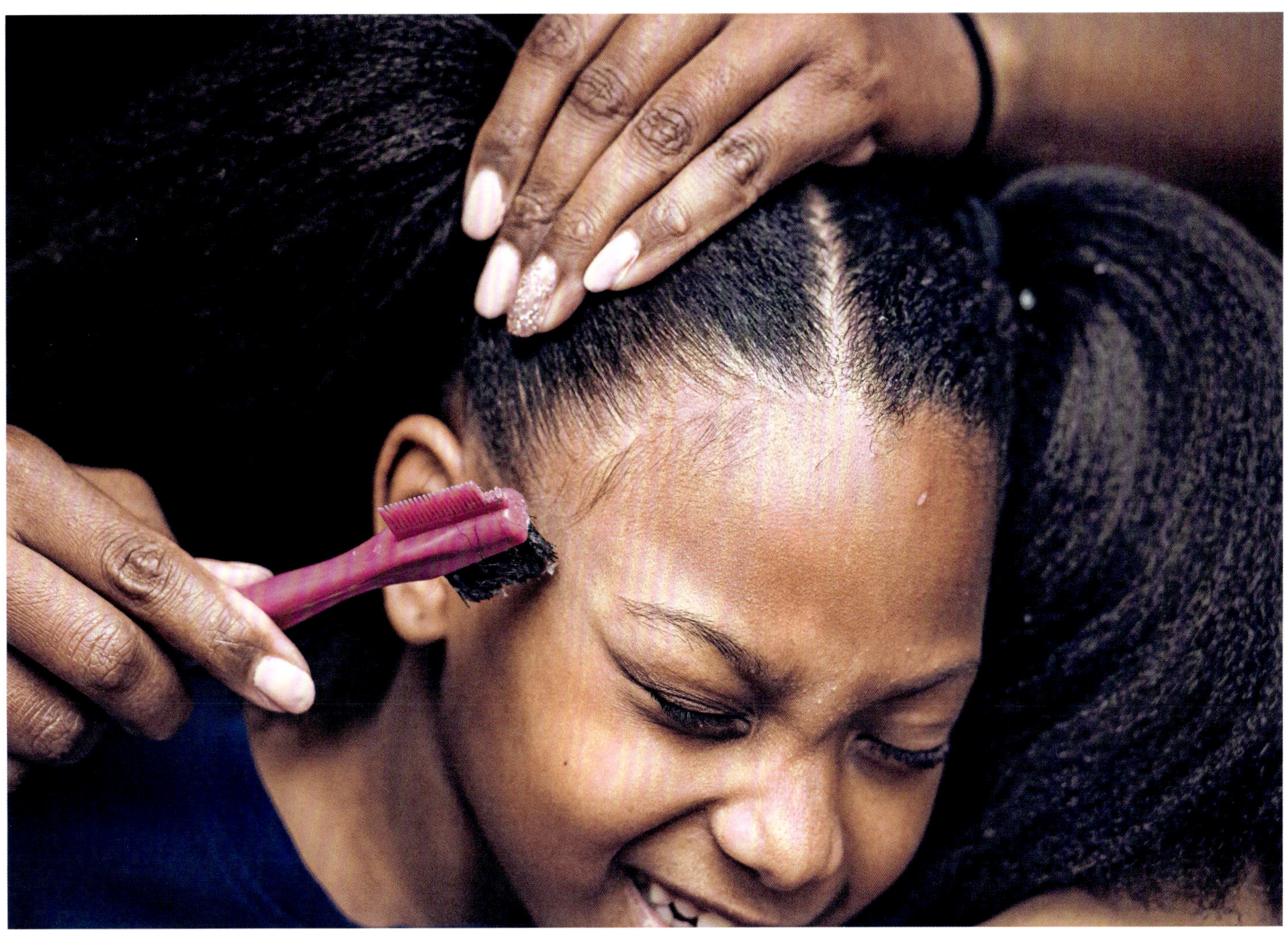

Opposite page: After washing, Kameron takes down each braid, adds deep conditioner and brushes each daughter's hair. She then places a heating cap on their hair for at least thirty minutes. After conditioning, she blow dries on low heat and styles their hair.

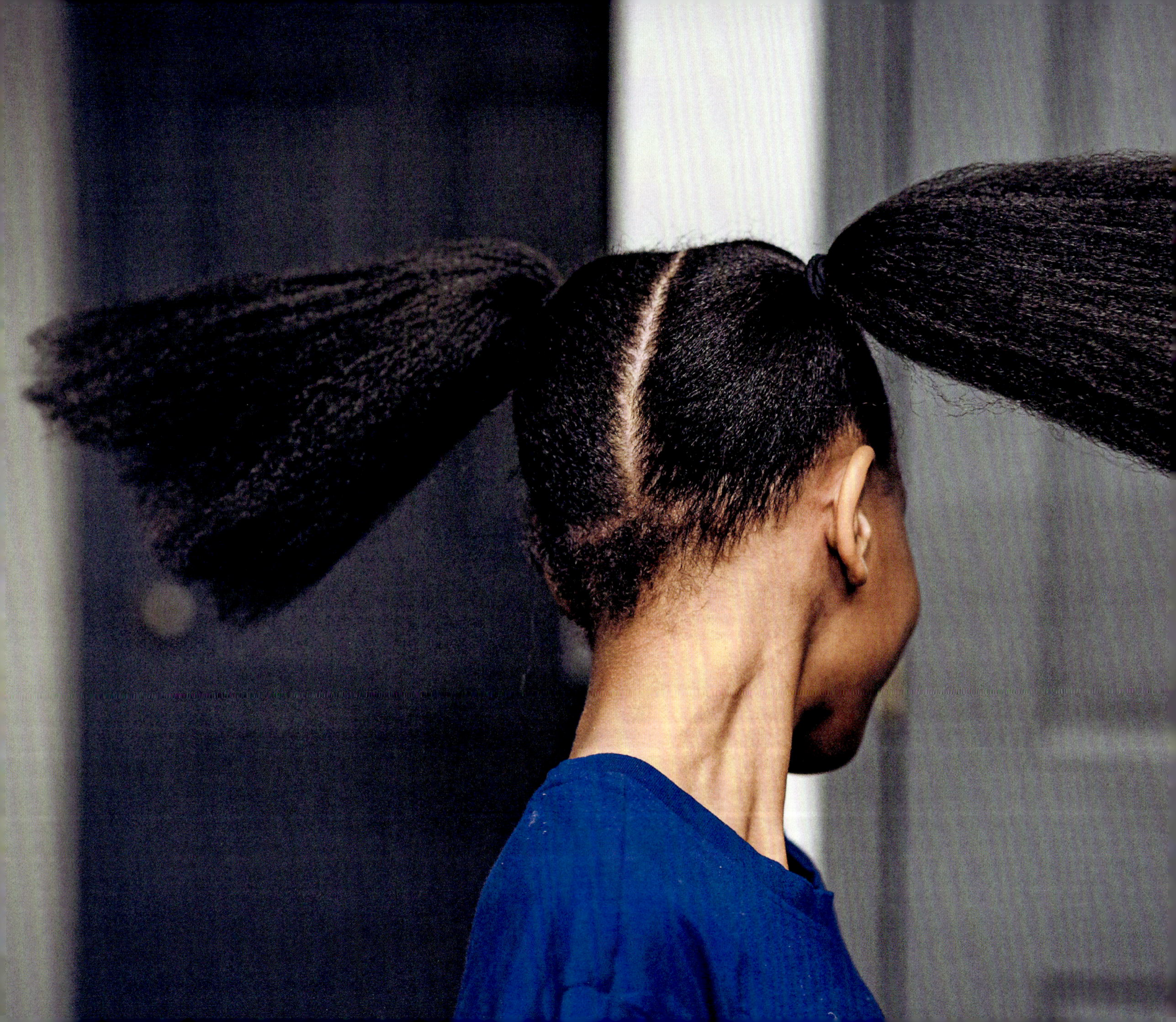

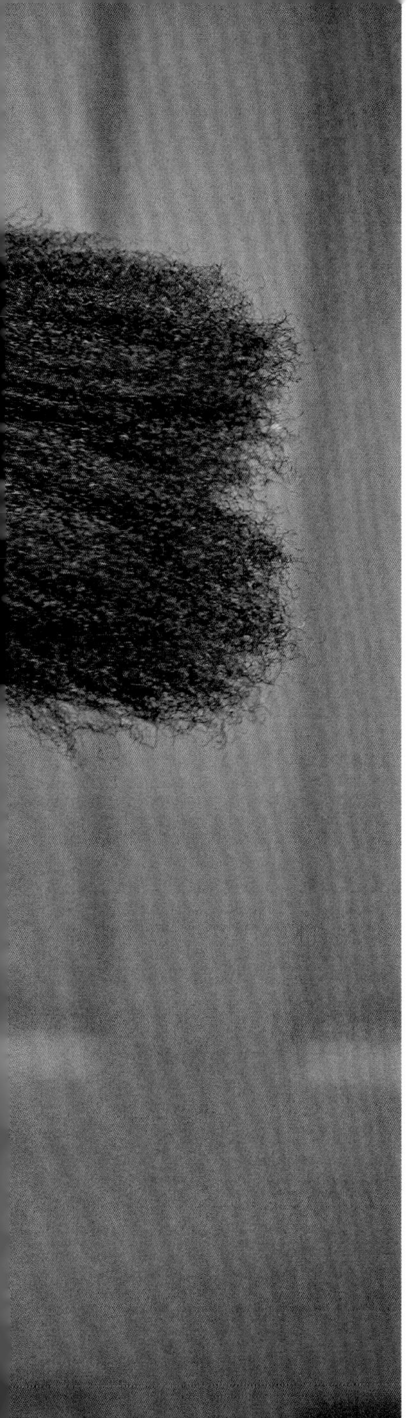

"I hope they will see their hair as an avenue for artistic and personal expression, and never as a limitation."

—KAMERON

Toni & Gabrielle

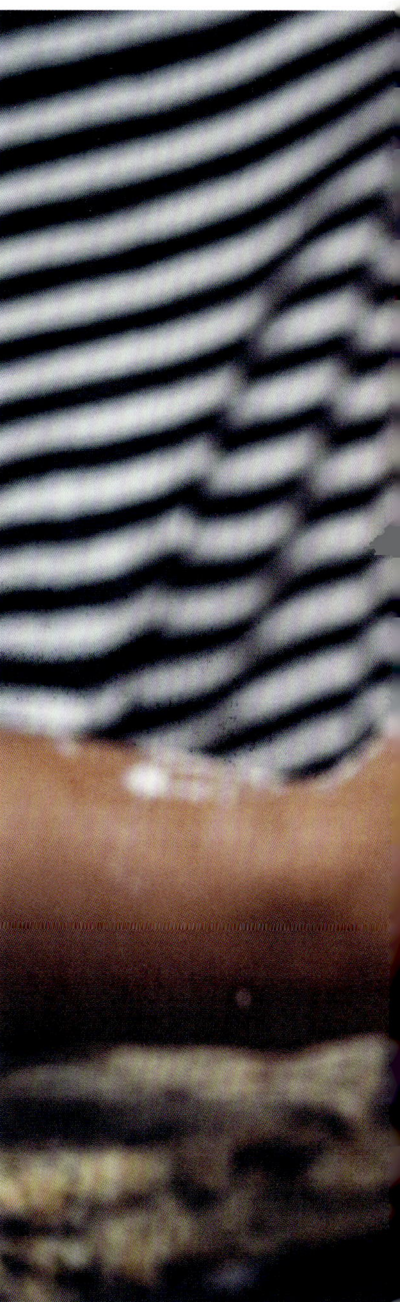

"I realize that for many situations and for many years, I had been often somewhat paralyzed by fear of water, which had sidelined me from many activities."

OH, the fear of water. Dreading the rain. Trying to avoid sweat if at all possible. This is the burden many natural-headed sisters carry when wearing their hair pressed, or in any elongated style for that matter. For water is the greatest enemy of many natural hair manipulations. I've been there, and I don't have a single natural-haired friend who hasn't. Some have gone so far as to tailor their workout regimens to account for their silk-press schedules. And forget about swimming.

Growing up, Toni experienced an excessive amount of negative commentary regarding her thick, curly hair. She

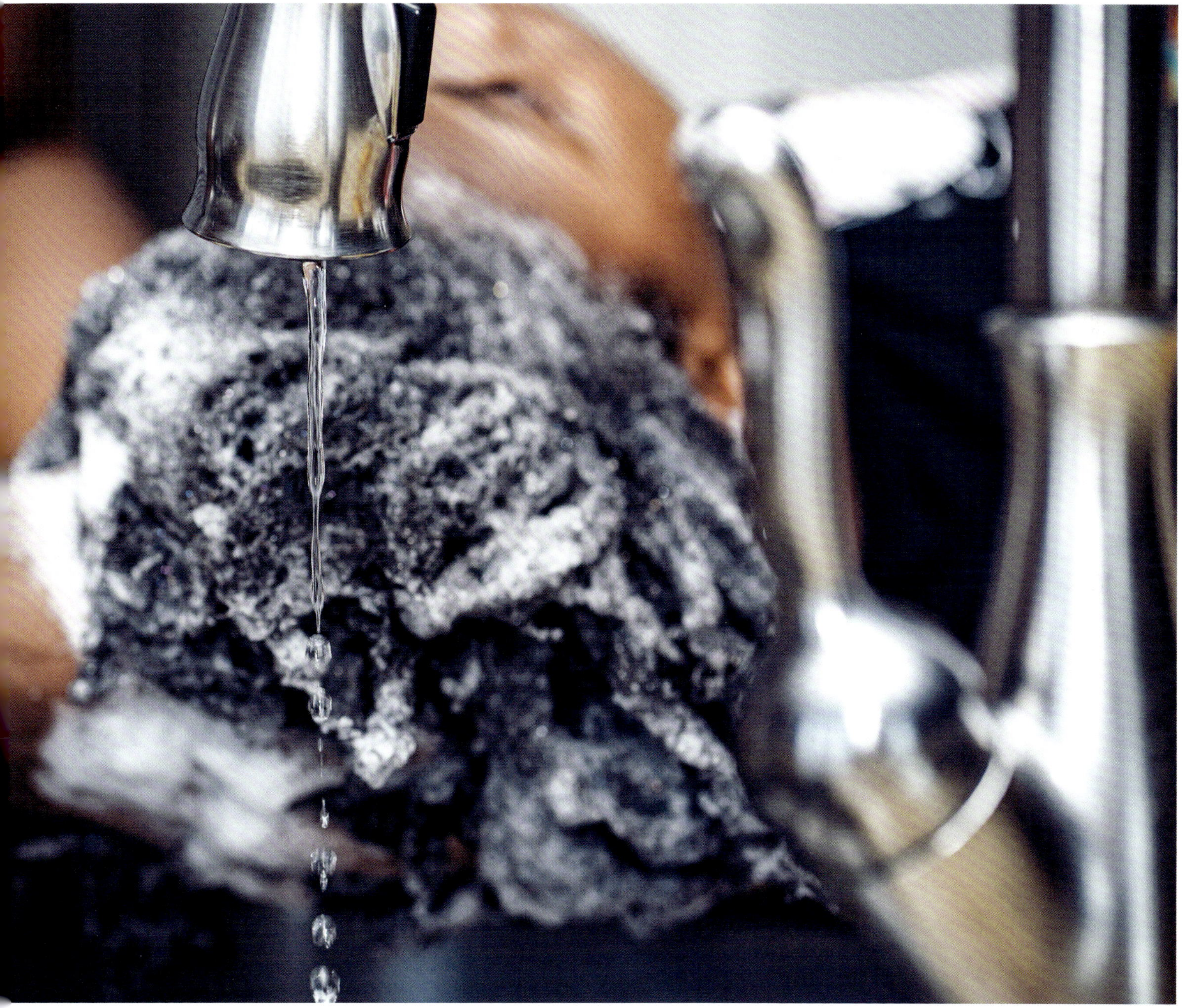

 I have been pleasantly surprised by the number of moms in this book who reported that their daughters swim competitively or very regularly. While my own childhood love of swimming was replaced with concerns about my hair as I grew older, I have spoken to many parents who prioritize swim lessons to combat the "Black people can't swim" stereotype.

Ironically, this trite one-liner is the offspring of Jim Crow–era prohibitions against Black people swimming in public pools and fears of civil unrest if Black people were allowed to swim with White people.[26] The sense of pride among Black people in 2016 when Simone Manuel became the first Black woman to win an Olympic medal in an individual swimming event was intensified given our history, which includes a hotel pool being drained and scrubbed after Dorothy Dandridge stuck her toe in it.[27]

grew accustomed to stylists using the word *thick* as a synonym for "coarse" or "unmanageable." This was evidenced by their tone of voice and the frequent sandwiching of the word *thick* between deep sighs and long exhales. She often found herself feeling like a spectacle when she went to the salon. Although these stylists should have been the ones apologizing, Toni was the one saying "sorry" and feeling embarrassed by the stress her hair seemed to cause. These experiences conditioned her to keep her curls at bay, and to view them as a problem to be solved.

Perms were the solution. While in high school, Toni got her hair relaxed faithfully every four weeks. In college, she decided to cut her hair short. To maintain the look, her stylist performed partial relaxers every two weeks and full relaxers every four weeks. While in graduate school, she decided to grow her hair out. Again, she was met with sly remarks from stylists. This reminded her that her thick curls were not only defiant, but also unwelcome. So, perms remained a critical staple in Toni's hair-care routine.

That is until 2012, when she was pregnant with her first child, Gabrielle. Her pregnancy made her reconsider exposing herself to chemical relaxers. She finally found a hair stylist, Chandi, who authentically celebrated her hair texture and made her feel safe enough to finally walk away from perms. But that past trauma still caused her to keep those curls at arm's length with regular silk presses.

For Toni, living with pressed hair meant avoiding water at all costs. Over time, this avoidance evolved into fear; the water became a sort of trauma trigger because it had the power to reveal the curls she had been hiding for so long. Chandi (who, again, was the first stylist to ever affirm her hair texture) would often tell her how beautiful her curls were as they were revealed in the wash bowl. But Toni dismissed her; she could not believe her curls could possibly be anything other than the source of shame previous stylists complained about.

That is until 2021; another milestone year for Toni. While swimming at a community pool with her kids, she found herself emboldened by the heightened sense of Black pride that 2020 prompted—one good thing that came out of that crazy year. She decided that this time, she would go ahead and let her hair get wet. She describes the moment she went under water and emerged with beautifully formed curls as a "baptism" of sorts. "I came out of the water a new woman!" She welcomed her curls for the very first time. Since that day, she has opted for wash and go styles over presses. She has even gained the confidence to wear her hair in its natural state to work, which, pre-pandemic, she wasn't brave enough to do. It's quite beautiful that the thing she avoided for so long turned out to be the very thing that set her free.

Toni's journey has formed her perfectly to be able to handle the strains of wash day with her daughter, Gabrielle (Gabby). Wash day lasts about four hours every three to four weeks. Just like Toni, Gabby has beautiful, thick hair. But unlike Toni, who experienced tons of negative commentary about the thickness of her hair, Gabby is blessed to experience the gentle touch of her mother. From the hot cocoa she sipped while getting her hair detangled, to the noodle used to cradle her neck, I watched as Toni made every effort to keep Gabby calm. I imagine the many tears she shed as a child while getting her hair done informed the way she cares for her daughter's physical and emotional well-being during this ritual.

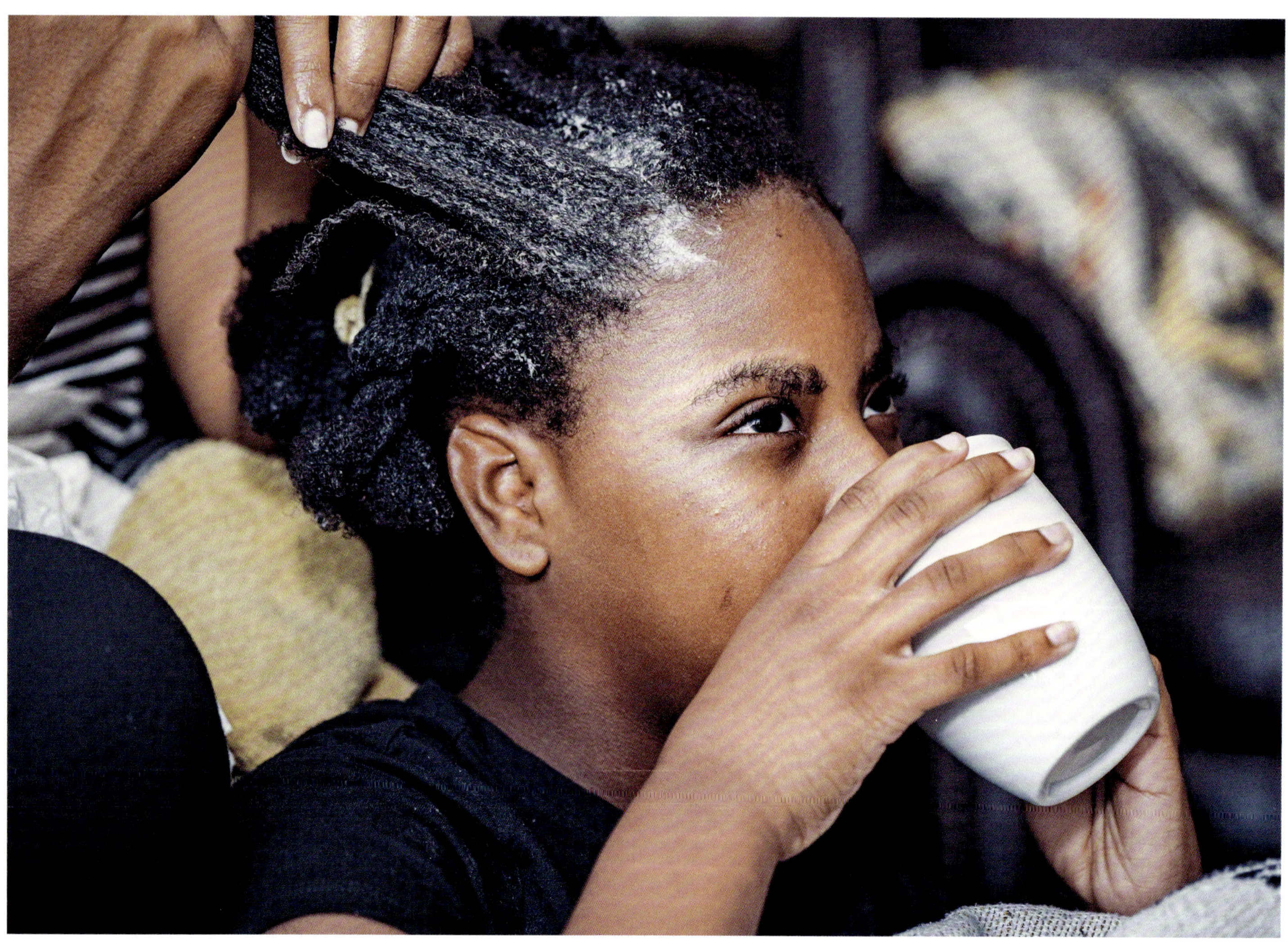

Gabby sips hot cocoa while Toni gently detangles her hair.

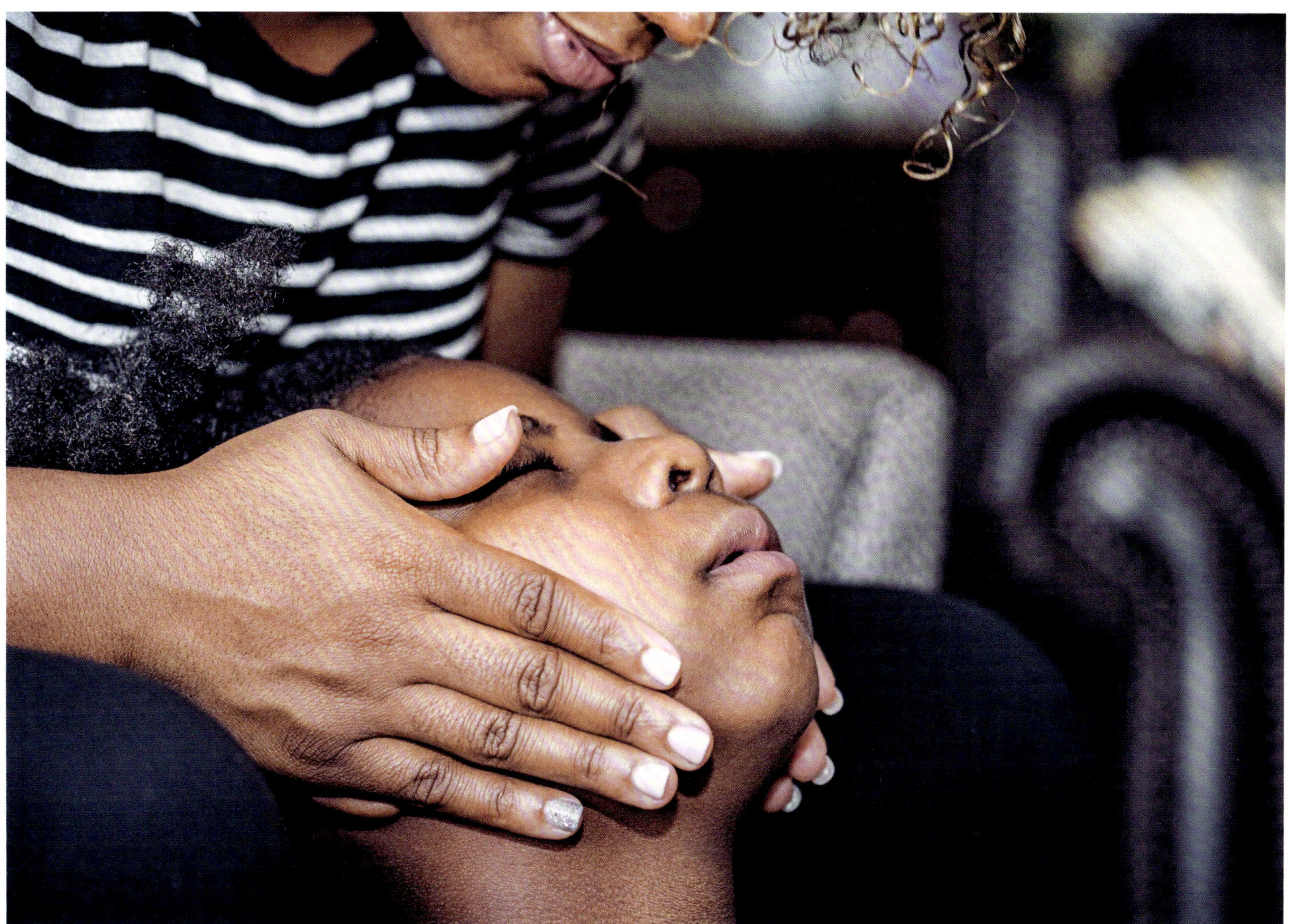

The detangling process is usually the hardest part of wash day. When it gets to be too much for Gabby, Toni helps her calm down with guided deep breathing.

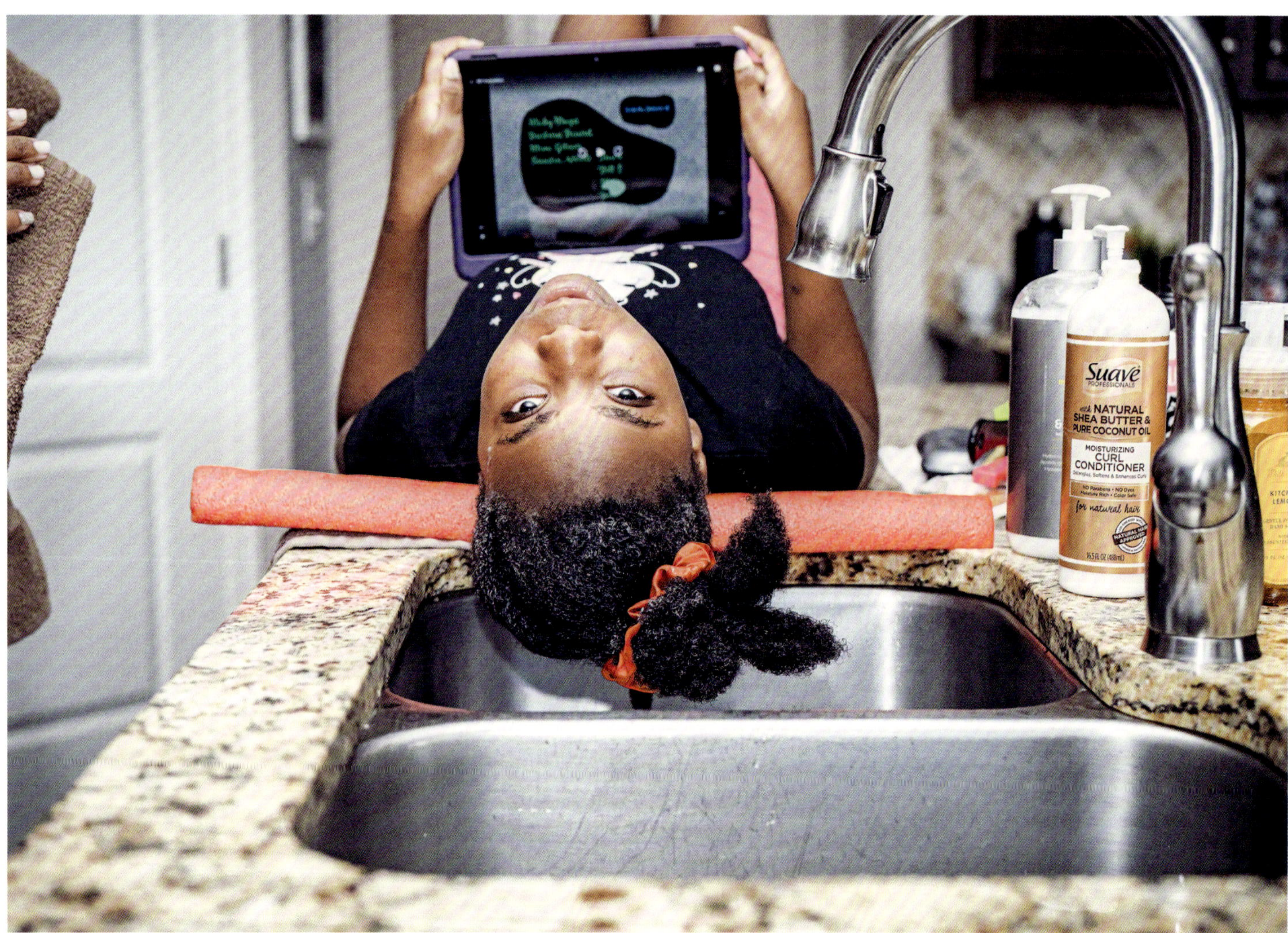

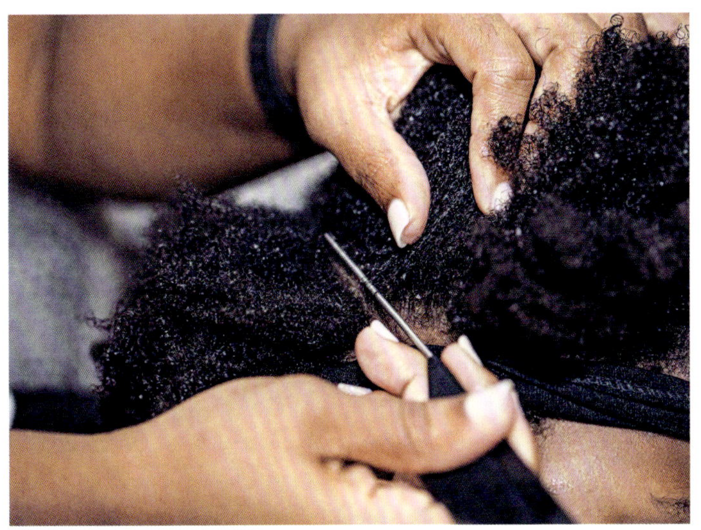
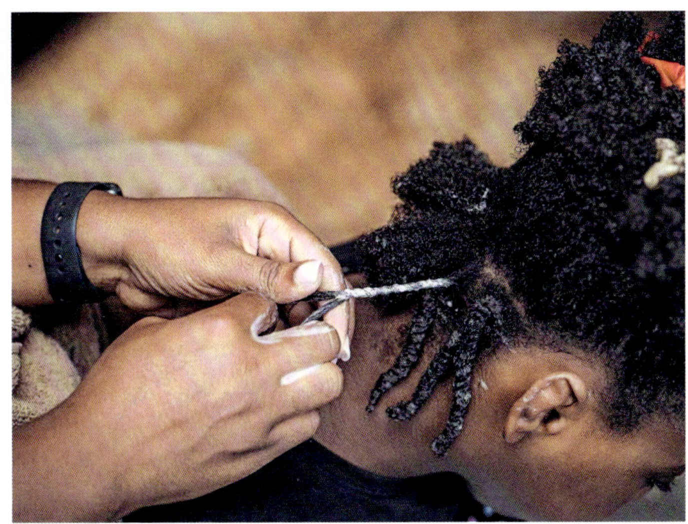
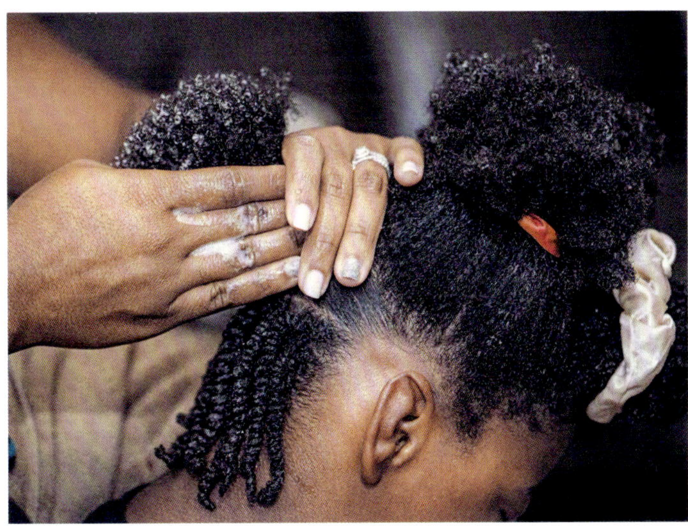
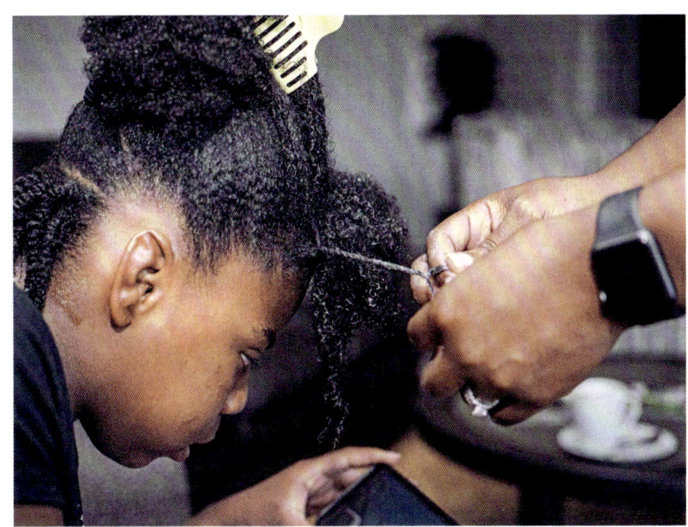

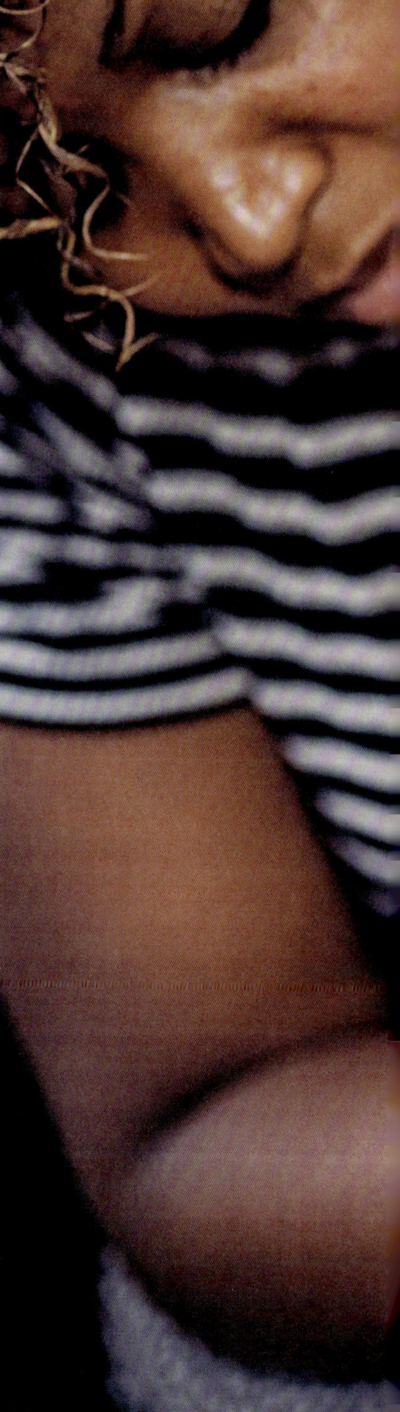

"[I hope to teach my daughter] that her hair is beautiful, a gift, and so very versatile. It is perfect because it is hers!" —TONI

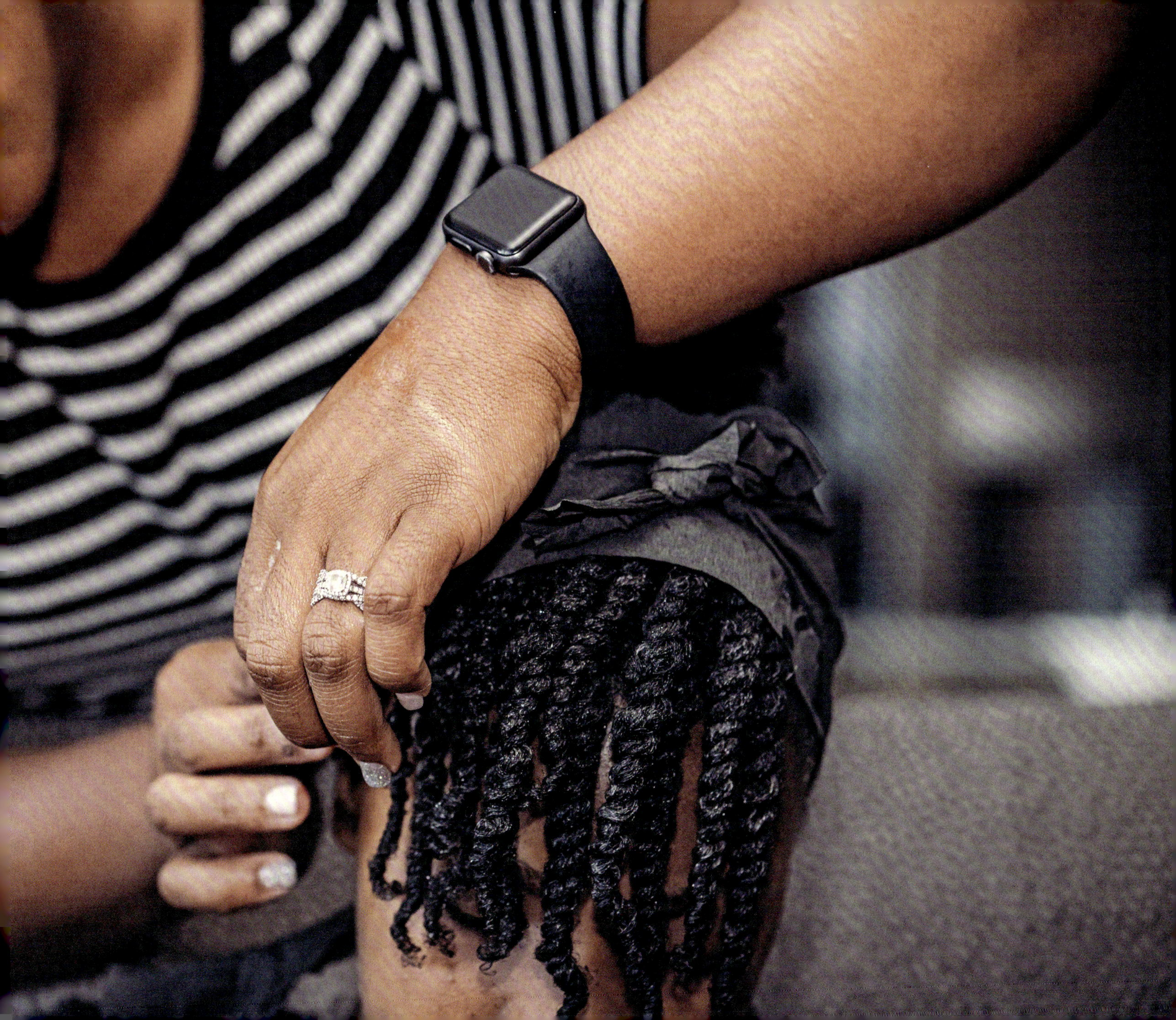

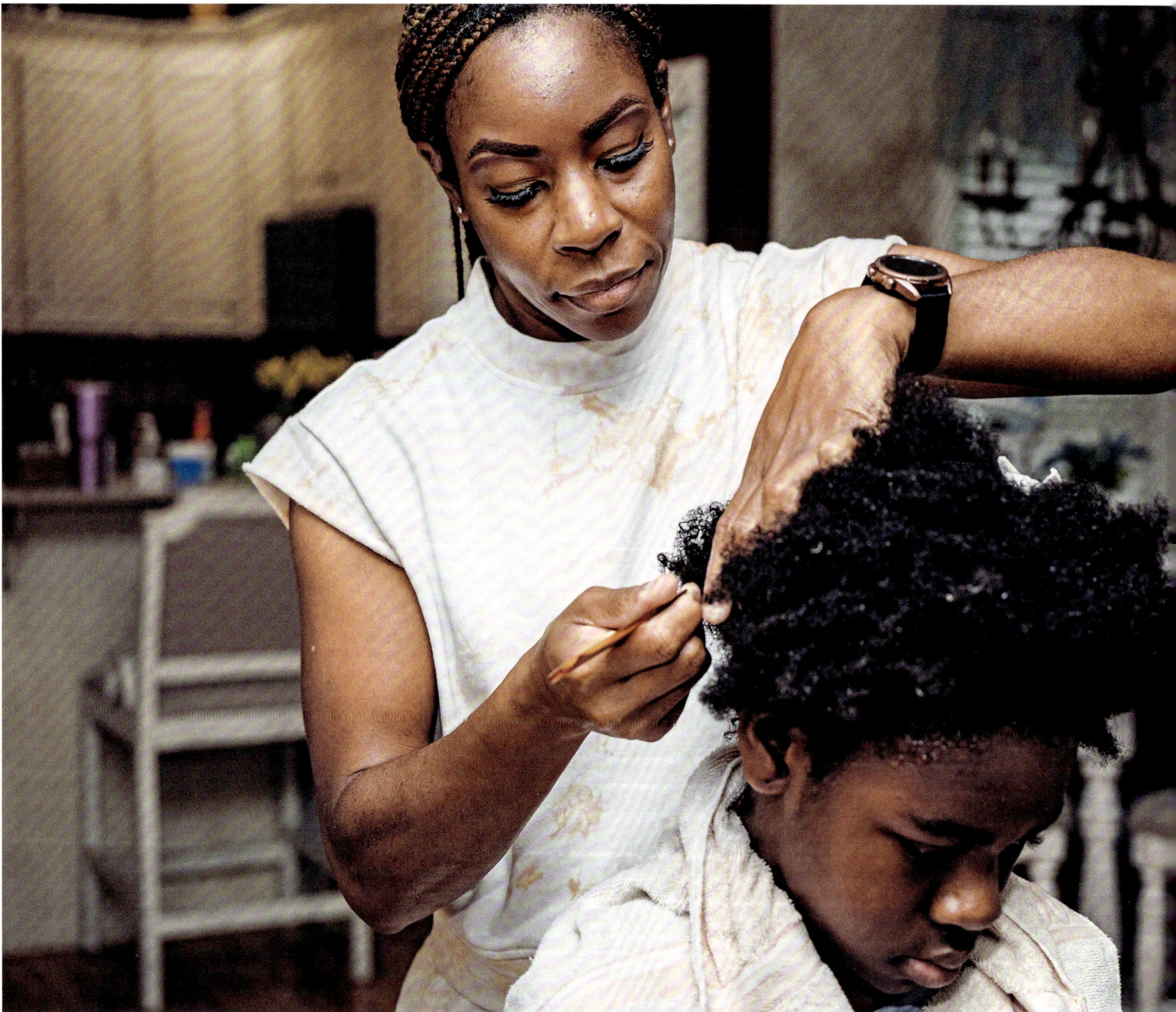

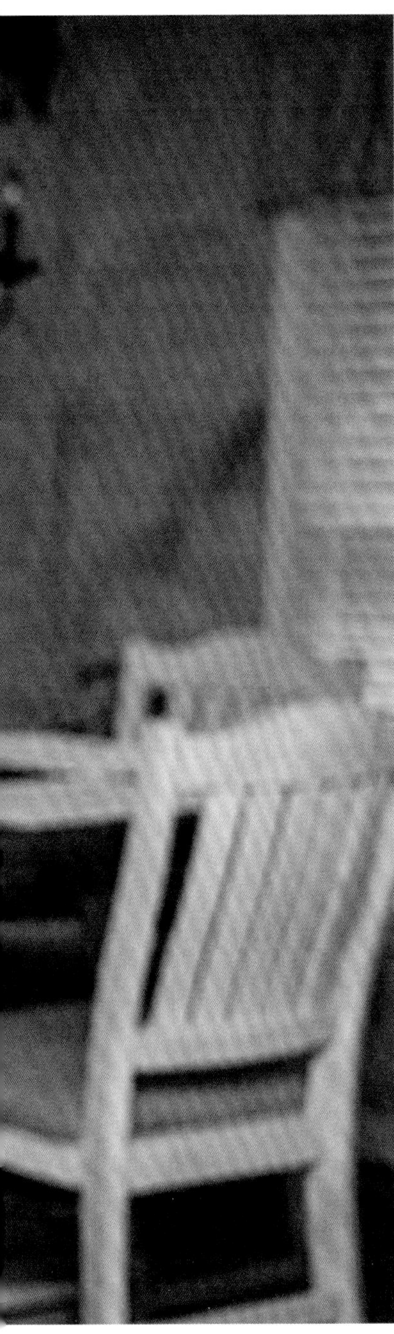

Vontressia & Kennadee

"I would like for her to learn to love her hair texture no matter how it is styled."

LET us observe a moment of silence in remembrance of '90s hairstyles. Finger waves. French rolls. And pour out a little liquor for the side swoop.

These are the styles that lured a young Vontressia into the world of relaxers. Growing up, Vontressia's mother opted for the hot comb (yes, heated on the stove top) rather than relaxers. Eventually, Vontressia began getting her hair regularly pressed at the salon. But back then, she wanted to rock those sleek 1990s styles and did not see how her natural hair could achieve them. She begged her mother for a relaxer. For her sixteenth birthday, her mother granted her wish and took her to the salon for her first perm. She was in teen heaven. She recalls:

I was so excited and nervous at the same time. The salon was full of people in the waiting area and in the salon chairs, and the aroma of shampoo and conditioners, relaxers, and hot combs were in the air. It was finally my turn in the chair to get my virgin hair chemically relaxed. It was a smooth transition; no scalp irritation and I loved my new hairstyle, a French roll with finger wave scrunch. You could not tell this sixteen-year-old nothing!

Well, fifteen years later, her hair told her something. Through breakage and shedding, it told her it was time to leave those relaxers alone. So, in 2008, Vontressia began transitioning to natural. The withdrawal was a struggle. It was not an easy transition for her, and she admits there were times when she hated her hair and considered going back to the creamy crack. Not to mention a set back after getting a Dominican blow-out. This treatment involves blow drying the hair at an extremely high temperature to straighten it, and unfortunately, due to heat damage, her curls did not return. On the recommendation of her stylist, she cut her hair to remove the damaged strands. She was understandably devastated to lose the growth she had worked so hard to achieve. But the damage her hair had sustained from relaxers reminded her that she needed to stay the course, no matter how difficult. She now loves and appreciates her hair texture, and is teaching her daughter, Kennadee, to do the same.

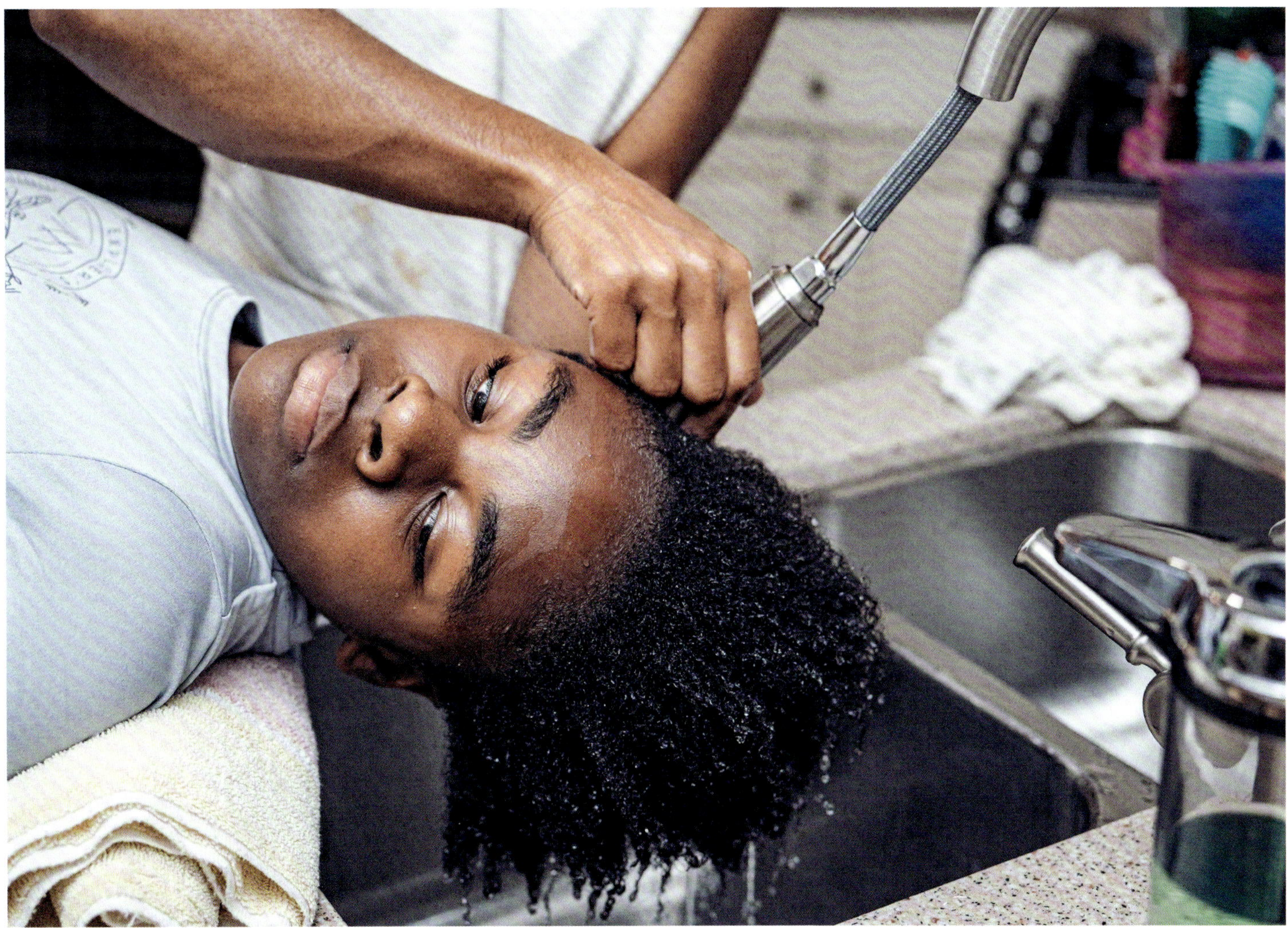

Page 66, top right and top left: Wash day takes place twice a month for Vontressia and Kennadee. Vontressia often uses fresh avacado, raw honey, hemp seed oil, and argan oil to make a conditioning mask for Kennadee's steam treatments.

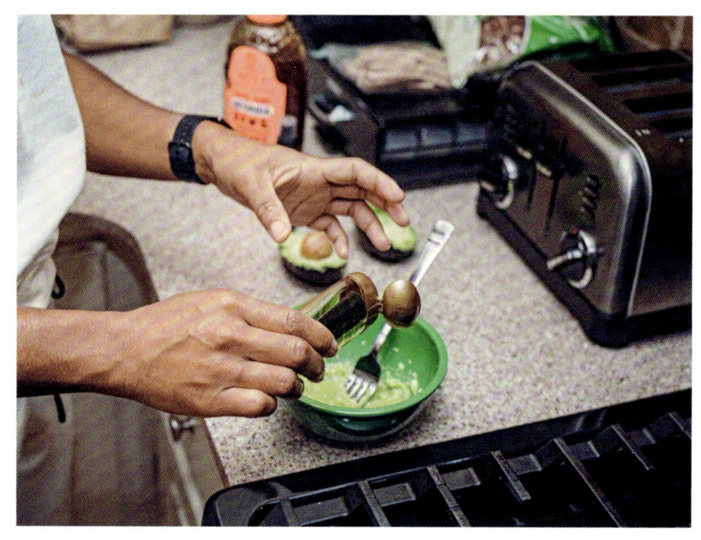
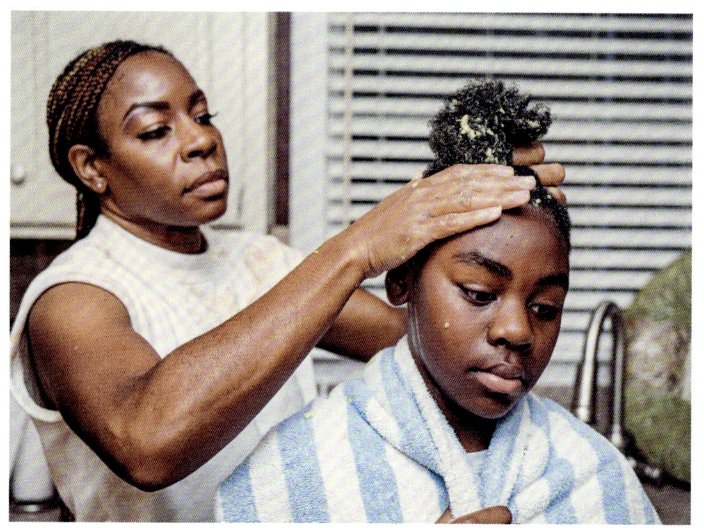
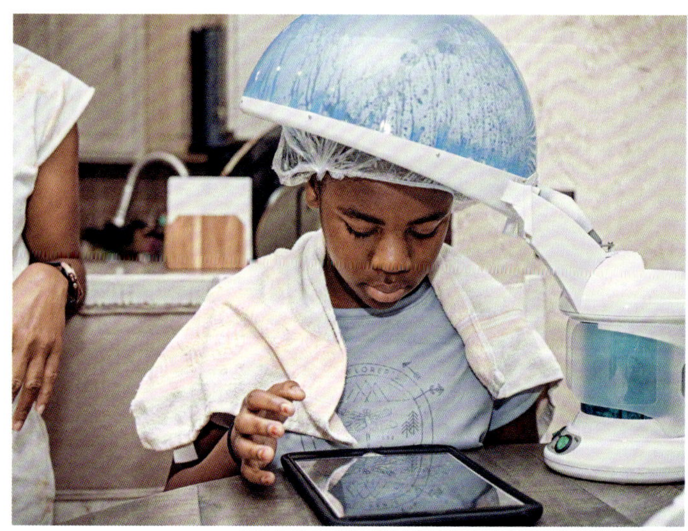
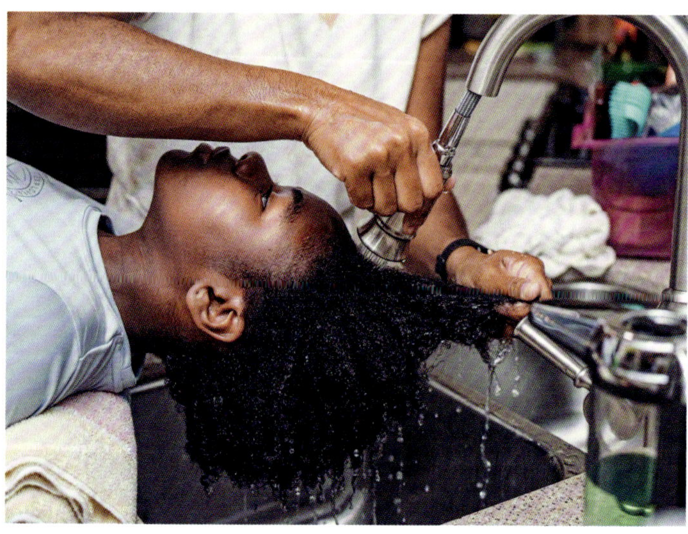

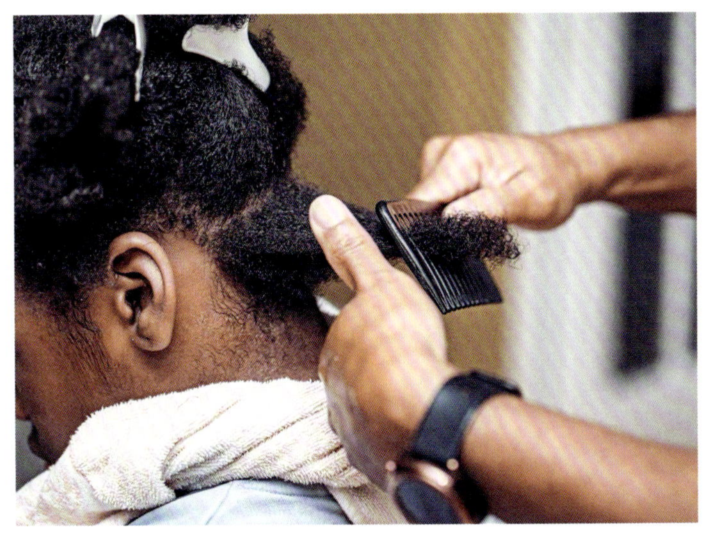
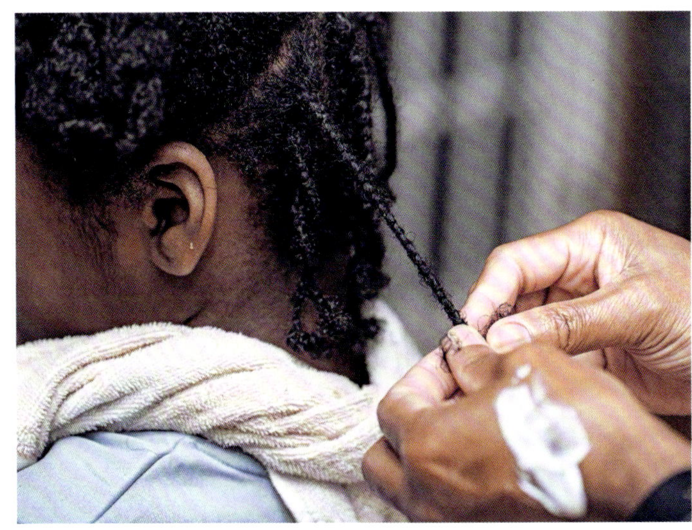
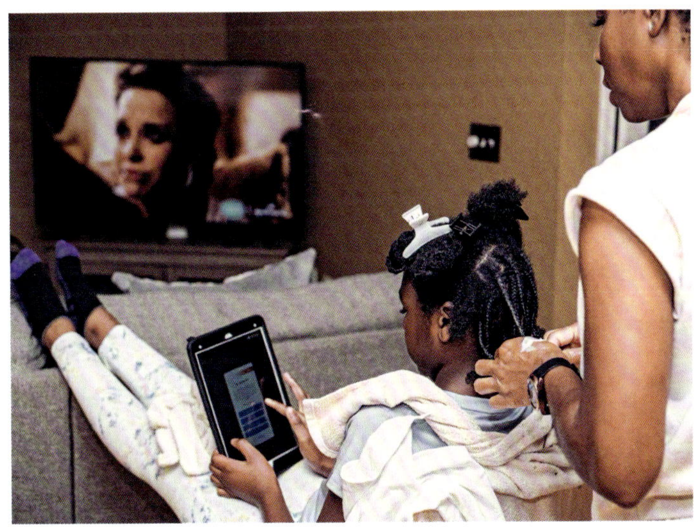
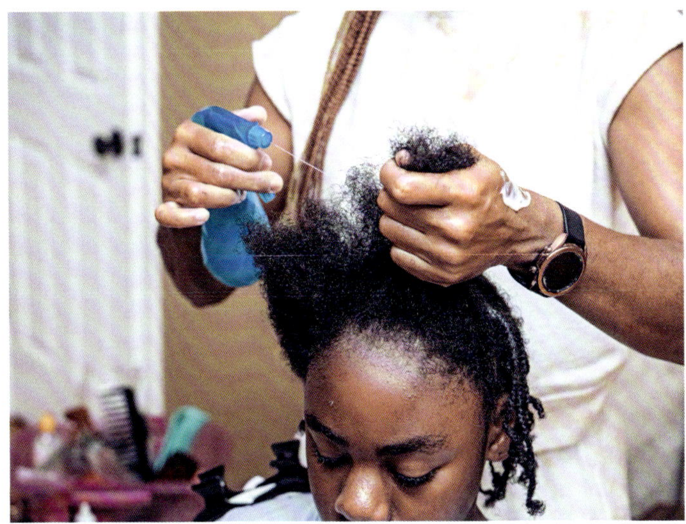

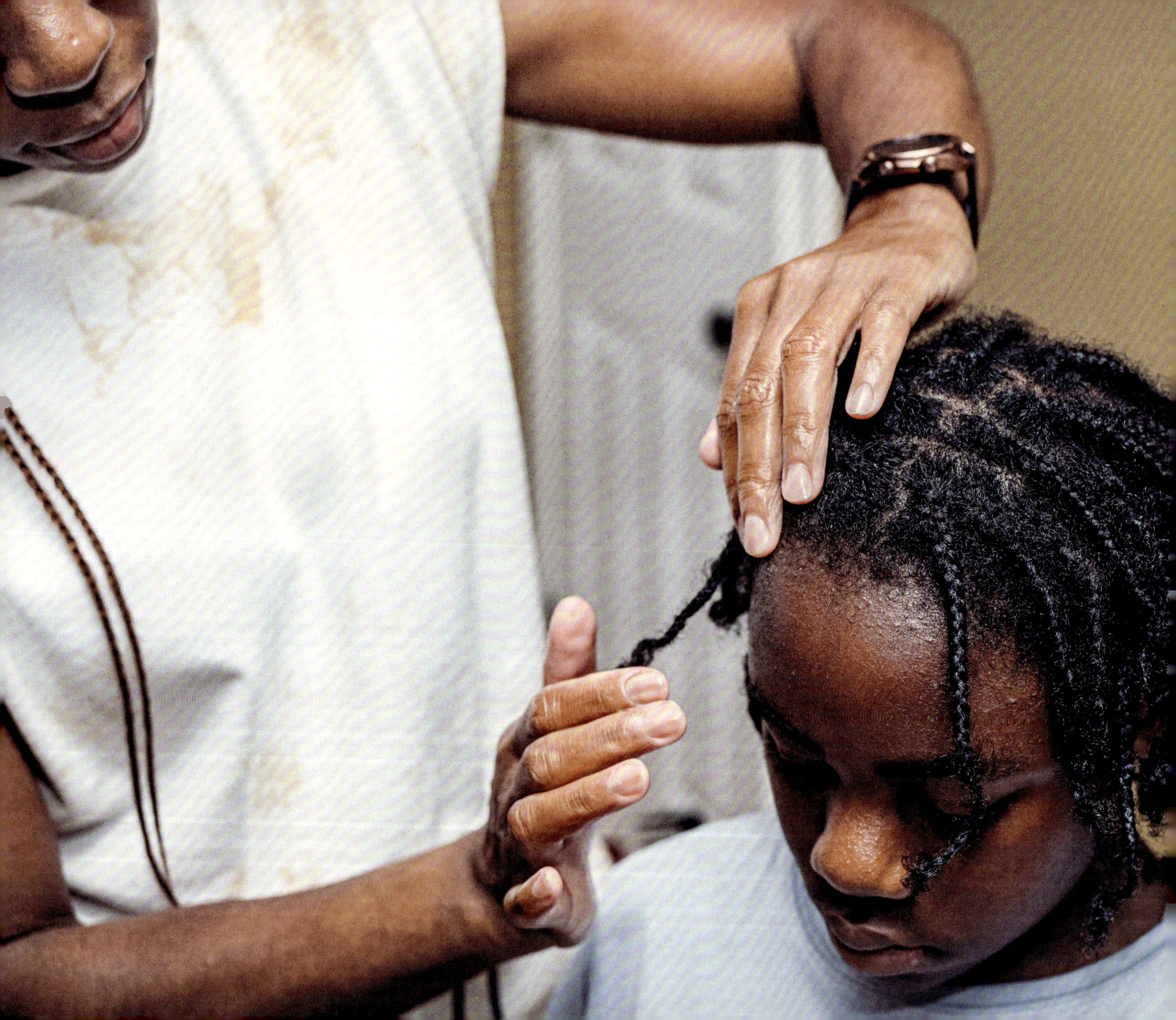

"I enjoy my hair. I love how fluffy, soft, and curly my hair is, and my hair makes me, me." —KENNADEE

Leslie & Arden

GROWING UP, I always understood long hair to be akin to "good hair." Length was probably the most coveted hair quality, next to loose waves or straight hair. Long hair has always been linked to femininity and beauty. This backdrop magnified the power of one aspect of the natural hair movement in particular: Black women, including myself, opting to cut off all of their relaxed hair. The big chop was disruptive; it stood in grand opposition to what we had been taught was beautiful or desirable.

So, when Leslie, a college student at the time, found herself with a T.W.A. in 1999, a few years before this style

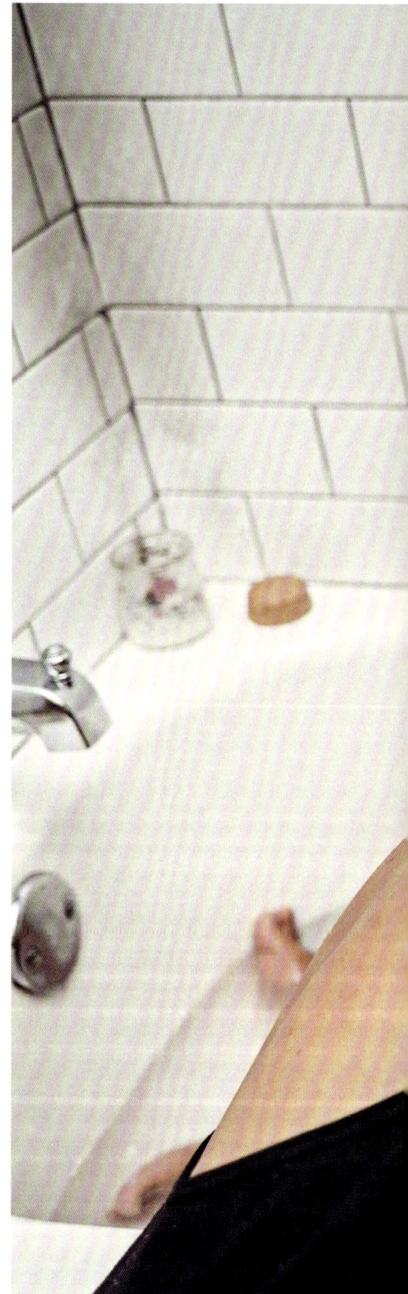

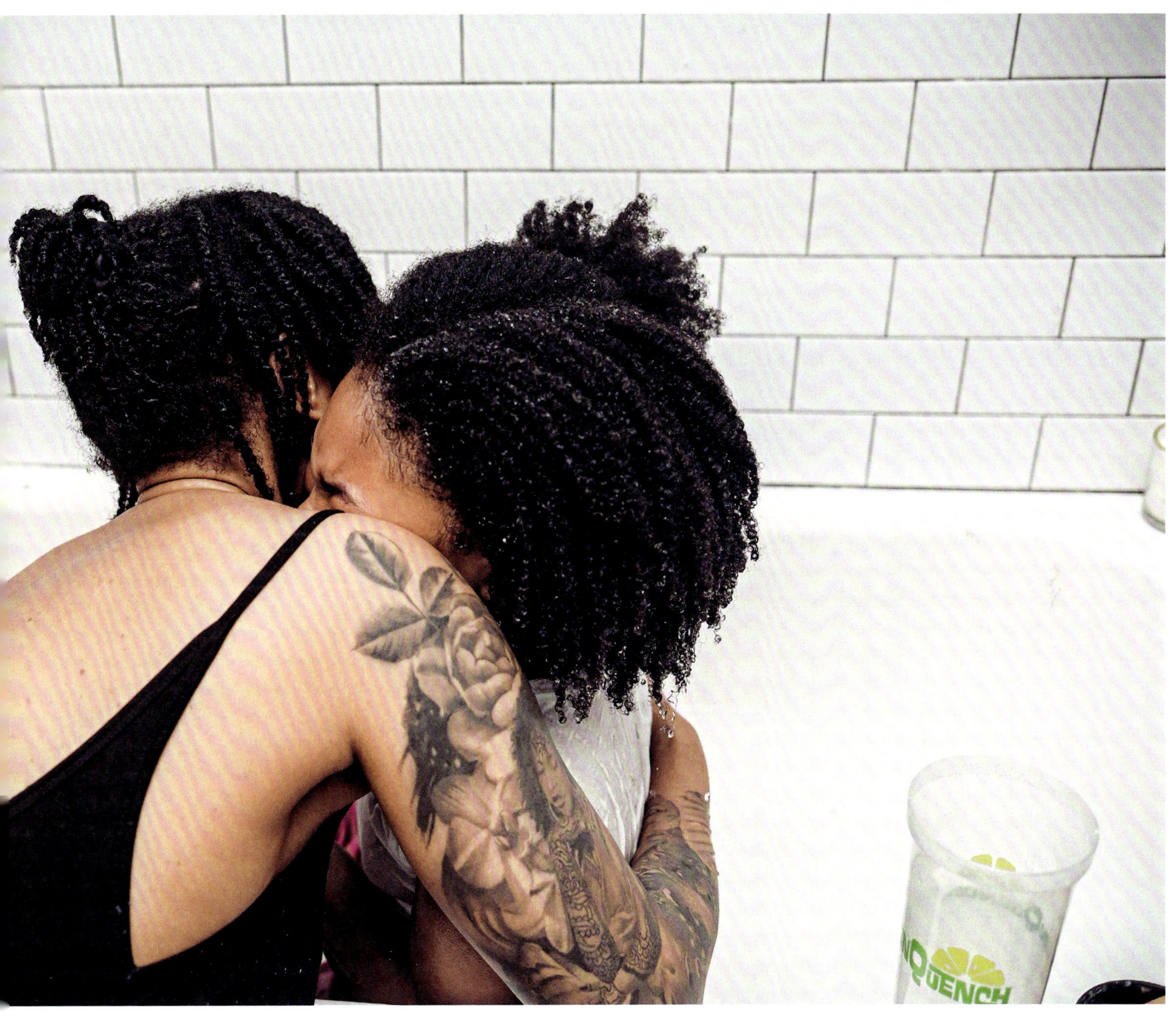

NO
QUENCH

started picking up steam, she struggled. The decision to cut her hair came on the heels of hair breakage from a relaxer. Notably, this was not the first instance of breakage Leslie experienced from a relaxer. In fact, her hair had broken so many times by that point that she promised herself that if it happened again, she would cut it off. Whether it was just a dare or a true desire to be free from the ongoing abuse of perms, she kept her word. She went to a barber to cut off her damaged, relaxed hair, but he went further and gave her a really short fade instead! She was not emotionally prepared for such a drastic change.

Leslie was understandably shaken. She stayed in her dorm room for two whole days trying to come to terms with her new, albeit short, head of hair. The shock of something so new coupled with the negative feedback from her family members who "believe in long hair no matter what" made it difficult for Leslie to embrace her new look. But knowing she couldn't hide out forever, she went to a stylist and got her hair further shaped and styled. She remembers feeling beautiful . . . and free. On top of this, she has since experienced the hair growth and health she has been desiring for so long.

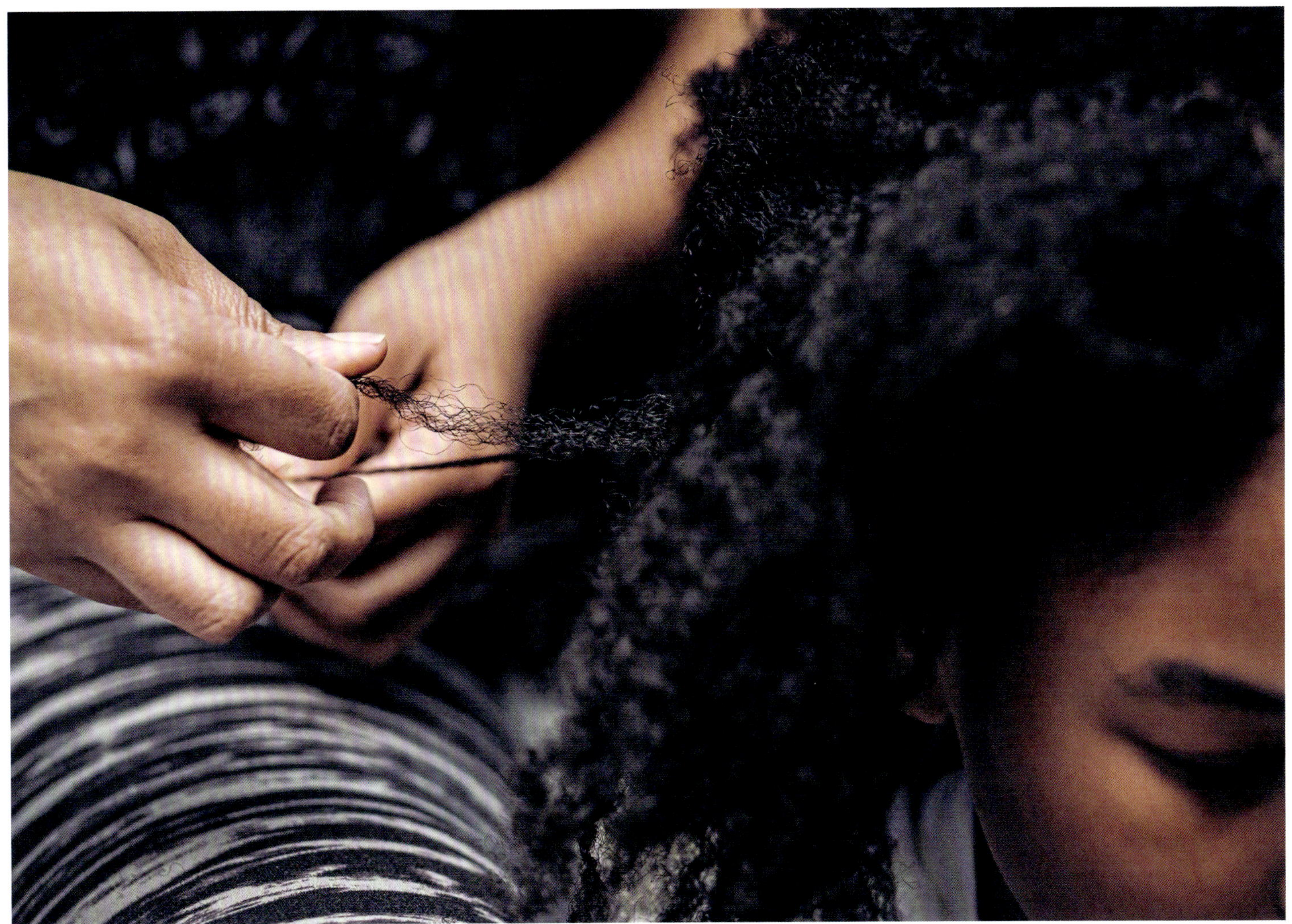

For Leslie and Arden, wash day lasts about five to six hours. In order to minimize the tears, Leslie carefully detangles Arden's hair by hand, avoiding brushes and combs. I watched as Leslie carefully detangled section by section. So much patience.

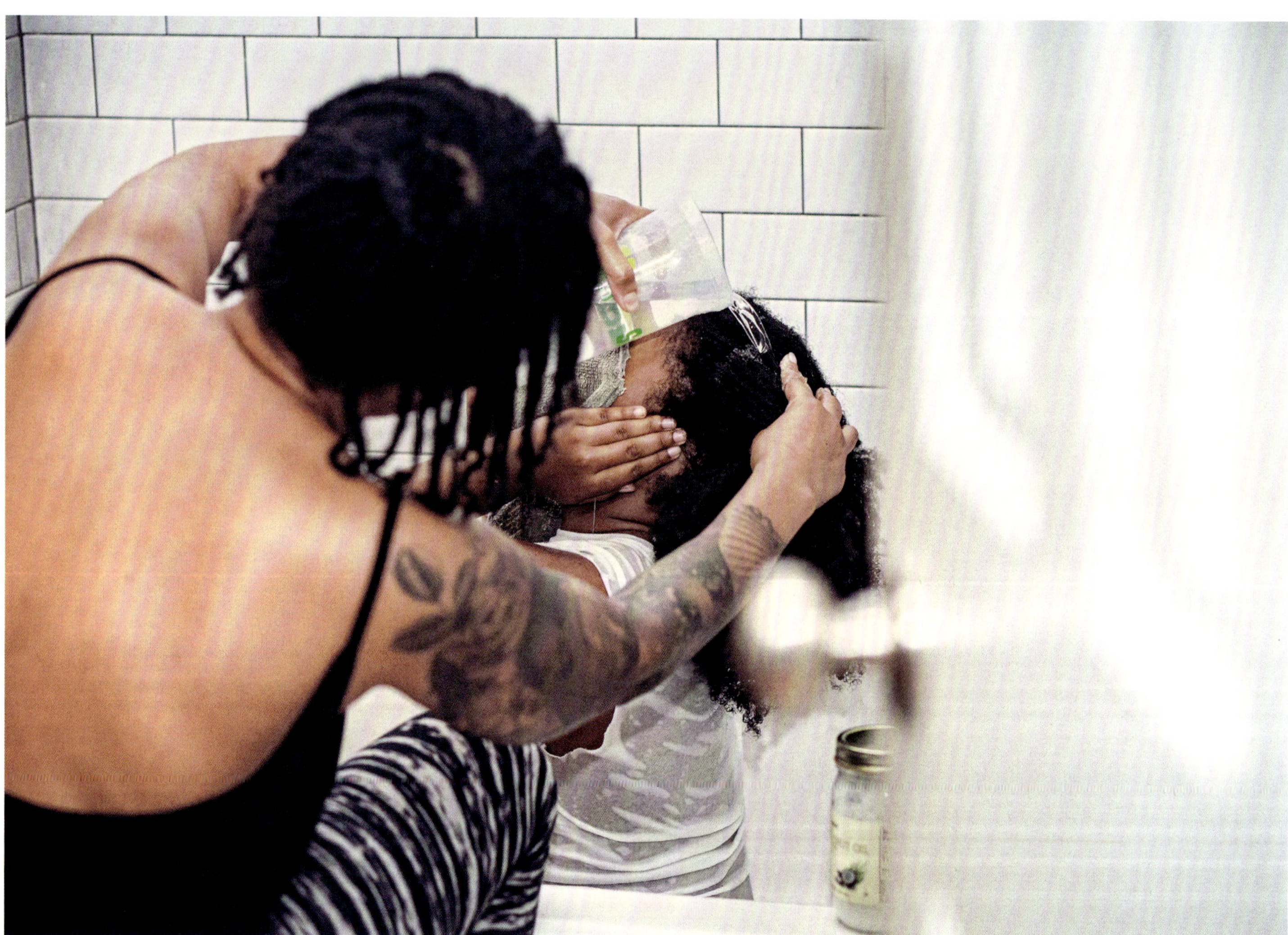

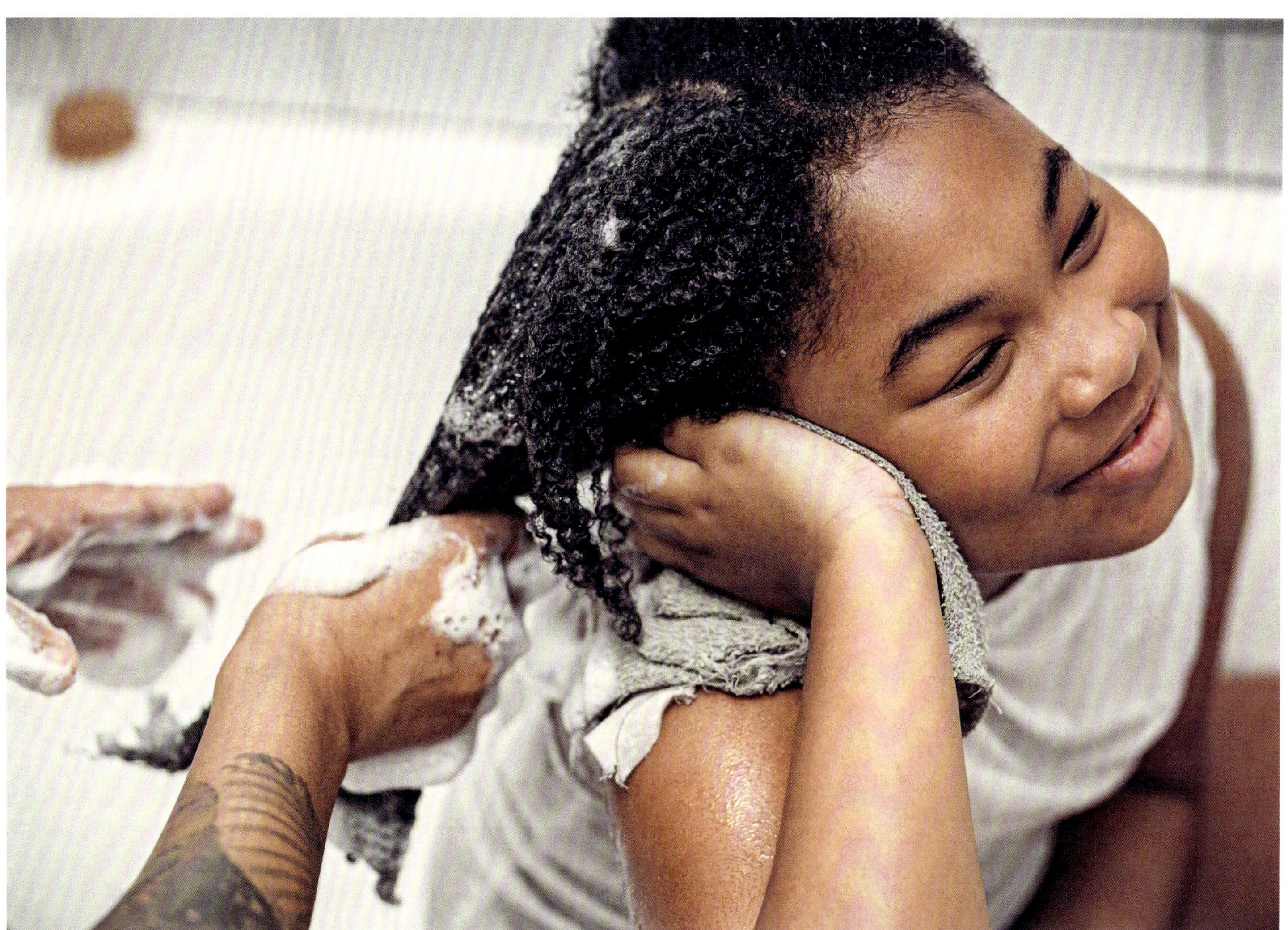

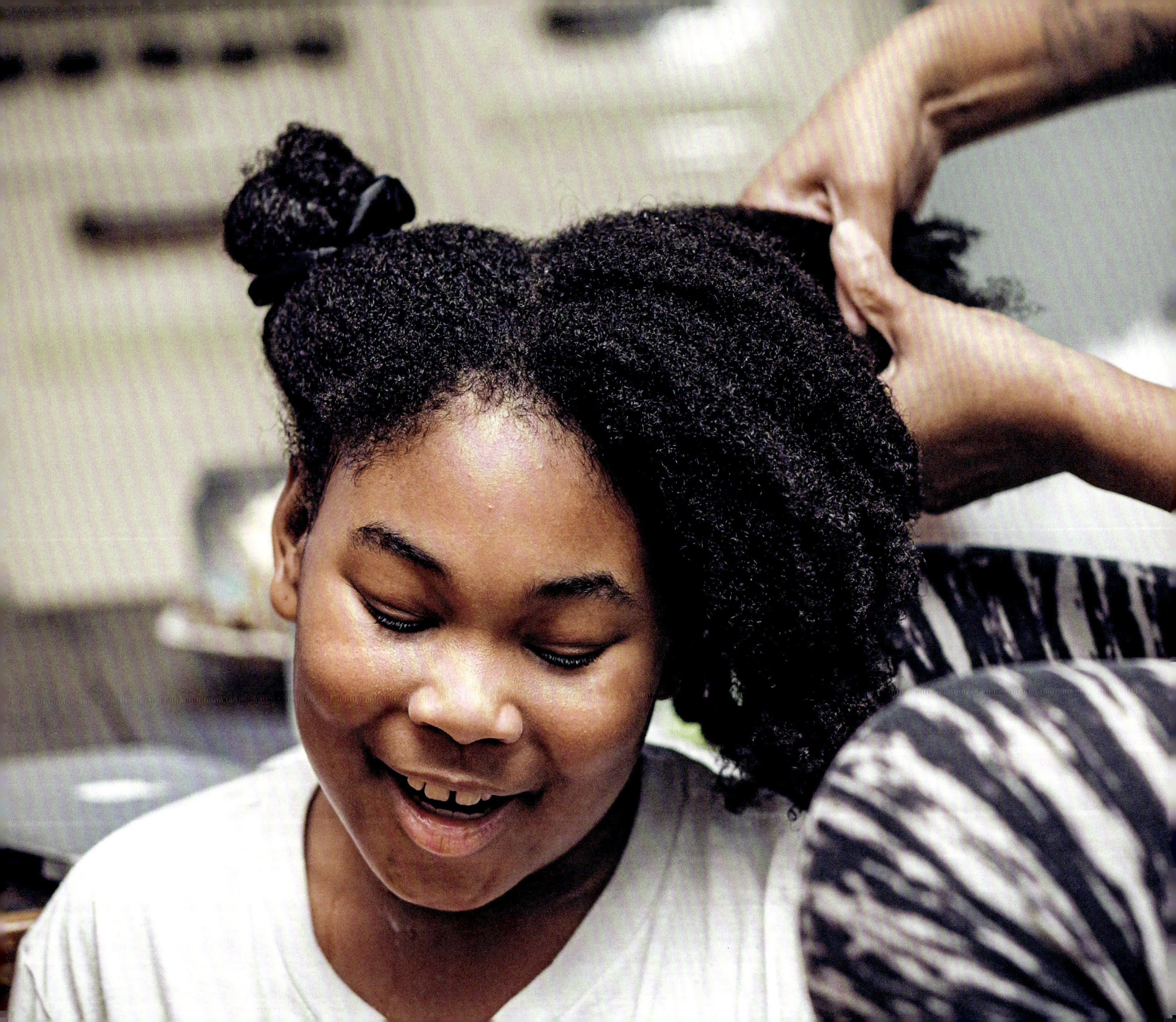

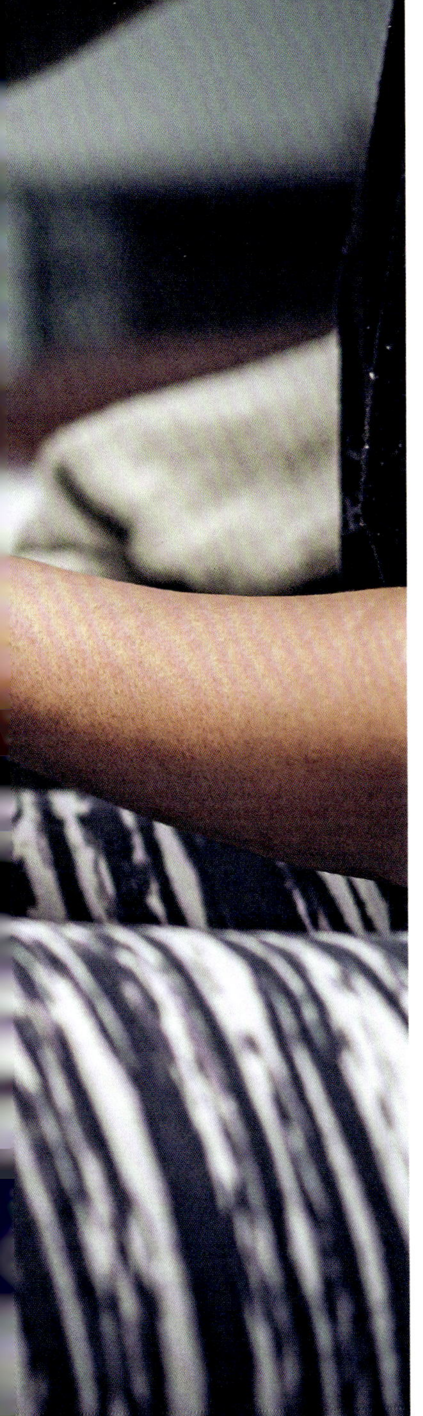

"Arden loves her hair. It's to the point that she expects to get compliments if it's out in a fro!" —LESLIE

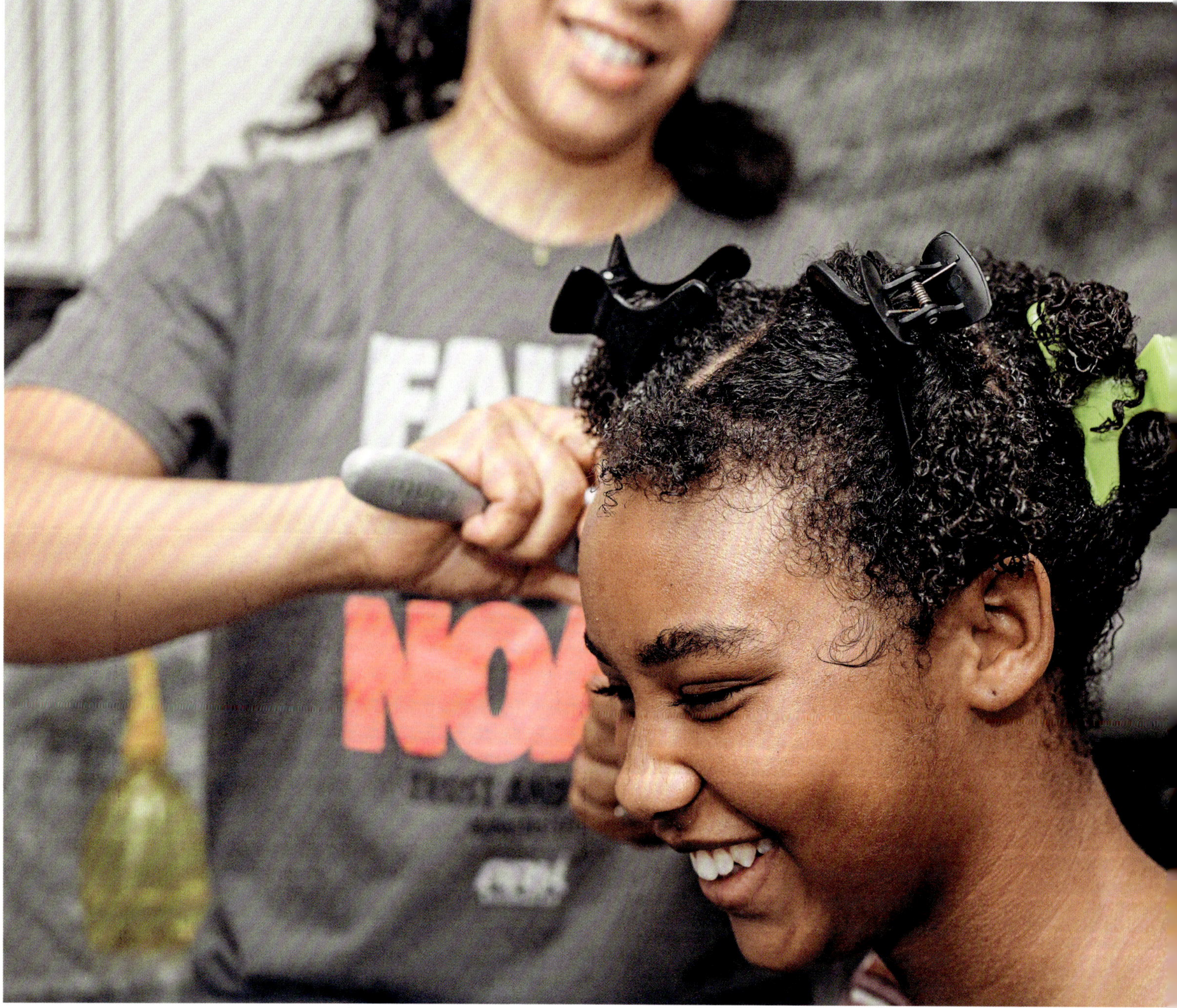

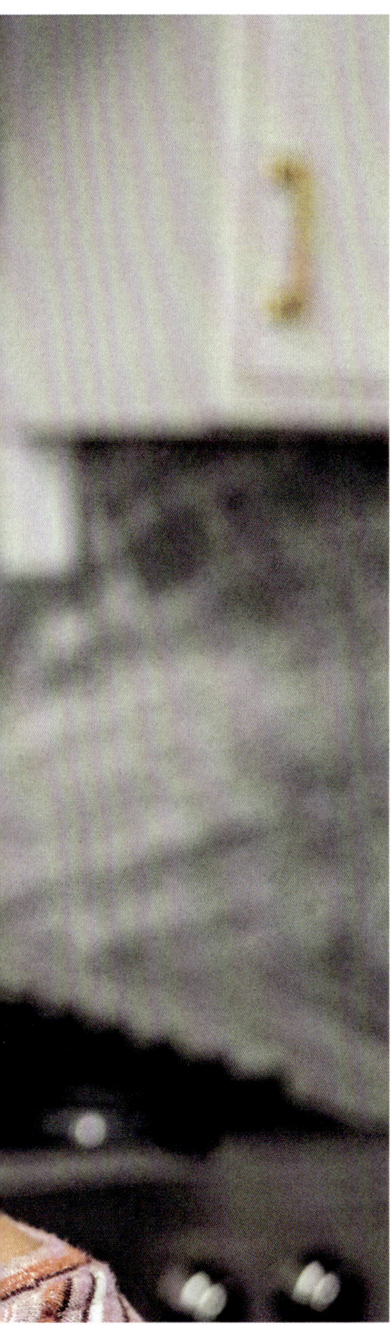

Latricia & Grace

"I received my first relaxer when I was twelve.
Over the years my thick hair became thinner,
the edges were lost and my hair length
decreased significantly."

I'VE had to come to terms with the fact that I have abused my hair. While not altogether knowingly, in hindsight, I imagine I had to have some sense that the chemicals and excessive heat were not exactly what my hair needed. I've suffered my share of scalp burns from relaxers and I recall a specific instance in college where I literally burned a chunk of hair off my head with a curling iron. And given the number of women I've spoken to who made the decision to stop using relaxers upon discovering they were pregnant, I believe we have always been somewhat aware of the inherent dangers of using these harsh chemicals on our bodies.

Perming breaks down the chemical bonds of the hair shaft and restructures it into a new shape. Over time, this deliberate destruction of the structure of the hair can cause weakening and breakage.

Sometimes, damage to our hair comes from simply not knowing how to care for it properly. Learning to appreciate and care for textured hair may take time. For many of us, meeting our hair for the first time in our twenties, thirties, and beyond, we didn't know what our hair needed or wanted. It has been a game of trial and error. And for some, more error than we'd like to admit. Adding to this lack of knowledge, many of us had preconceived ideas about how our hair should and should not look. This often leads to overmanipulation of our hair to *make* it look a certain way, which, in the long run, can also damage it.

Latricia is well versed in the many errors that come from trying to force hair to be what it isn't. She received her first relaxer when she was twelve years old. She hoped that the relaxer would give her what she truly desired; long, shiny, straight hair like the "pretty girls." However, the relaxer that she had hoped would make her "beautiful" only resulted in making her once thick hair much thinner, her edges balder, and her length shorter. She realized that she needed to get away from the harsh chemical relaxers and rebuild her hair, so she stopped using them while attending college. But she still wanted the look of long, straight hair, so she started getting regular blow-out treatments. Eventually, she found her hair suffering once again, this time from heat damage.

She decided enough was enough. She became dedicated to learning what her hair actually needed. She spent hours in the library and on YouTube studying how to care for her hair. Like many of us, she was not able to ask elder family members because they did not know either. She had to figure it out on her own. Through the application of the techniques she learned in her research, she has been able to restore the health of her hair. She has found that sowing seeds of acceptance and love into her hair, rather than rejection and hate, has caused it to finally thrive.

Latricia's time, energy, and studying, along with her trials and errors, have built an inheritance of wisdom, and her twelve-year-old daughter, Grace, is the beneficiary. Grace loves her hair, but understandably struggles at times with how much work goes into maintaining it. For the sake of ease, she sometimes wishes for straight hair like the White girls. She attends a predominantly White school and her hair has been the punchline of an insensitive joke or two (or three) from White peers. But Latricia, having served her time in the "I want that kind of hair" penitentiary, reminds her often that altering her hair may likely damage it. On top of that, she reminds Grace that her peers' straight hair cannot do the magical things that Grace's natural hair can. Rather than desiring something different, she wants Grace to celebrate what she already has.

A beautiful example of this is how Grace dominated her school's spirit day for years. The rules were simple. Each clothing item or accessory that a student wore that was in the school colors counted as one point for that grade. Latricia knew what to do. She would put Grace's hair in braids, then attach beads to each braid. With over seventy braids, each having about ten beads each, no one at the school could touch Grace's high score. Thus, her class won for a straight two years in a row. In light of this, the principal changed the rules to give other classes a fighting chance of winning. What an awesome example for Grace as to how our hair (and specific to this story, our cultural hairstyles) are not only beautiful, but also literal game changers!

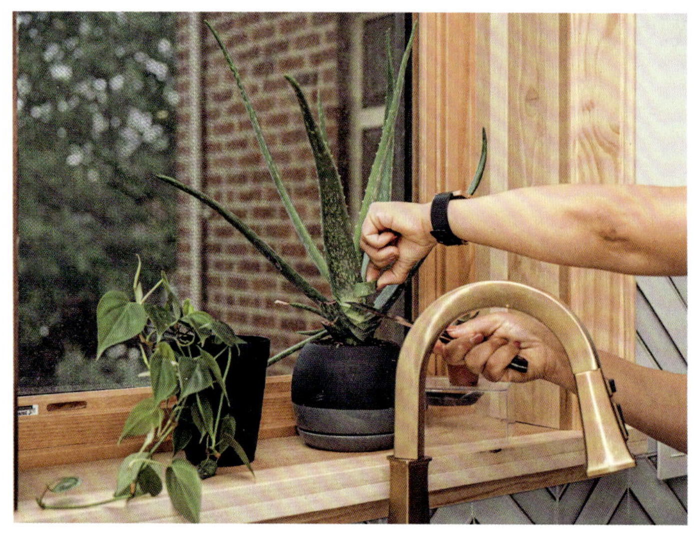
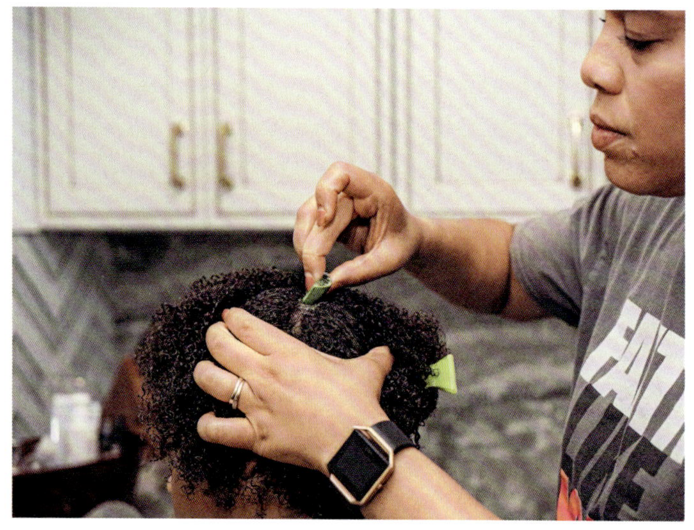
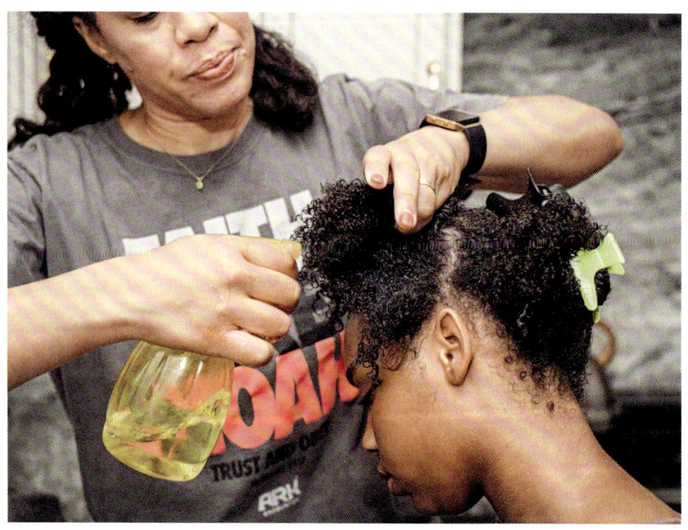
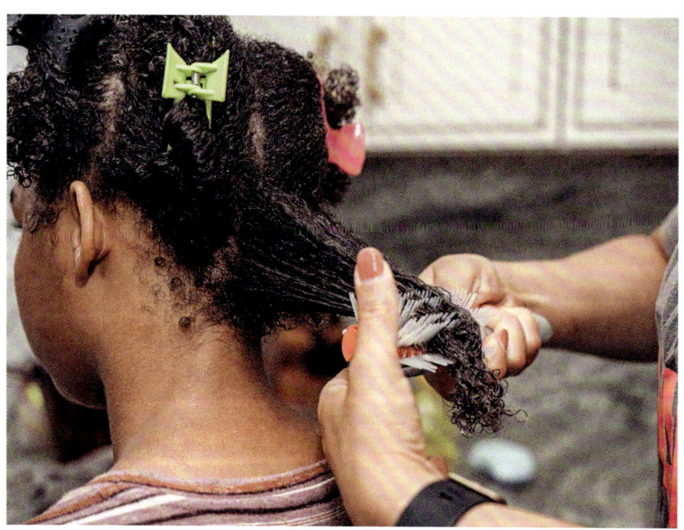

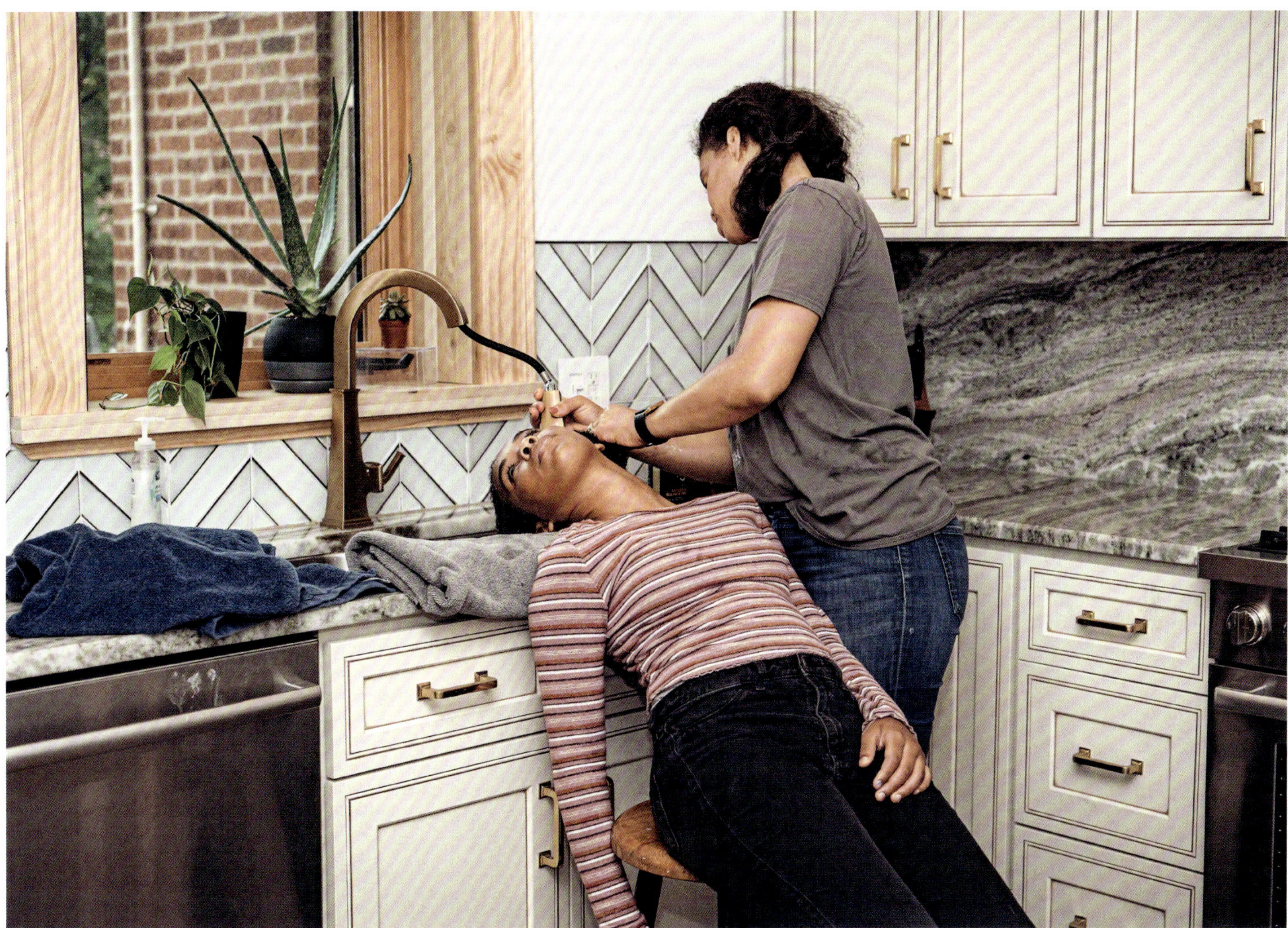

Wash day for Latricia and Grace lasts about two hours every two weeks. Latricia's hours in her own personal cosmetology school have turned her into a pro. *Opposite page, top left and top right:* The aloe plant that sits beautifully in the windowsill above her kitchen sink speaks volumes. I watched curiously as she cut a piece from the plant to rub onto Grace's scalp and hair. She then added water and olive oil for detangling.

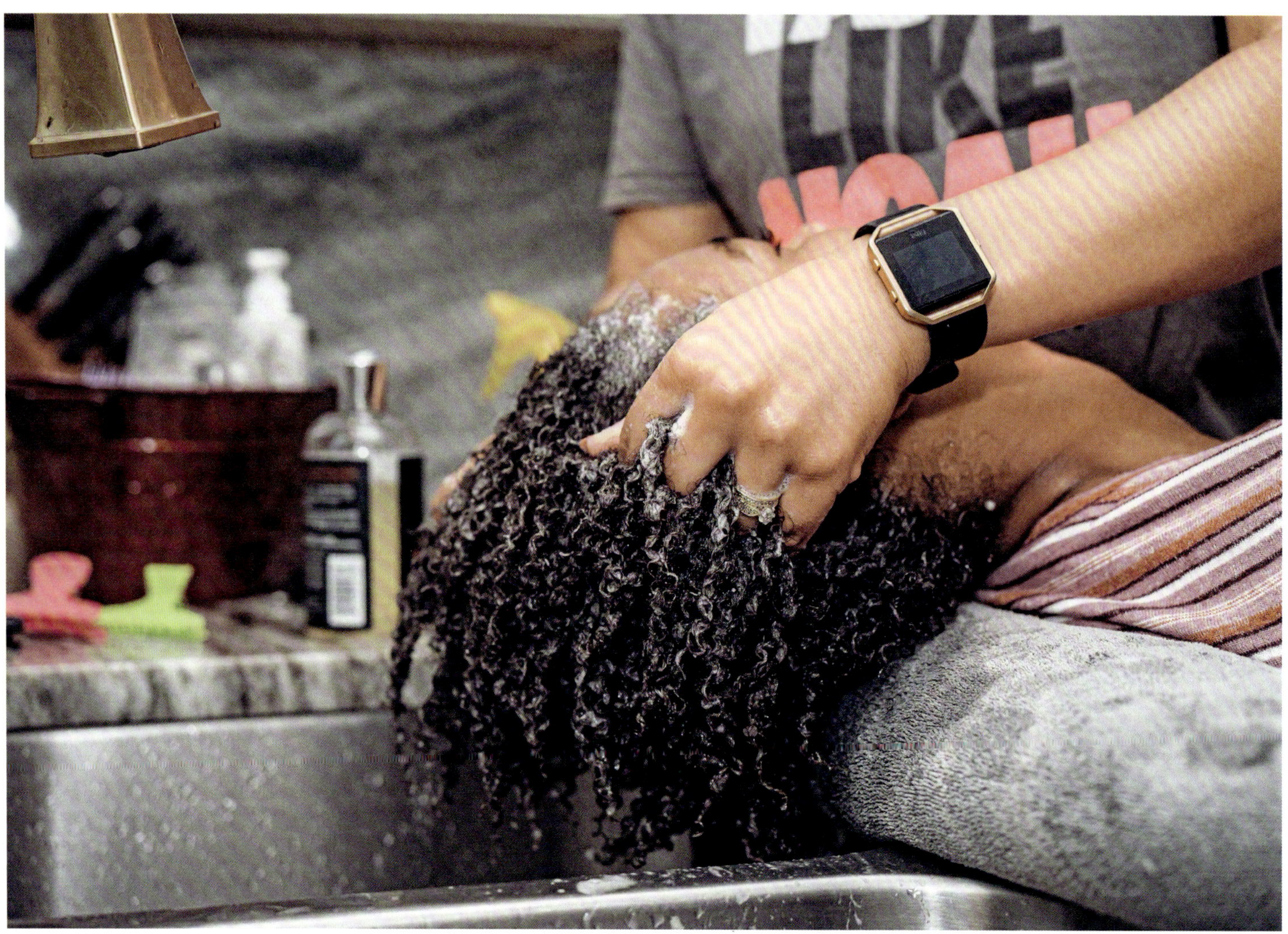

After washing, Latricia applies a mixture that includes hibiscus and fenu-greek seed powder to Grace's hair, then covers her hair with a warm, damp towel for deep conditioning. She then rinses with lukewarm water while further detangling Grace's hair. Finally, she rinses with cold water to seal the cuticles.

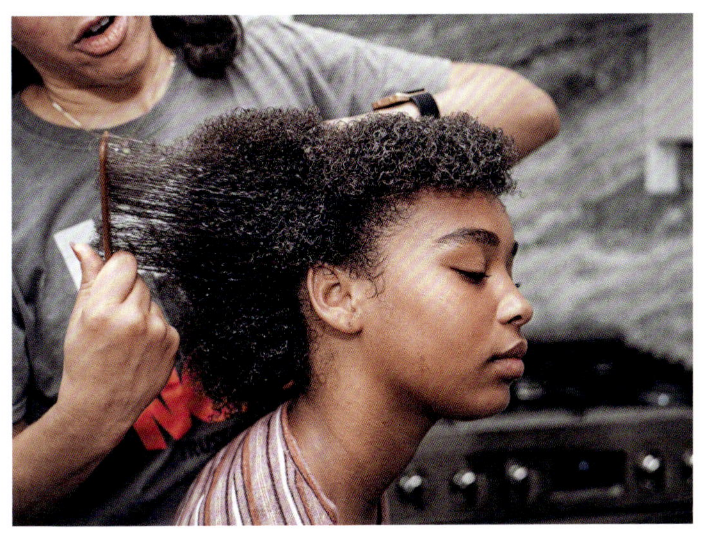
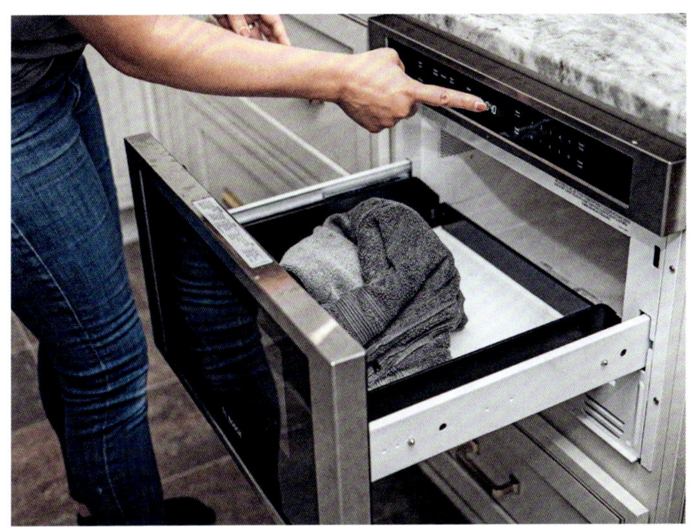
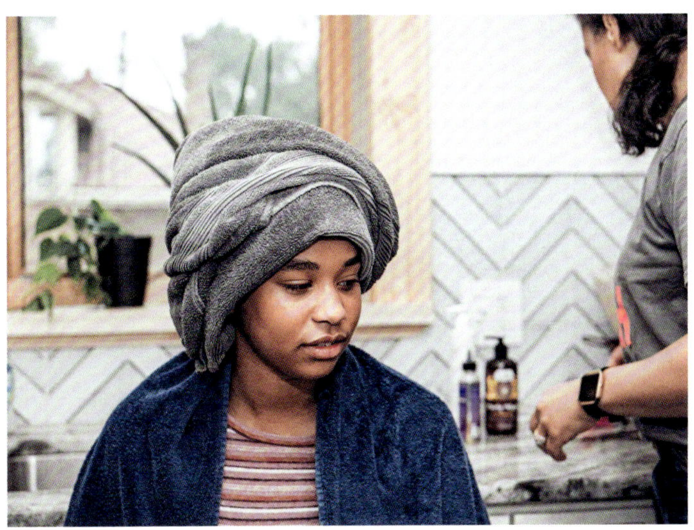
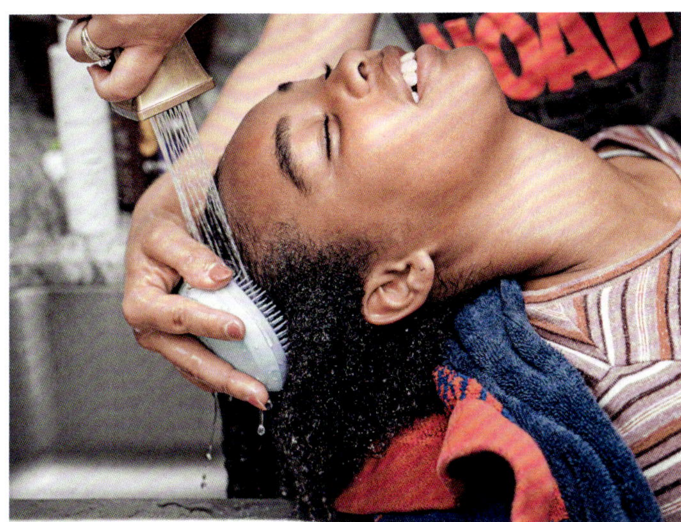

"[Our hair] is beautiful, grows up toward heaven as a crown, and has the best diversity of texture and style than any other texture." —LATRICIA

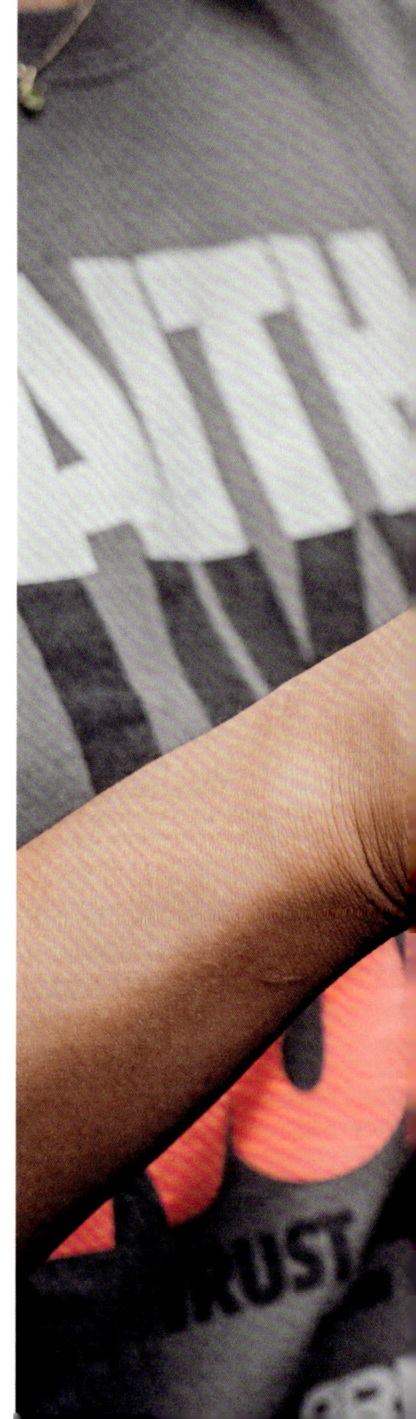

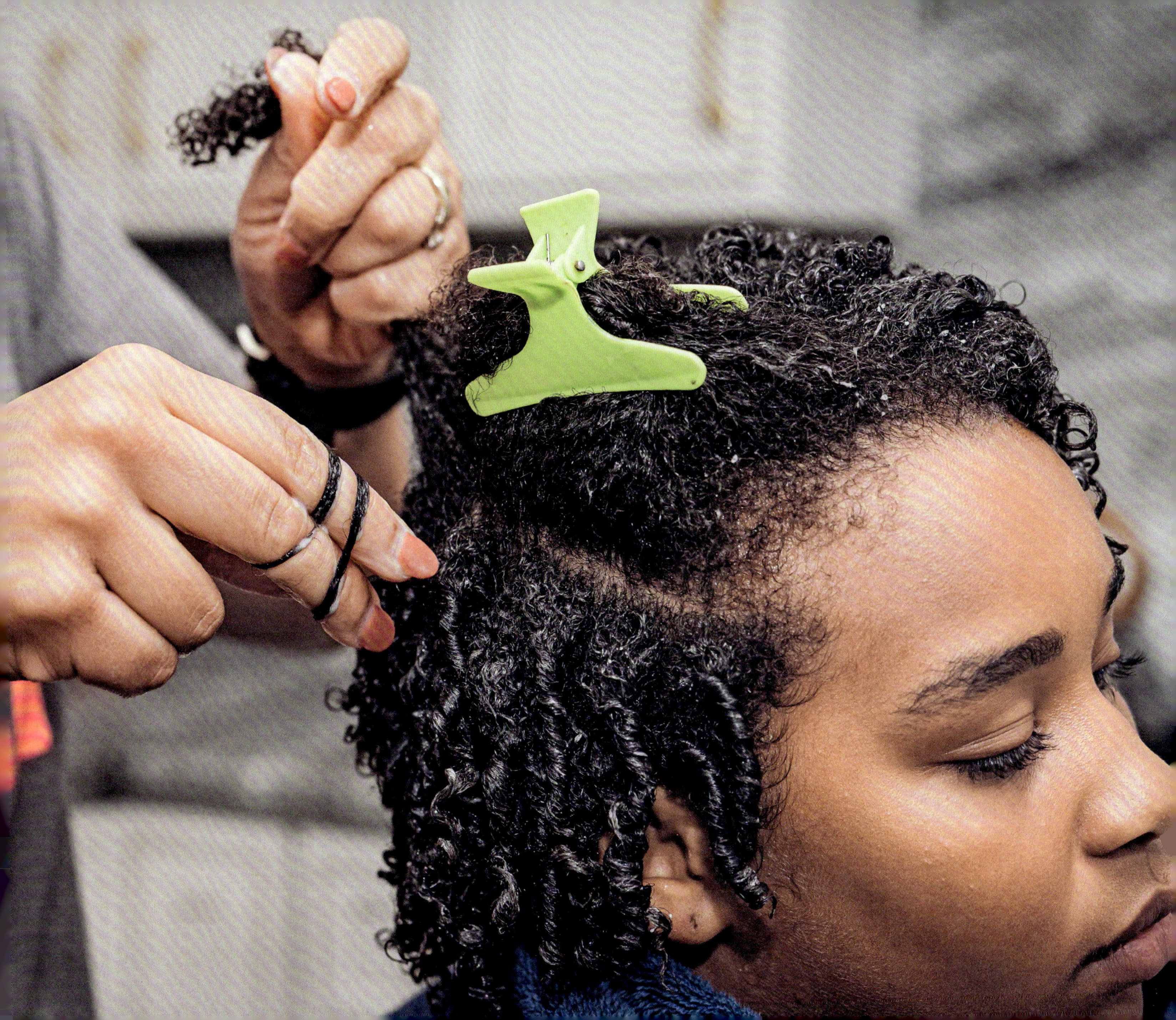

Sharifa & Laila

WHEN I was growing up, it was rare to see a Black girl with natural hair. Perms were everywhere. They were seemingly the norm. In *Hair Story,* Ayana D. Byrd and Lori L. Tharps report that in 1997, about two-thirds of Black women were wearing their hair straight and many Black men were getting their hair texturized.[29] I had a few biracial friends who flat ironed their hair but let their "good hair" curls out occasionally. I grew up believing my hair was simply meant to be straightened. Thus, in my mind, so was everyone else's. I mean, who wanted nappy hair? No one I could think of. Too many of us believed that our hair, the way it grows,

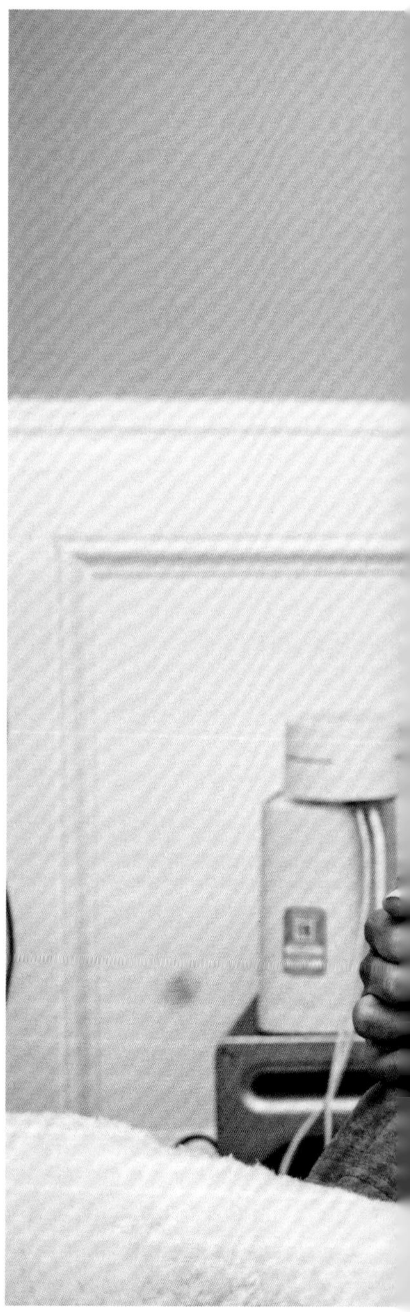

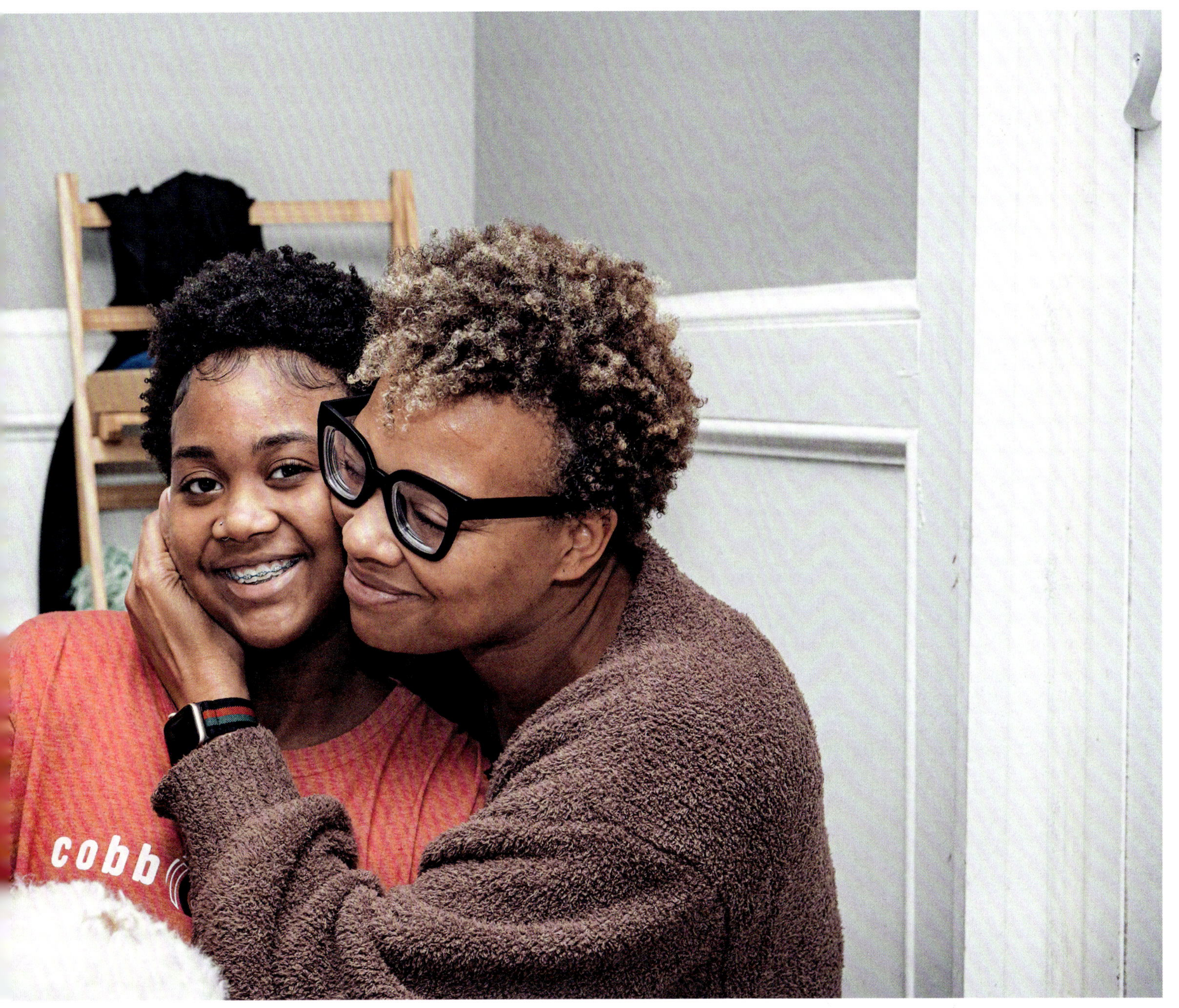
cobb

looks, and behaves from the scalp, was unwanted. We did not realize this rejection of our natural texture was, in essence, a rejection of our own Blackness.

Sharifa was part of that one-third of Black women who did not have straight hair in 1997. She grew up natural. Her mother was a hard "no" on hair straightening and did not allow Sharifa or her sister to get relaxers or even press their hair. While Sharifa now understands what her mother was doing, she was definitely not feeling it at the time. She had every intention of getting a relaxer as soon as she got to college. Her sister didn't want to wait until she moved out, so she tried to straighten her hair on an ironing board. Desperate times, right? But Sharifa's mom never budged.

Sharifa's hair sparked confusion among her classmates. Her peers could not understand why she did not have a relaxer. Sharifa was bullied for having natural hair at a time when it was neither popular nor socially acceptable. She recalls comments like, "You would be so pretty if you could get your hair together," and "Why doesn't your mom want you to look nice?" She even remembers being placed on an "ugly list." The reason for her "ugliness" was written next to her name. It simply said, "nappy hair."

The unfortunate reality is that these were Black kids doing all the bullying. Black kids who, like so many of us, had been socialized to believe that natural hair was a problem to be solved. They believed kinky hair was not pretty, thus, Sharifa, as beautiful as she was, and still is, couldn't possibly be pretty to them. Not with that nappy hair!

And this, my friends, is what internalized anti-Blackness looks like.

Despite the haters, Sharifa maintained a high self-esteem. She had lots of friends, had straight As, was active in student government, and boys still thought she was cute. I imagine that her mother, who instilled in her the value of embracing her whole self, helped to counter the messages she was receiving from her peers. Sharifa realized that her mother established a different tone for how she perceived herself that set her apart from others. She learned the value of marching to her own beat.

And the beat goes on. Sharifa's daughter, Laila, loves her natural hair and embraces her curl pattern more than most. When she was seven, she wanted to loc her hair and Sharifa allowed her the freedom to do so. At the age of twelve, Laila wanted a change, so she decided to cut off her locs. Sharifa was amazed and proud that Laila was secure enough to cut off all of her hair. Laila now proudly rocks a short afro.

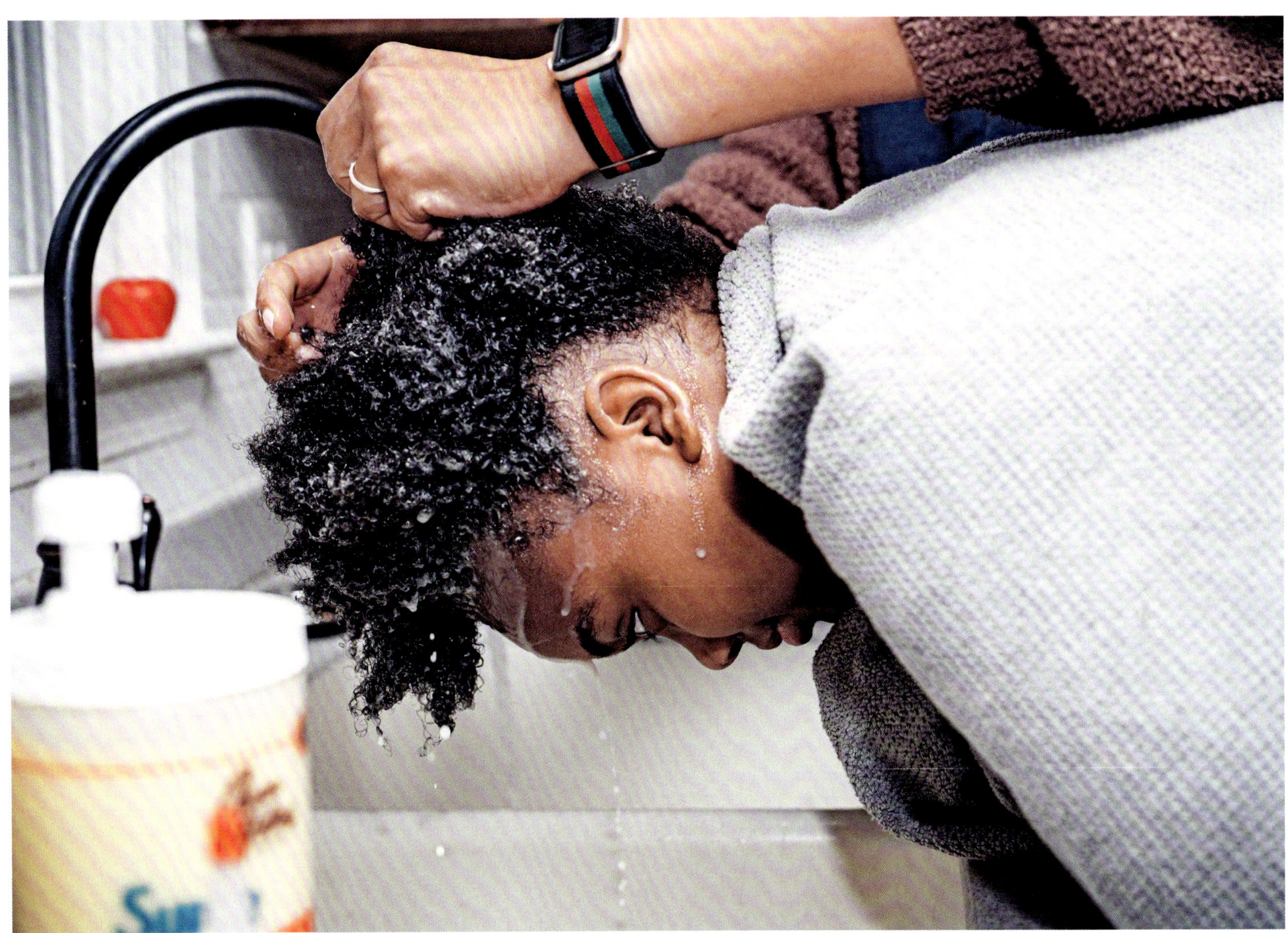

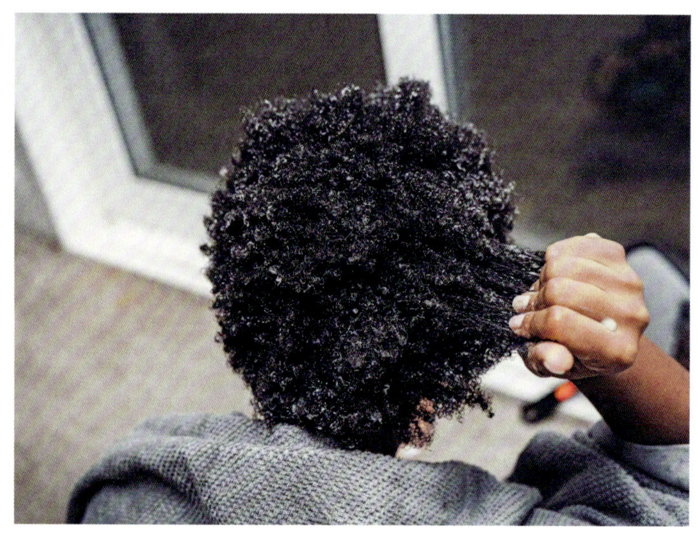
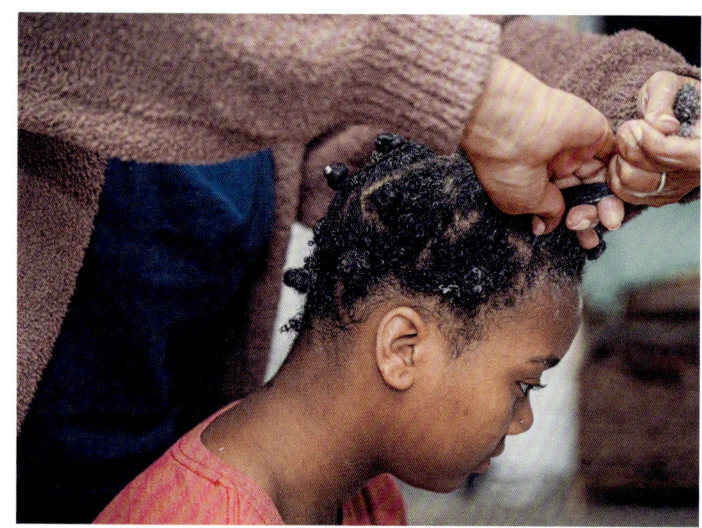
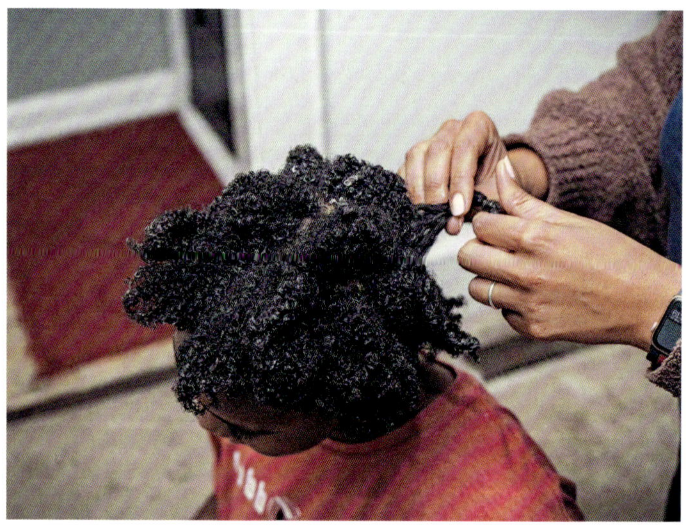
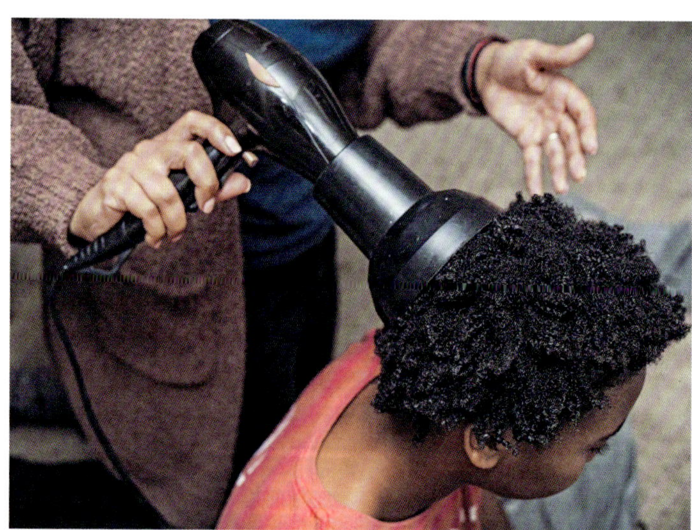

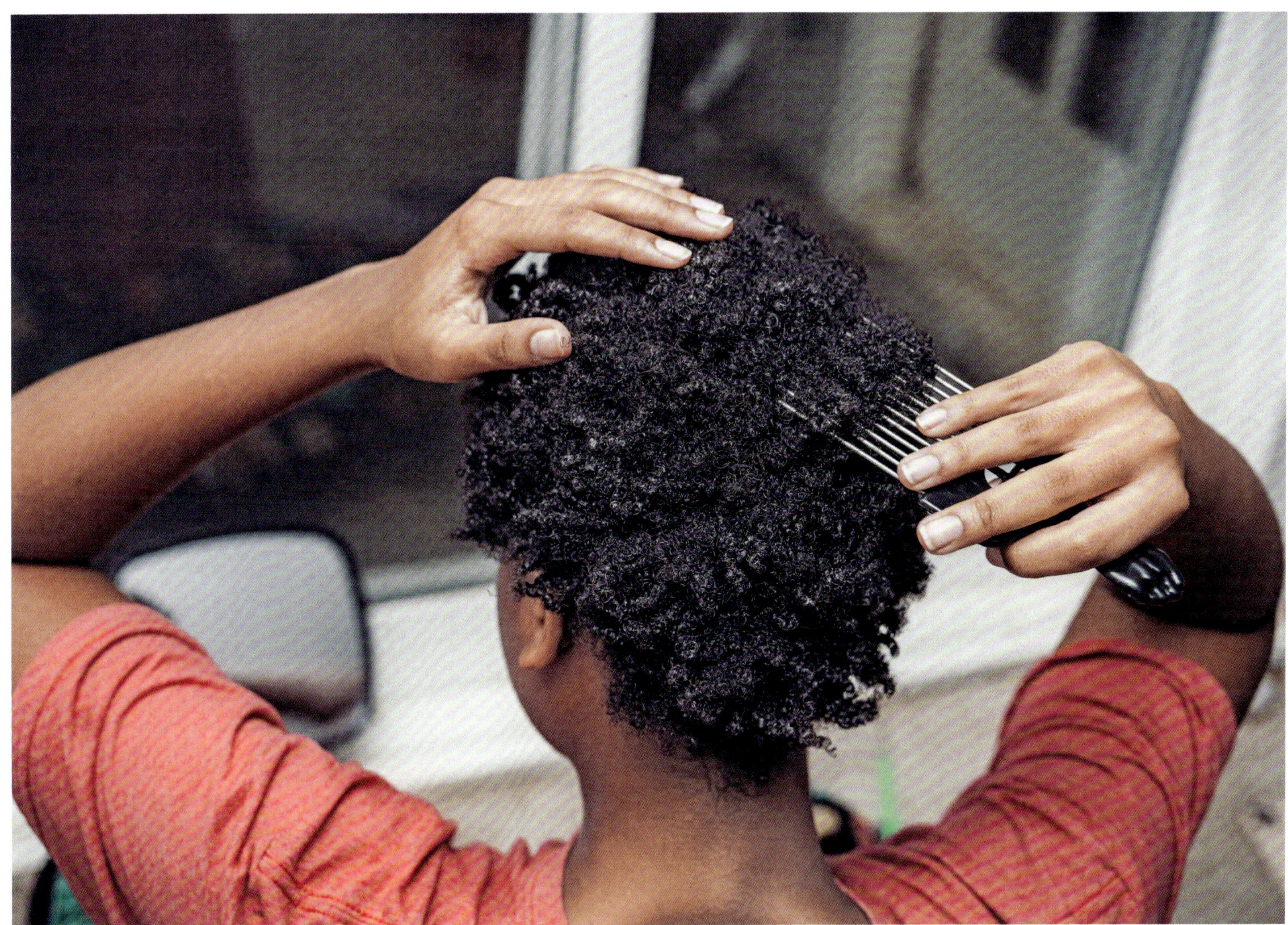

While Sharifa may help out occasionally, Laila usually washes and styles her own hair using techniques learned from her mother. It takes her about an hour to complete her weekly wash-day routine. After washing, Sharifa and Laila define her curls with bantu knots. Then, they carefully separate them before diffusing her hair to keep her curl pattern in tact. Finally, Laila uses a pick to shape her afro.

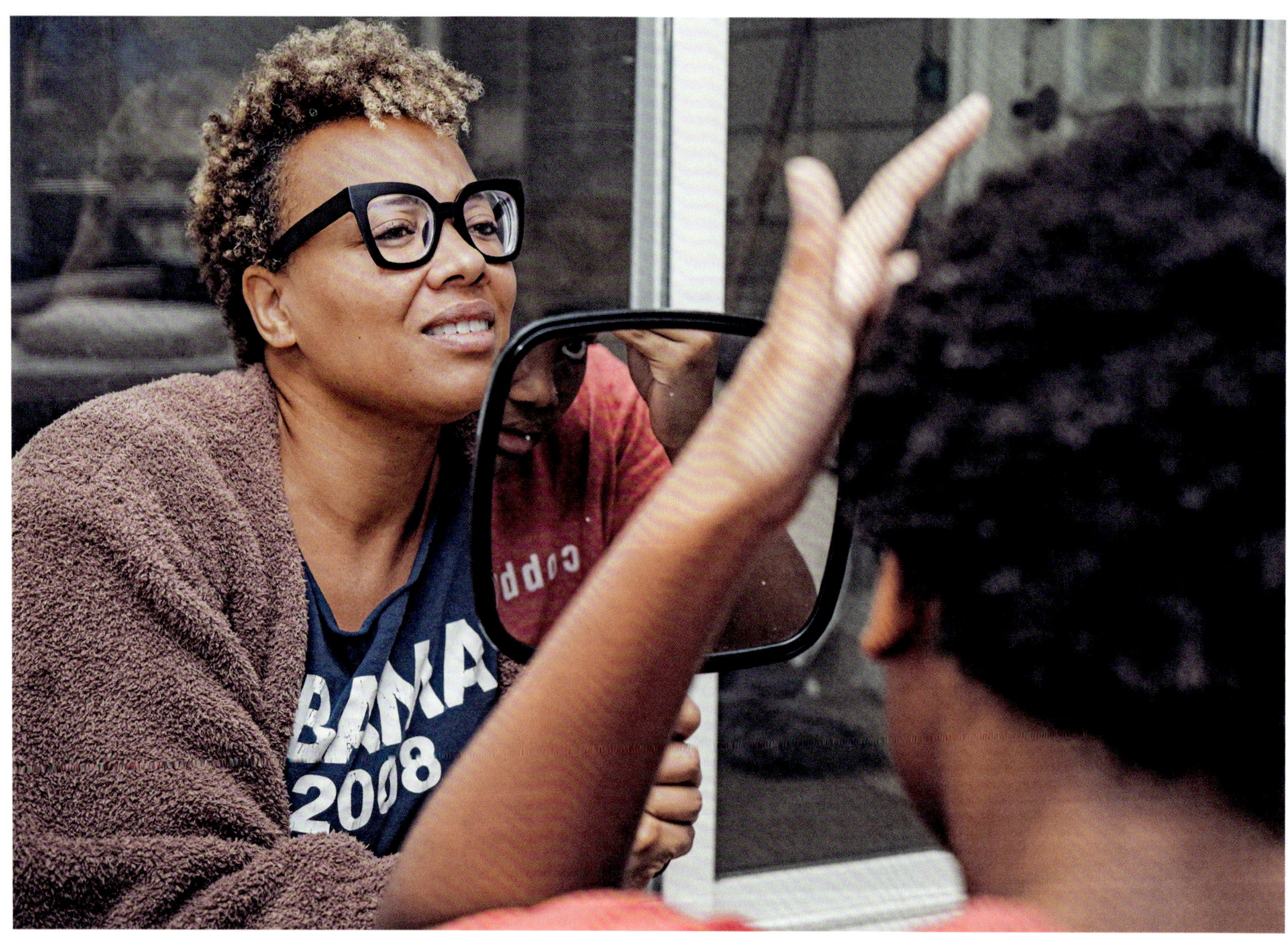

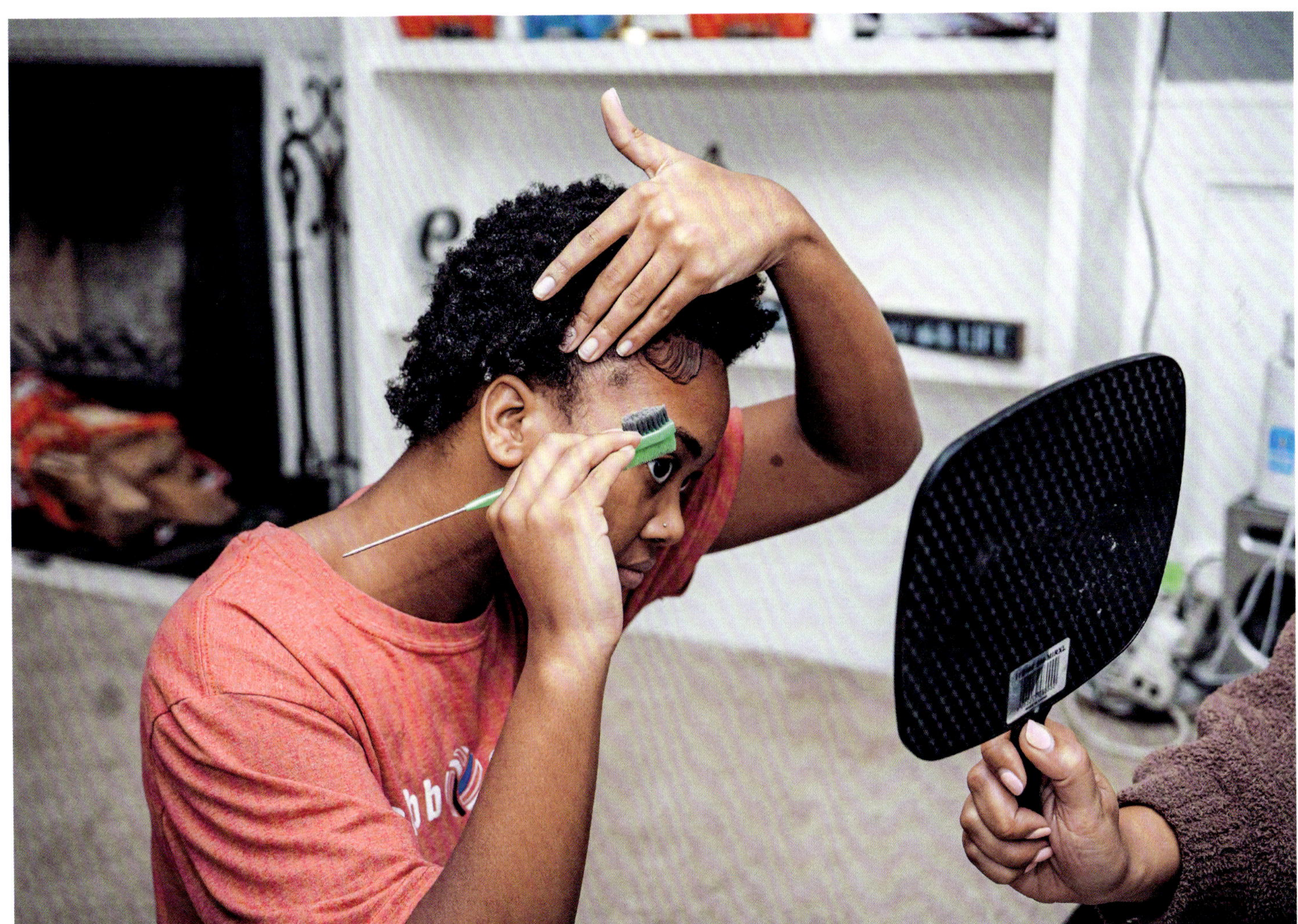

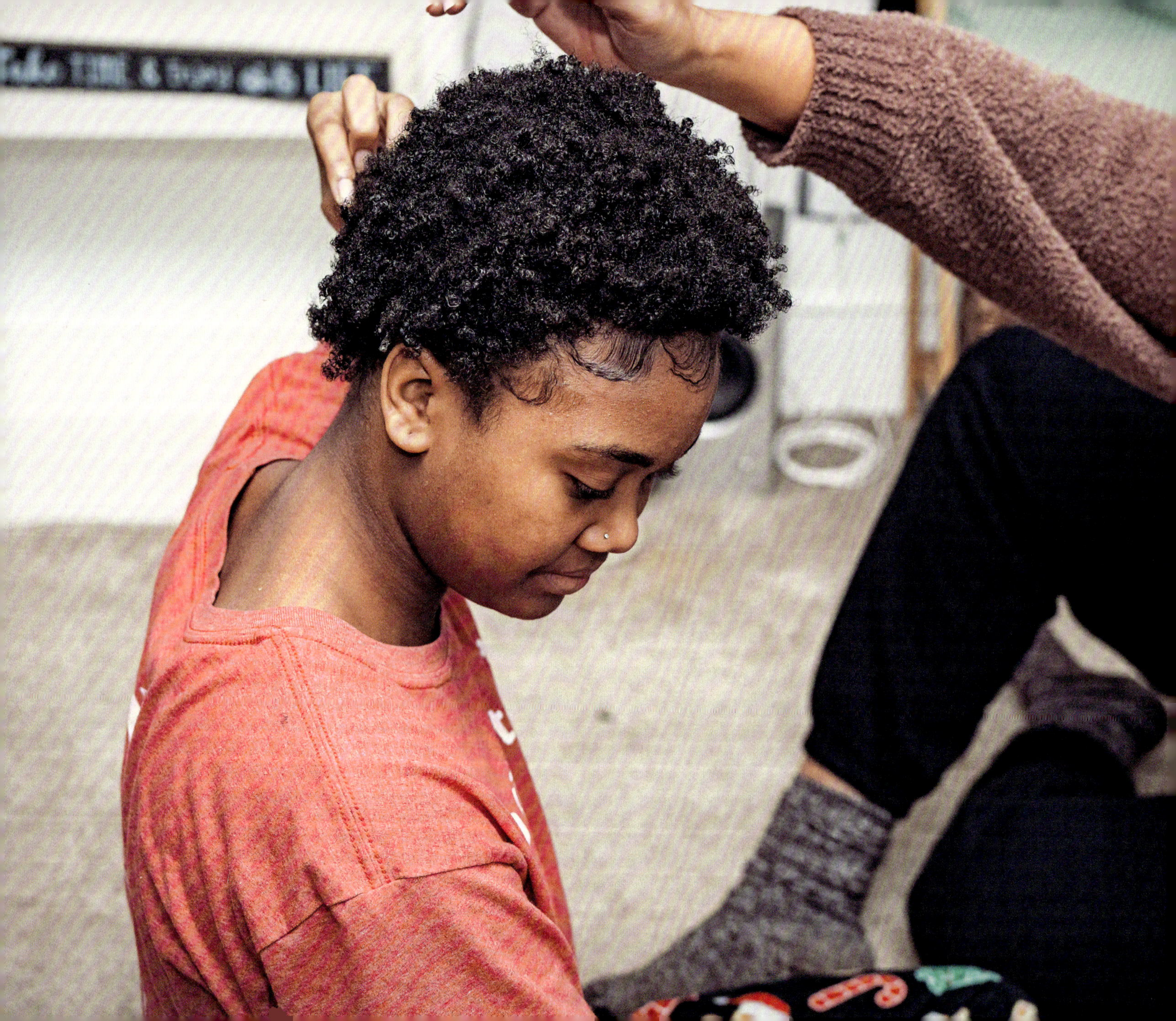

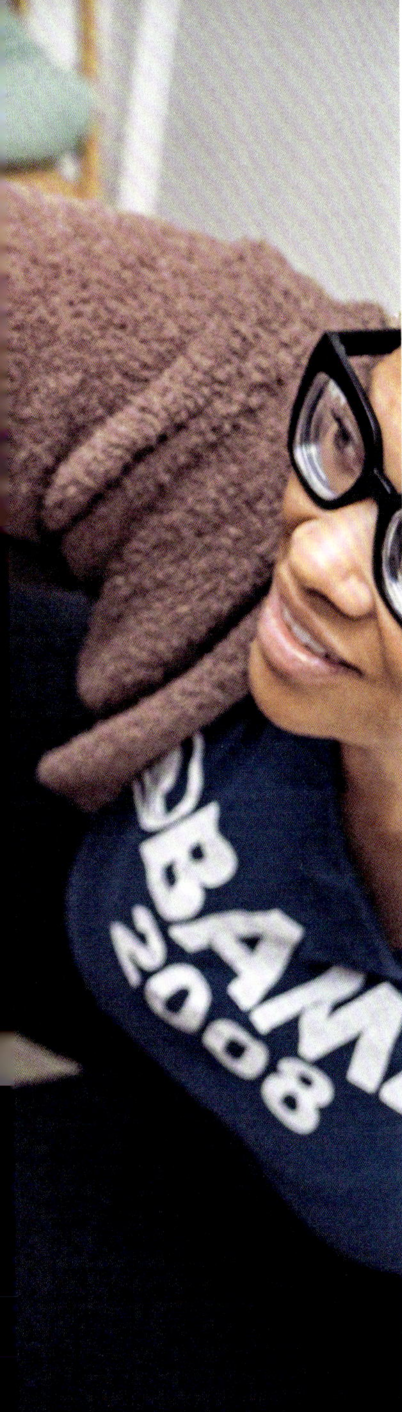

"I tell her all of the time that she was blessed with strong and beautiful hair. She is proud of her natural texture. I often have tried to make her do other styles like twist-outs and braid-outs, but she prefers her afro."

—SHARIFA

Elisa & Madison

"God did not make a mistake with the hair texture that comes out of my scalp . . . why not rock his beautiful creation! It took me a while to get here . . . but I'm glad I'm finally here!"

NOT EVERYONE who goes natural stays natural. And not everyone who makes the decision sticks with it at first. A number of factors play a role in making it difficult to stay on the natural path. Internalized beauty standards that do not include kinky hair, negative feedback from others, the demands of daily life making it hard to devote the time deemed necessary to care for natural textures, and even the difficulty of learning how to care for a completely new head of hair can weigh against the decision to stay natural.

Elisa has experienced all of these. She has gone natural four times.

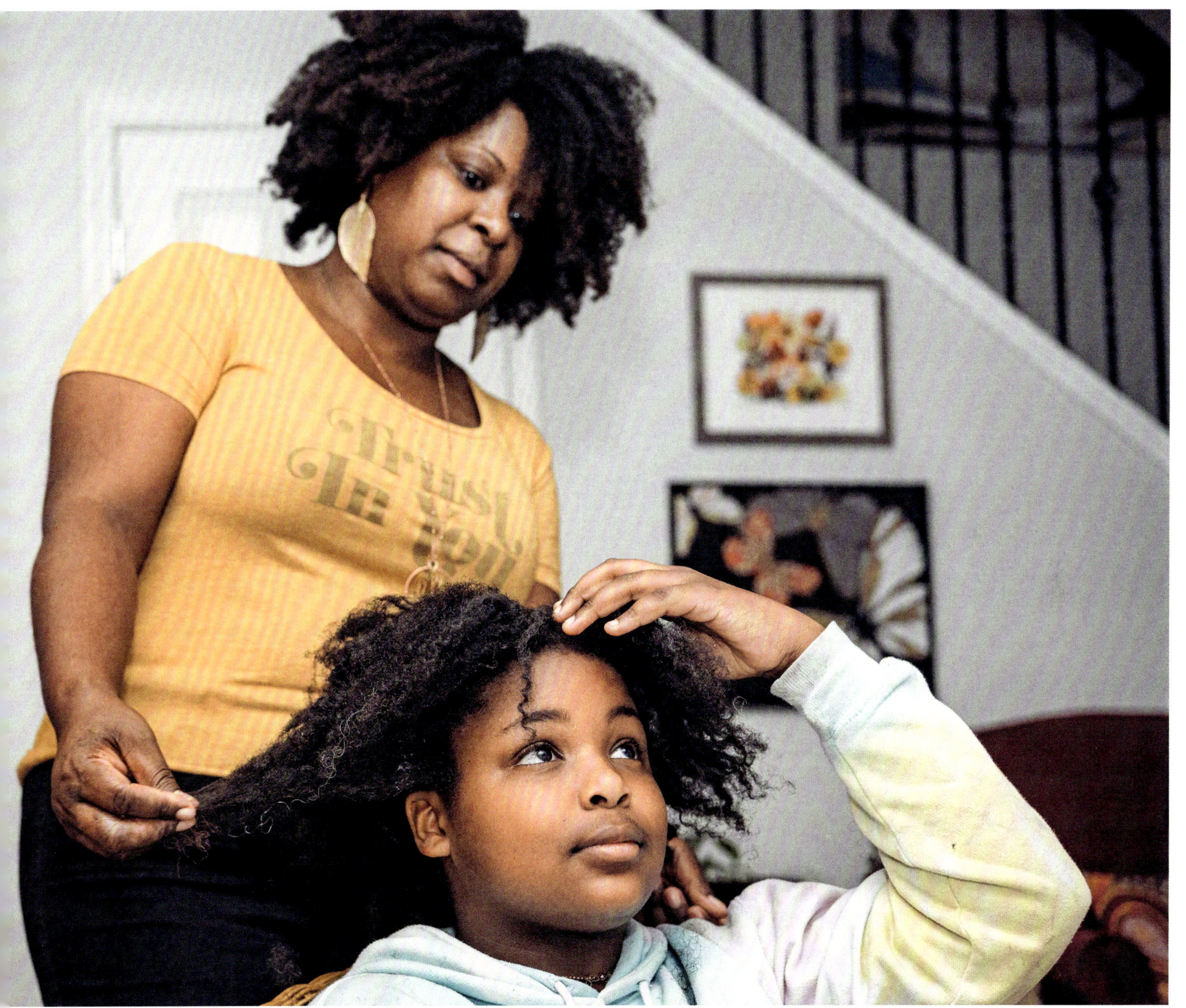

First. Elisa grew up going to the salon to get a press and curl for holidays and special occasions, while her mother tended to her and her sister's natural hair on a regular basis. However, due to her mother's busy schedule as an elementary school teacher and the director of a community school on the weekends, she had a hard time maintaining their hair. In an effort to make their hair easier to manage, her mother took them to a salon to get Jheri curls. By age eleven, Elisa had started getting relaxers. Elisa grew accustomed to the compliments her long, straight hair received.

However, in 2004, while attending graduate school in Harlem, New York, Elisa saw Black women rocking natural hair and discovered natural hair salons. Natural hair started to look like a legitimate option for her, which inspired her to try it. She loved it! However, since she was so used to straight hair, she opted to keep her hair pressed. She quickly found that maintaining pressed hair in often-rainy conditions was stressful. On top of this, there was not much information available about how to care for her hair on her own. For ease, she went back to the relaxer.

Second. When information regarding the dangers of chemical relaxers began to surface, Elisa took notice. This prompted her second attempt at going natural. This time, she really went for it. She did the big chop, and rather than pressing it, she tried to embrace her short natural fro. Sadly, she was met with negative feedback about the look. One of the most hurtful comments came from a family member who told her, "Your hair looks like Frederick Douglass." Wow.

This feedback was not unlike the negative commentary she grew up hearing about her natural texture. As a kid her hair was often compared to hair deemed to be a "better grade" than hers. She was often told her hair was nappier than so-and-so's hair. These comparative statements caused her to believe that her texture was inferior to looser textures, and that the "best hair" was closest to straight hair.

The criticism of her short, natural hair stood in stark contrast to the compliments she was so fond of receiving for her once long, straight hair. She didn't feel beautiful, so she decided to start wearing weaves. Eventually, she went back to relaxers.

Third. This time, her decision to go natural was prompted by a bad relaxer experience. Her stylist left the relaxer on too long, leading to damage and breakage. After this, she was determined never to return to perms. Rather than a big chop this go around, she decided to transition slowly. She utilized roller and straw sets to ease the transition process. After two years, she achieved her desired length and had gotten rid of all the relaxed hair. She made it!

But then, something crazy happened. Elisa was in a wedding and decided to get her hair pressed for the ceremony. She visited a Dominican salon. The advertised process included wash, deep condition, roller set, and blow-dry. However, when she washed her hair a week or so later, the curls did not return. She suspected that the salon may have somehow slipped relaxer into the process without her knowledge or consent. She later visited another salon, where it was confirmed that her curls were completely gone. She could not believe it. This sounds unbelievable to me as well. Unconscionable even. Unacceptable for sure. But since it was easier for Elisa to keep her hair relaxed after the blow-out incident, she kept getting perms.

Finally, in 2012, Elisa walked away from relaxers for the *fourth* time. By then, she had gained the knowledge, desire, and confidence to stay the course. While she recalls being proud of the styles her relaxed hair could achieve, she is now even more proud of her big curly twist-outs. She is a principal at a majority-White school and loves that she can wear her hair in its natural state as an example to the young Black girls at her school, including her own daughter, Madison.

In order to ensure that Madison is able to see the beauty of her hair, Elisa is very intentional about the messaging Madison receives on wash day. Elisa stated:

I always stay positive about her hair. I never complain if it is tangled or takes a while to comb out. I promote positivity in her hair. This includes music, dancing at times, and watching fun shows on TV. I usually include Madison in the styling of her hair. I want her to feel empowered and proud of her hair.

This intentionality started early. When Madison first started attending elementary school, she would tell Elisa she wanted her hair in a ponytail like other girls at her school. Elisa realized what she meant and started buying books and watching programming geared toward Black hair pride. They had the Sesame Street "I Love My Hair" song on repeat. Elisa quoted Proverbs 22:6 as she reflected on her efforts. "'Train up a child in the way they should go, when they are old, they will not depart from it.' Hopefully, this works for hair also!"

It's working. Madison is confident wearing both afro puffs and braids. She does not shy away from curious questions from her White peers regarding her hair texture or styling choices. And because Elisa has discussed how to handle wandering hands, Madison is comfortable telling others not to touch her hair. She is empowered in a way that many of us are still striving toward.

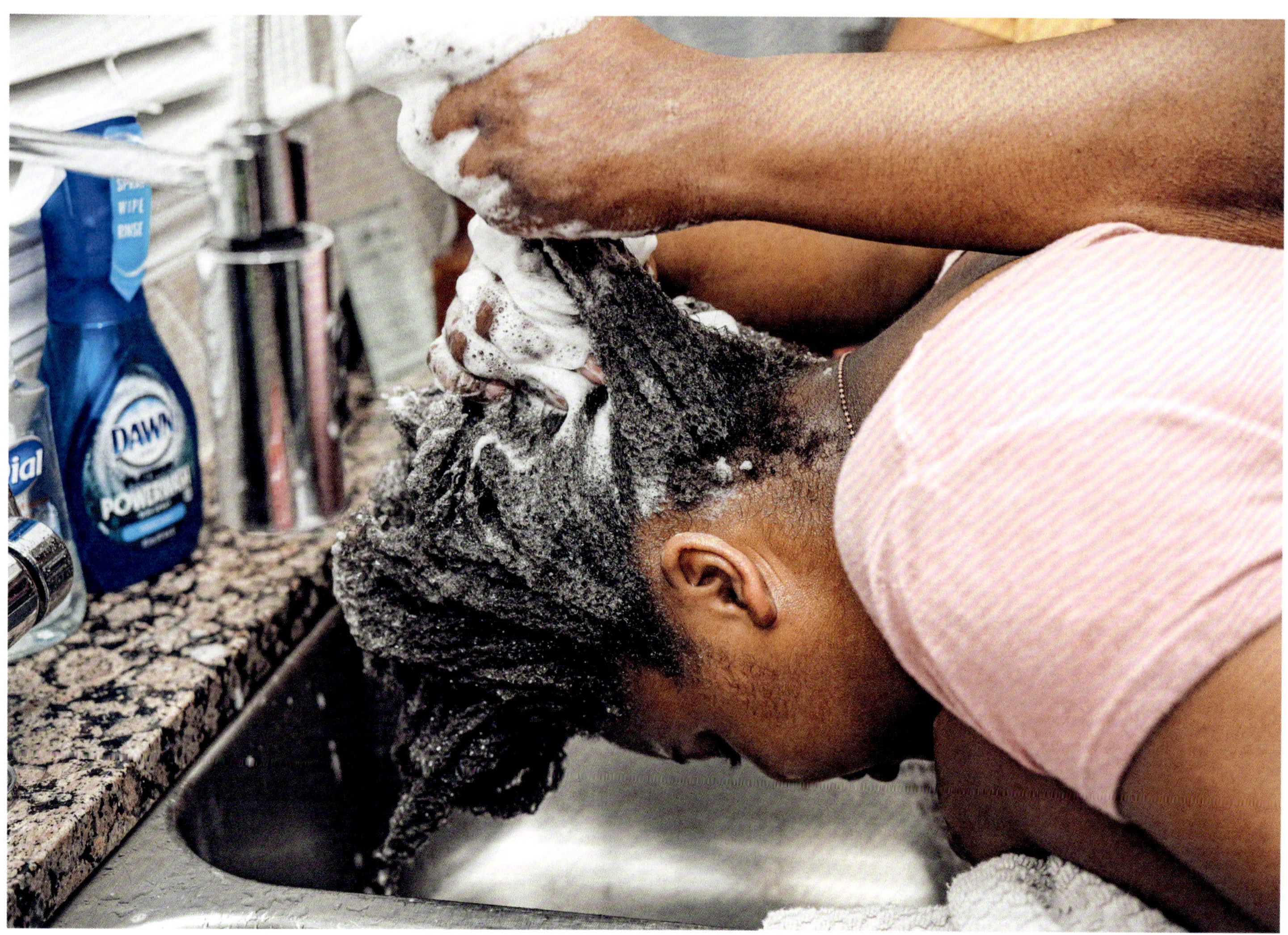

For Elisa and Madison, wash day lasts about three hours every two weeks.

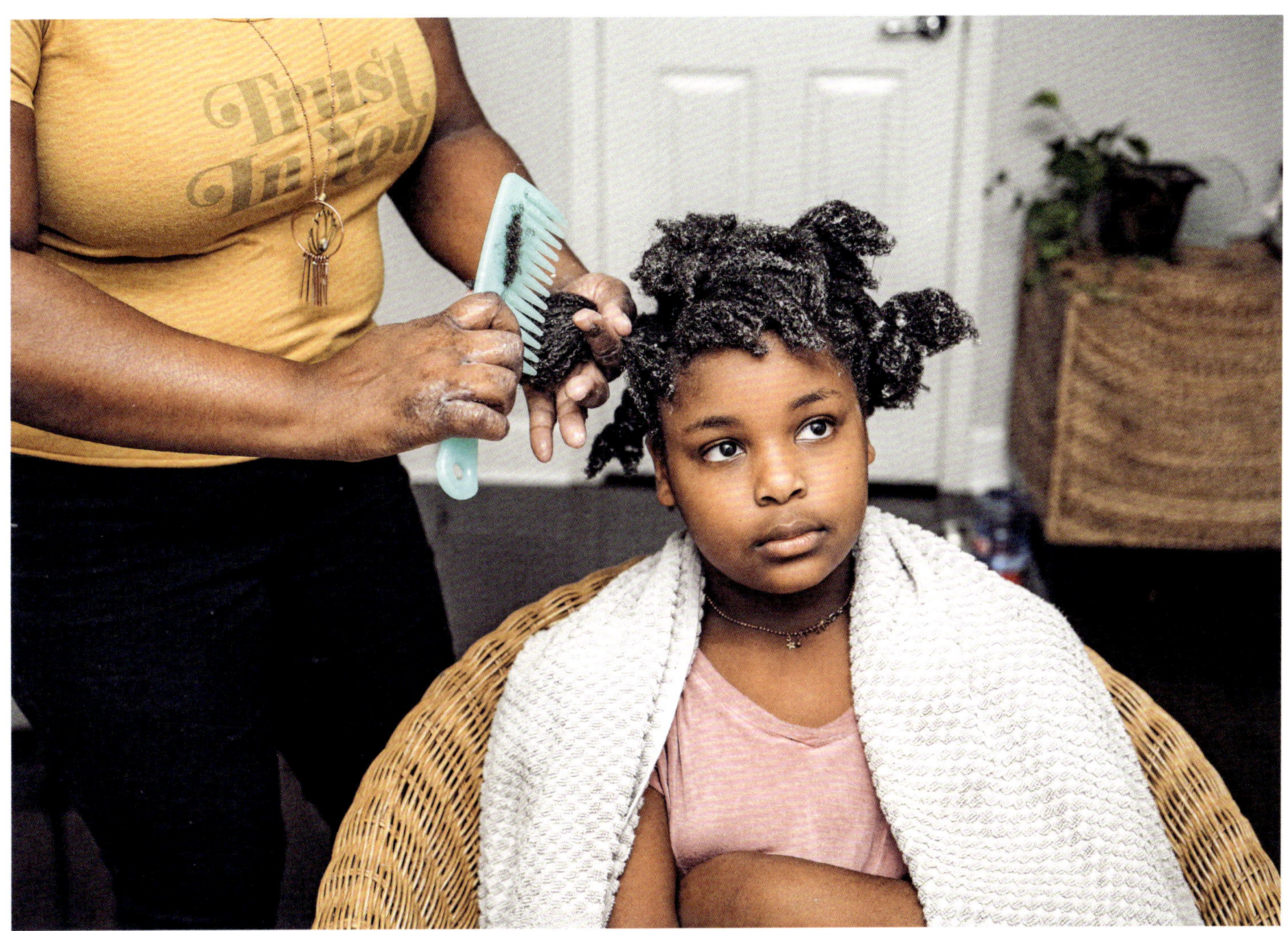

After washing, Elisa adds deep conditioner and detangles Madison's hair.

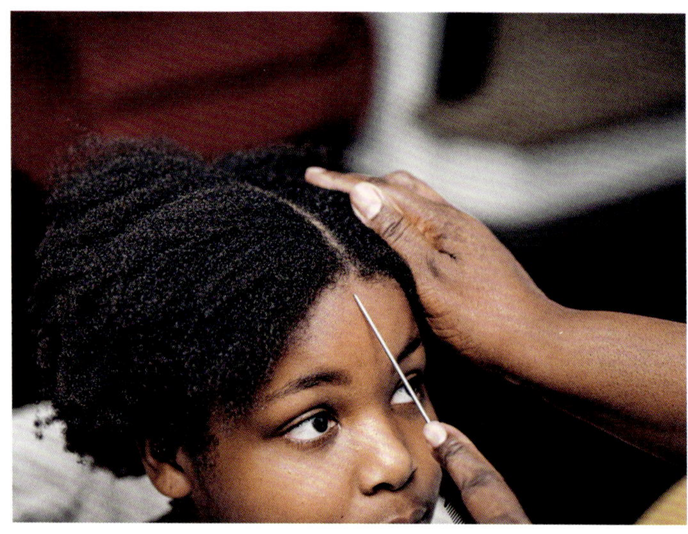
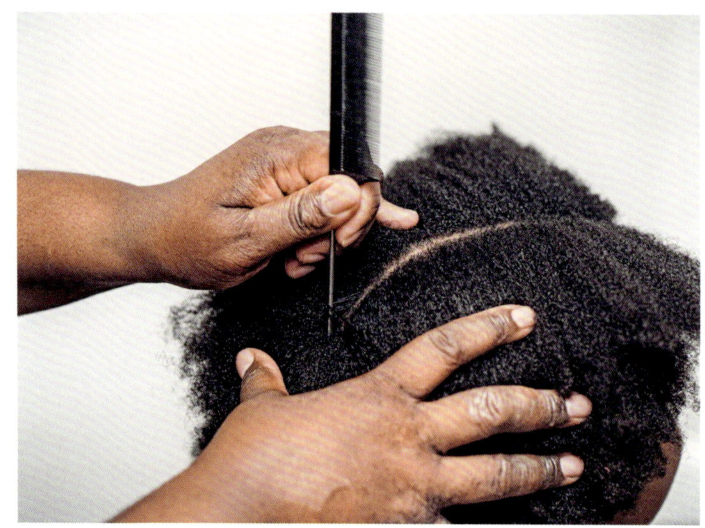
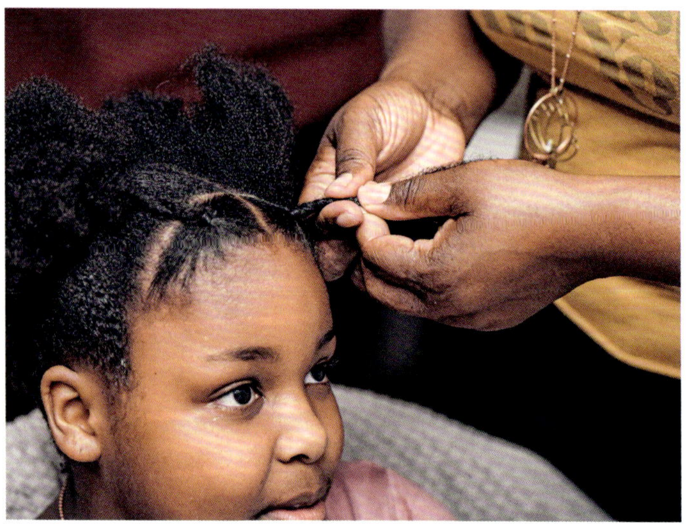
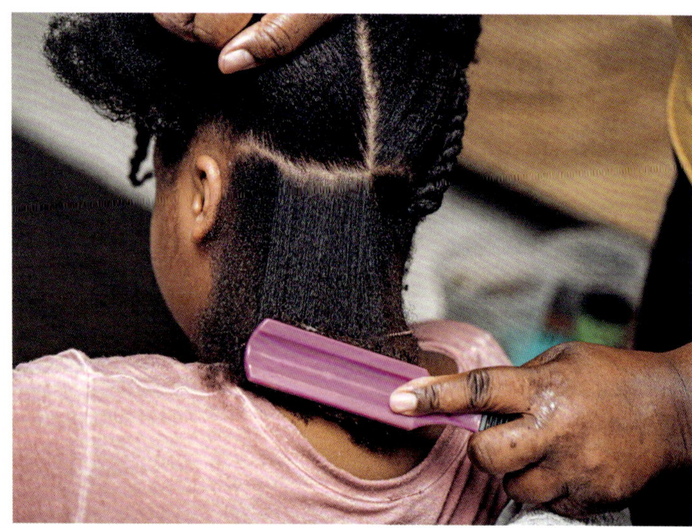

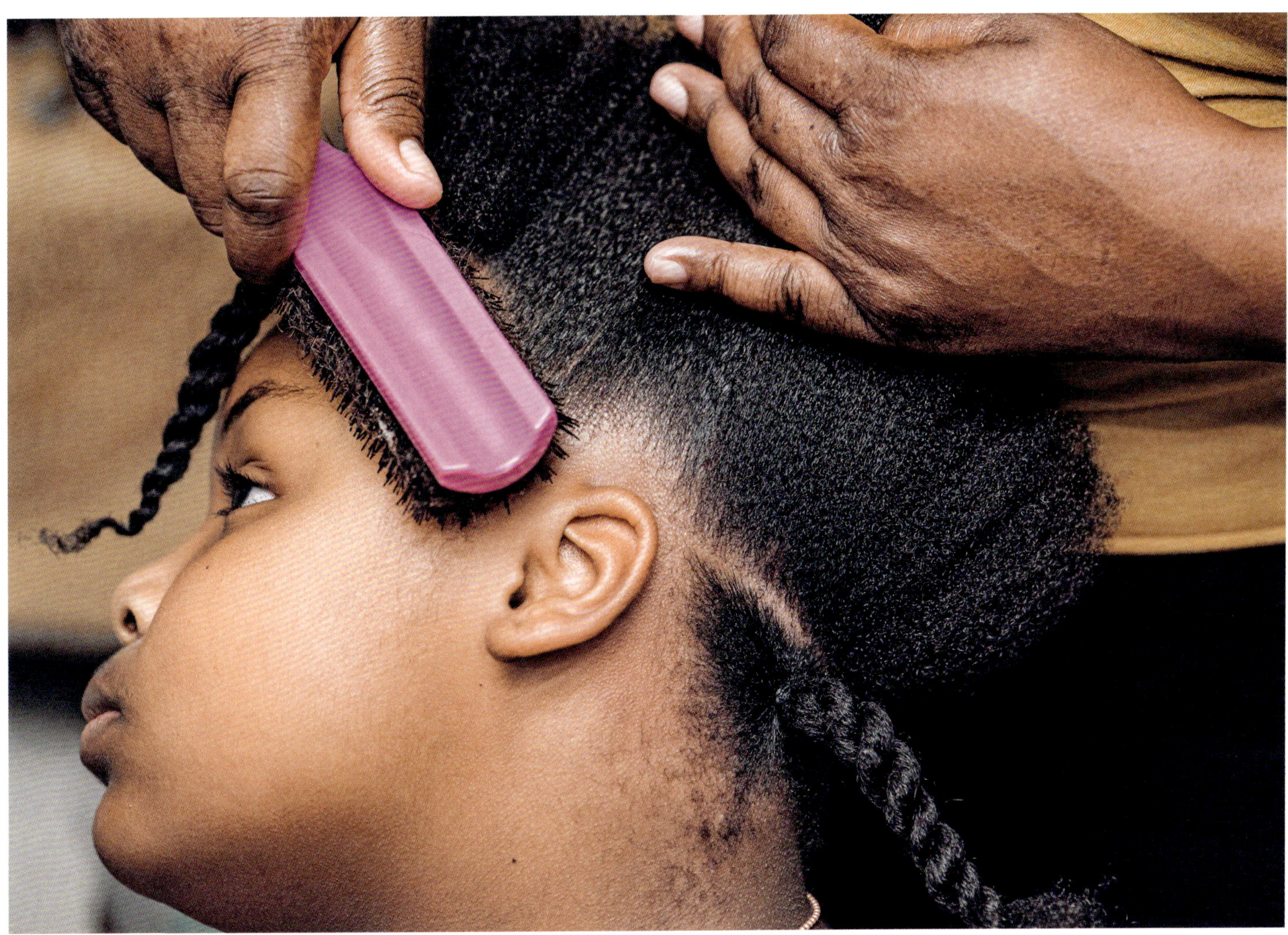

After conditioning, Elisa blow dries and styles her hair.

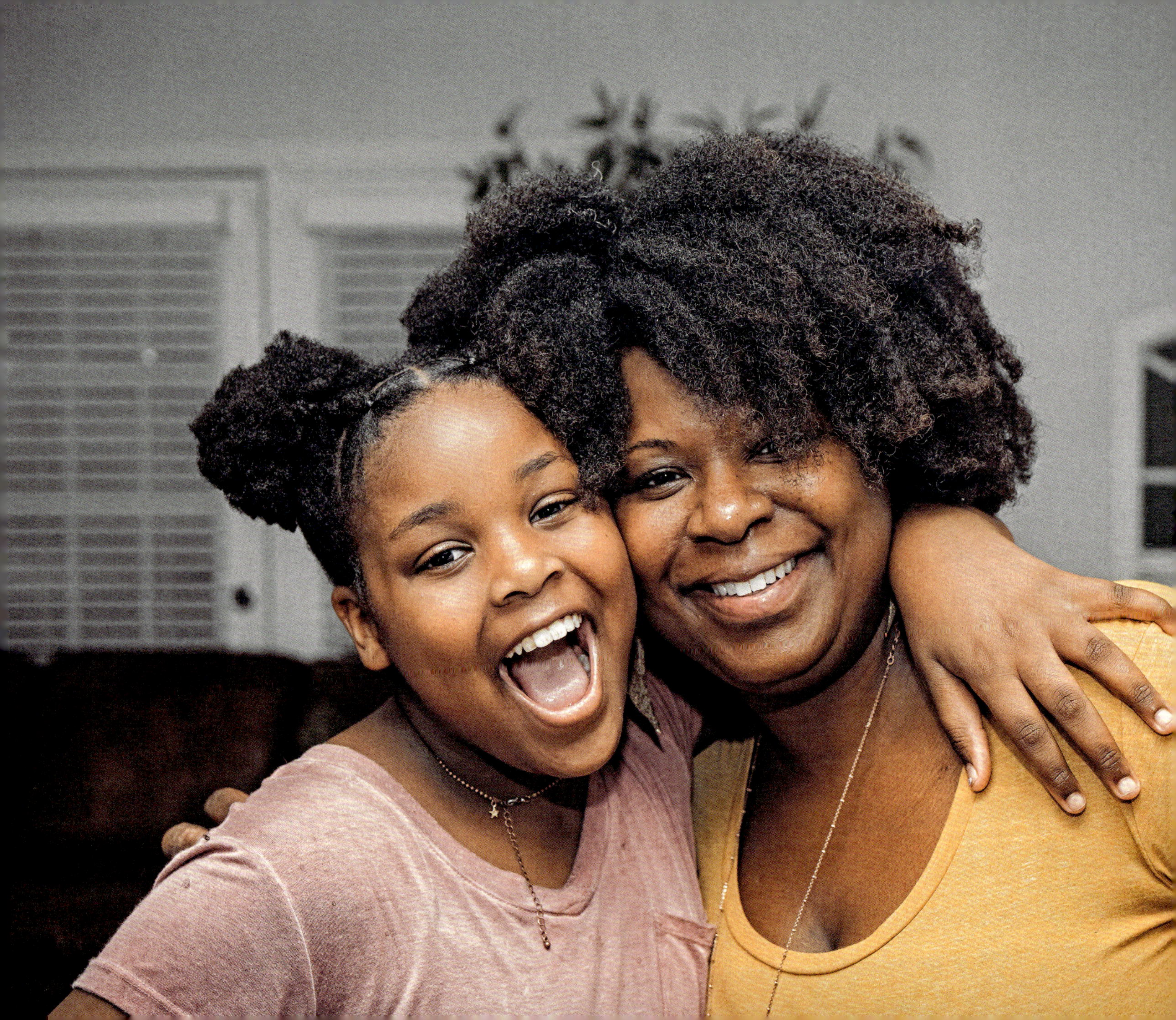

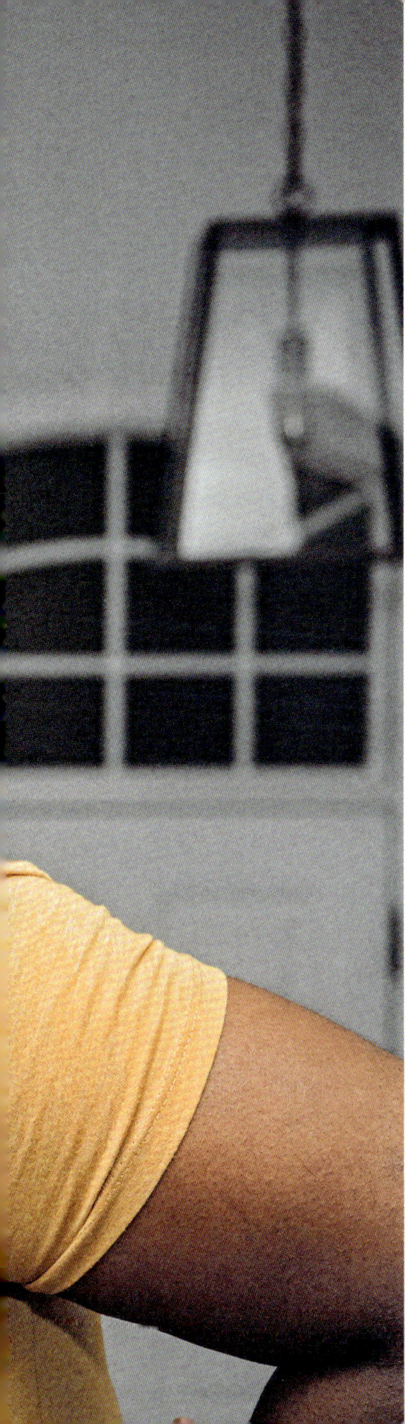

"Her hair is a gift from God . . . be proud of it . . . ROCK it! Don't hold back!" —ELISA

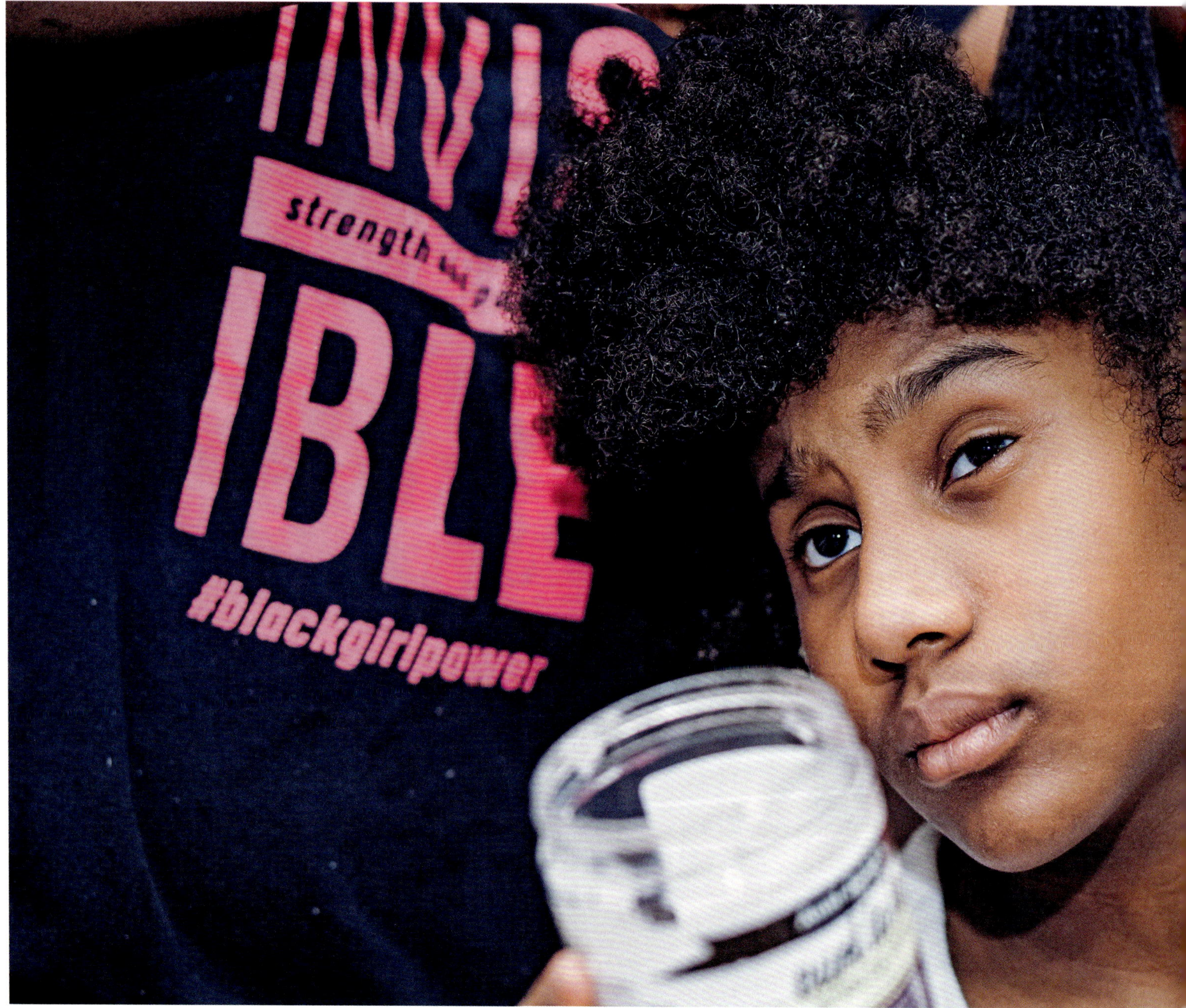
INVIS
strength
IBLE
#blackgirlpower

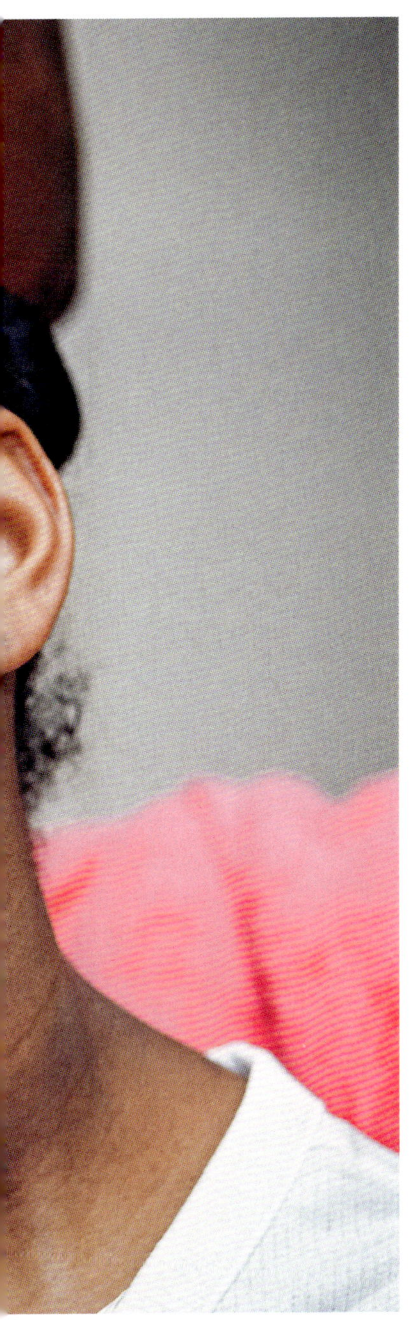

EuLisa & Shelisa

"Once someone called my natural hair aggressive. In hindsight, I should have smacked her!"

EULISA has always felt free to try new things with her hair. Seeing it as an accessory, she has worn it in a variety of styles over the years. In 2014, she went natural because she wanted something more practical and manageable. Pause. She is one of the few women I've heard use these two words, or even descriptions remotely similar, in association with natural hair, but I digress. While EuLisa found some simplicity in her hair-care routine after going natural, things at work got a bit more complicated. After being told that her natural hairstyle was "aggressive" by a co-worker (yes, someone actually had the audacity), EuLisa found herself rethinking the free-spirited approach she had once taken to hairstyling. Though she maintained her natural hair, she wore it in styles that she believed would avoid such an impression.

Enter 2020. Working from home became the norm for many, and EuLisa finally saw an opportunity to try locs for the first time.

I honestly can't believe that as I write this line Black women *still* feel pressured to "tame" their natural hairstyles for the workplace. Some have avoided hairstyles that have wrongfully been deemed "unprofessional." Indeed, our beliefs about how we are allowed to show up to the office have been shaped by the lengthy history of Black women being fired from jobs because of their cornrows, braids, and locs. Where did all those afros from the 1960s and '70s go in the '80s? Well, I imagine they got pressed or relaxed in order to fit into cubicles.

Natural hair discrimination in the workplace is well documented. A 2023 study found that over 20 percent of Black women aged twenty-five to thirty-four have been sent home from work because of their hair.[30] A 2020 study found that "Black women with natural hairstyles were perceived to be less professional, less competent, and less likely to be recommended for a job interview than Black women with straightened hairstyles and White women with either curly or straight hairstyles."[31] Further, a 2019 study supports the claim that Black women's hair is more policed in the workplace.[32]

Because our hair and hairstyles continue to be "othered," the CROWN (Creating a Respectful and Open World for Natural Hair) Act was created in 2019 by Dove and the CROWN Coalition, in partnership with then State Senator Holly J. Mitchell of California, to protect against race-based hairstyle discrimination in schools and in the workplace. It includes both hair texture and styles such as braids, locs, twists, and other styles that are rooted in Black culture. Thus far, it has been passed in twenty-three states.[33] It's difficult to accept that we *still* need legislation to guard against the discriminatory policing of Black bodies. It's no wonder that sheltering in place in 2020 gave many Black women the hall pass they needed to finally wear culturally significant hairstyles.

While we still have a way to go regarding natural hairstyles in corporate spaces, I would be remiss to not acknowledge the progress we have made. Although it is true that *the* Michelle Obama understood the sad reality that America just wasn't ready for a First Lady with kinky hair, many of us celebrated Ketanji Brown Jackson, the first Black woman to serve as a justice on the United States Supreme Court, proudly wearing locs as she was sworn in. Slow progress is still progress.

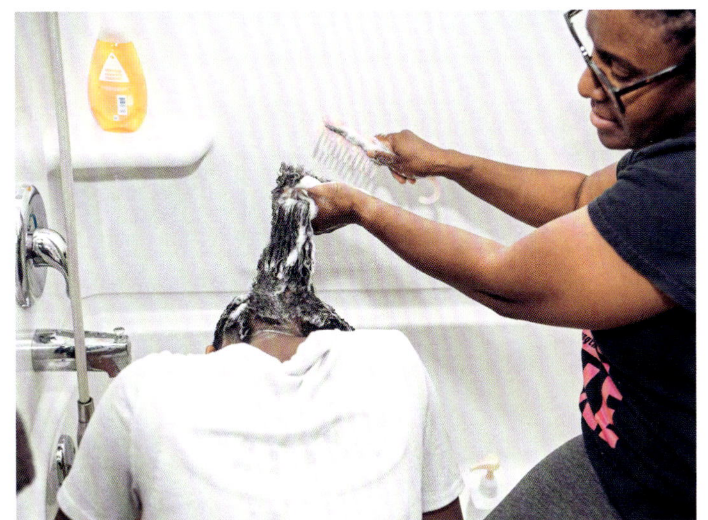 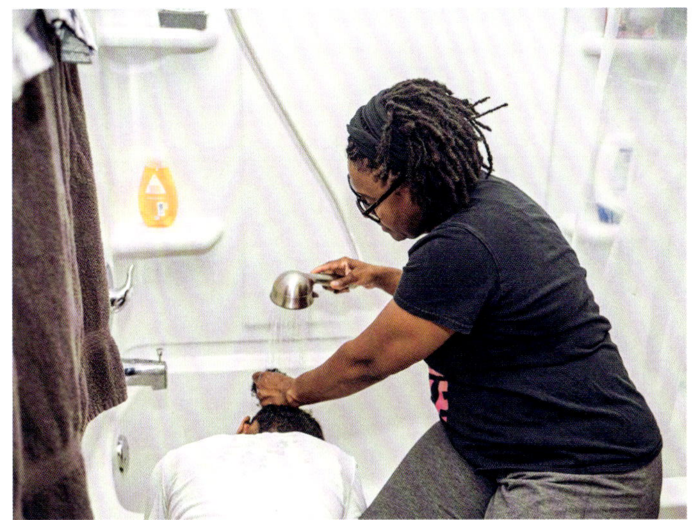

Wash day for EuLisa and Shelisa takes place every two or three weeks for about two to three hours. EuLisa takes a "less is more" approach. I counted a total of three products as I observed EuLisa's wash-day routine. THREE!

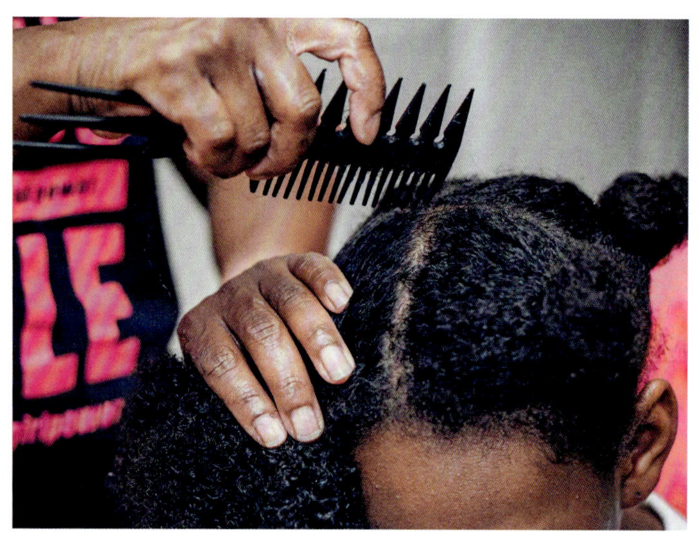
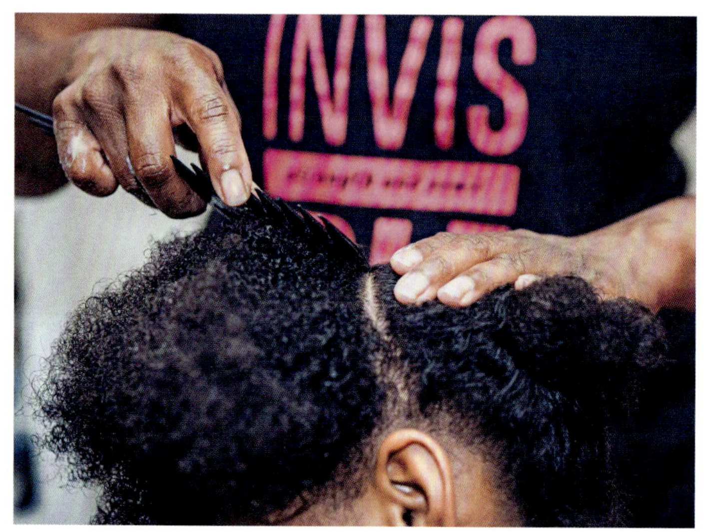
INVIS
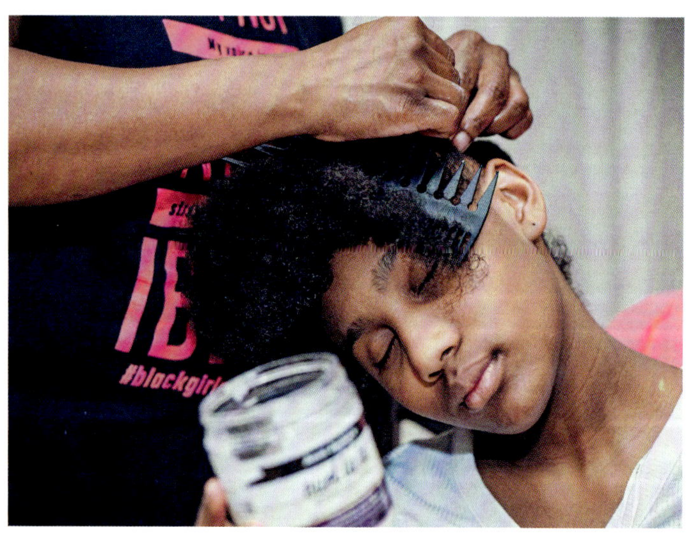
#blackgirl
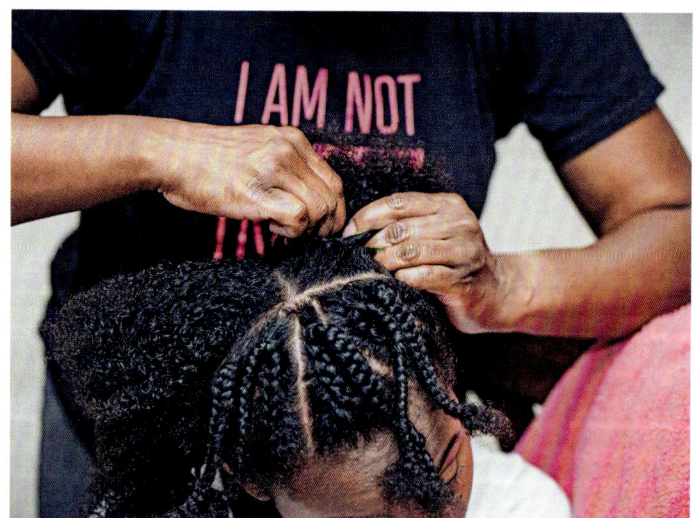
I AM NOT

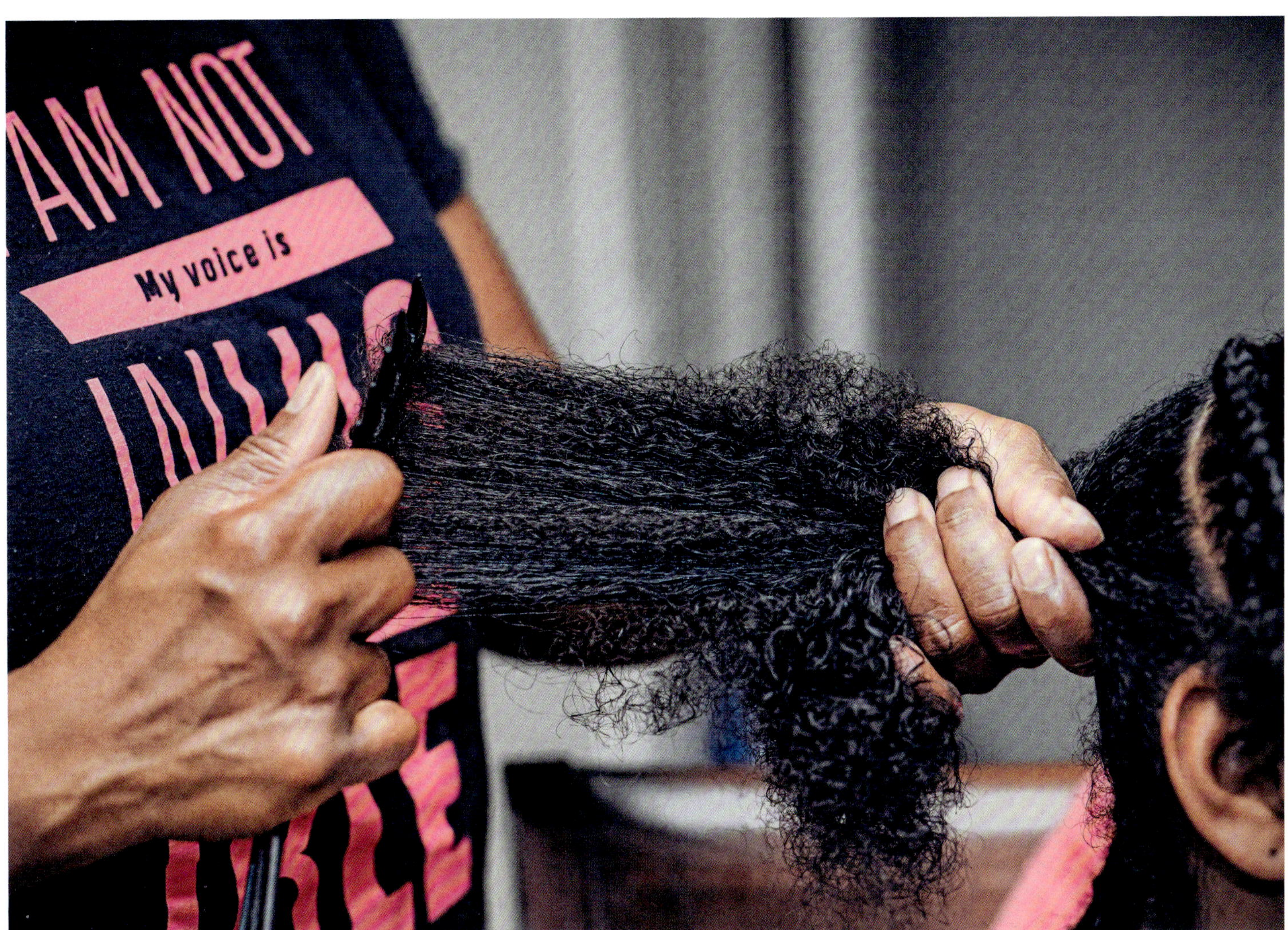

AM NOT
My voice is

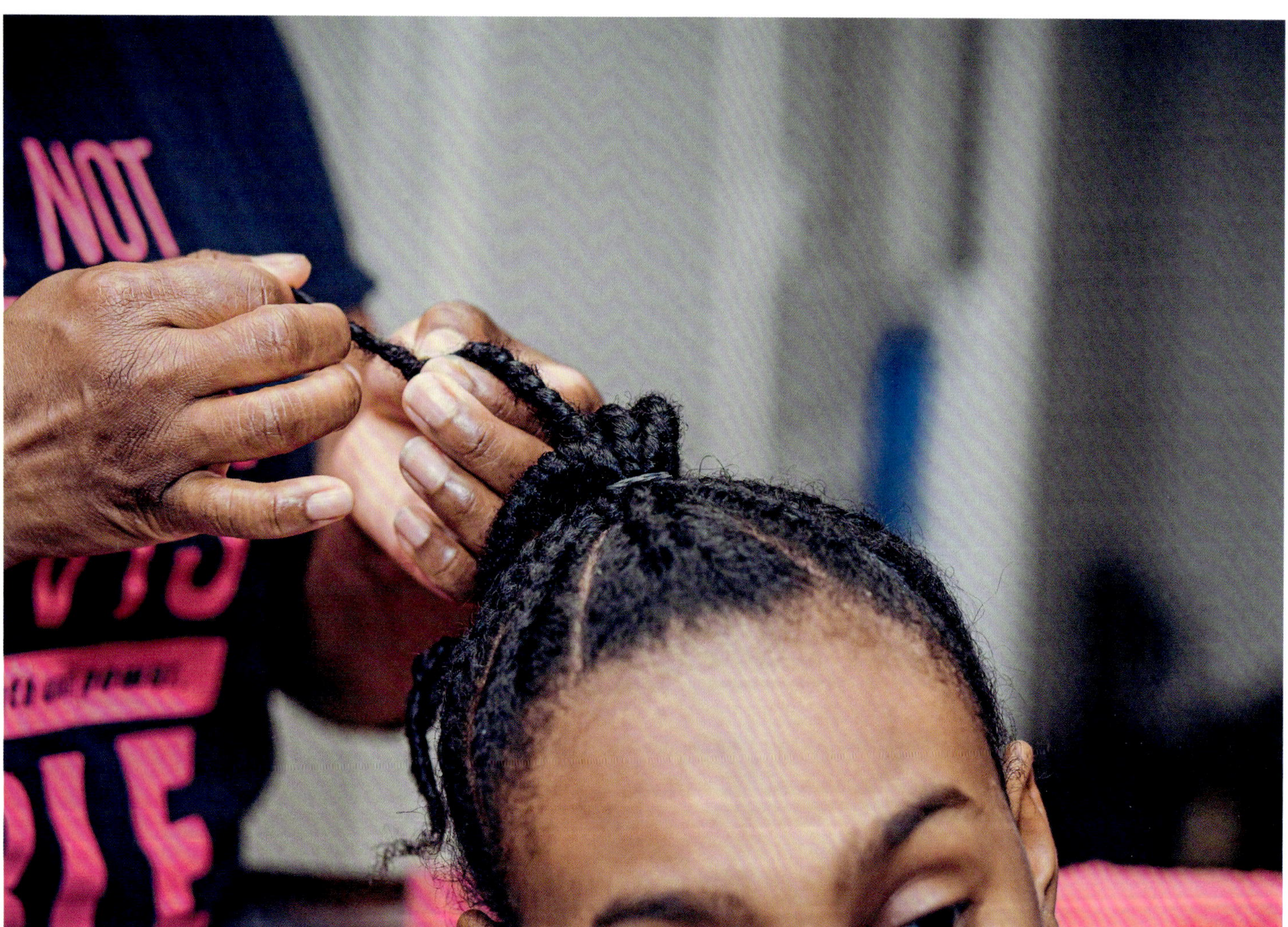

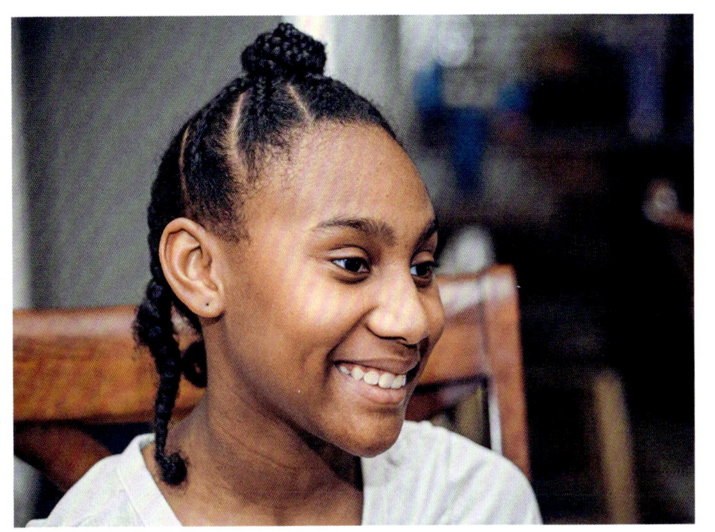 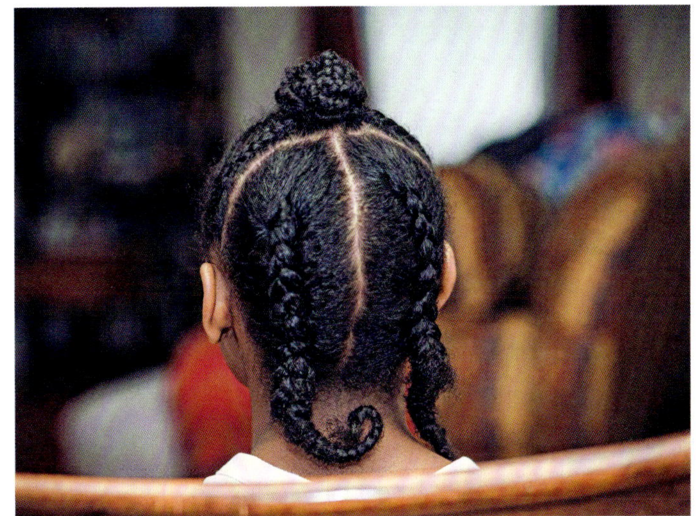

"[Shelisa] loves the length [of her hair] and the natural shape it grows in. She does want to wear it straight, but I encourage her and let her know how beautiful her hair is!" —EULISA

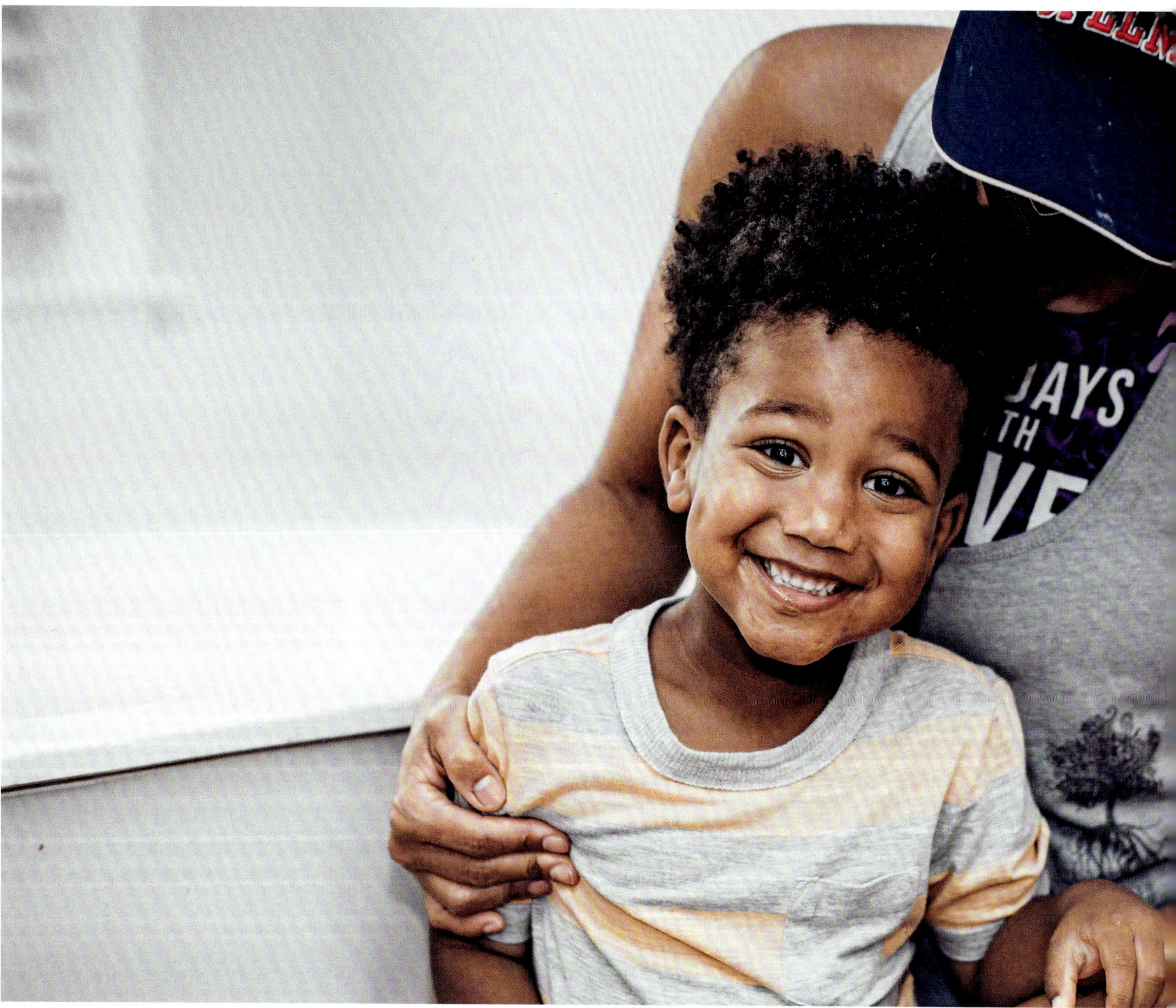

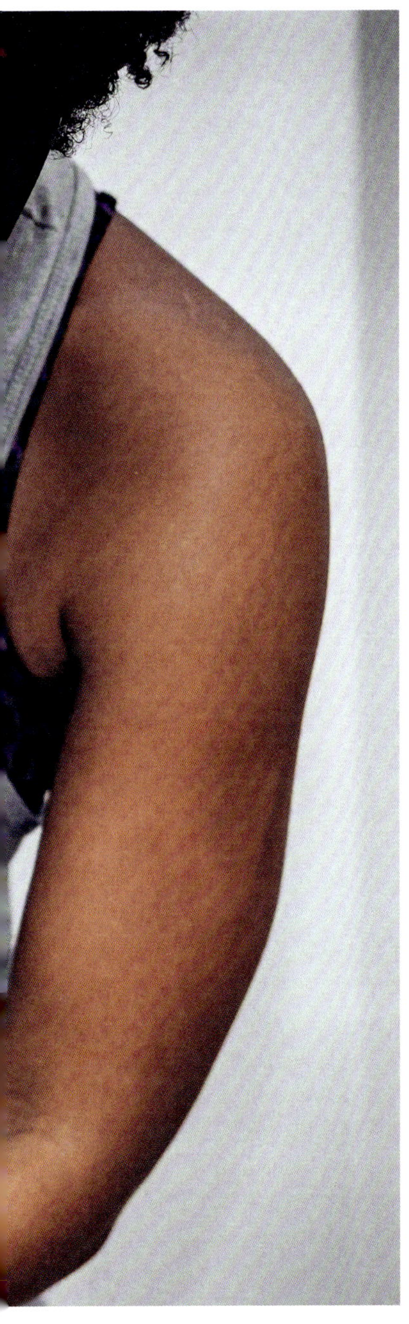

Emily & Coleman

"I love that young Black boys and men and their parents are embracing longer natural hair for themselves and their sons."

GROWING UP, I did not see many Black boys wearing their hair long. Those who did would often wear it in corn-rows or plaits and were perceived to be "thugs." If their hair was in locs, it seemed to indicate that they were either an artist or an activist. I imagine that in addition to these stereotypes regarding long hair, pervasive anti "nappy" sentiments kept many Black boys and men from wearing their hair long. When my dad was nine years old, a boy in his neighborhood told him that his hair was so nappy, it looked like ten thousand soldiers with their fists balled up. The popularity of the conk hairstyle in the 1950s and s-curls in the '90s shows that Black men have been on their own journey toward natural hair acceptance. The preference for straight hair or looser curl patterns does not discriminate based on gender.

When I started creating this book, I had no intention of photographing mothers and sons. I'm a mom of two girls, so wash day including boys just wasn't on my radar. However, I have recently become aware of the growing trend of Black boys growing their hair longer, thus requiring more regimented hair care beyond just visits to the barbershop. For some Black boys, wash day is replacing the barbershop altogether. I believe relaxed gender norms regarding hair length, coupled with the increased normalization of natural hair textures have made long hair a suitable option for Black men and boys. A few of them are featured in these pages.

For Emily, a mom of three boys, "it's just hair!" She's not afraid to experiment. From nearly bald, to braided styles, to weaves, Emily has tried more than most with her hairstyles. She loves experimenting with her hair and enjoys frequently changing it up. She loves the freedom her natural hair provides.

Emily hopes to pass this freedom on to her three sons. Her older twins, Lathen and Zachary, have chosen to wear their hair short like their father. However, her youngest son, Coleman, wears his hair long. She wants to show them that they don't need to feel bound by racial or gender-based stereotypes—they should be free to express themselves and tell a story with their hair, no matter how they decide to wear it.

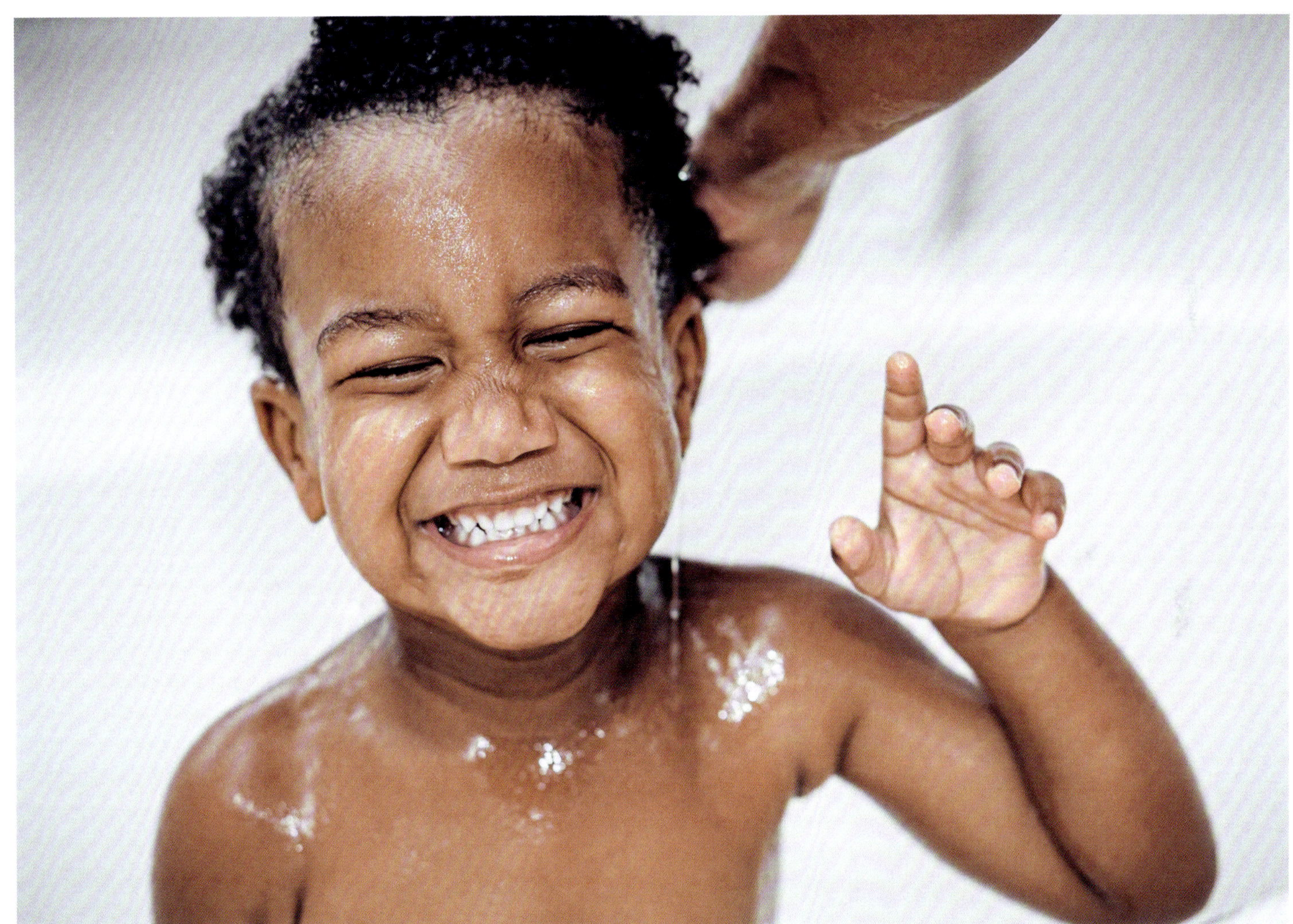

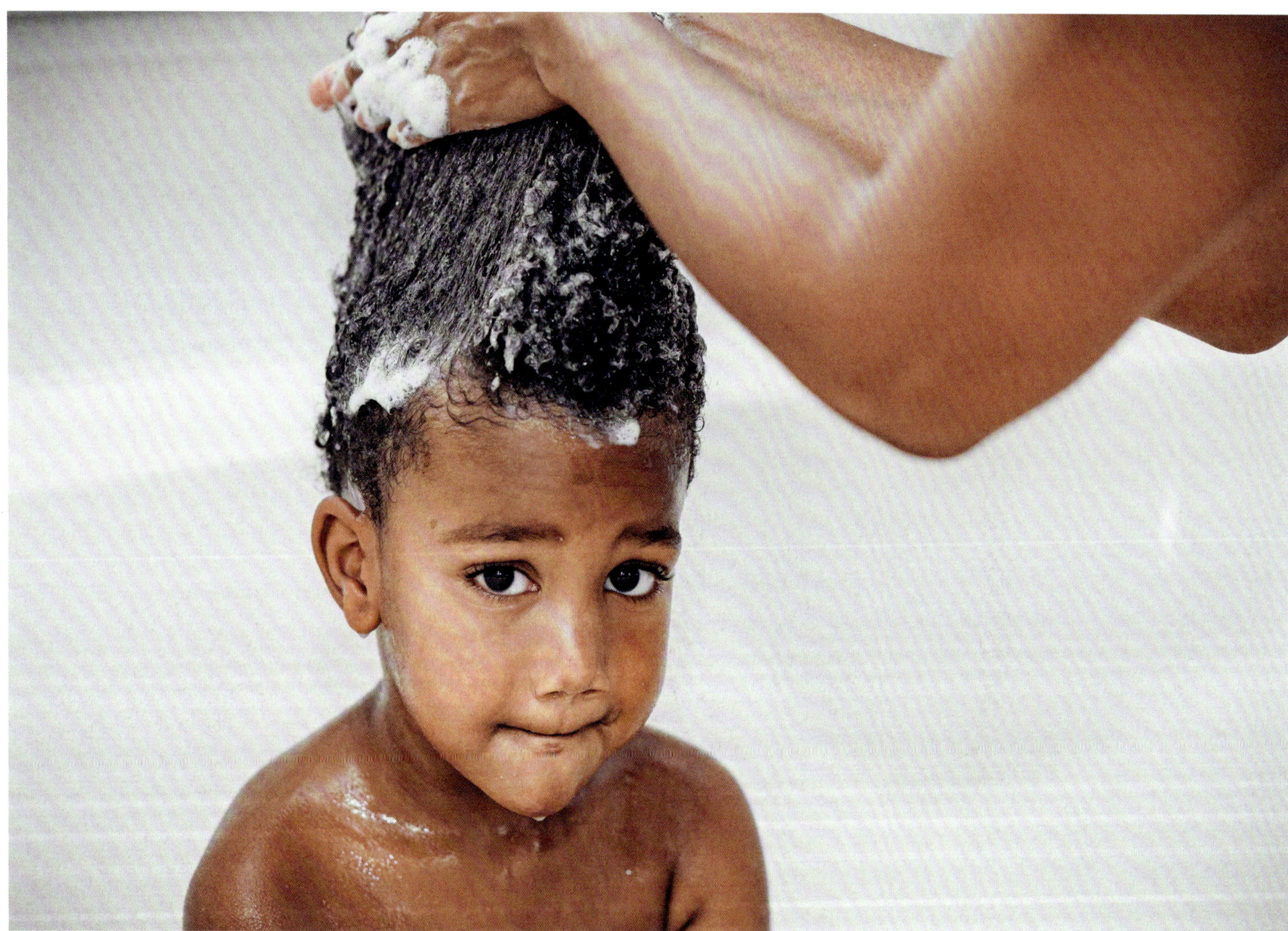

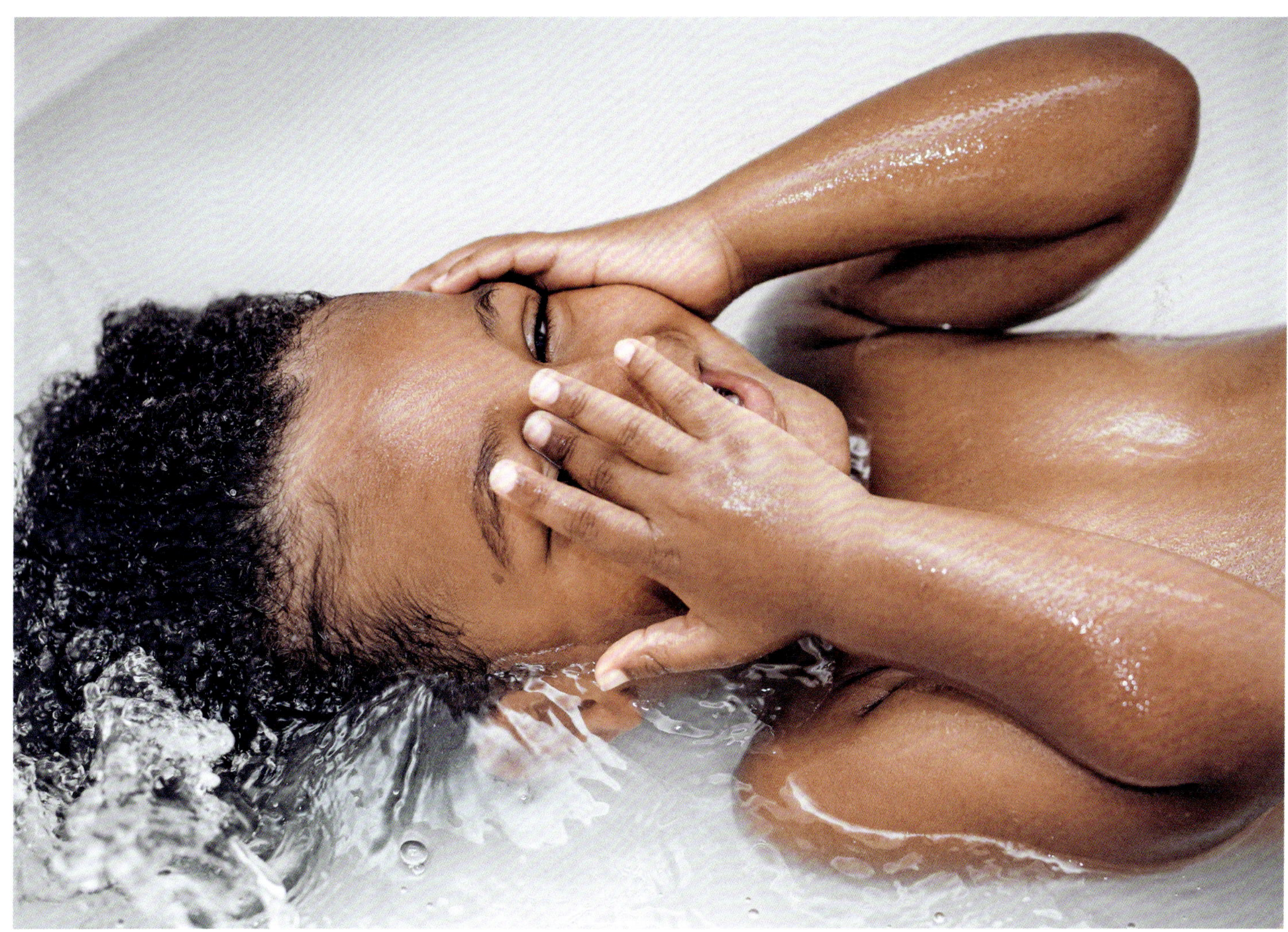

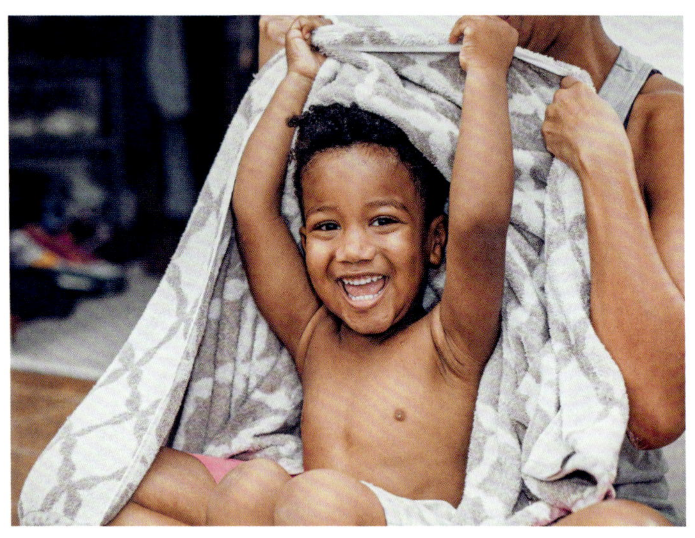

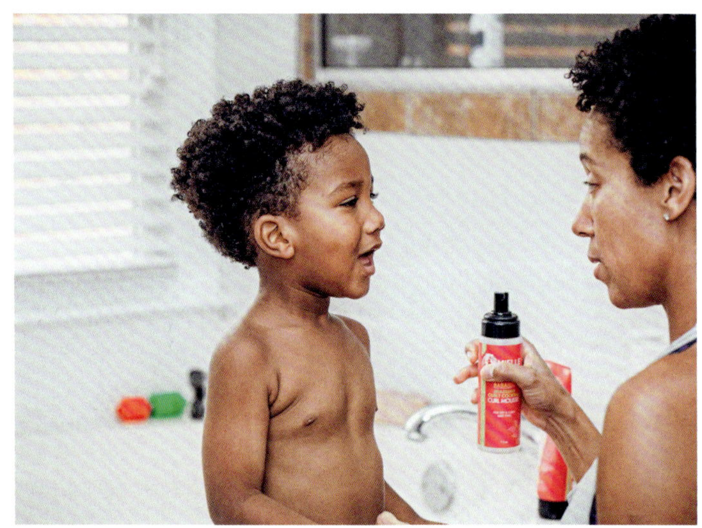

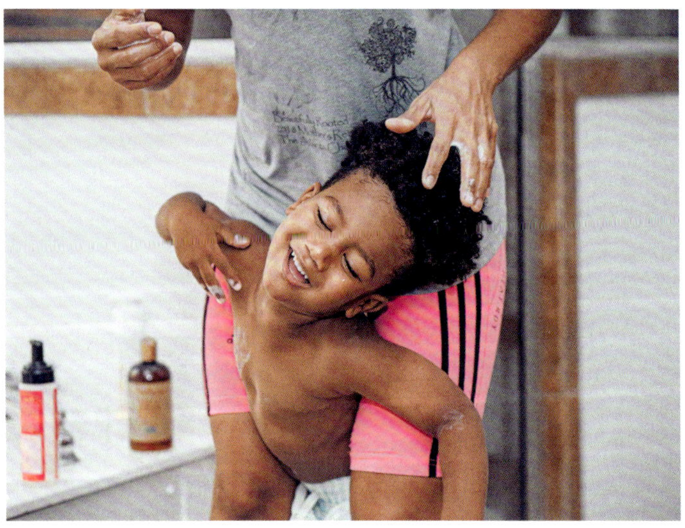

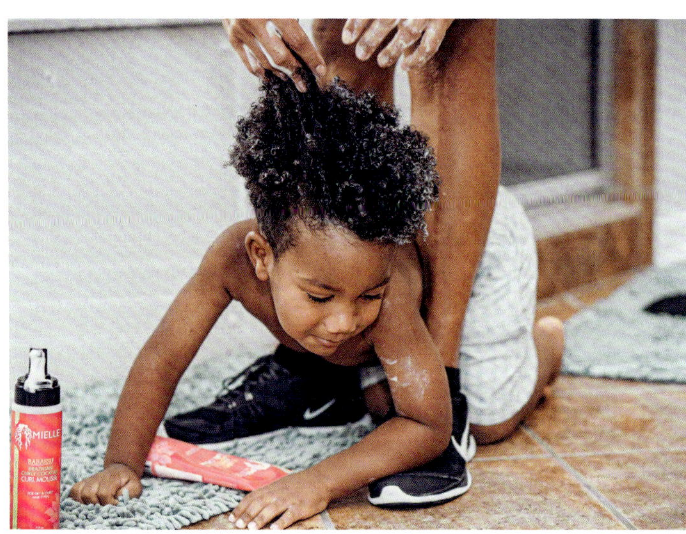

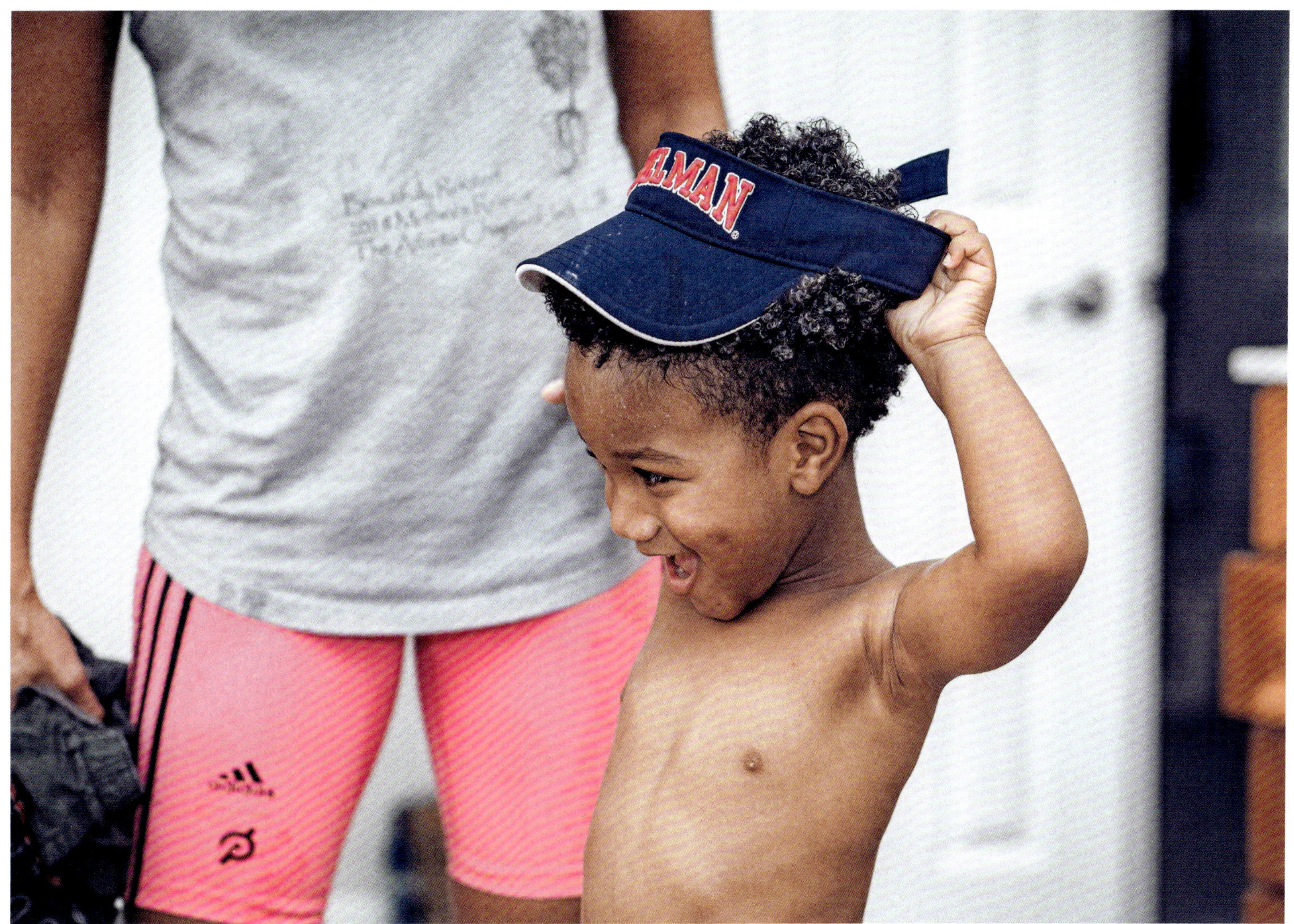

After washing, Emily applies styling foam to Coleman's hair. Well . . . she tries to apply it while Coleman squirms.

Somehow, by the end of it, Coleman has Emily's visor.

Tonya, Briana, Grace & Evan

SOMETIMES, it be your own people.

After her hair fell out from a relaxer, Tonya recalls family members singing "Tonya bonya is a bear. Tonya bonya has no hair." I can only imagine how those words, put to melody, had to sting, especially to a child living in a culture that places so much emphasis on hair length. And especially coming from her own family.

Despite the harm that chemical relaxers caused, and the fact that relaxed hair wasn't something she actually wanted (or even liked), Tonya continued to relax her hair. She felt pressured to conform to commonly held beliefs

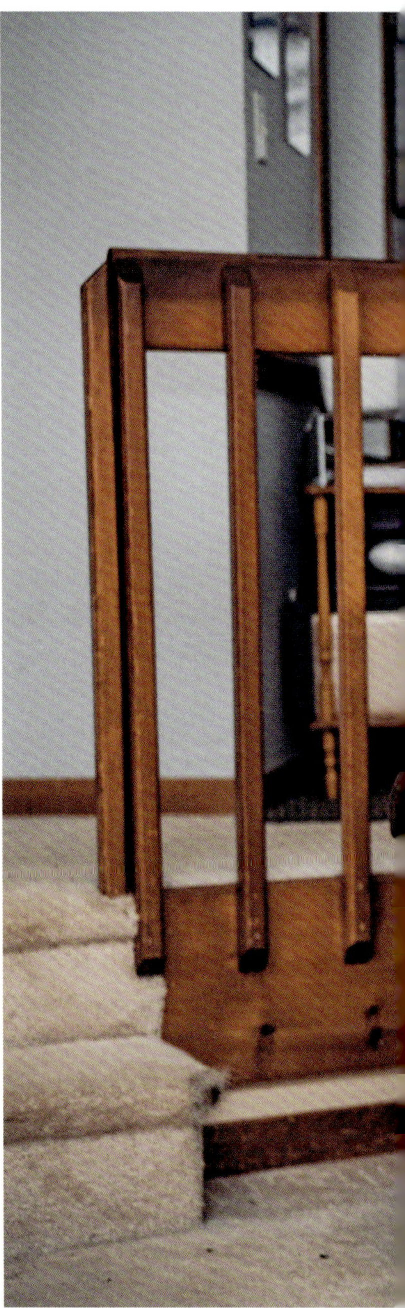

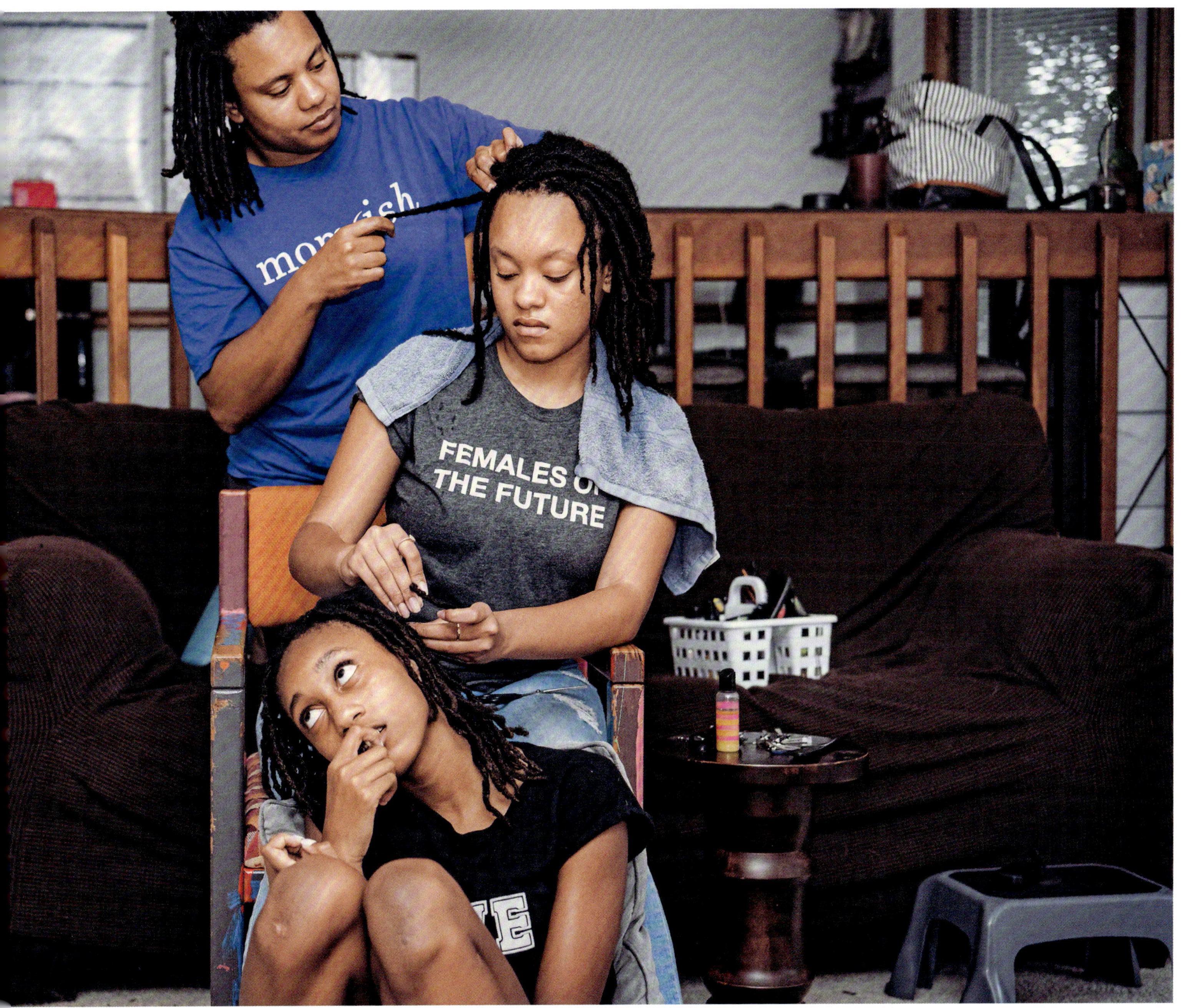
mom-ish.
FEMALES OF
THE FUTURE

within her family, and within the Black community at large, about what Black hair was *supposed* to look like. Relaxed hair didn't reflect who she really was, but she believed, as many of us did at that time, that it was just what we were *supposed* to do.

As a freshman at Spelman College, Tonya was inspired by the unadulterated Blackness that surrounded her. She was encouraged to embrace her whole self, which included her hair. This was 1999, which was prior to the natural hair movement, so this decision had not yet achieved the popularity or acceptance it reached in the late 2000s. Needing support to take the next step toward self-love, Tonya locked arms with her best friend and they made a pact to graduate with natural hair. In the fall of 1999, Tonya walked into a barbershop with hair past her shoulders, and walked out with a very short fade.

Her decision to do the big chop and begin embracing her natural hair texture was met with extreme opposition from her family. "My family was traumatized," she recalls. They constantly reminded her that they were not fans of her decision. This type of response isn't unique to Tonya. I've spoken to quite a few Black women who have recounted story after story of a grandmother, mother, or auntie who responded negatively to their decision to go natural. Assimilation often presents itself as harsh criticism of "nappy" hair.

Rarely is this done out of malice. Most often it comes from a desire to *protect* one another from negative perceptions and stereotypes about Black people. We don't want to give anyone an opportunity to see us as less than. Sadly, aligning with Whiteness, or assimilating, has historically been our best defense against having our humanity questioned.

In *Hair Story*, Ayana D. Byrd and Lori L. Tharps note, "To gain access to the American dream, one of the first things Blacks had to do was make White people more comfortable with their very presence."[34] Black people were forced to adopt White norms about physical appearance in an effort to "become" American and refute racist stereotypes. Assimilation became a necessary survival technique.[35] Its perceived importance to the greater good of all Black people meant that it became *expected* of all Black people.

This expectation evolved into criticism of hairstyles that didn't fit the image many were collectively trying to portray. As Byrd and Tharps state, "Cicely Tyson recalled in *Jet* magazine how the harshest critics of the braids and cornrows that she wore on her CBS series were other Black people, who 'were irate because they felt that I was portraying a negative image of the Black woman.'"[36] More recently, some Black people reacted similarly, stating that Gabby Douglas's hair did not appear, to them, to be presentable enough for public display at the 2012 Olympic Games. Rather than focusing on Gabby's historic win, some took to Twitter to call attention to her kinky edges. *Daily Beast* published a quote from a Black woman who stated, "I wish someone could have helped her make [her hair] look better since she's being seen all over the world. She's representing for Black women everywhere."[37] When photos of a fifteen-month-old Blue Ivy went viral in 2013, comments about her "nappy" and "uncombed" hair were widespread, along with harsh judgment of Beyoncé and Jay-Z for allowing her to be seen in public that way. The fear of being perceived as less than can cause us to reinforce the very non-inclusive beauty standards we have been trying to destroy.

Unfortunately, Black people are often seen as a monolith, and we're still fighting against being collectively judged based on the actions of a few. If one of us is perceived negatively, we fear that it will reflect on all of us. We are constantly negotiating between respectability and freedom. Because of this, we sometimes feel the need to "correct" one another. We want people outside of our community to see us at our best. And unfortunately, "best" has traditionally aligned with White standards of beauty. But once we can separate the many layers of White supremacy from our beliefs about our hair, we will clearly see that "good hair" is simply healthy hair, whatever the curl pattern.

Tonya can attest to this, as she has experienced the longest, healthiest hair of her life since returning to natural.

Tonya has been intentional about teaching different ideas about natural hair to her children. Her oldest, Briana, followed in her footsteps and is currently a student at Spelman College; she rocks beautiful locs, just like her mom and younger sister. Her middle child, Evan, has allowed his hair to grow long and routinely wears it braided. Her youngest, Grace, was actually the first to decide to loc her hair and inspired her mom and sister to follow suit! What a departure from Tonya's own childhood experience!

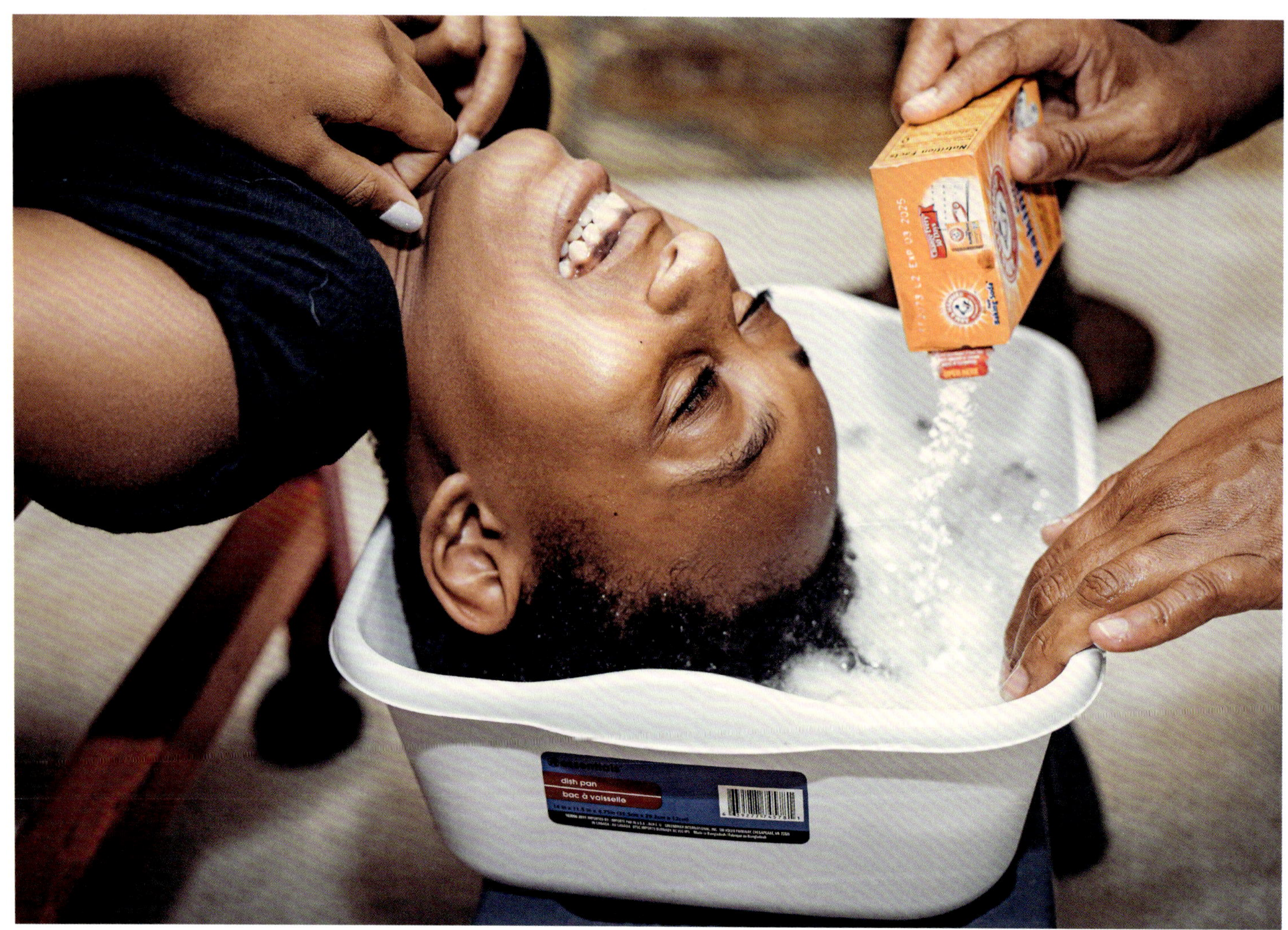

Every three months, Tonya deep cleans and interlocks Grace's and Briana's hair. This process begins with an apple cider vinegar and baking soda soak.

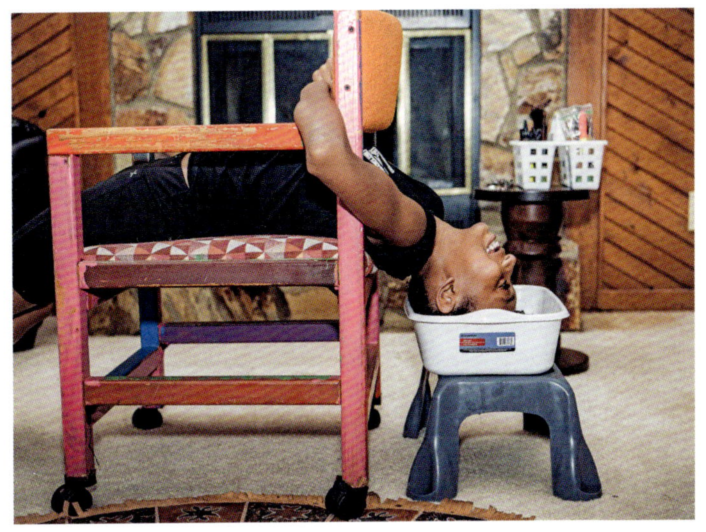
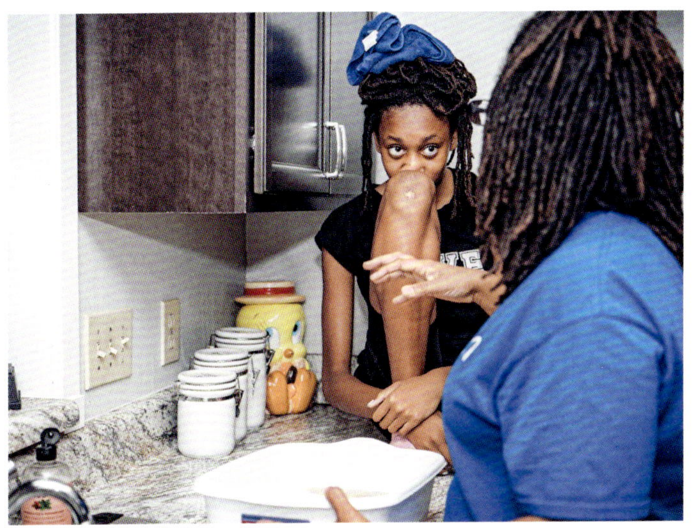
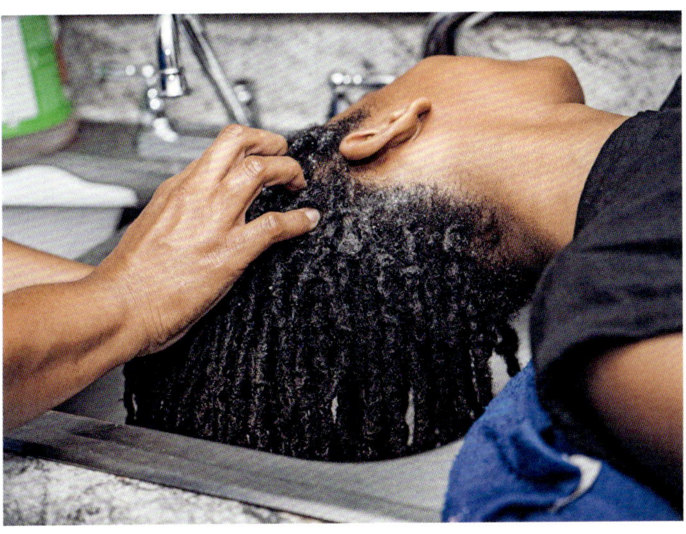
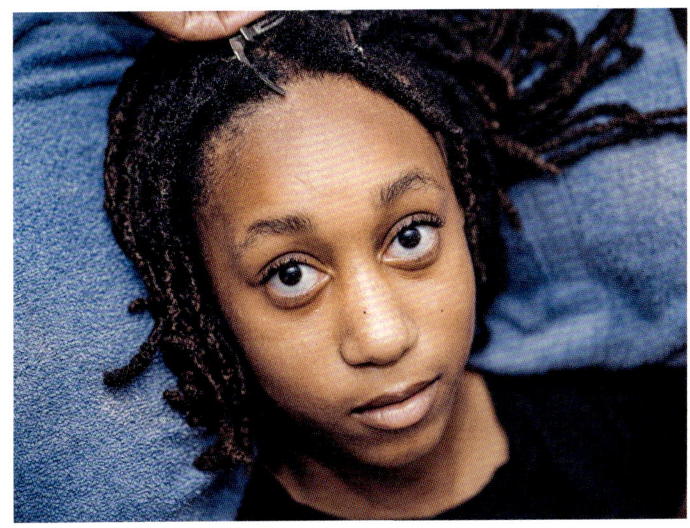

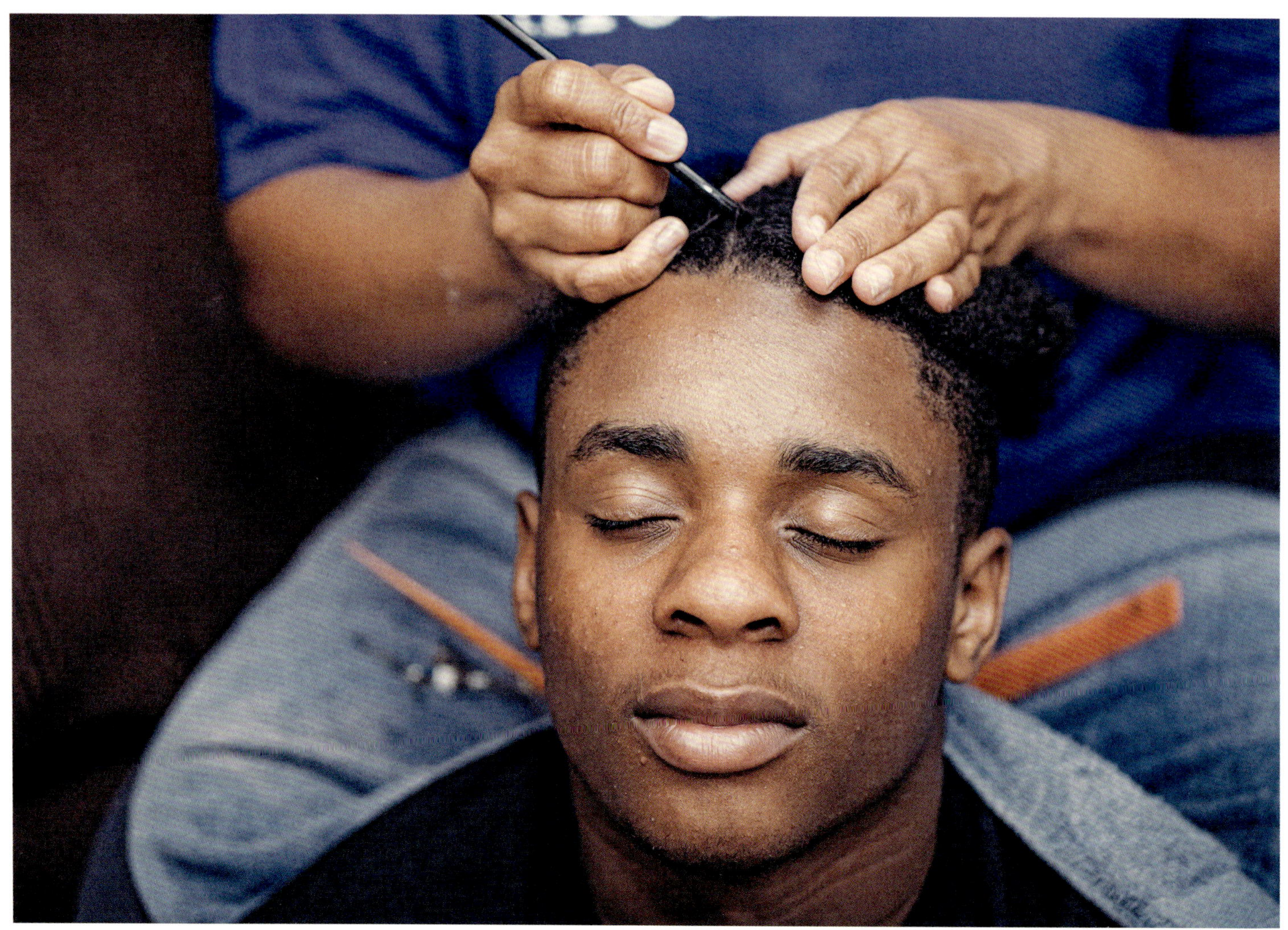

Since Evan wears his hair long, Tonya also washes and braids his hair.

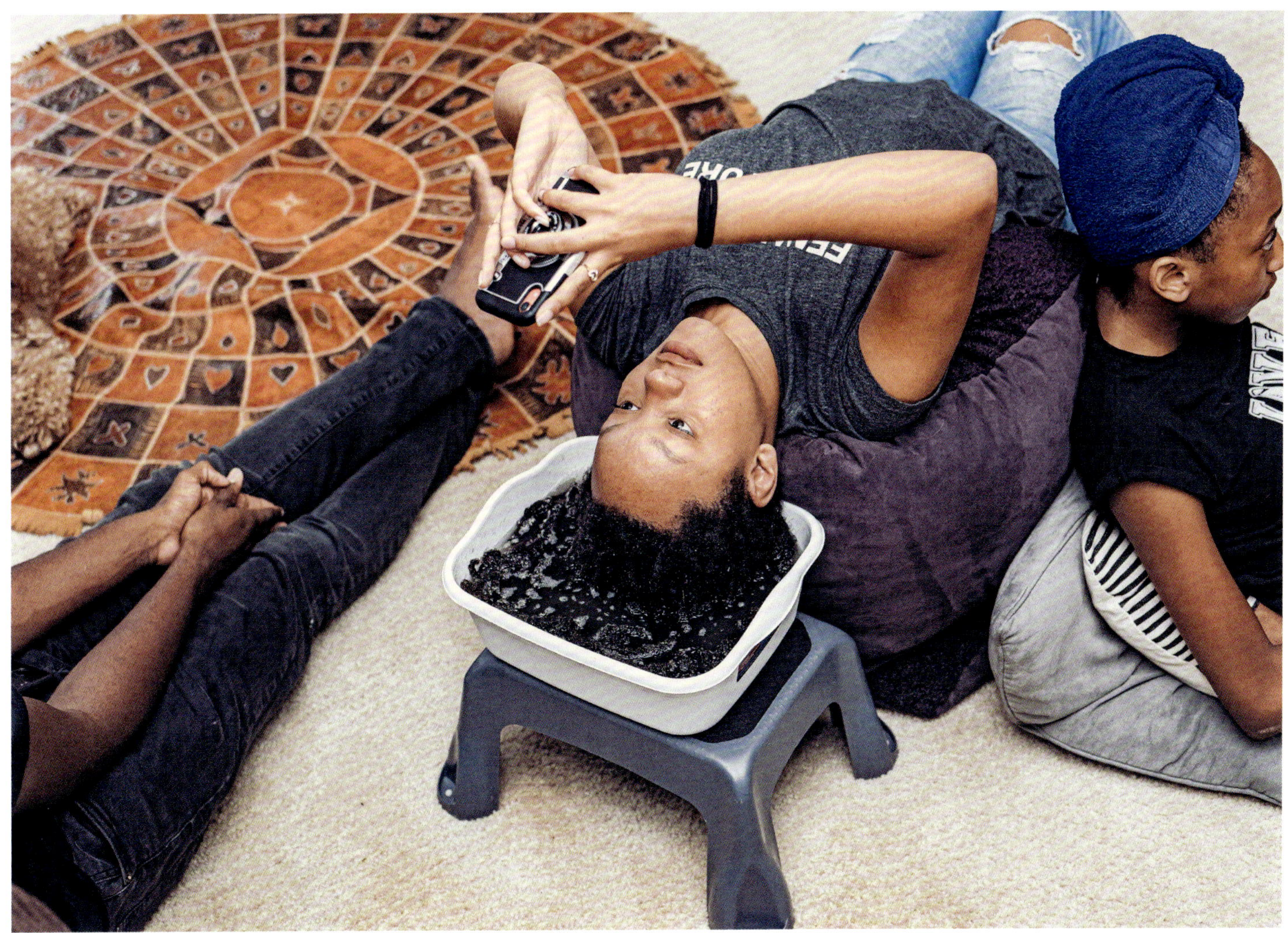

Even though Briana is in college, she still returns home to have Tonya do her hair. Here, she soaks her locs while Tonya braids Evan's hair.

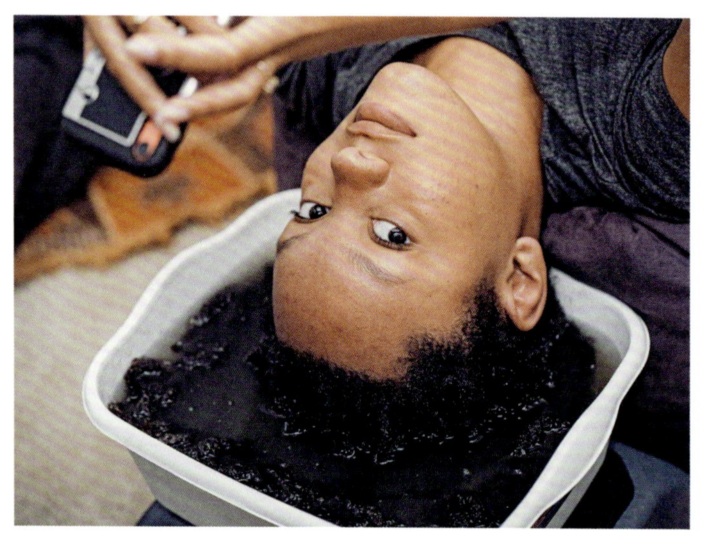
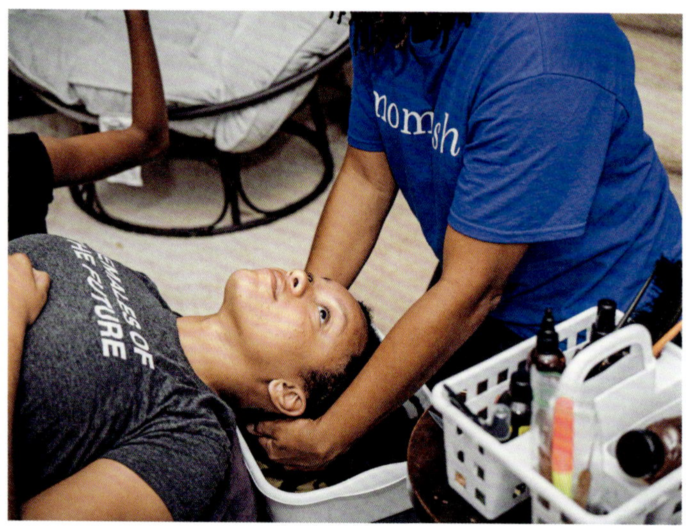
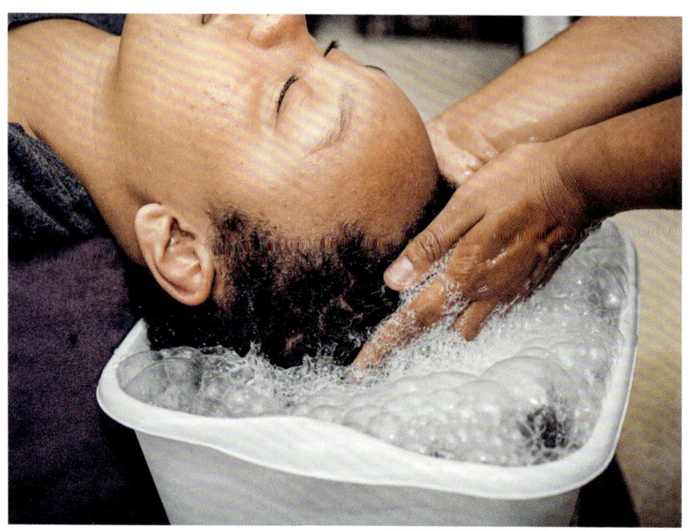
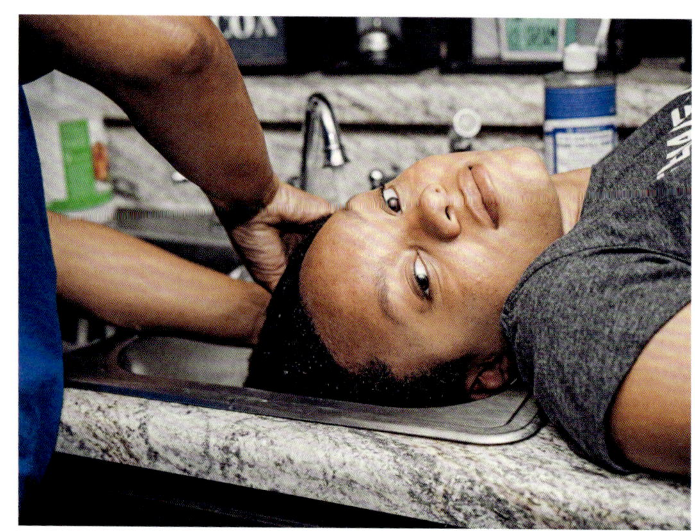

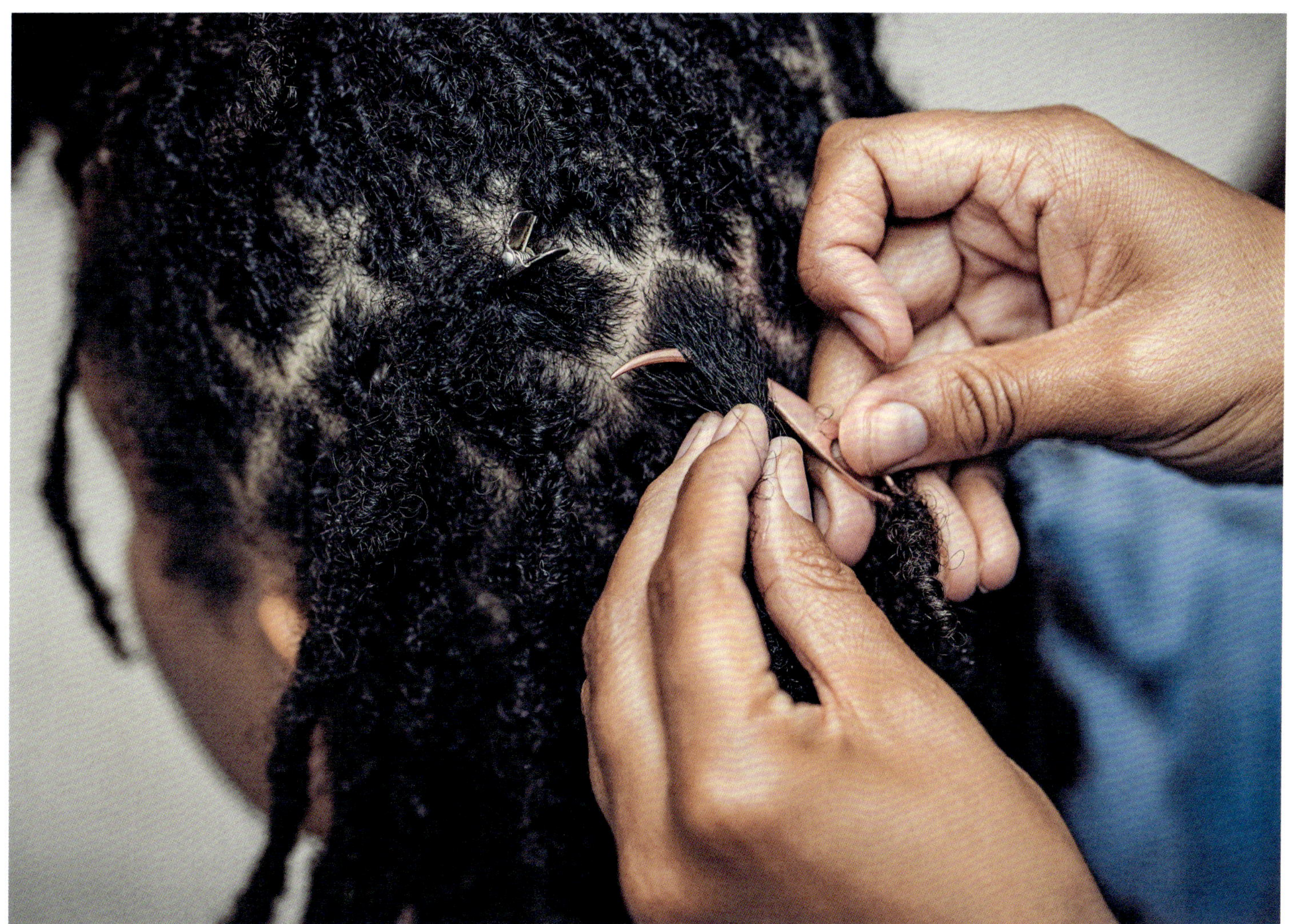

Tonya uses the interlocking method to tighten Briana's locs.

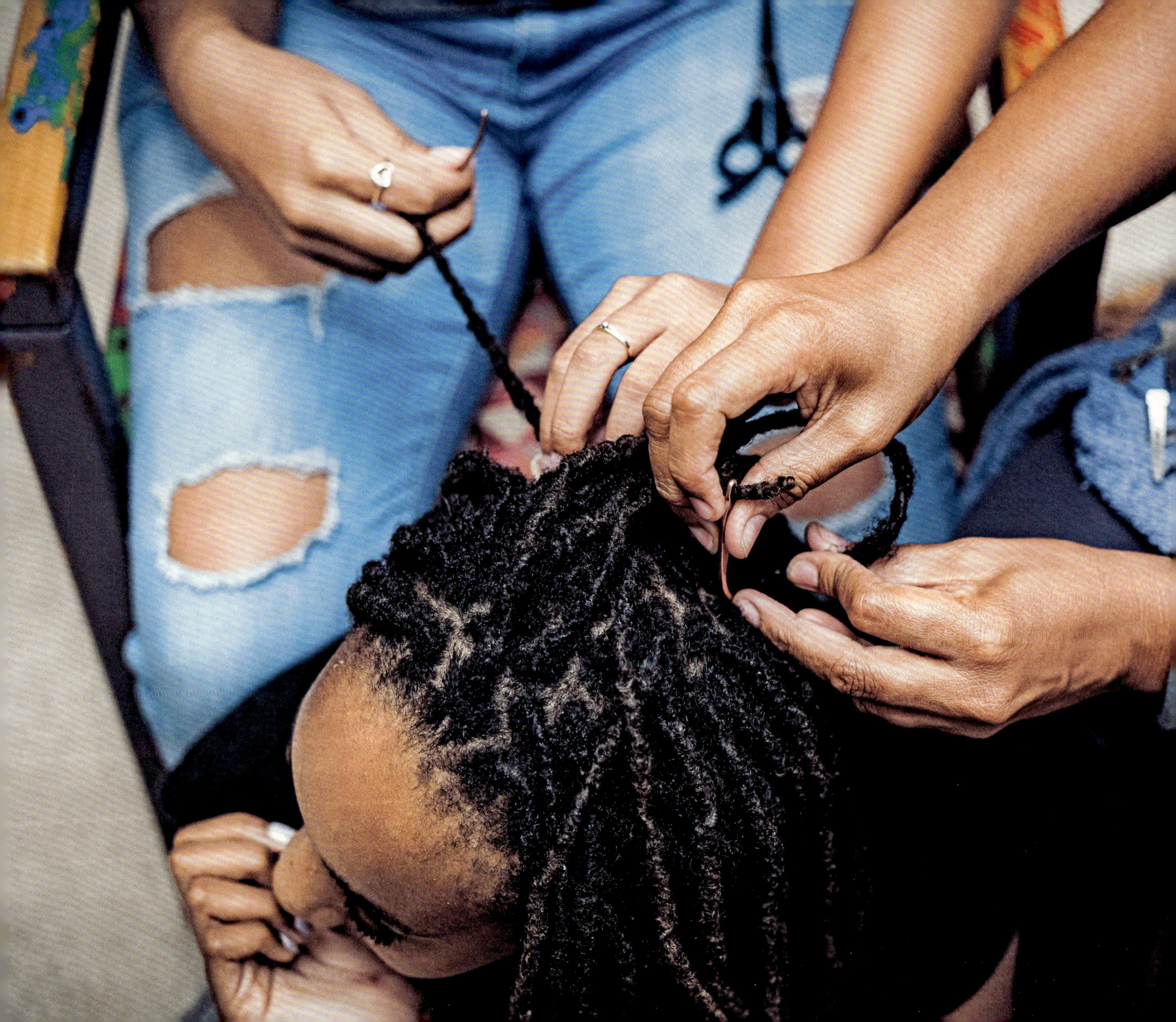

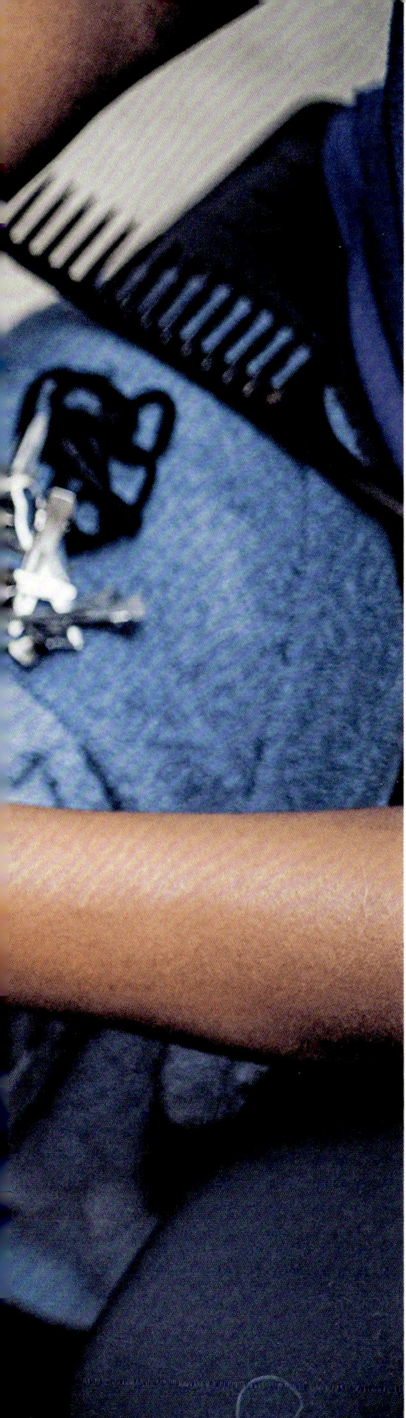

Having learned techniques from her mother, Briana pitches in to help Tonya with Grace's hair. On occasion, Briana also helps tighten Tonya's locs. I'm in love with this illustration of the generational nature of wash day.

"Take care of your hair and it will be 'good' for you." —TONYA

Stacia & Harper

"I did the big chop. I felt so different but free.
I had long hair all my life, so it took some
adjustment, to say the least."

FOR MOST, the big chop and resulting T.W.A. are a through phase, not the final destination on their natural hair journeys. But for some, the style just sticks. I know from experience. I big chopped in 2008, grew my hair out, then chopped it off again in 2012. I'm pretty sure Tyra would have told the stylists to cut off my hair if I was a contestant on *America's Next Top Model.* From 2012 to 2019, I went from short to shorter to shortest, and I loved it. I hit my shortest length right after *Black Panther* came out, and it was a hit (both the movie and my hair).

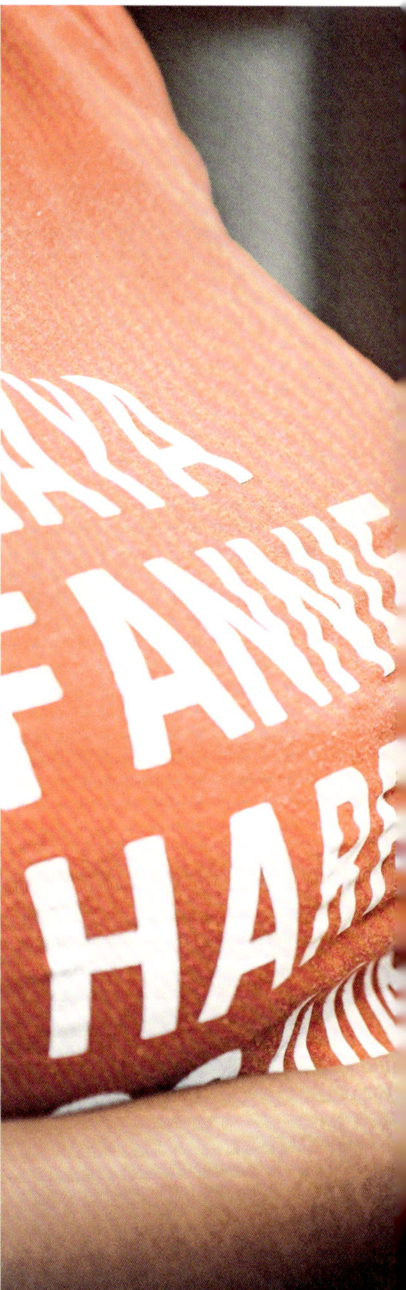

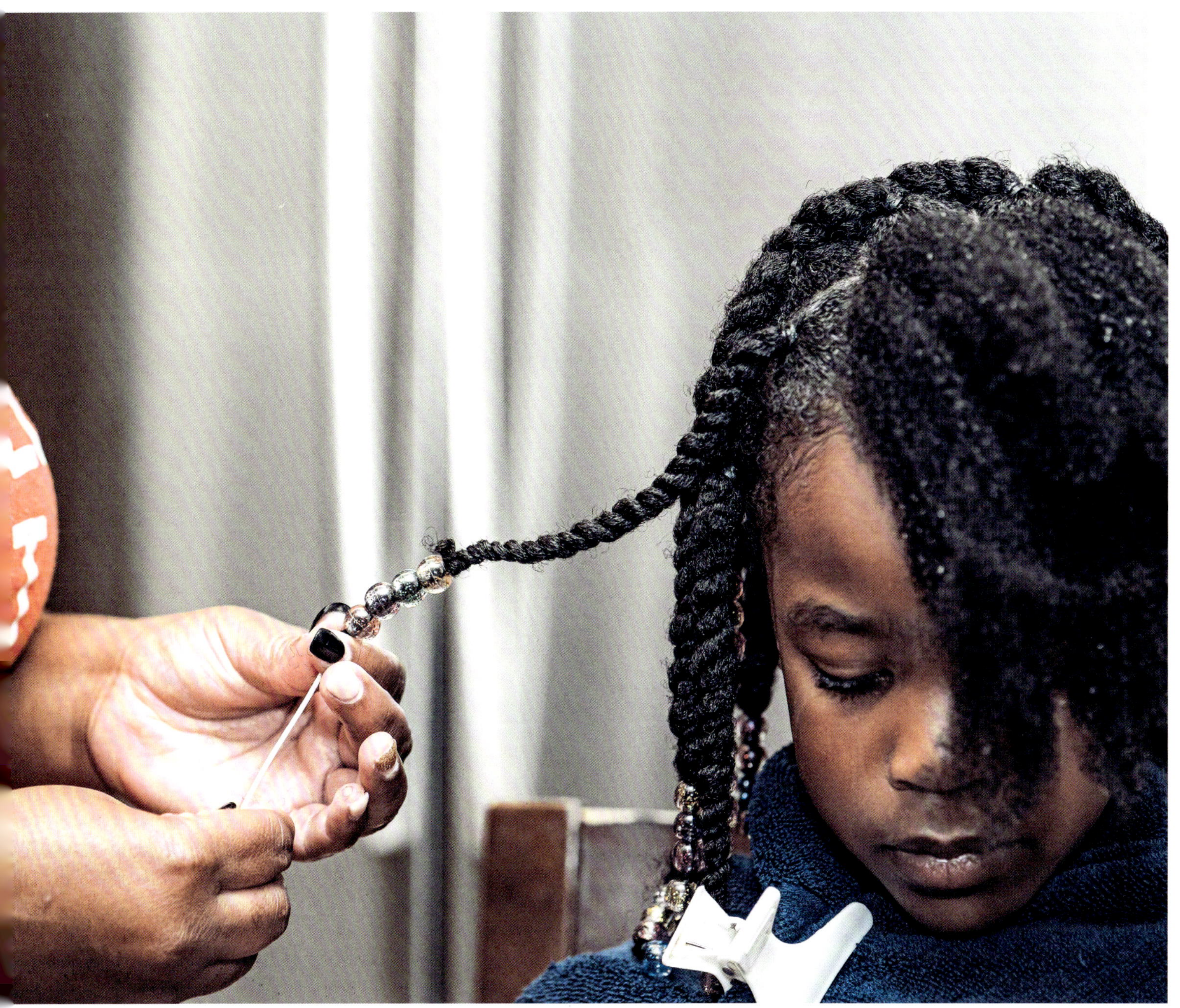

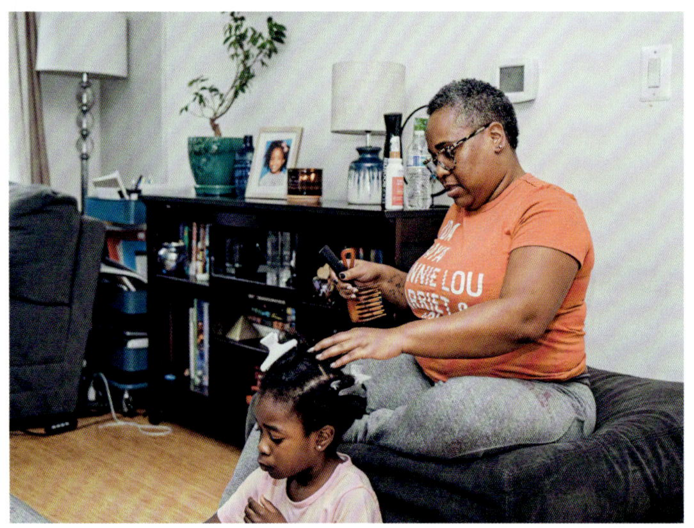

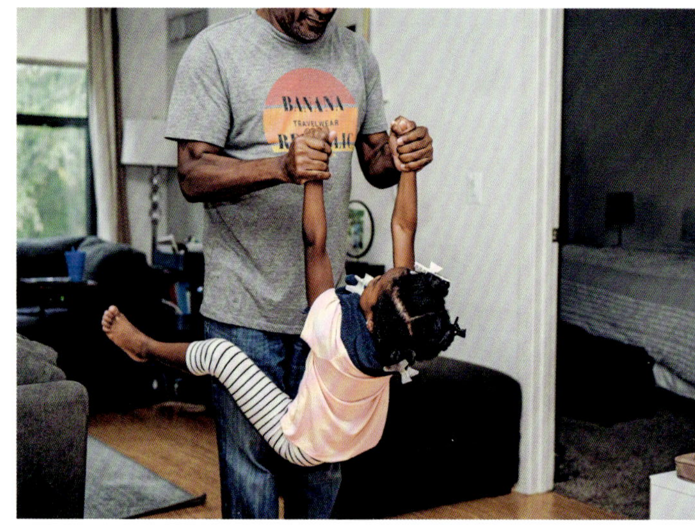

In 2020, I decided to let my hair grow, and I've enjoyed the diversity of styles that length can bring. But, I honestly miss the short look. The ease. The simplicity. Not to mention, I looked dope. Seriously, I have *never* received more compliments than when I was basically rocking a buzz cut.

Stacia knows what I'm talking about. She has cut off all of her hair four times. The first big chop followed her realization in 2008 that relaxers and color treatments do not get along well. After suffering substantial breakage, a choice was made. She valued the color more than the relaxer, so the relaxer had to go. Stacia had enjoyed long hair all of her life, so the change was certainly an adjustment. For some people in her life, it prompted concern. They wondered why in the world she would cut off her long hair. She received both positive and negative feedback, but at the end of the day, Stacia recalls feeling free. That sense of freedom trumped the negative commentary. She's still rocking her short natural hair, and loving it.

Page 140, top left: Wash day takes place every two weeks and lasts about four hours. On wash day, Stacia aims to avoid traumatic hair experiences for Harper, who snacks and watches her favorite show while getting her hair done.

Page 140, bottom left and bottom right: Stacia's husband, Barry, often steps in to comfort Harper if, despite Stacia's efforts, the tears come. *Page 141:* After washing, Stacia deep conditions with a processing cap, then detangles, and styles Harper's hair with twists and beads.

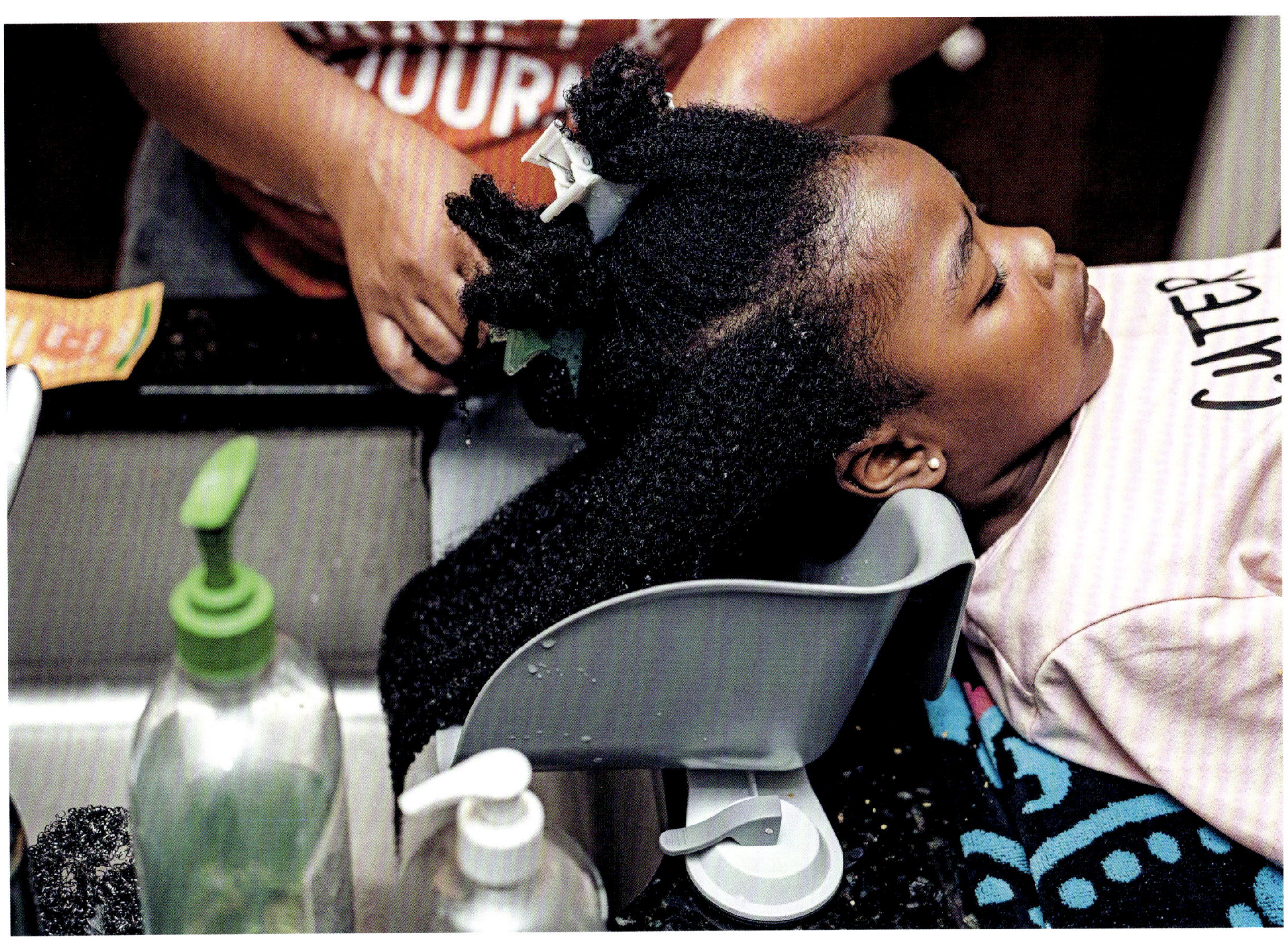
CUTER

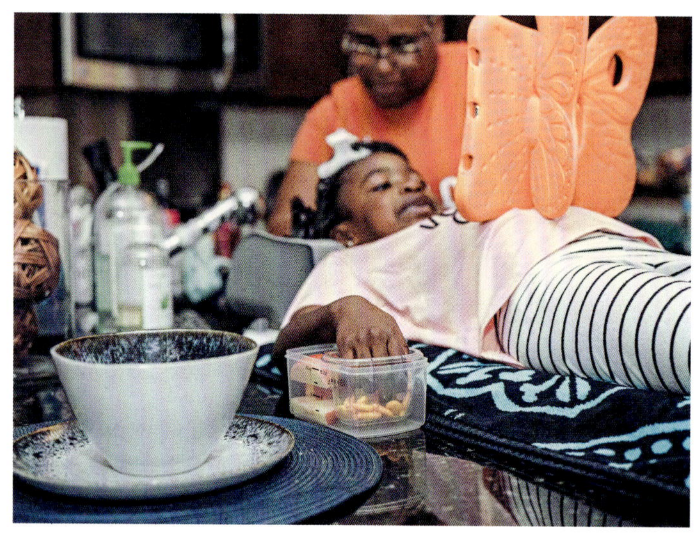
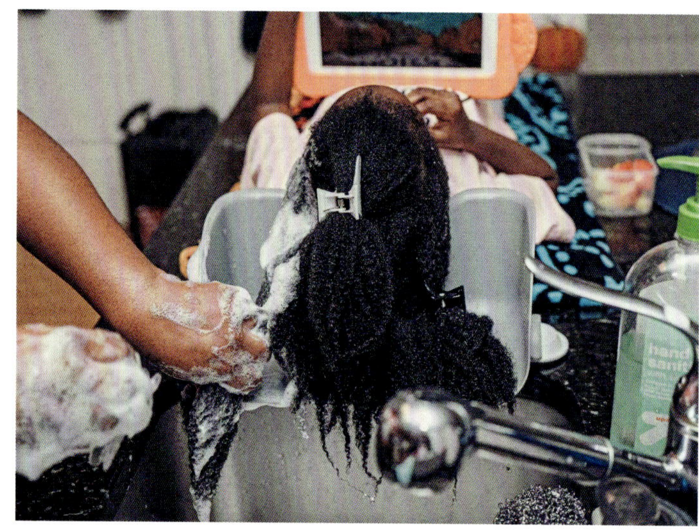
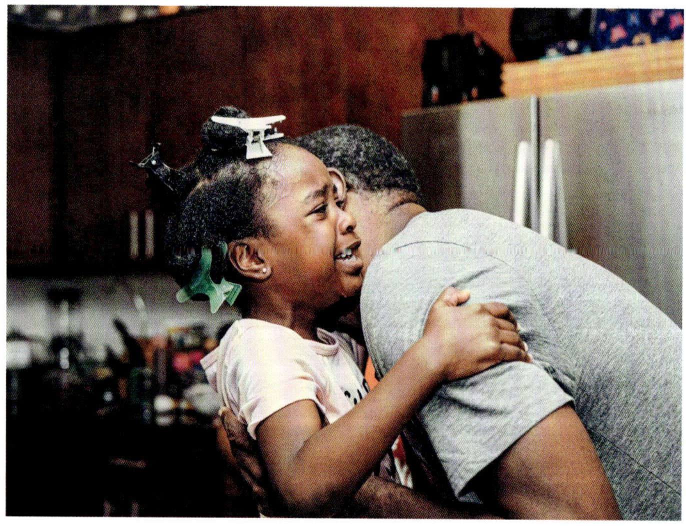
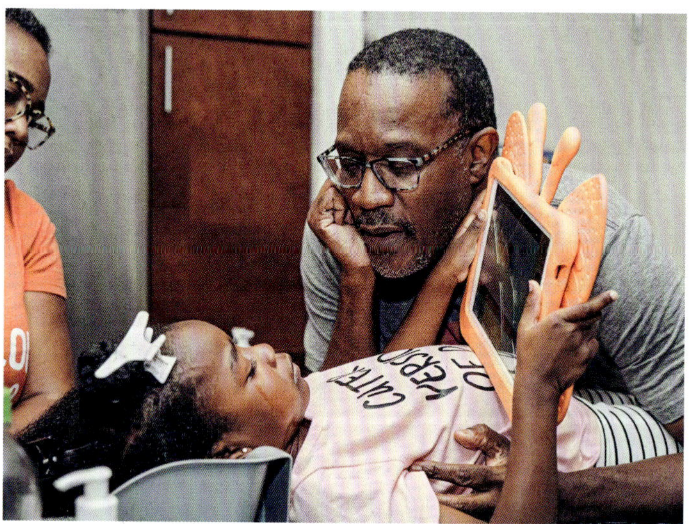

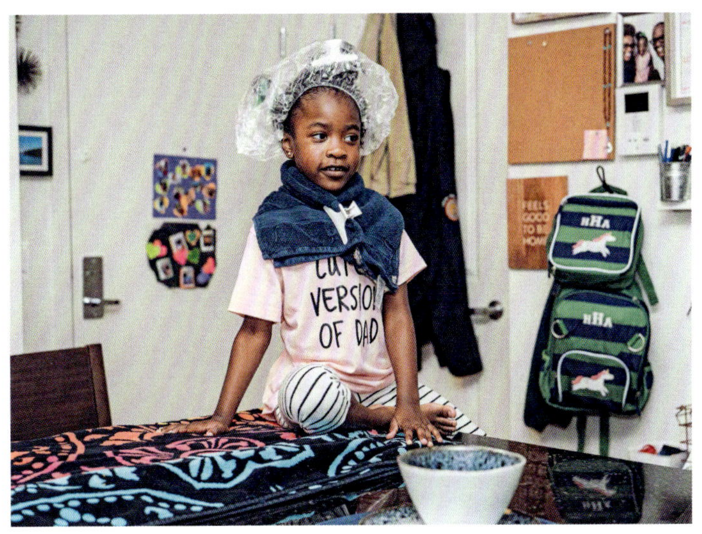

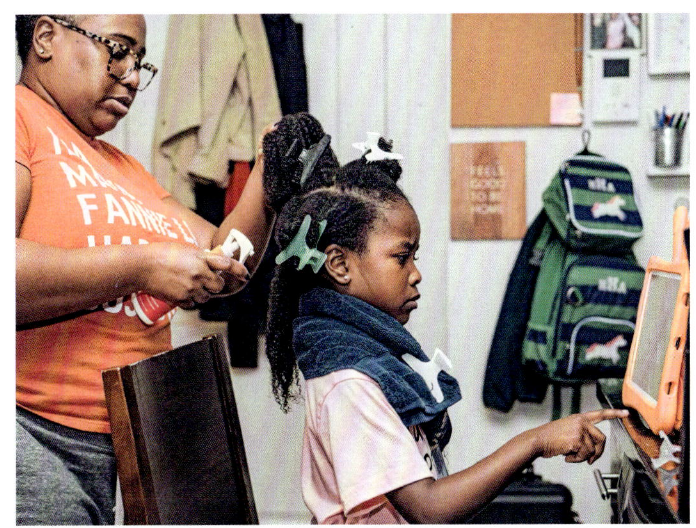

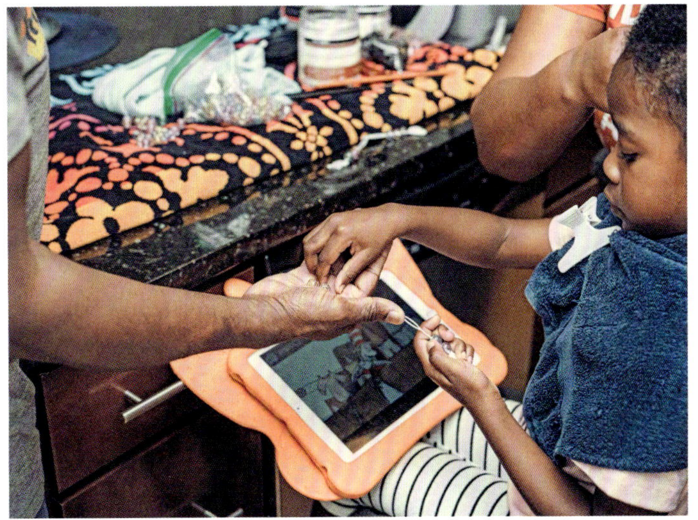

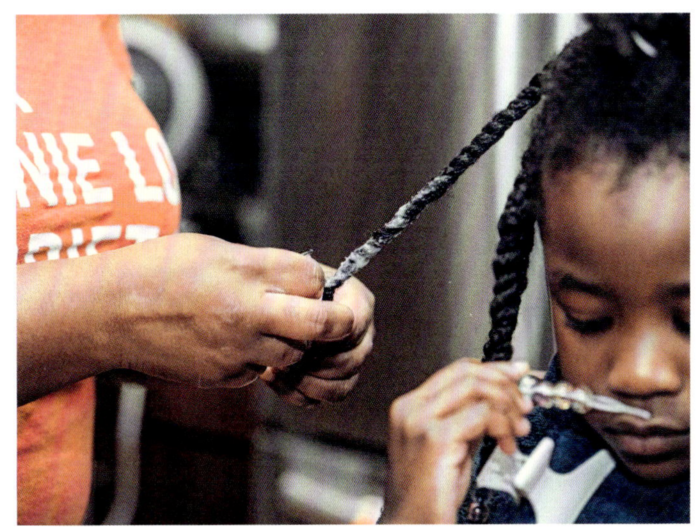

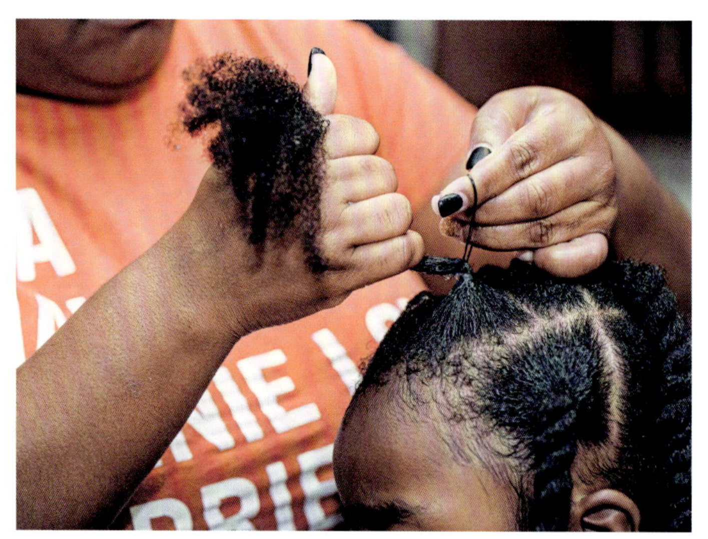 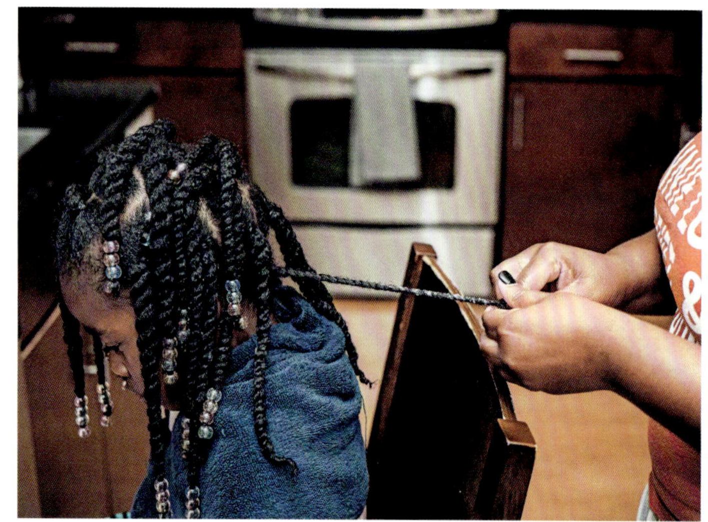

"[I want to teach my daughter] that her hair is beautiful and that it is her crown and glory. That her worth is not defined by it. That true beauty comes from within ourselves." —STACIA

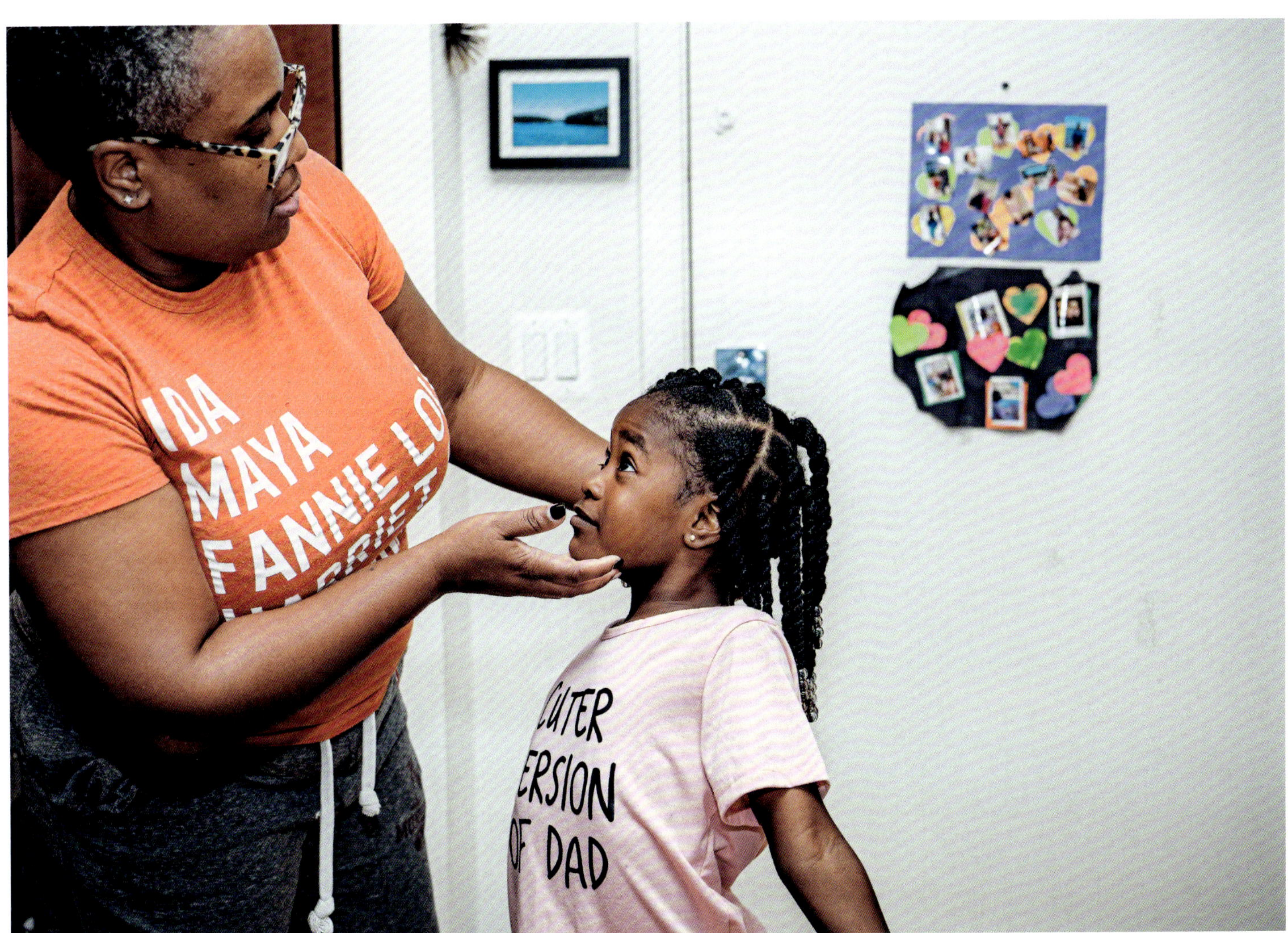
IDA
MAYA
FANNIE LOU
HARRIET
CUTER
ERSION
OF DAD

Tanika & Azaria

"I know I'm beautiful! I look in the mirror
and I like what I see. But I know that I don't
fit today's standard definition of beauty. "

TANIKA'S JOURNEY sheds light on the work we still need to do within our own community as it pertains to full acceptance of all skin tones and hair textures. Black is indeed beautiful and natural hair is currently being celebrated like never before, but deep, deep, *deep* down, many of us are still bound by centuries of anti-Black history, trauma, and socialization.

Let me start by saying this: Tanika has done the work to overwrite much of the anti-Black programming she received while growing up. Her experiences with anti-Black criticisms of her appearance have caused her to dig deeper into why

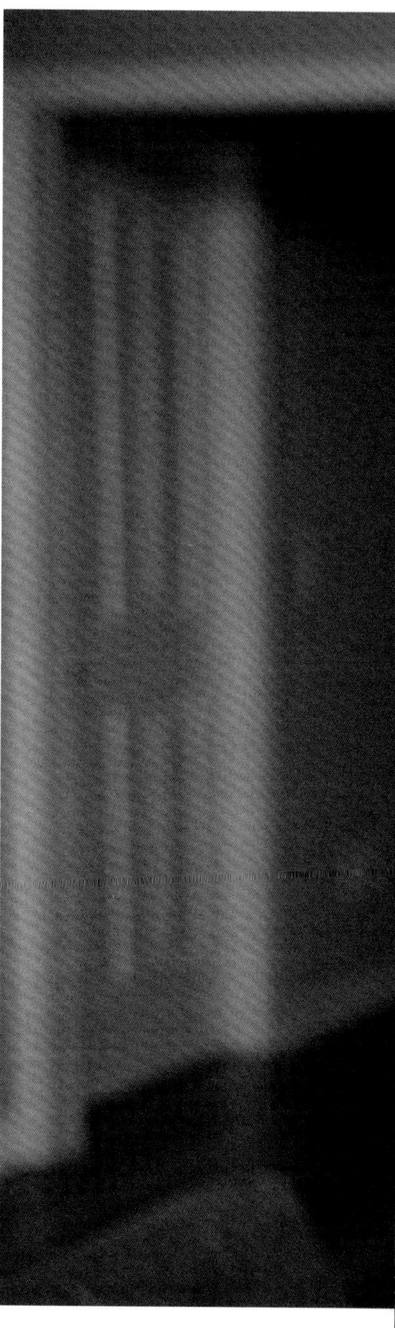

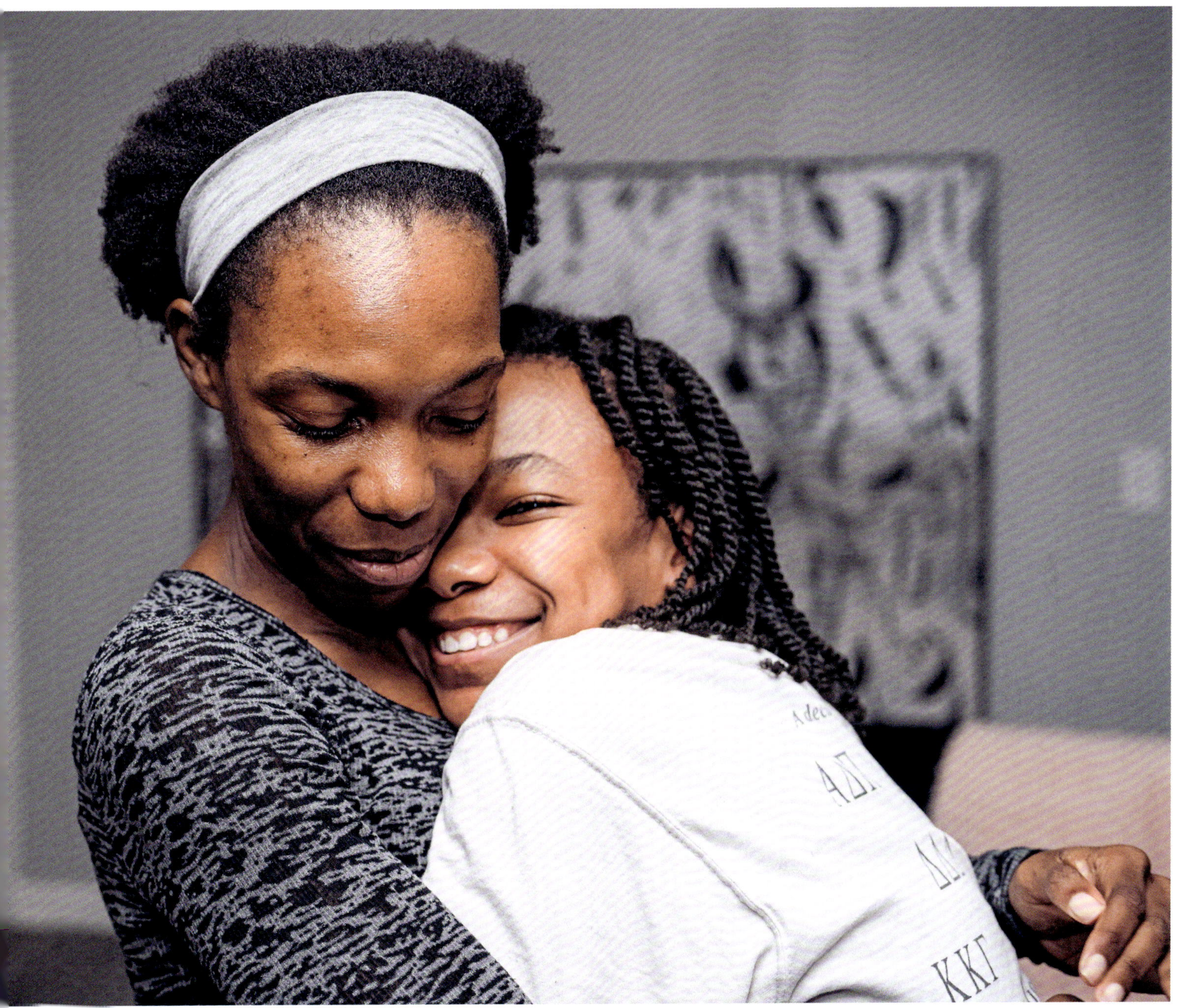

these mindsets exist. She understands that the prevailing Eurocentric beauty standard intentionally excludes her. She knows why some are uncomfortable with her kinky hair, dark skin, wide nose, and prominent cheekbones.

The root of this discomfort can be traced back to the days when African ancestry became a source of shame for Black people. Because Europeans had to justify the race-based institution of slavery, they created the narrative that Africans were savages, among other terrible things. Numerous theories were spouted to "prove" the inherent inferiority of Africans. Thus, dark skin, wide noses, full lips, and kinky hair became associated with being uneducated and unciv-ilized. Oh, and don't forget ugly. In his speech, "Not Just an American Problem, but a World Problem," Malcolm X stated:

> We hated the African characteristics. . . . We hated our hair. We hated our nose, the shape of our nose, and the shape of our lips, the color of our skin. . . . This is how you imprisoned us. Not just bringing us over here and making us slaves. But the image that you created of our motherland and the image that you created of our people on that continent was a trap, was a prison, was a chain . . . [38]

To avoid being buried by the avalanche of criticism she has received over the years, Tanika pushed herself to explore the inherent beauty of Black people and how our appearance links us to a beautiful, but stolen, heritage. Tanika knows from experience, however, that not everyone has done this work.

Prior to going natural, Tanika had on many occasions been told she was "pretty, for a dark-skinned girl." We are well aware of the lies that colorism tells. It says that dark skin just isn't beautiful. As a result, Tanika grew accustomed to these backhanded compliments.

In 2004, Tanika, a college student at the time, realized that years of getting relaxers had taken a toll on her once thick, long hair. By this time, her hair had become limp and thin. She hated it. Furthermore, she had never really learned how to care for it herself. She was tired of having to rely on friends to do her hair when she could not afford to go to a professional stylist. So tired, in fact, that she marched into a random salon, sat down in a random stylist's chair and asked her to cut off all of her hair.

Many people in Tanika's circle voiced their displeasure with her new look. Again, this was 2004, so natural hair was still pretty rare to see. Tanika shared, "See, my natural hair isn't soft and wavy. It's dry and kinky. Very dry and very kinky. In 2004 and 2005, Black natural hair was not popular. Only the girls with the 'good hair' wore their hair natural. Many people did not understand or like my choice." On one occasion, she overheard a group of family members talking about her haircut. One of them stated, "She used to be so pretty." No one disagreed. It's as if she went from being "pretty for a dark-skinned girl" to not being pretty at all.

While the definition of "beautiful" has certainly broadened since her family declared her "unpretty," Tanika continues to find herself on the outskirts. Some of the harshest critiques of her appearance have come at moments when Tanika did not have her hair "done" as is commonly defined. You see, Tanika has never really learned how to style her natural hair, so she usually just lets it be. This should not be considered problematic, but we are conditioned to expect Black women, especially those with the kinkiest textures, to manipulate their hair in some way. Tanika has found that "done" means braids, weaves, wigs, twist-outs, controlled edges, blown-out and/or curled hair. It's not enough for her hair to be clean, moisturized, and detangled. "The times I'm asked, 'What are you going to do with your hair?' are the times when my hair is in its unmanipulated, natural state. No gel, no edge control, no twist-out, no sponge, no braids, no weave, no wig." Apparently, just letting her hair be is not sufficient.

A comment she gets quite often when her hair is not done is that she looks like Celie from *The Color Purple*.[39] While Whoopi Goldberg is beautiful, it's pretty well known within the Black community that being told you look like the character Celie is definitely not a compliment. I've always understood this to be a common way to tell a Black woman that her hair looks shabby, *especially* when the texture is on the tighter side. I suppose the reason Celie has become synonymous with unkempt hair is due to how she is portrayed in the film; her hair is typically in plaits or "undone" as we tend to define it.

As if that weren't enough, Tanika has also been told that her undone hair makes her look like a "field slave." Let that sink in for a moment. This comment says so much more about the mindset of the person making it than the actual condition of Tanika's hair. Given the historical context underlying the house slave / field slave hierarchy that led to the "good hair / bad hair" lie, this comment demonstrates the resilience of the racist value judgments that still govern some of our perceptions of natural hair.

Quite frankly, Tanika is over it. She feels pressured to expend tons of energy and use tons of product to achieve the looks that are deemed "done" and "presentable" by others. Furthermore, she has found it difficult to find products and how-tos that apply to her texture. She shared:

Even today, I'm in some 4C hair groups on social media and guess who's in there declaring they have 4C hair . . . the wavy naturals. I don't say that to be exclusive. It's just that it's a challenge for people like me to truly find methods that work and empowering messages that celebrate that tough, kinky, non-curly, zig-zaggy texture.

Miraculously, Tanika's experiences with negative reactions to her natural hair have not polluted her own views of what is beautiful. But knowing the culture she is raising her daughter in, Tanika is very intentional about ensuring her daughter sees her own beauty as well. Tanika recalls:

When she was under five, maybe about three or so, she wanted long, yellow "pinktails." She'd cry when I'd give her puffs. And she'd still cry when I would twist them. I took those moments to pour into her and talk to her about the beauty and uniqueness of her hair. I told her that her hair would never technically be long because it didn't grow down to the earth, but instead, it grew up to the heavens in reverence to God, therefore, she could have "big" hair but not long hair. We read books celebrating big, cotton candy hair. And she was fortunate to see other Brown girls with all different hair types and *she learned to appreciate the diversity of textured hair.* Now she loves her hair. I'm sure she wishes I knew how to do fancy styles, and I know she wishes I'd let her wear it out more. *She loves her fro.*

Although Tanika will tell you she is not good at doing hair, she sure did teach me some new tricks. Prior to washing, Tanika applies shampoo and water and massages Azaria's scalp. I've since combined this pre-wash technique with detangling, using shampoo as the detangler. Game changer. Tanika also uses a triple twist method (twisting each strand while creating two-strand twists) that I've also adopted.

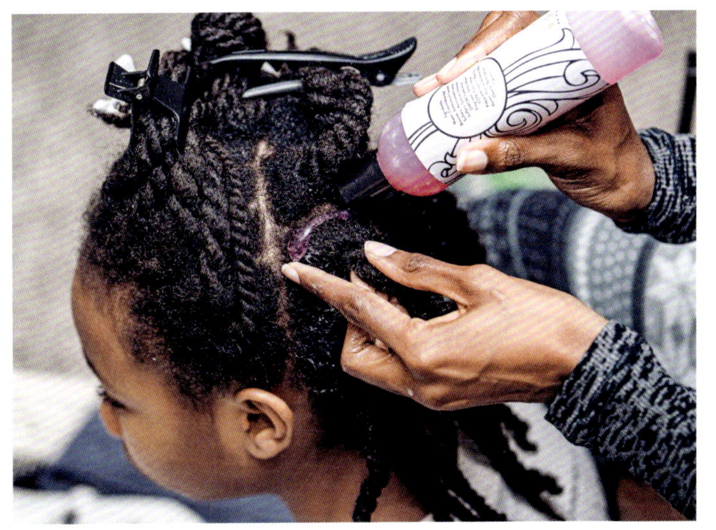
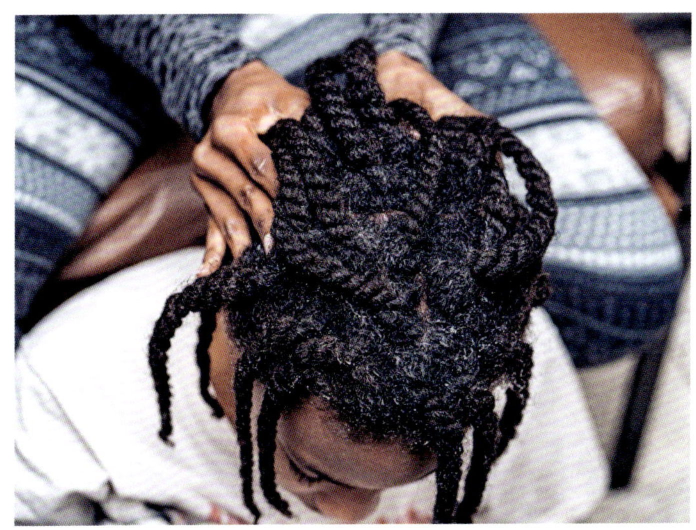
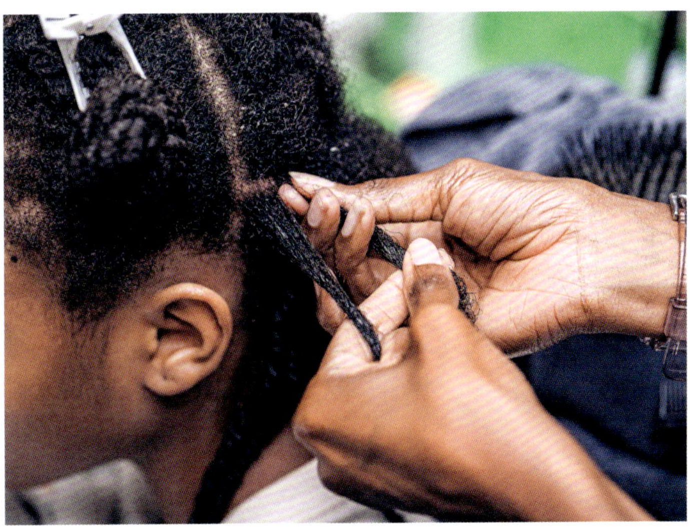
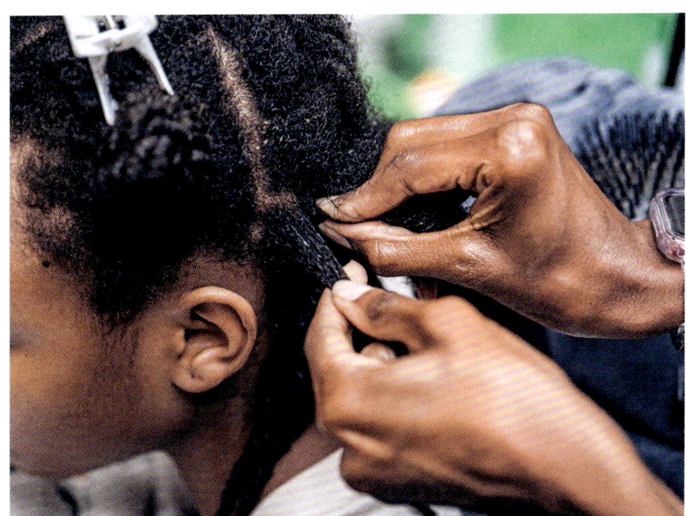

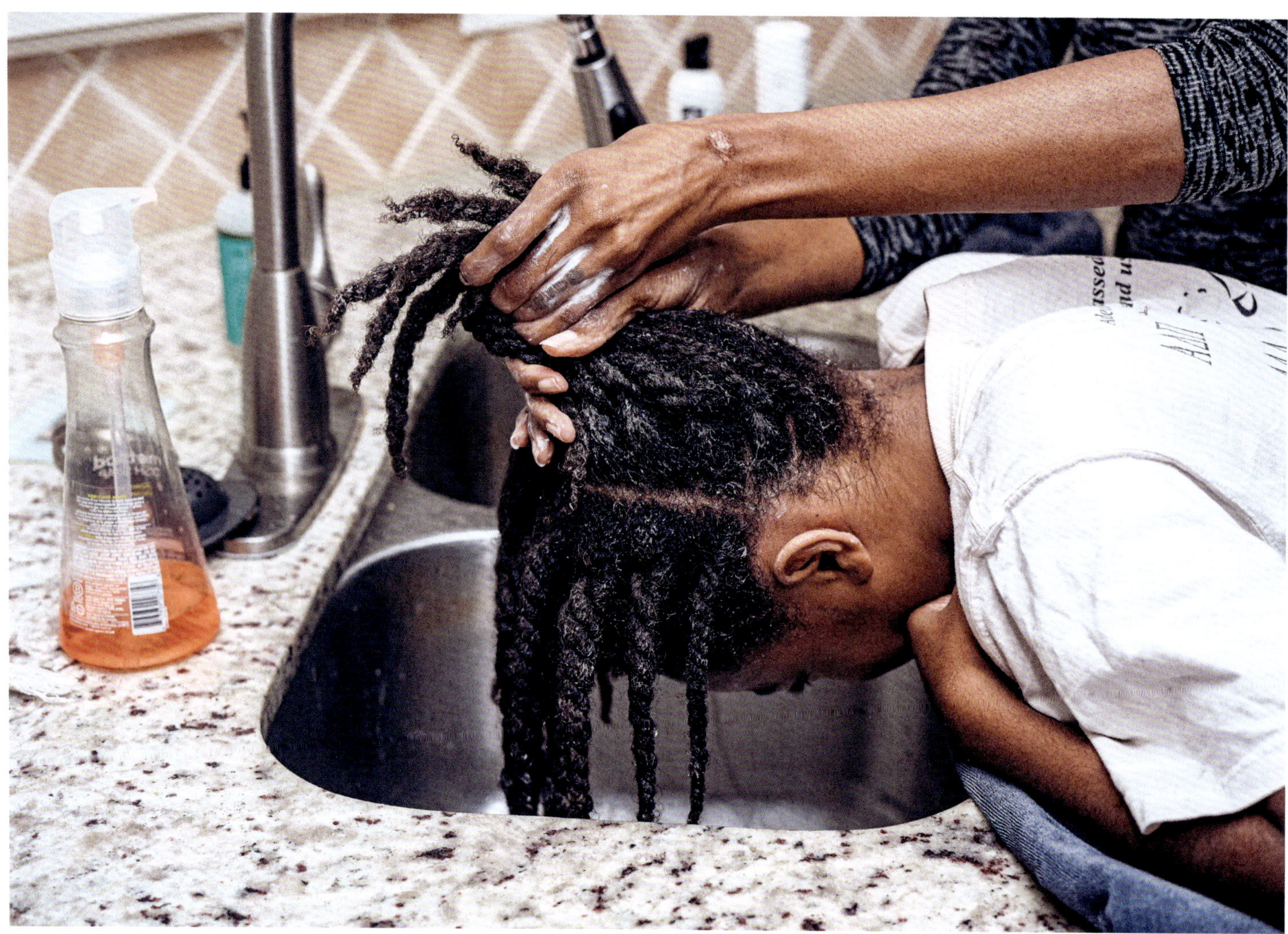

After the pre-wash, Tanika does a full wash in the kitchen sink. She keeps Azaria's hair in twists to reduce tangling.

Although Tanika's wash-day process usually lasts twelve hours, she condensed the process during my visit.

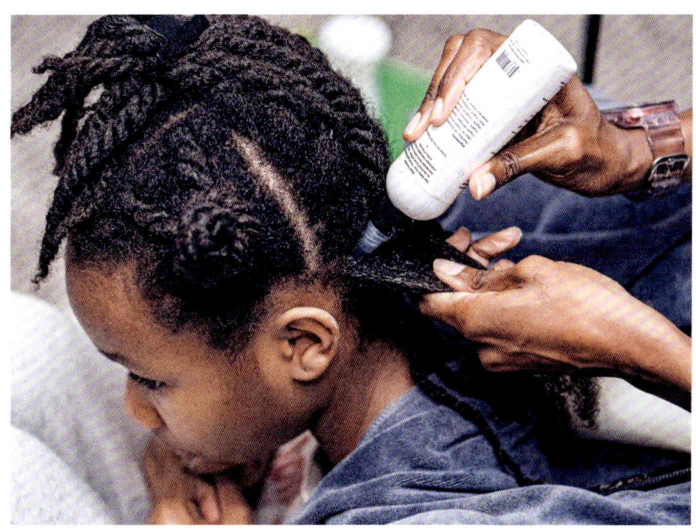

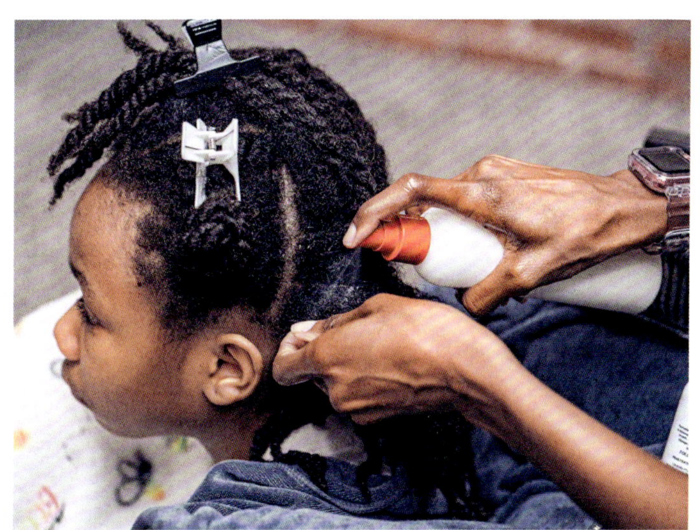

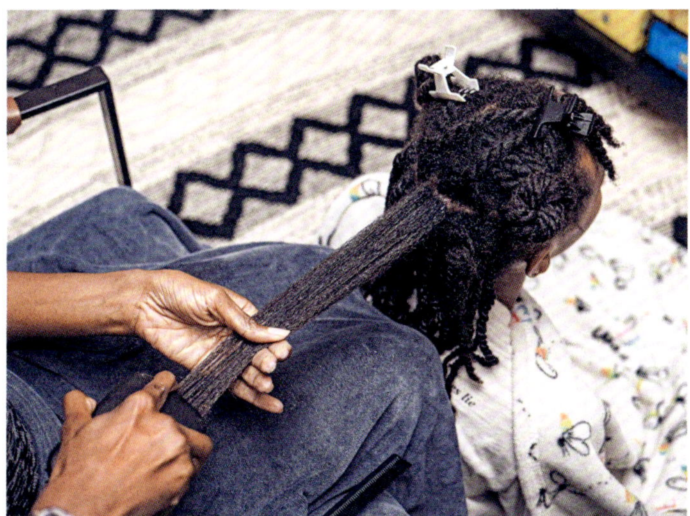

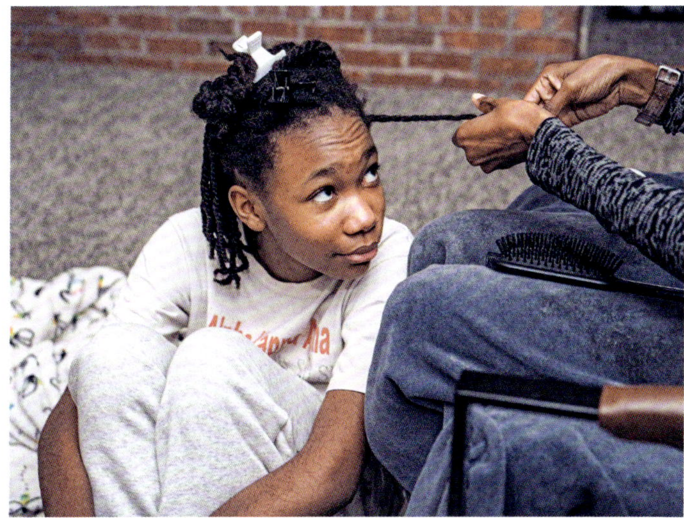

"I like it! I like how fluffy it is! And I like it when it's blow-dried and when it's out. And I like that it's curly and that it changes all the time randomly for no reason." —AZARIA

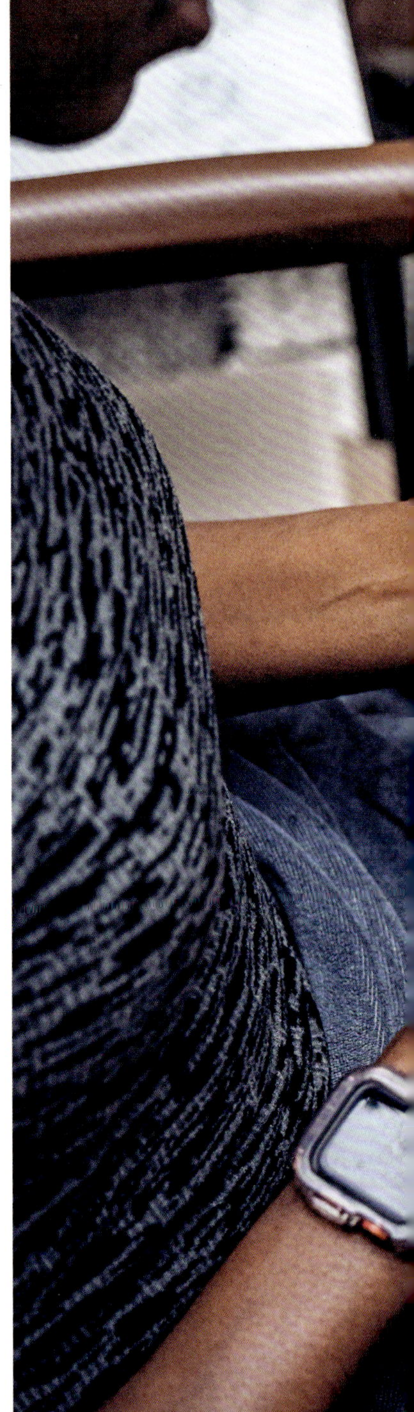

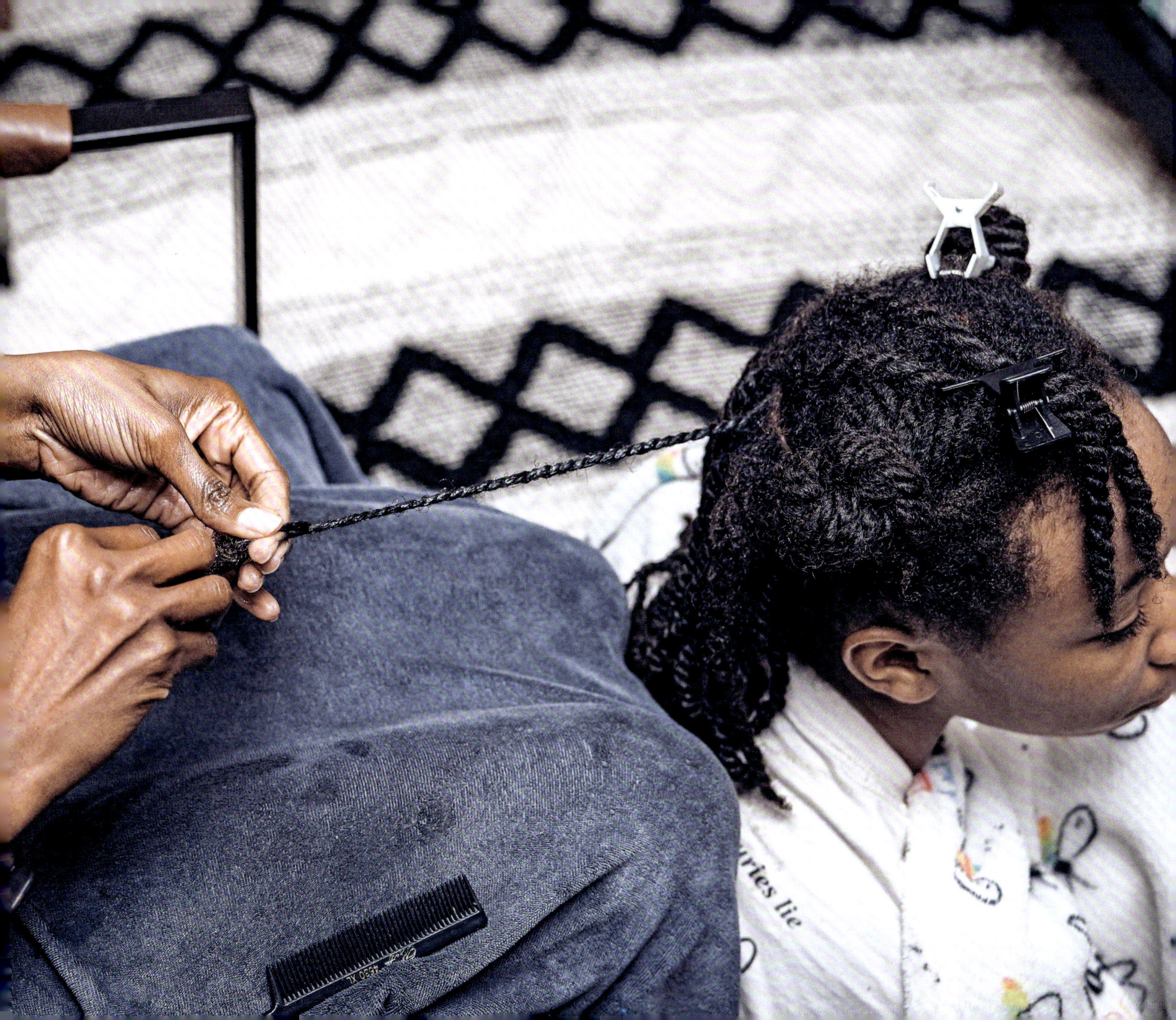

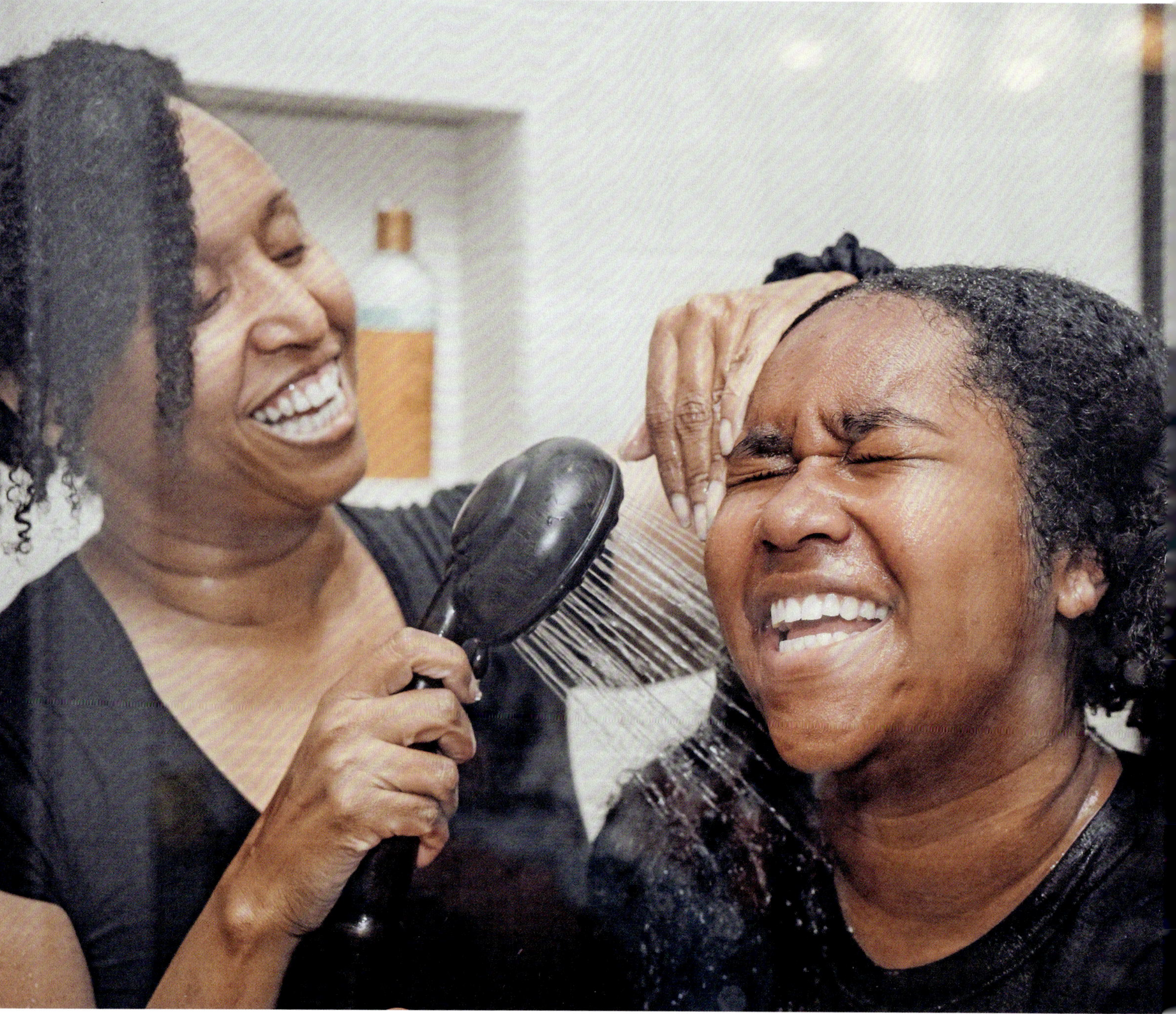

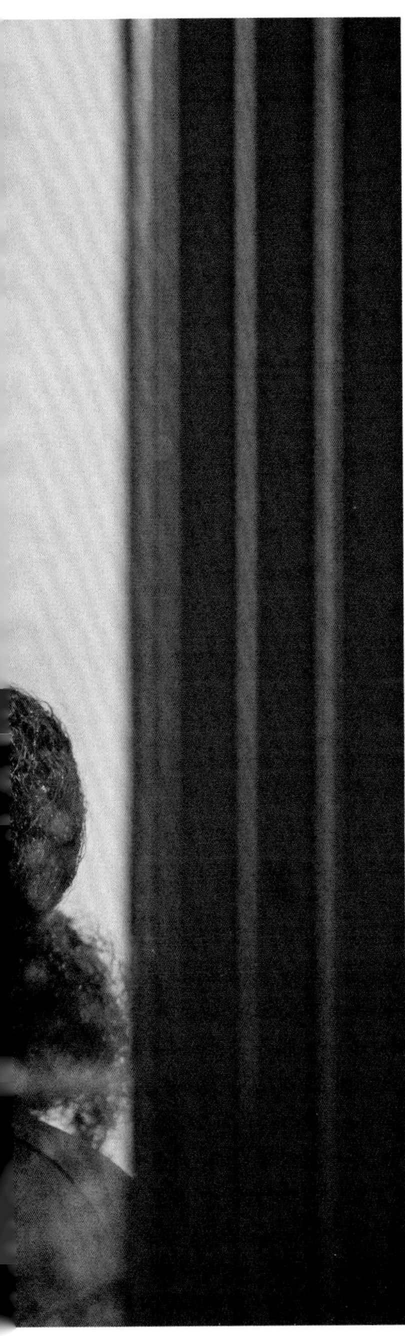

Cherise & Kira

"My grandmother and aunts had straighter, silkier, shiny hair that was a lot easier to do than my own."

TEXTURE ENVY is real. Very, very real. Overexposure to straight hair and underrepresentation of kinkier textures has led many of us to believe straighter is better. Even after going natural, many of us tighter-coiled sisters were met with visual representations of natural hair that highlighted looser textures as #goals. Many of us found ourselves attempting to achieve these textures with products and techniques that promised silkier, more elongated curls. I recall believing that my 4C texture was lacking something, simply because of the way it presented itself in its unadulterated state.

The idea of "good hair" being that kind of hair that was just a bit closer to Whiteness, not to mention, growing up with a grandmother and aunties who had loose, shiny curls, made Cherise want something different from what was growing from her scalp. She saw those looser textures highlighted as beautiful over and over and over again in the media. So, who could blame her for wanting to be considered beautiful as well?

In addition to being surrounded by familial reminders of the hair she wished for, hers was different from everyone else's and required a different care regimen. This resulted in her hair being kept in braids because it was easier for her family to manage. I imagine that, with her texture being different from other family members, there may have been less knowledge among them with regard to the options available for her tighter coils. Eventually, Cherise's aunt, a singer, started taking her to a fellow bandmate to get her hair done. Without consulting her grandmother, Cherise decided to get a relaxer during one of these visits. Grandma was not happy, but Cherise wanted that glossy, shiny, straight hair, and the relaxer gave it to her.

Cherise maintained the relaxer until 2001 when she realized it just was not worth it. She recalled:

One day I was in the chair, "feeling the burn" . . . it really hit me that I was sitting there, voluntarily, paying to torture myself, that I was saying yes to abusing myself, my being, my beautiful God-given skin . . . to do something unnatural . . . something outside of how God designed me. So that was my last relaxer . . . ever.

Cherise realized that her hair was an extension of her identity. And rather than embracing that part of herself, she had been destroying it. She quit relaxers that day and never looked back. Now, her goal is to ensure that her daughter, Kira, understands that her hair is uniquely hers and is a part of her, but at the same time, does not define her. At times, Kira struggles with shrinkage and insecurity about her tight curls, but Cherise does what she can to reinforce the beauty of her hair, just the way it is.

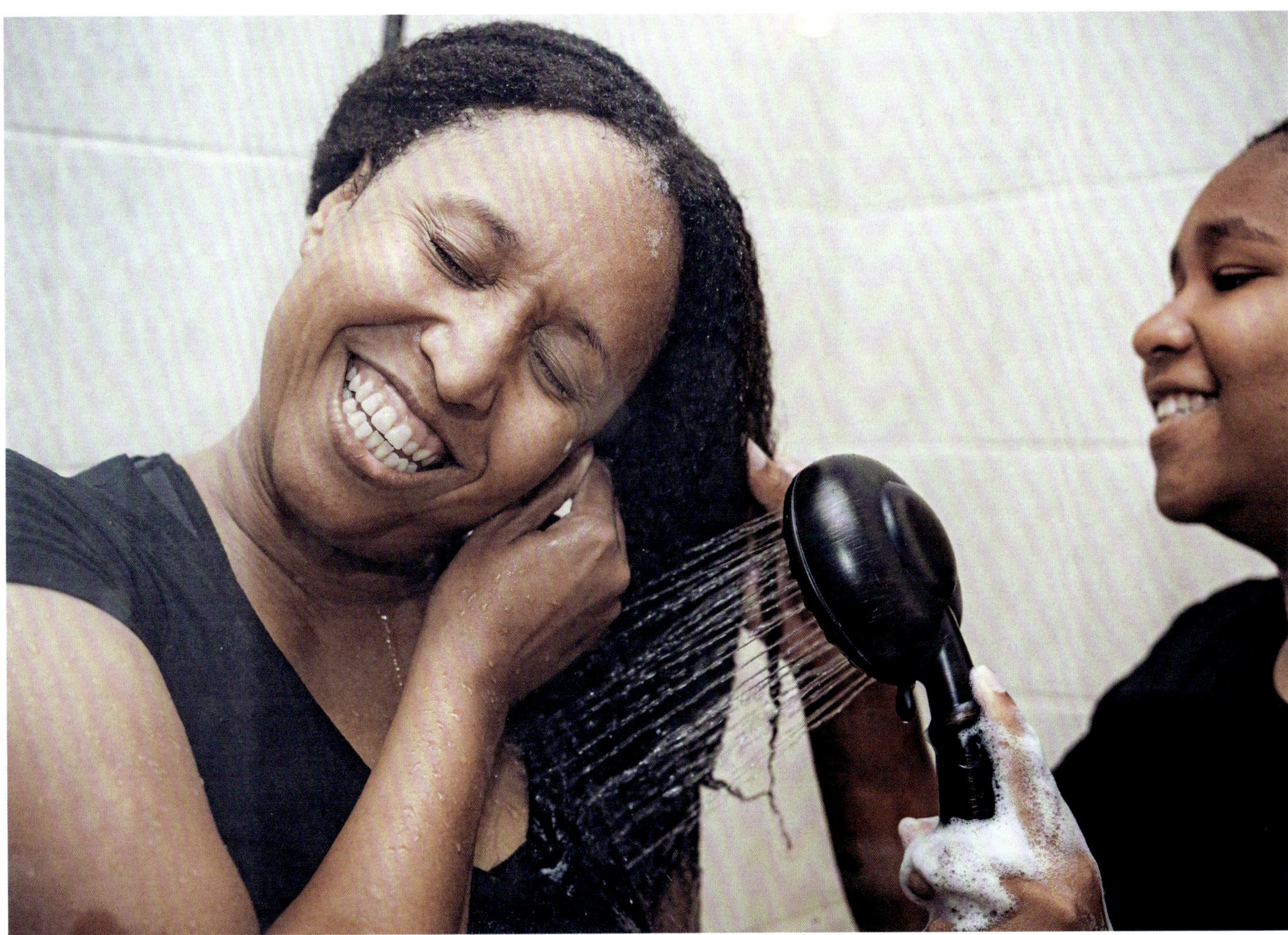

Page 158: While Cherise and Kira occasionally wash each other's hair, Kira often washes and styles her own hair, which takes about three and a half hours.

Page 159: For them, wash day and hair care in general is an exchange of ideas, techniques, and knowledge. Cherise has set a foundation for Kira, but Kira also shares newfound knowledge with her mother.

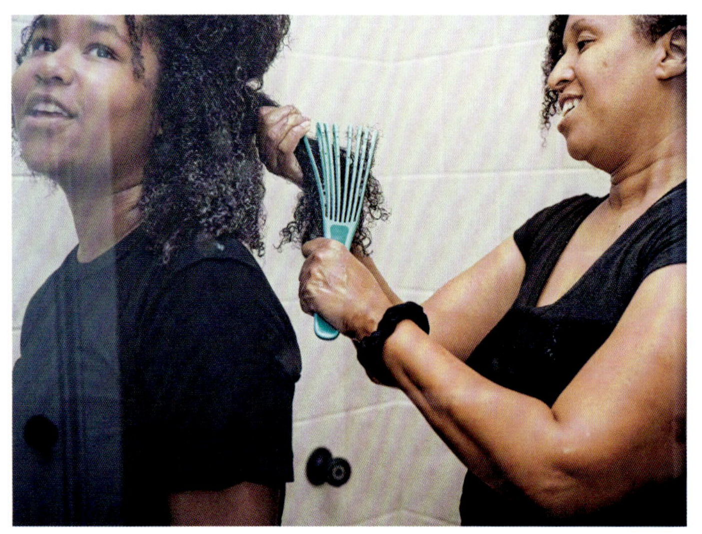
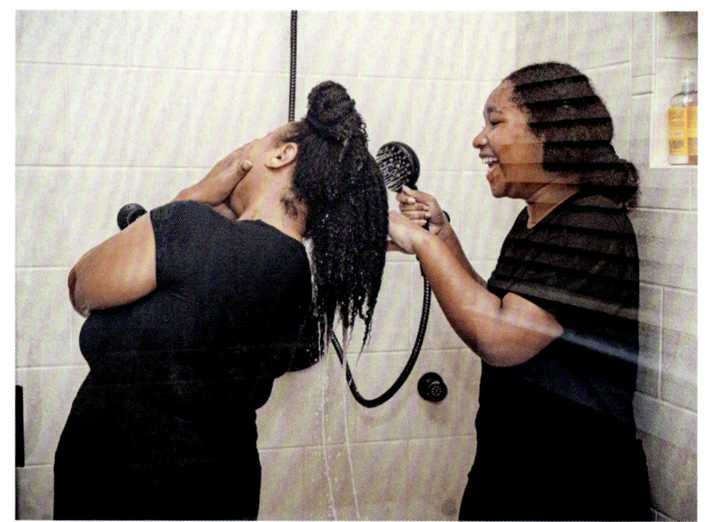
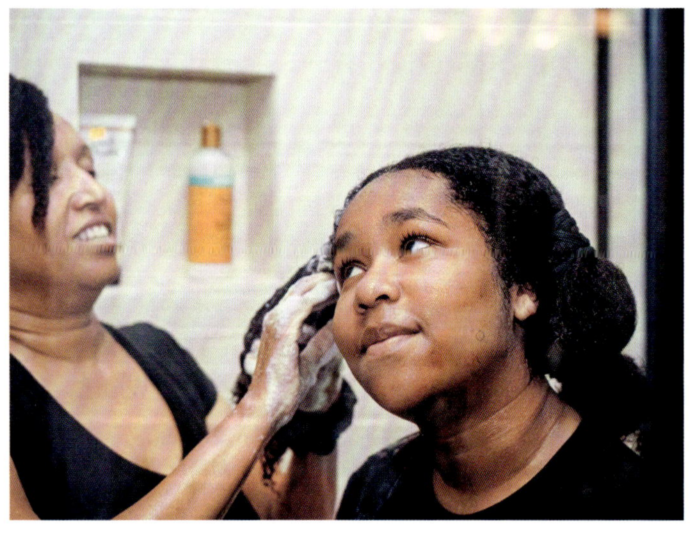
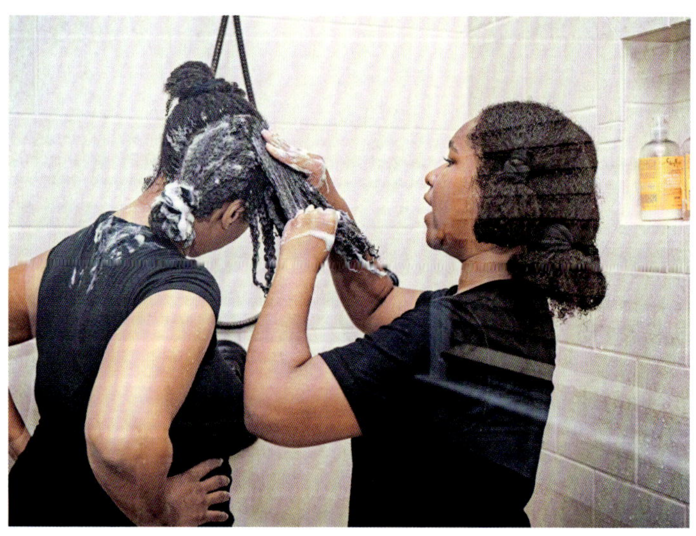

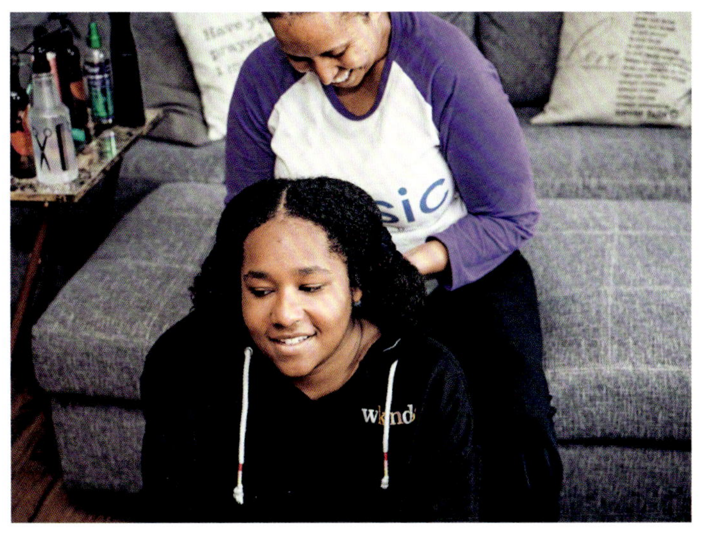
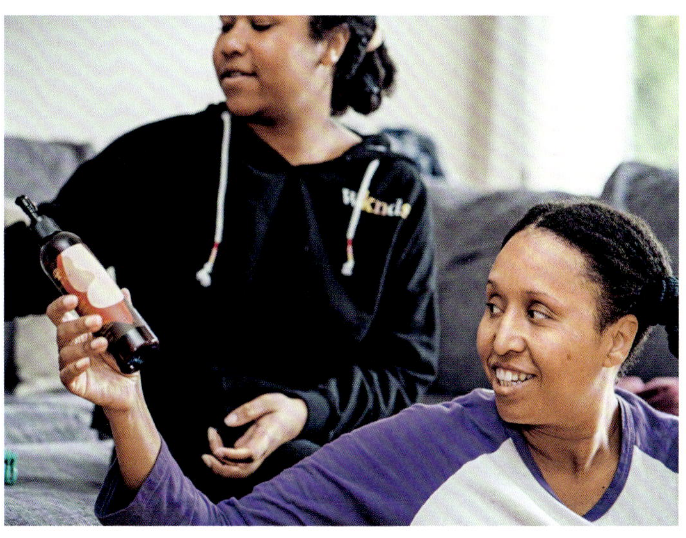
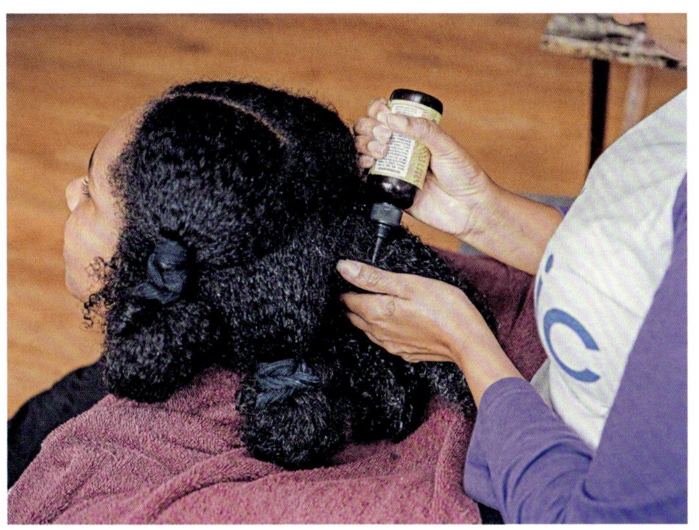
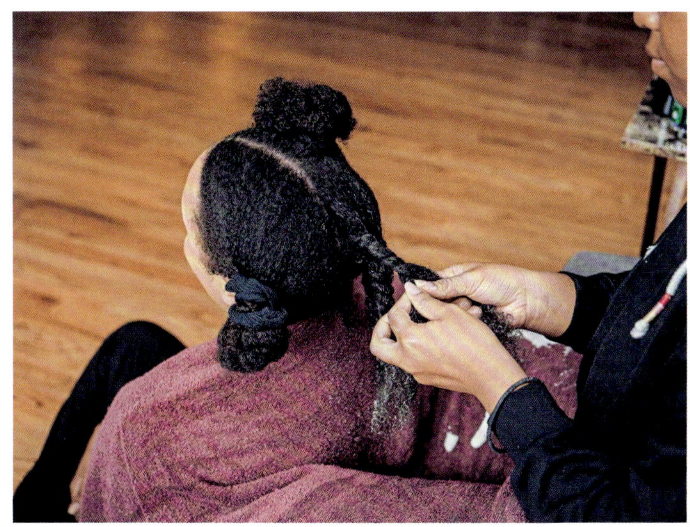

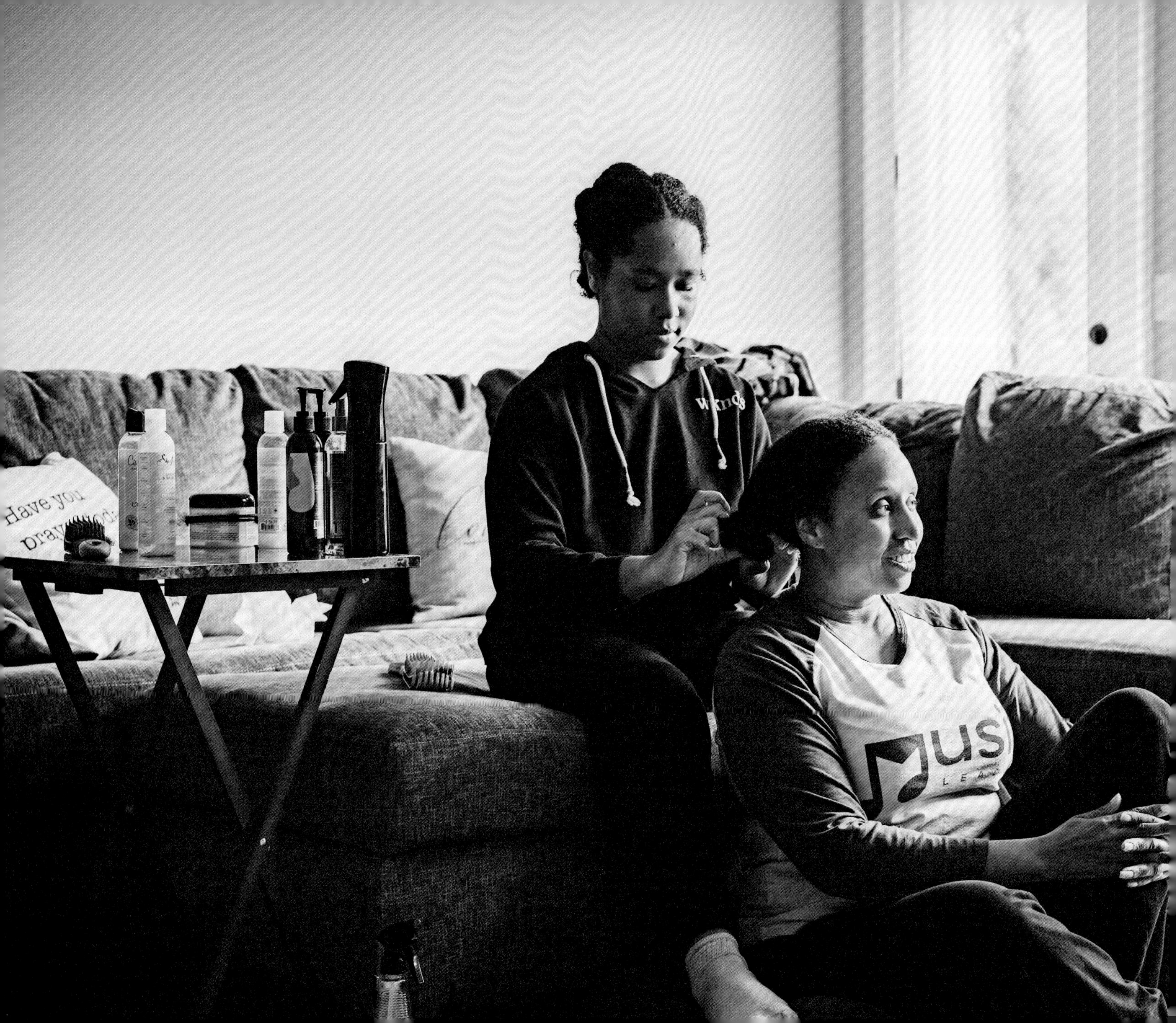

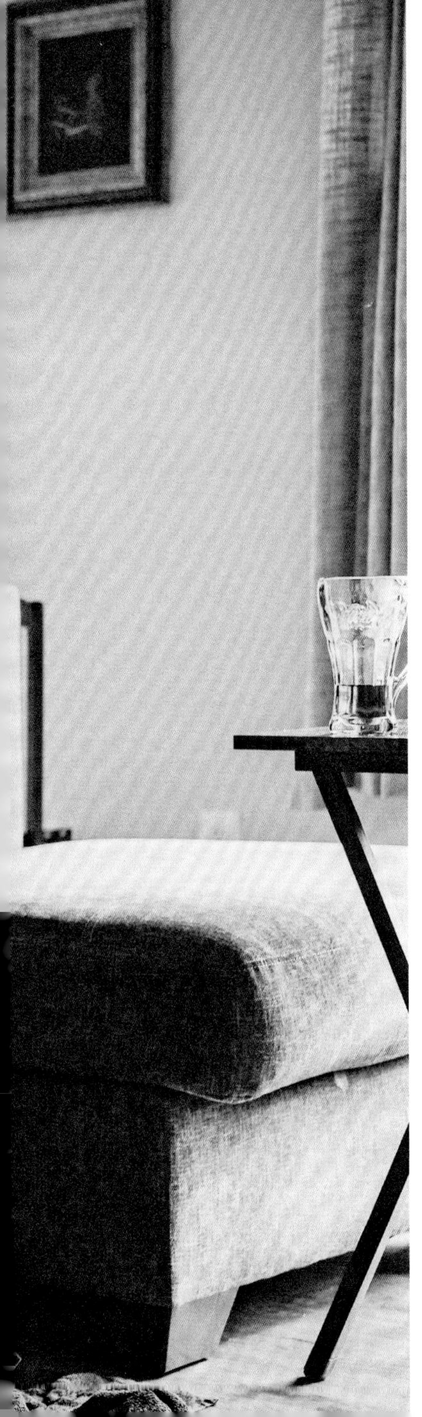

"I want to teach her that [her hair] is a beautiful extension of wonderful, unique, amazing her—that at the same time, it does not define her."

Tyrese & Catelyn

"I got to a point of feeling some type of way about [my hair] because my different hairstyles always became a point of conversation in my meetings with senior leaders."

ALTHOUGH Tyrese went natural in 2011, she kept her hair in various protective styles for ease and time management. These styles, and the frequency with which Tyrese changed them (you know how we do), were met with much commentary from a White female coworker. As many of us know, White people tend to be quite curious as to how we can change our hair from short to long (or vice versa), or curly to straight, and so on. Well, this coworker was quite comfortable making her curiosity known with each of Tyrese's new hairstyles.

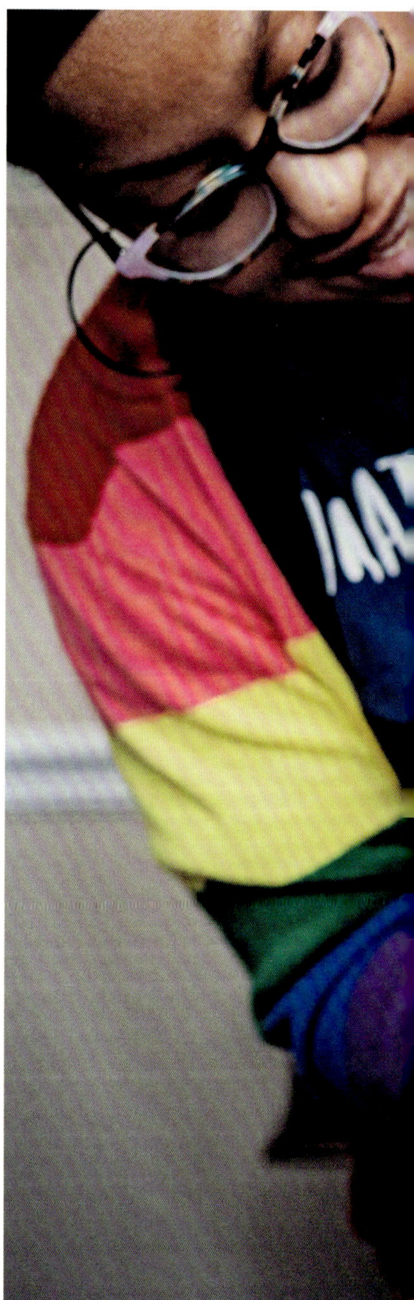

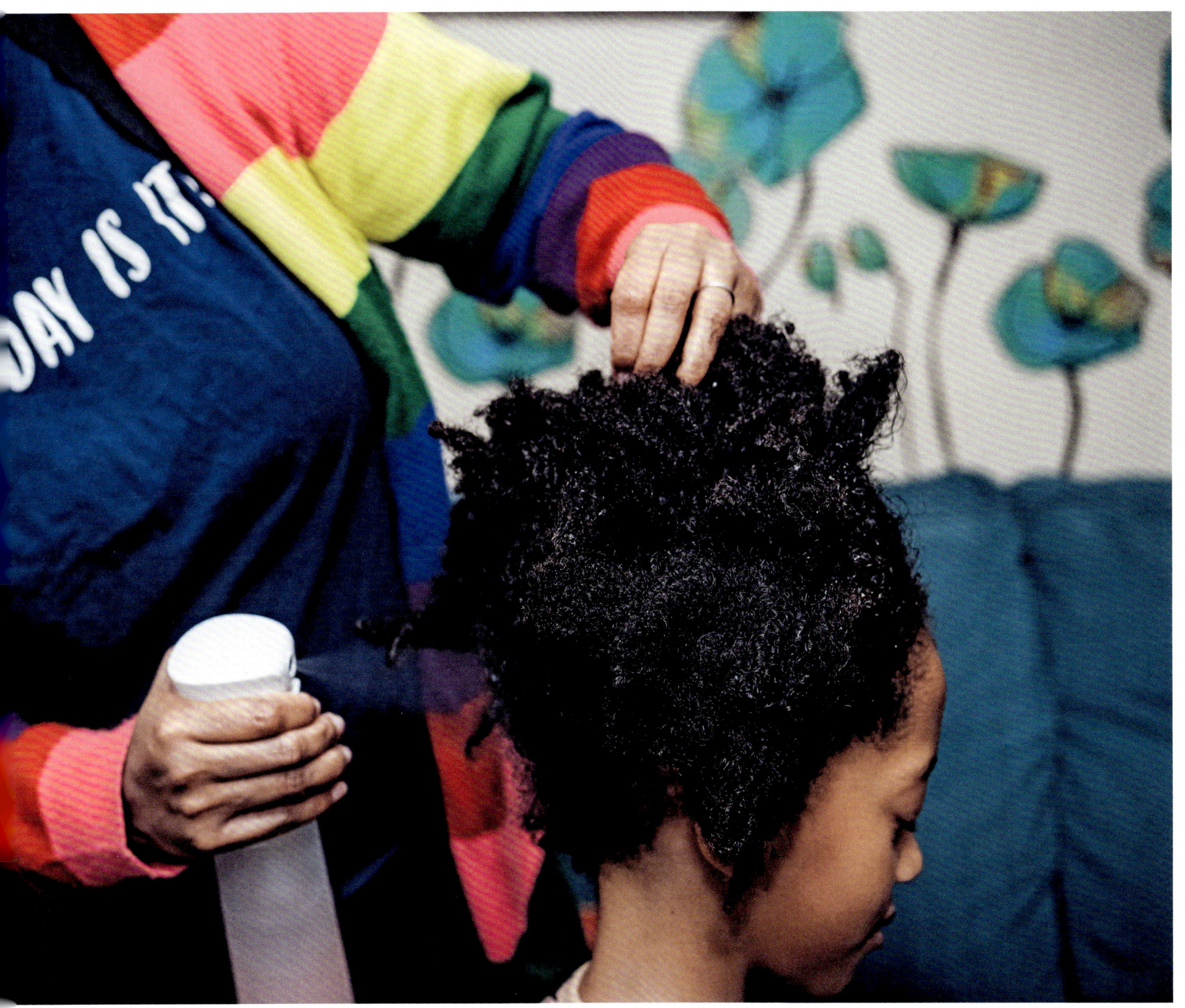
DAY IS IT

When the pandemic hit in 2020, Tyrese found herself working from home. This gave her space to finally give protective styles a break. She cut her hair short and began investing time into caring for her own curls. She loved it. However, the same coworker who used to comment on her protective styles pre-pandemic was the first to take note of her new natural style during a virtual leadership team meeting. Other coworkers followed suit, and Tyrese's natural hair became the center of attention. This continued week, after week, after week. I should also mention that Tyrese was the only Black person (or even person of color) in these meetings. And this probably goes without saying, but no one else's hair was being discussed.

Although many would consider it harmless, singling out a Black person's hair *is* a microaggression, as is commenting on how often it changes. A 2023 study found that Black women with coily hair are two times as likely to experience microaggressions at work than Black women with straighter hair.[40] Dr. Chester Pierce, a Black psychiatrist and Harvard professor, coined the term *micro-aggression* in the 1960s.[41] Dr. Pierce explained:

> In fact, the major vehicle for racism in this country is offenses done to blacks by whites in this sort of gratuitous, never-ending way. These offenses are micro-aggressions. Almost all black-white racial interactions are characterized by white put-downs, done in an automatic, preconscious, or unconscious fashion. These mini-disasters accumulate. It is the sum total of multiple micro-aggressions by whites to blacks that has pervasive effect to the stability and peace of this world.[42]

The definition has since evolved to include "brief and commonplace daily verbal, behavioral, or environmental indignities, whether intentional or unintentional, that communicate hostile, derogatory, or negative racial slights and insults toward people of color."[43] Research has shown that microaggressions are associated with a number of nega-tive mental health consequences.[44] As clinical psychologist Monnica T. Williams explains, "Reactions following experi-ences of microaggressions may include confusion, anger, anxiety, helplessness, hopelessness, frustration, paranoia, and fear. . . . Because microaggressions are so common, they can be conceptualized as a form of chronic stress that may also result in physical problems . . ."[45] Unfortunately, most people making these remarks are completely clueless as to their racist implications, as well as to the harm they may be causing.

This constant othering of Tyrese's hair made her un-comfortable. So, when her company announced its plan to have employees return to the office in a hybrid capacity, she decided to return to a look that would garner less at-tention. She decided to texturize her hair in order to keep some of the curls she had worked so hard to grow out, but also allow her to easily straighten her hair for office days. Tyrese shared, "I have no clue why I associated straight hair with 'professional,' but I did." No one had to tell her directly to straighten her hair; being singled out because of her natural hair took care of that. The commentary from coworkers only added to the internal struggle she already had regarding whether natural hair is appropriate for the workplace. In order to avoid being treated like a spectacle, Tyrese found herself straightening her hair every time she went to the office. Unfortunately, the texturizer plus the fre-quent heat resulted in damage and breakage. Her hair fell out completely and she had to start all over again.

This experience convinced Tyrese that she was done with chemicals. Despite the concerns surrounding her nat-ural hair at work, she has chosen to prioritize the health of her hair. To keep from having to worry about styling, she has her twin sister braid her hair into simple updos. This way, she can maintain the ease of protective styles, protect her peace, and minimize unsolicited commentary about her hair at the office.

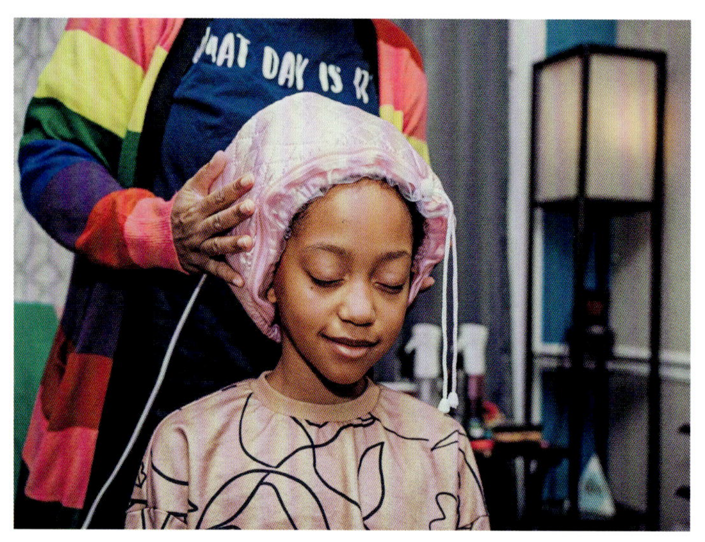
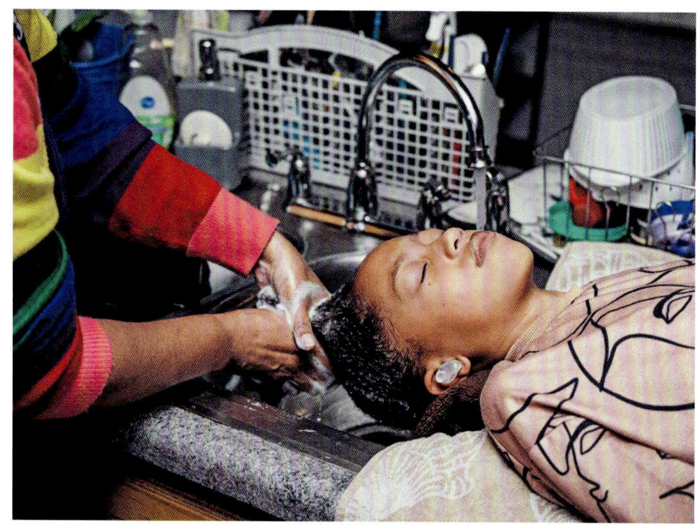
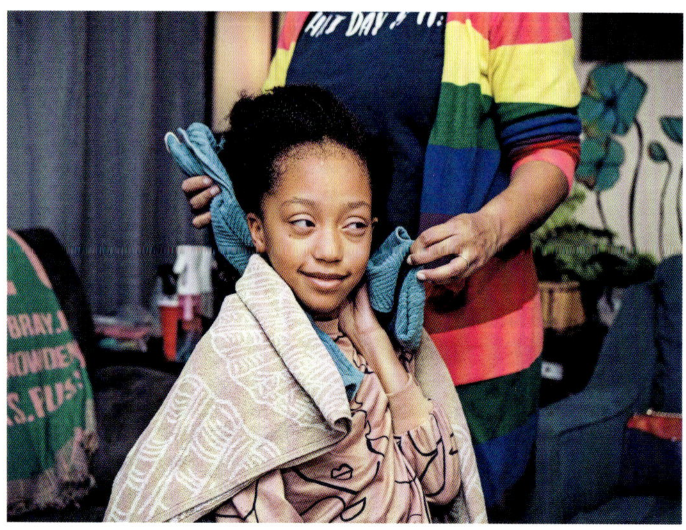
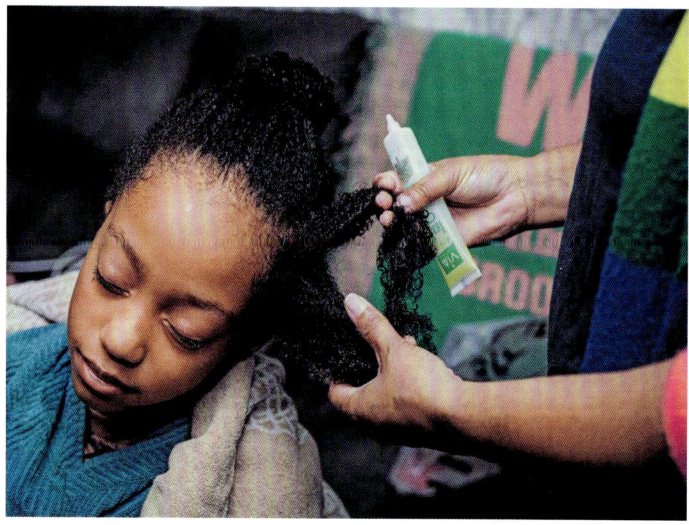

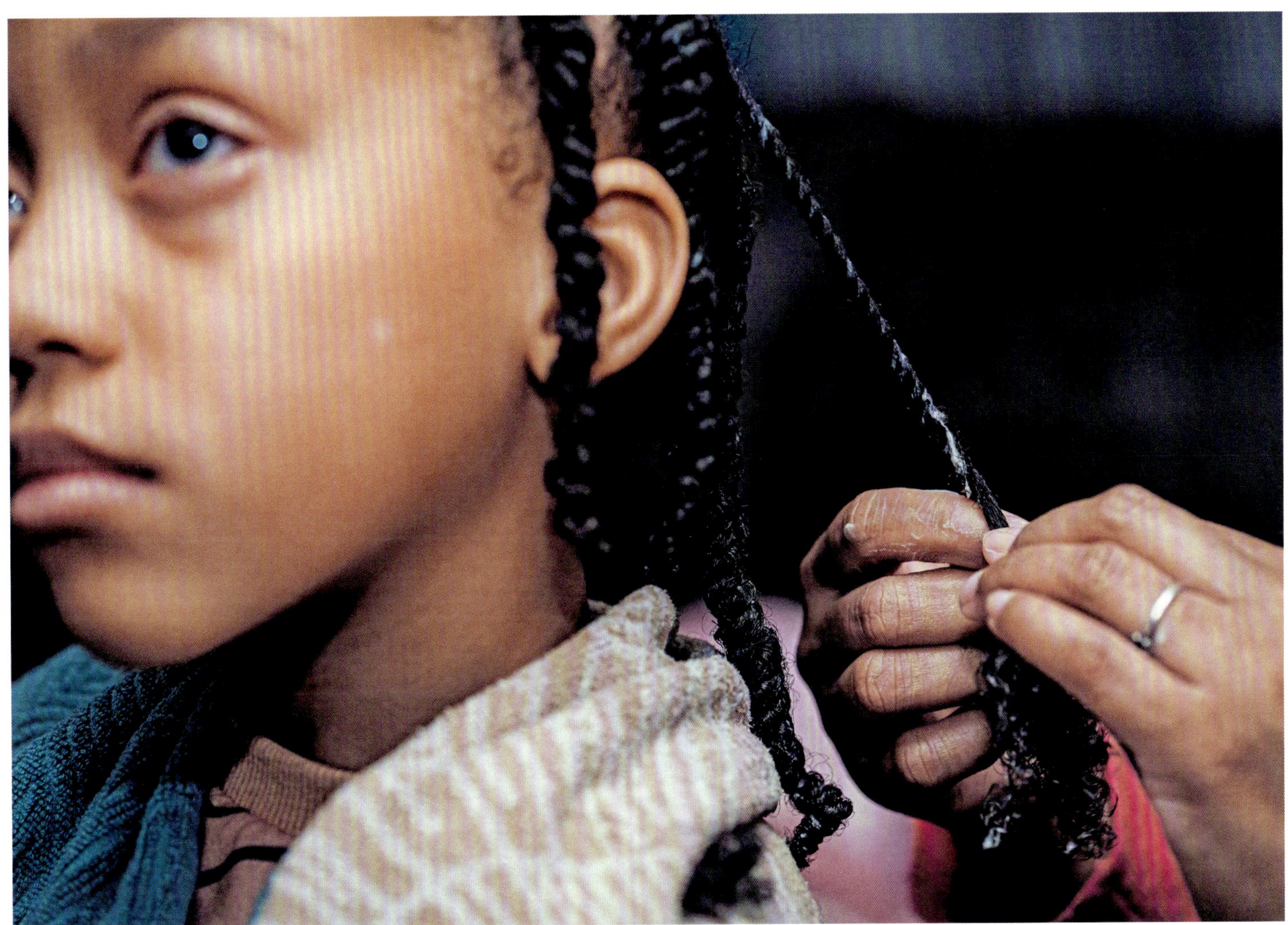

Opposite page, top left and top right: Wash day for Tyrese and Catelyn takes place every two to three weeks and lasts for about two to three hours. Tyrese begins by putting a clay mask in Catelyn's hair and applying a heating cap to loosen any product build up and soften her hair. She washes her hair with ear plugs since Catelyn hates getting water in her ears. For styling, Tyrese usually opts for two-strand twists.

Though I'm unable to include all of the snacking photos I've captured while photographing these families, snacks are essential to the wash-day routine. For many, it's a long process, so it is typical to take a snack or meal break or, as seen here, to snack during the process.

"She absolutely LOVES her curly hair! If she could wear an afro every day, she would! Her words!"

—TYRESE

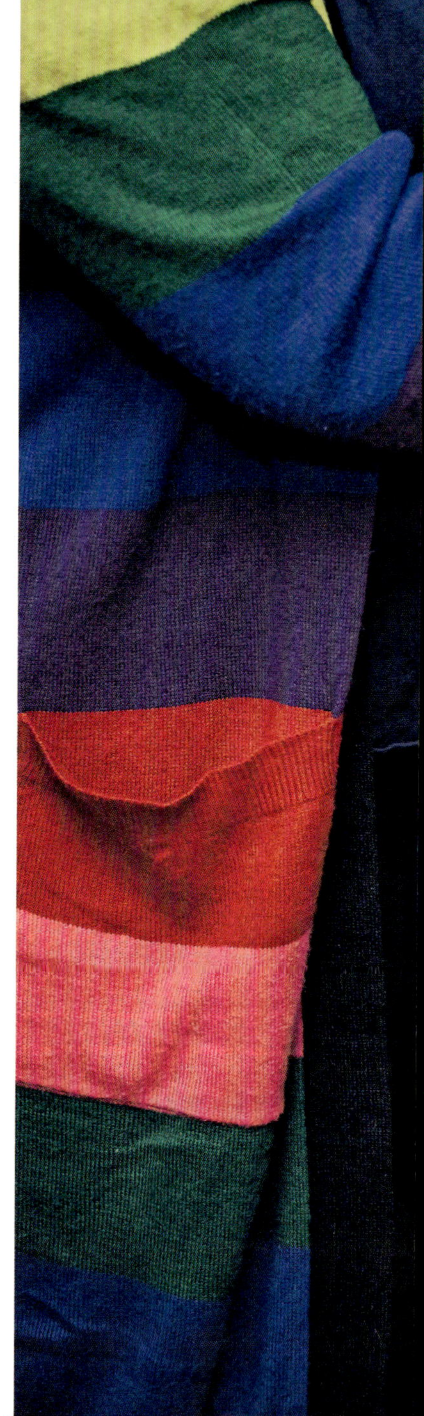

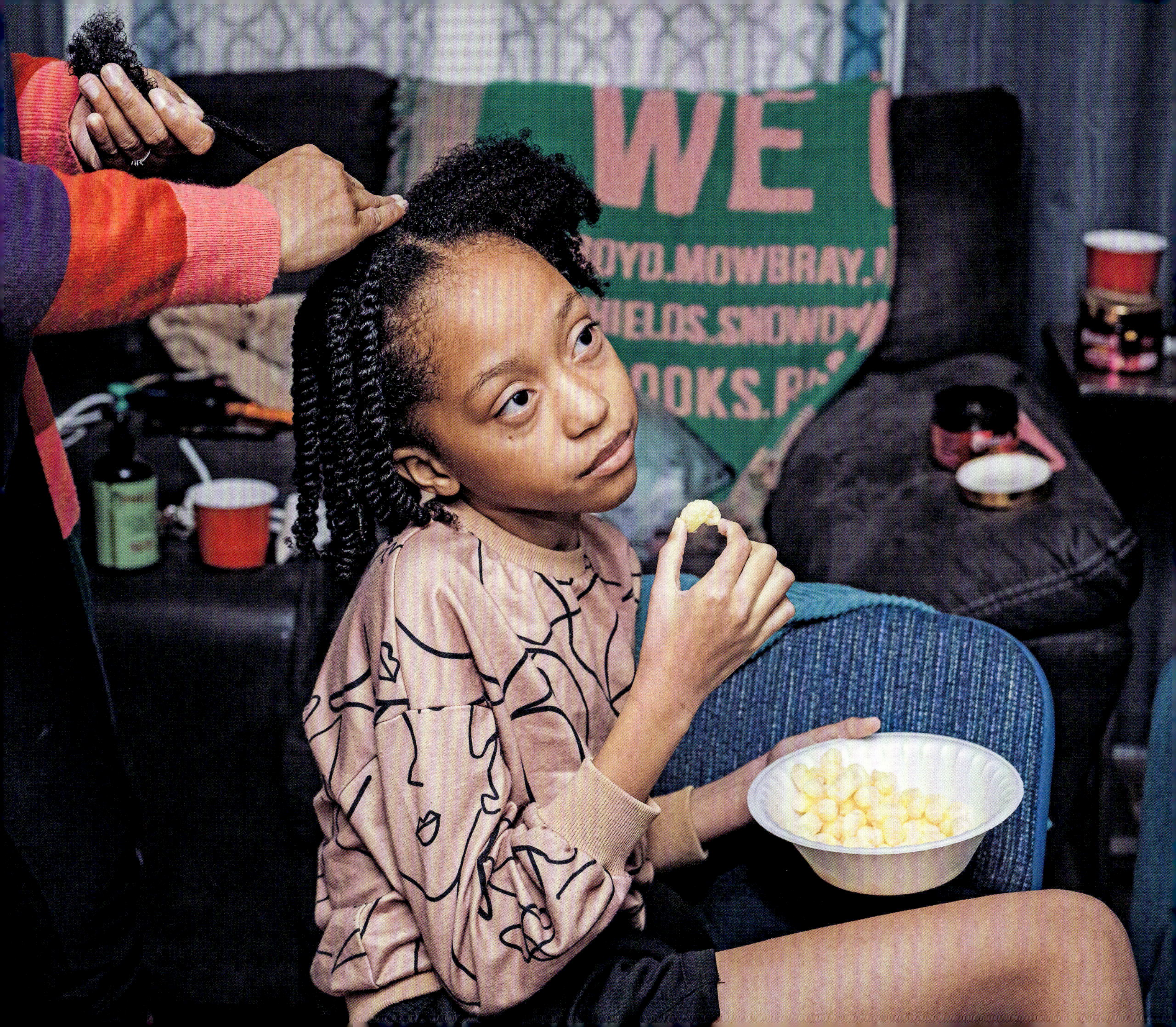

WE
OYD.MOWBRAY.
HIELDS.SNOWD
OOKS.P

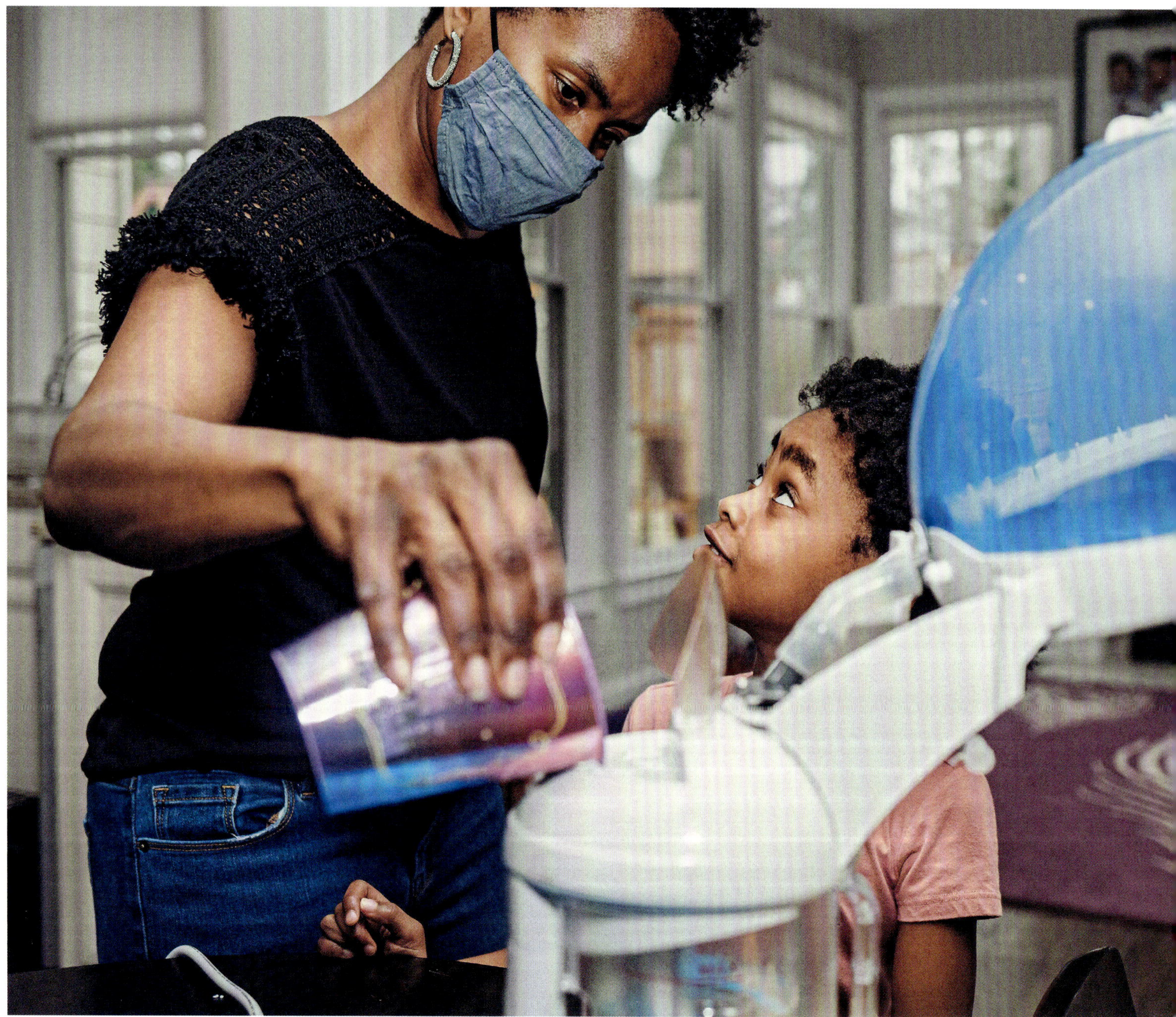

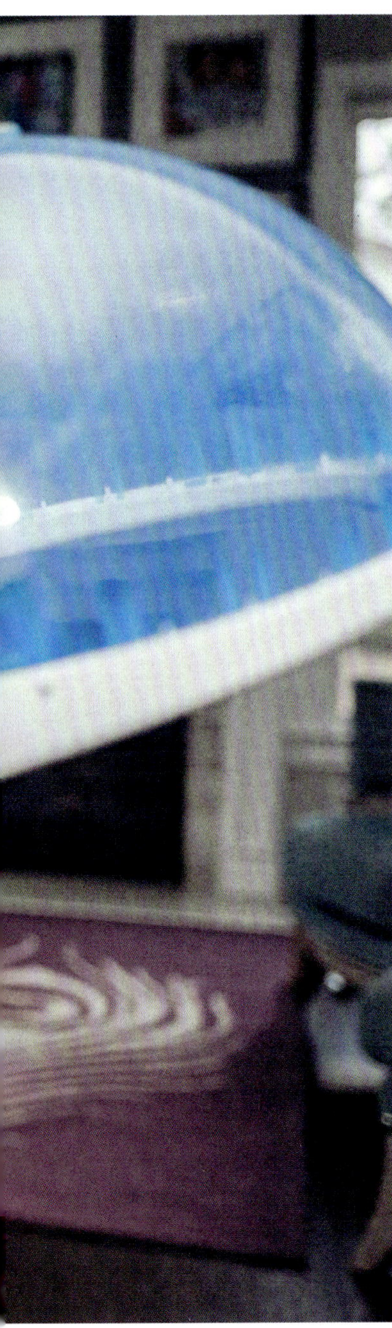

Nadia & Kinsley

THESE DAYS, while Black women *can* choose to wear curly or straight hair to work, oftentimes, their choice is heavily influenced by their work environment. In Tyrese's story, I discuss the microaggressions she experienced at work and how they impacted her hairstyling choices. She chose straight hair in order to end the cycle of unsolicited comments from her White coworkers that were a source of anxiety for her. But when that choice resulted in damage to her hair, she made a different call; she chose herself. Nadia faced a similar crossroads.

SIDE NOTE: Nadia's stylist was not alone. One of the driving forces behind the natural hair movement was the collective desire to live a greener lifestyle. People in general were taking a closer look at product labels, and for Black women, this included the ingredient lists for hair relaxers. In fact, research has shown that chemical relaxers are associated with a higher risk of uterine cancer.[46]

For years, Nadia struggled internally with whether she should wear her hair natural to the office. She feared criticism, and was concerned that wearing her natural hair might impair her chances of upward mobility within her company. Relaxers were the standard for her until 2007, when her hair stylist, who was diagnosed with cancer in her hand, told her that she suspected the chemicals in hair relaxers contributed to the diagnosis. Nadia was convinced of the potential dangers of perms, so she discontinued chemically straightening her hair.

However, since she was still concerned about how her natural hair would be perceived at work, she began pressing it weekly. As she was promoted, she became more and more comfortable with trying out curly styles. Sometimes, she would press her hair straight, then twist it to give it a wavy pattern. Over the years, Nadia has received a mixture of comments regarding her hair when worn curly or wavy at work. She has received many compliments, as she should. But she was also told by a male coworker that she looked like she stuck her finger in a light socket. Whether good or bad, Nadia has often found her hair to be a topic of discussion at work.

On a particular occasion in 2019, she wore her hair in a twist-out without pressing it first, so it looked much kinkier and closer to her actual curl pattern. Upon seeing Nadia's hair at a corporate event, a White male coworker had the nerve to ask her, in front of others, "Did you get caught in the rain?" She was shocked. The comment really stung, but Nadia tried her best to play it off in the moment.

Later, she found herself struggling. It's already difficult enough for Black women to overcome negative perceptions of natural hair in the workplace, but the added anxiety caused by *actual* negative comments from coworkers can be a bit too much for some (heck, maybe even most of us). The comments made her wonder if she should continue down the path of wearing her natural hair to work. Though she was an executive by this time and was no longer worried about moving up in the company, she still found herself confronted with the very criticism that kept her from exploring curly styles in the first place. Similar to Tyrese, Nadia felt the real impact of what her coworker believed to be a harmless comment. Insensitive jokes and unsolicited comments about a Black woman's hair are microaggressions that happen way too often.

Despite her coworker's hurtful joke about her hair texture, in 2020, Nadia chose to lean in. All the way in. She cut off the heat-damaged hair she sustained from her weekly presses and started wearing it curly from then on. Like many Black women in 2020, Nadia found renewed freedom while sheltering in place. Being away from that corporate environment gave her the space she needed (space away from comments about "rain" and "light sockets") to confidently begin rocking her curls on the regular. Nadia felt empowered to choose the hair that grows from her scalp, rather than changing it to make her coworkers comfortable. She now boldly wears her kinky-textured hair. Thankfully for her, the comments have ceased, and she is hopeful that her courage has shifted the climate and opened the door for acceptance of Black hair textures in her workplace.

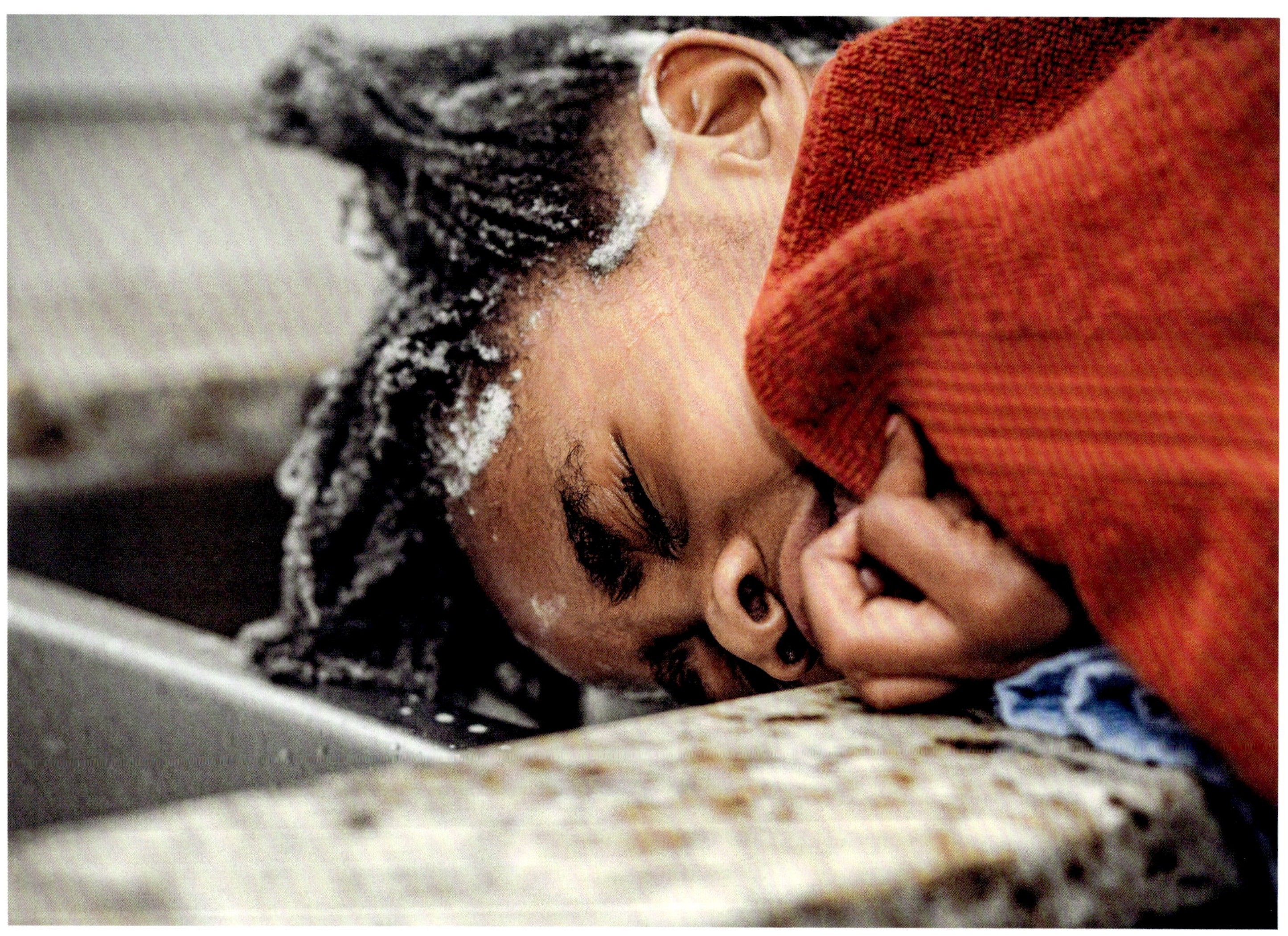

Nadia and Kinsley have wash day weekly. Her process includes a deep conditioning steam treatment and blow drying.

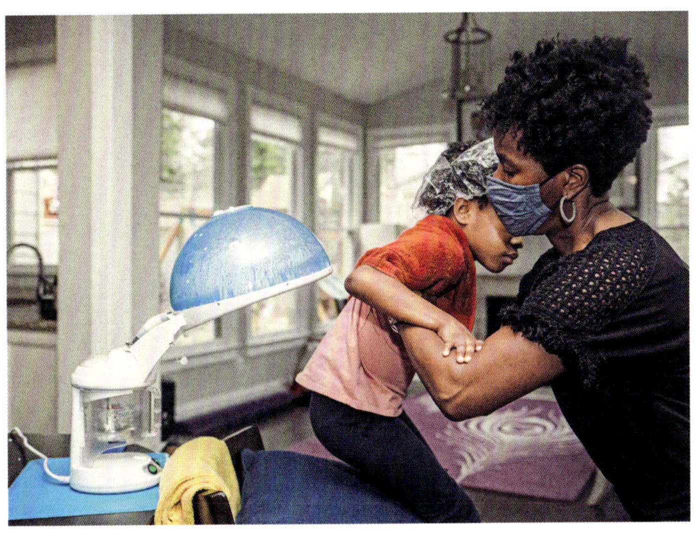
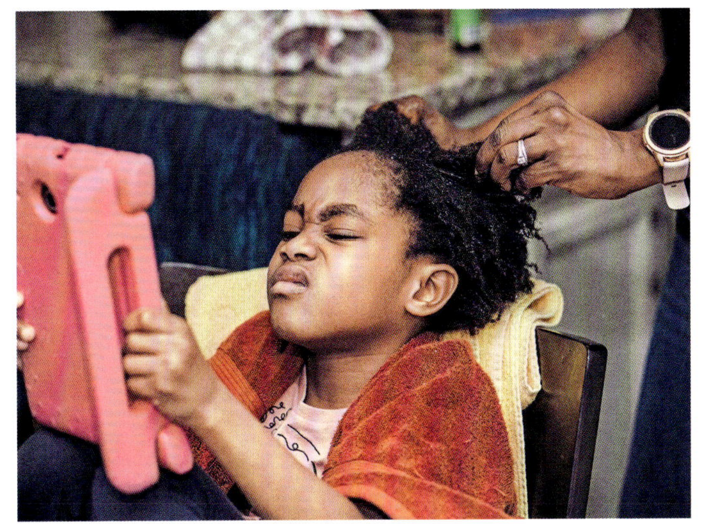
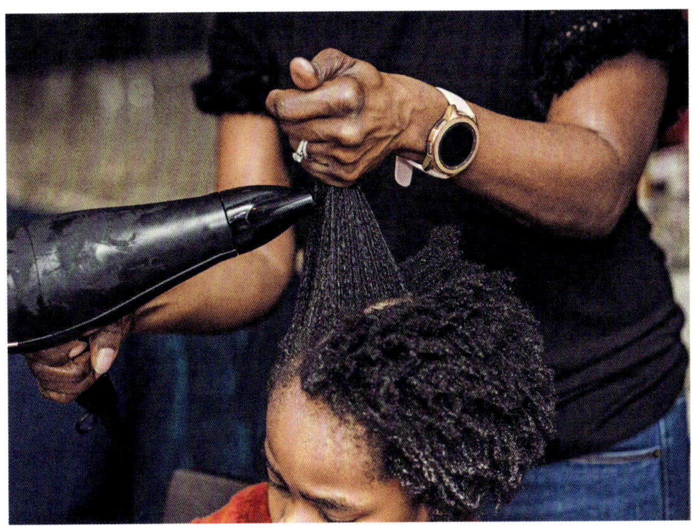
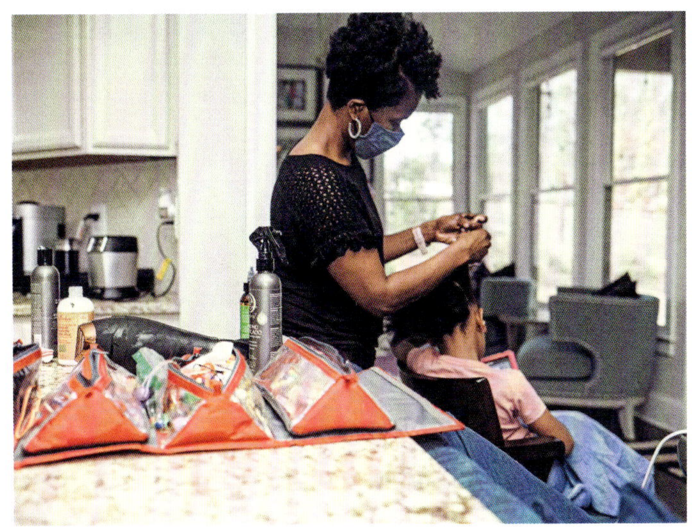

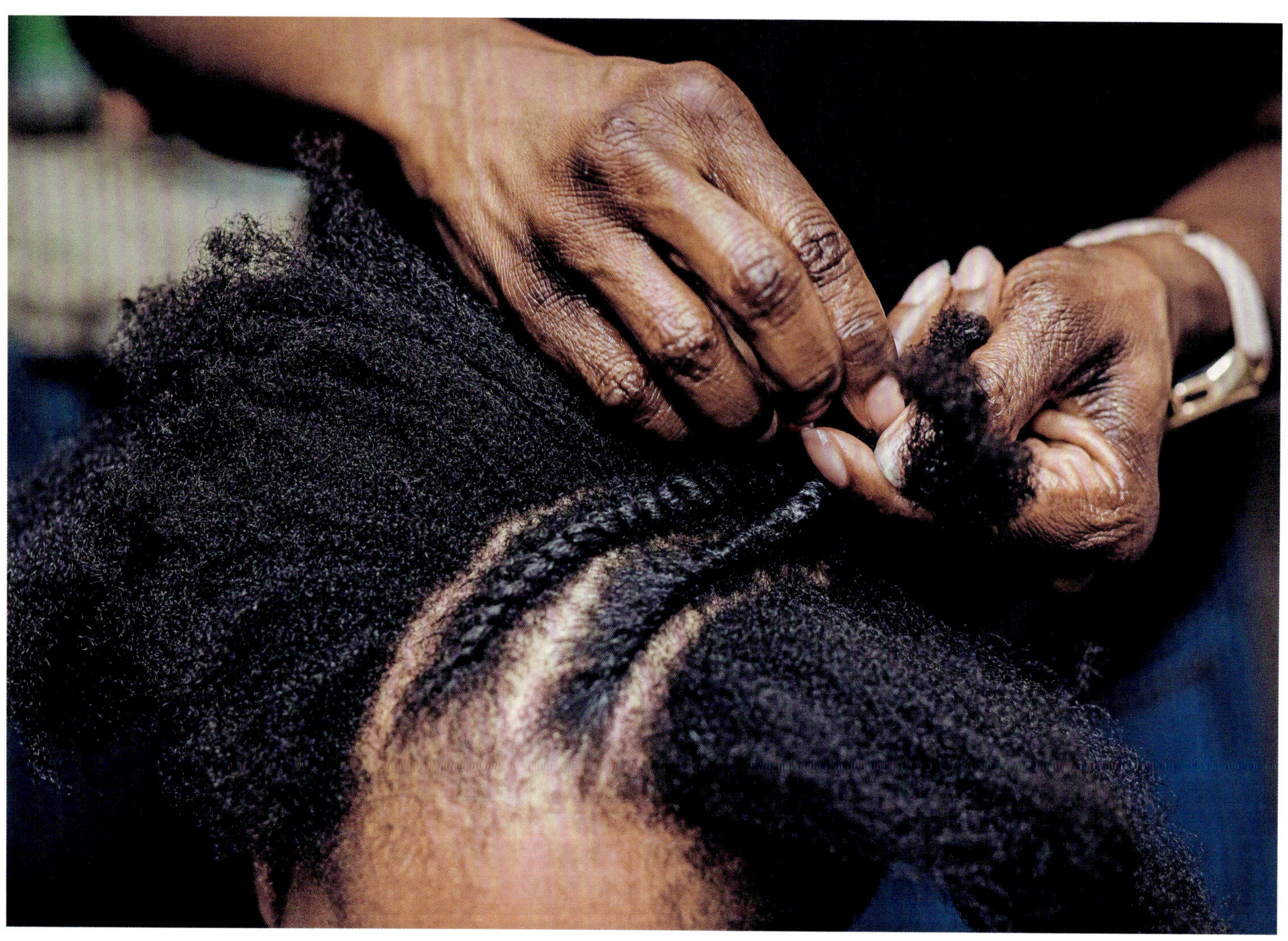

Nadia flat twists Kinsley's hair using styling mousse.

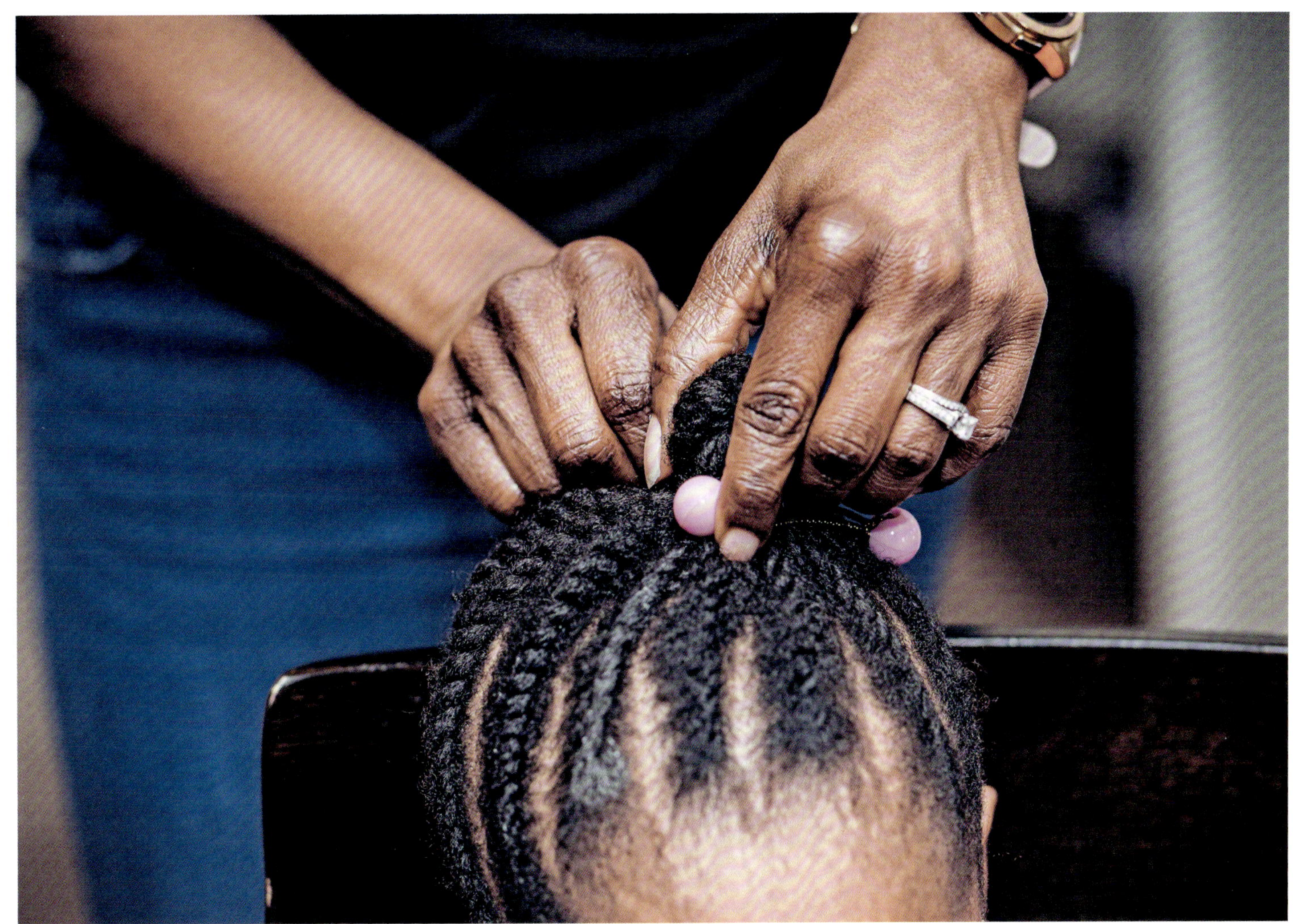

Nadia wraps Kinsley's hair to keep her new style intact while the mousse dries.

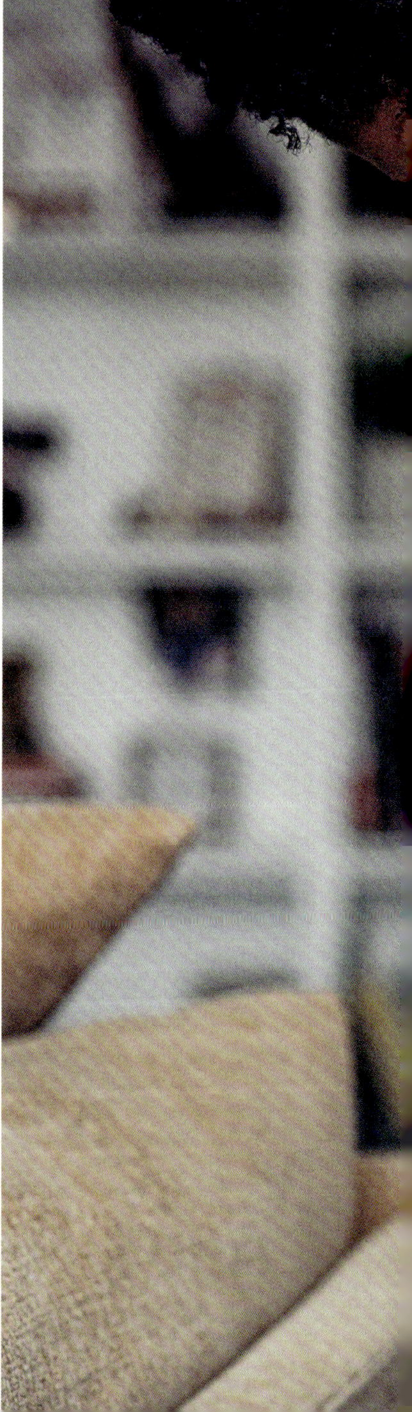

"I'd like her to see the beauty in her texture but also know that it's just hair and it complements her, not defines her." —NADIA

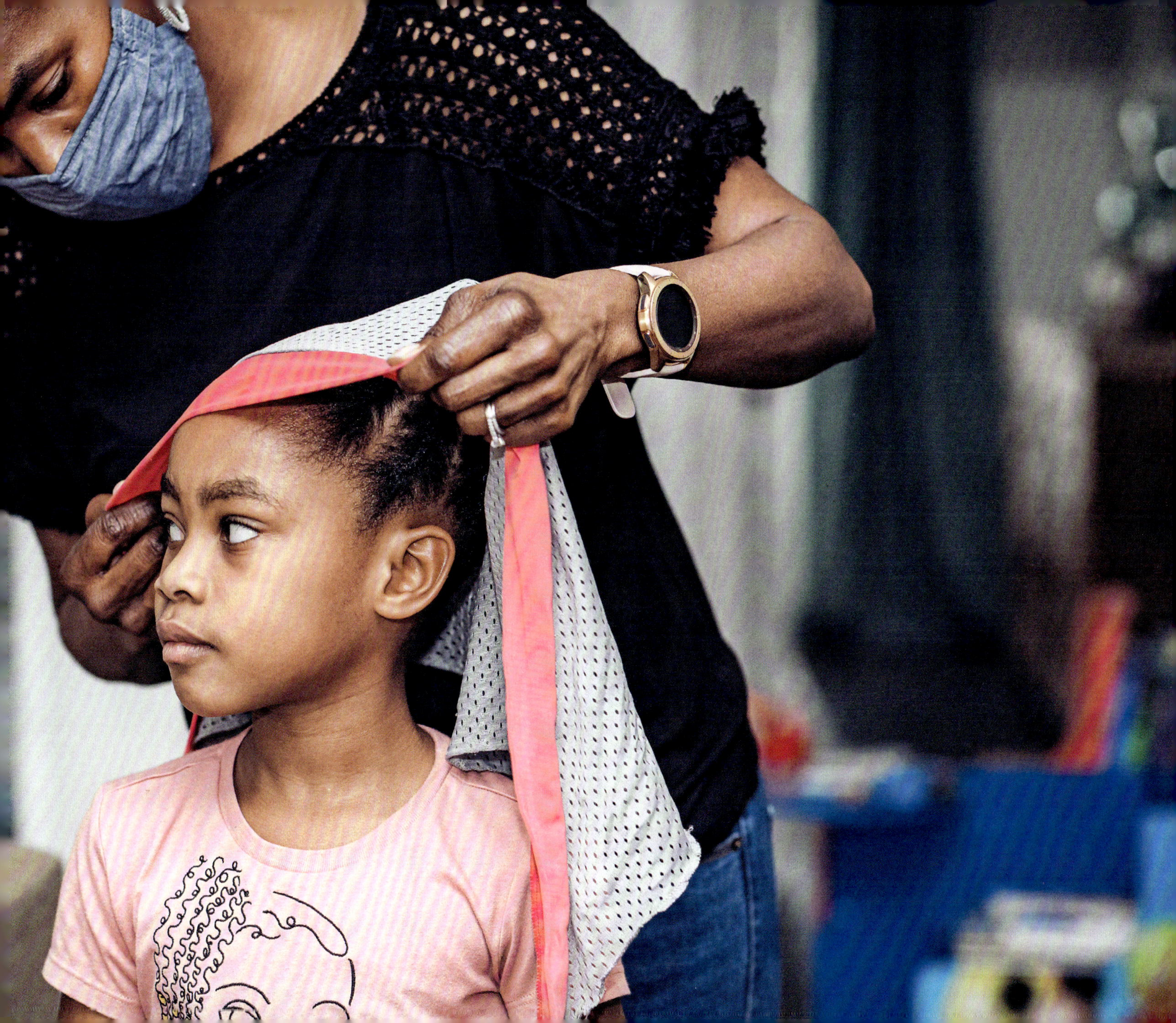

Jerolyn & Drew

"The ebbs and flows of my natural hair journey have been both gratifying and challenging."

LIKE many Black women, Jerolyn has found it tough to negotiate between having straight hair (which we have been taught is more desirable and even necessary for certain hairstyles) and having healthy hair.

Growing up, Jerolyn was used to being told her hair was "too thick" and that it would be easier to manage with a relaxer. Her friends, and even her hair stylist urged her to get a relaxer. Add to all of this, the lure of '90s hairstyles, which Jerolyn was not able to achieve with her thick, natural hair. So, in the eighth grade, Jerolyn decided to go ahead and get a relaxer.

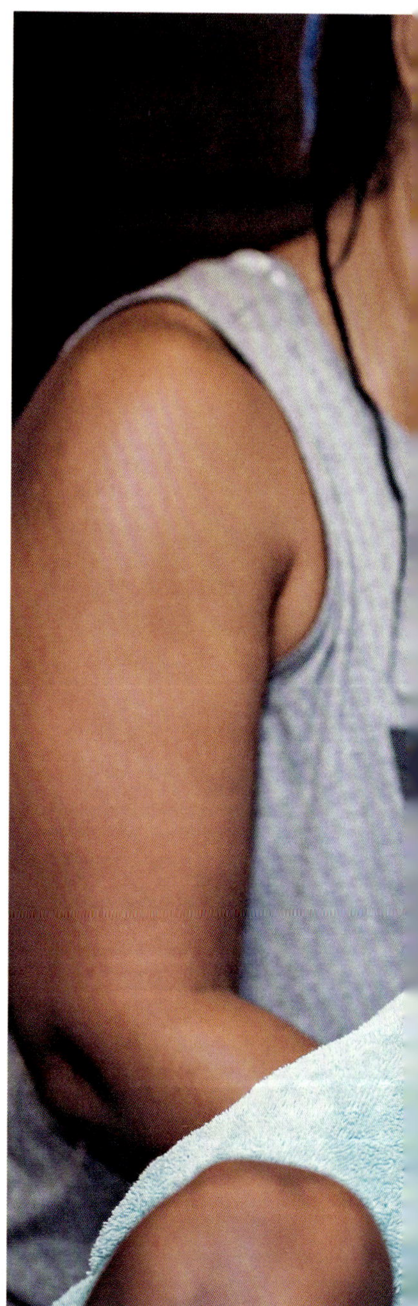

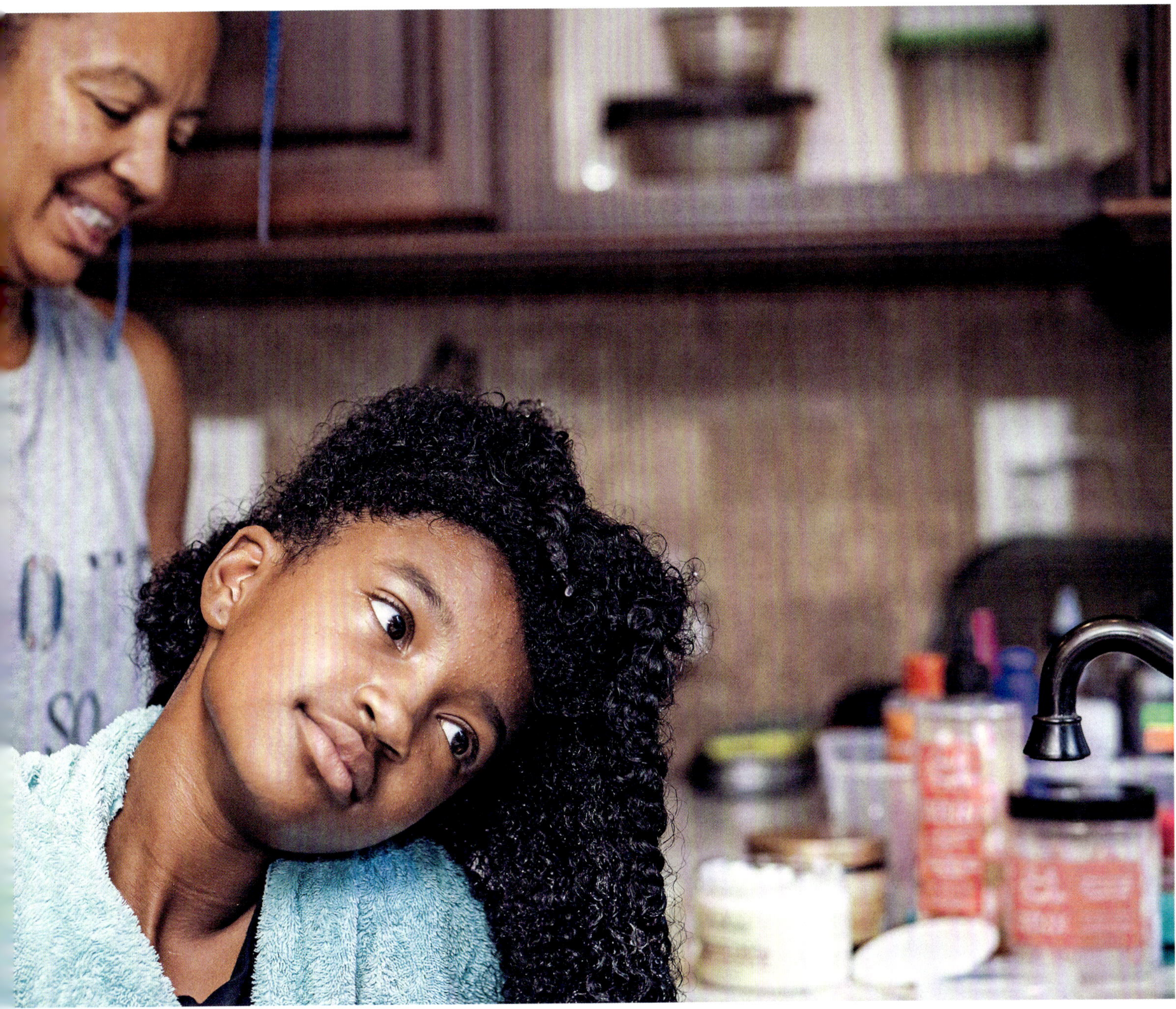

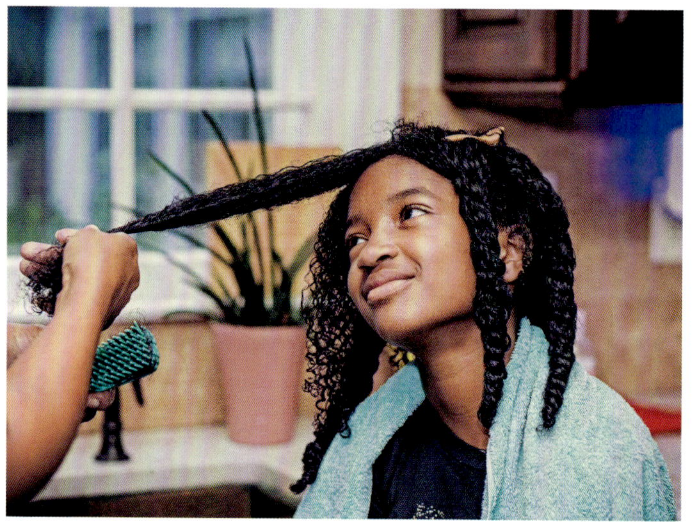

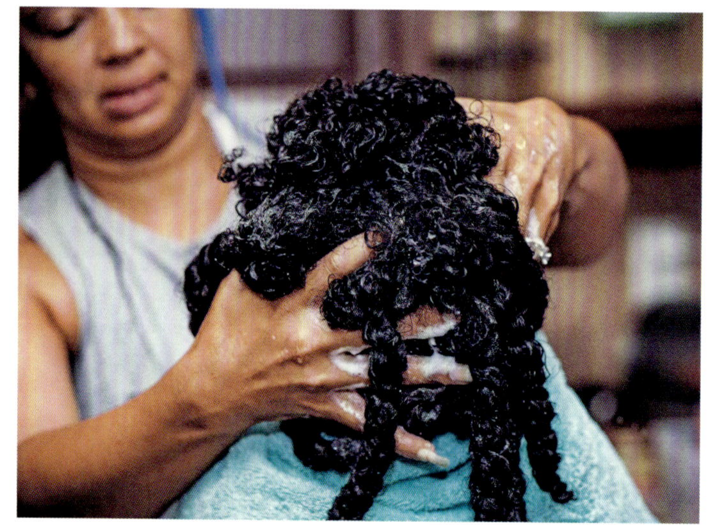

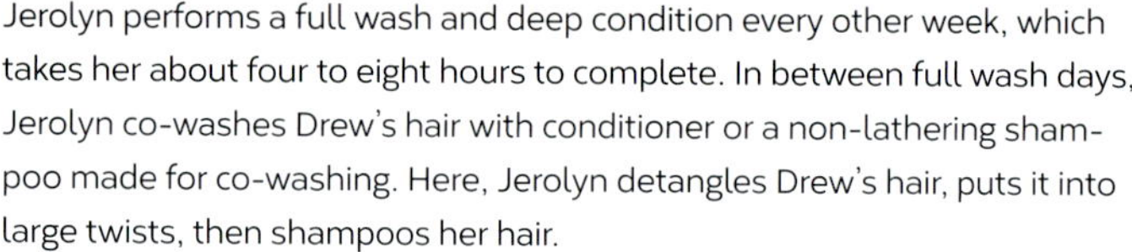

Jerolyn performs a full wash and deep condition every other week, which takes her about four to eight hours to complete. In between full wash days, Jerolyn co-washes Drew's hair with conditioner or a non-lathering shampoo made for co-washing. Here, Jerolyn detangles Drew's hair, puts it into large twists, then shampoos her hair.

Jerolyn found herself in a tug of war between relaxed and natural hair over the years. The desire for easier maintenance and the ability to wear short, straight styles has nudged her toward relaxed hair. However, the desire for healthy hair keeps calling her back. Overall, she has gone natural three times. The third time was in 2015, and she has been natural ever since. Ultimately, she has found that she loves and appreciates her natural texture much more than straight hair. Her goal is to pass on this same love and appreciation to her daughter, Drew.

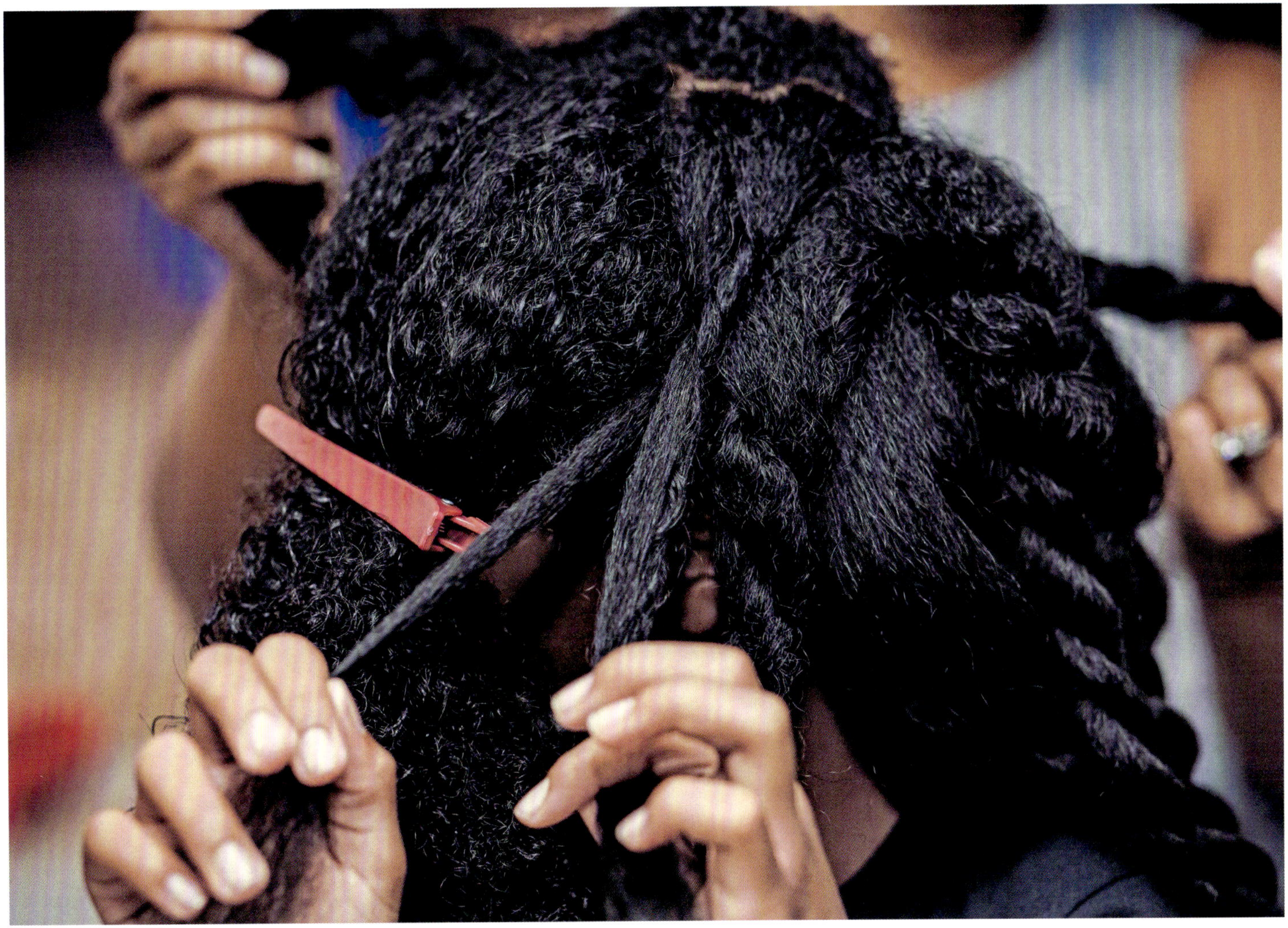

When I got a good look at Drew's gorgeous and bountiful head of hair, it was clear that Jerolyn's wash-day process would be quite the endeavor. But rather than communicating to Drew that her thick hair is a problem to be solved, Jerolyn invests hours into Drew's hair each wash day, teaching her the techniques that will help her maintain the health of her hair.

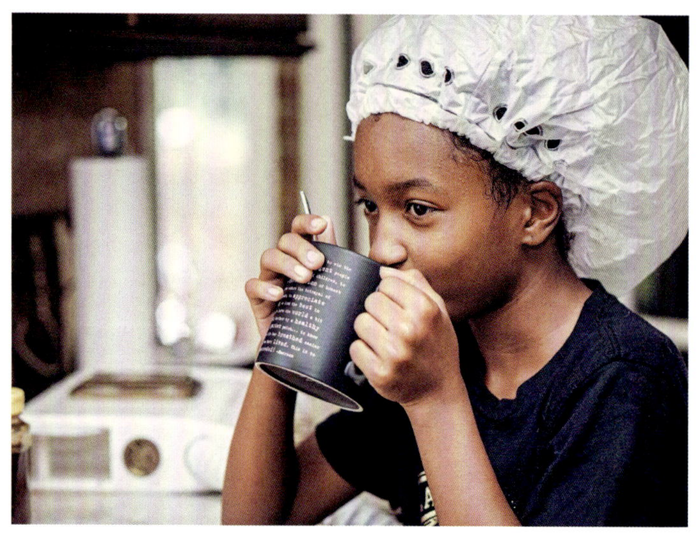
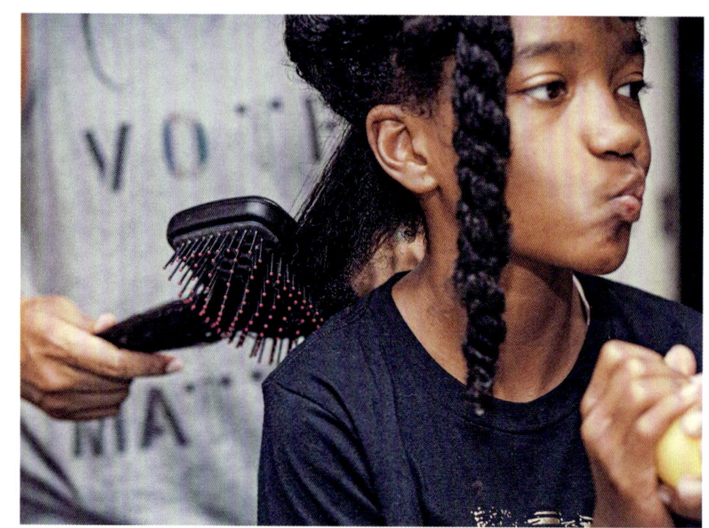
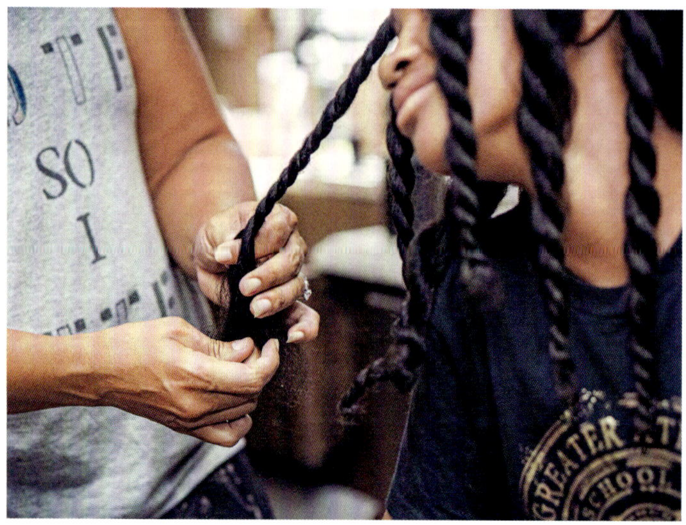
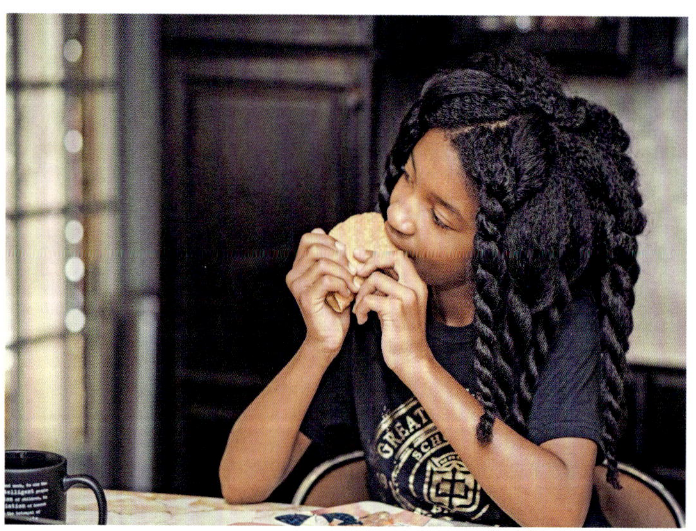

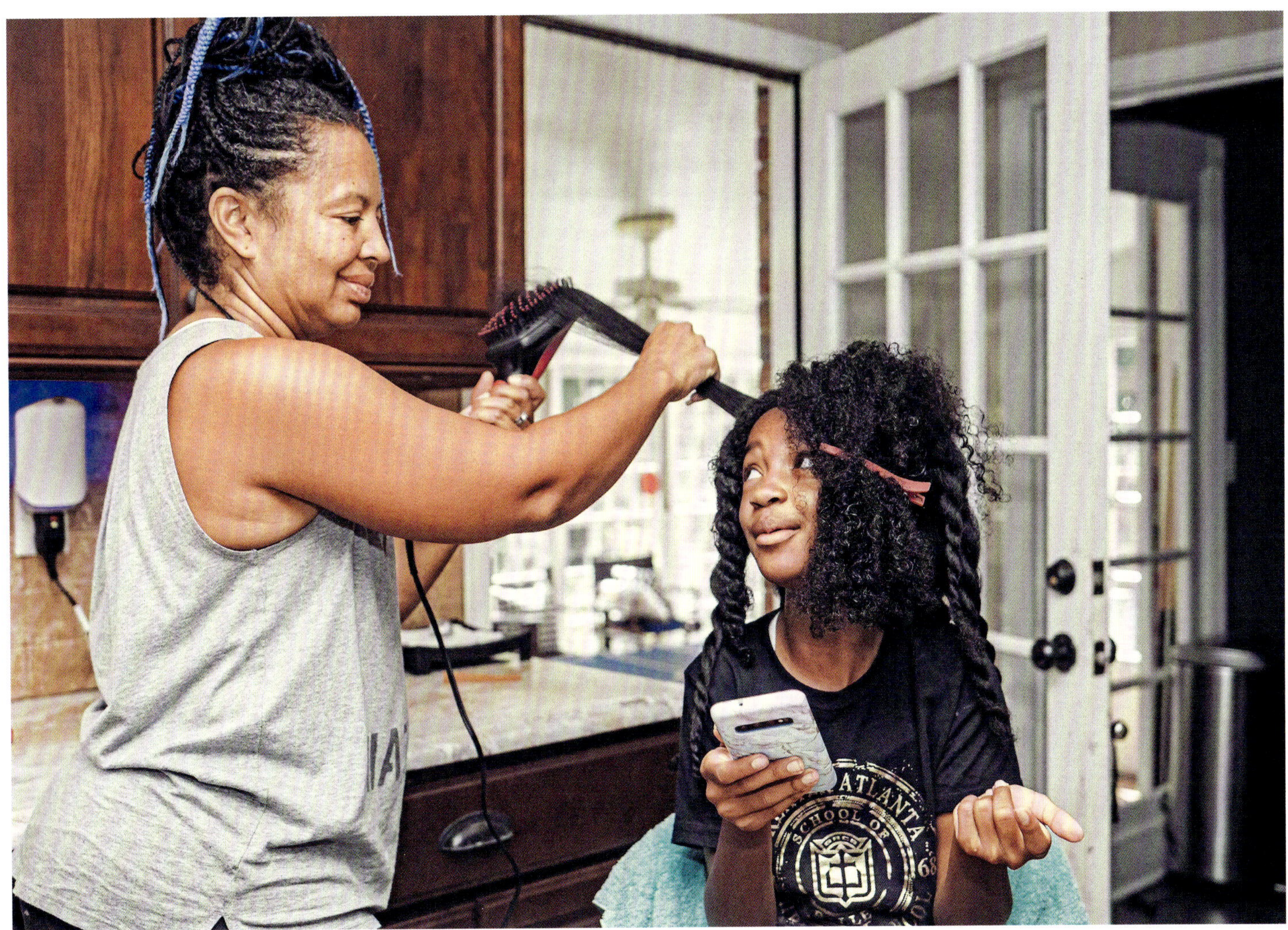

Opposite page, top left: After washing and detangling, Drew enjoys a cup of tea while she sits under the heating cap for her deep conditioning treatment. *Opposite page, top right and bottom left:* After rinsing, Jerolyn then blow dries Drew's hair and places it in large twists. *Opposite page, bottom right:* Then comes the most critical part—a taco break!

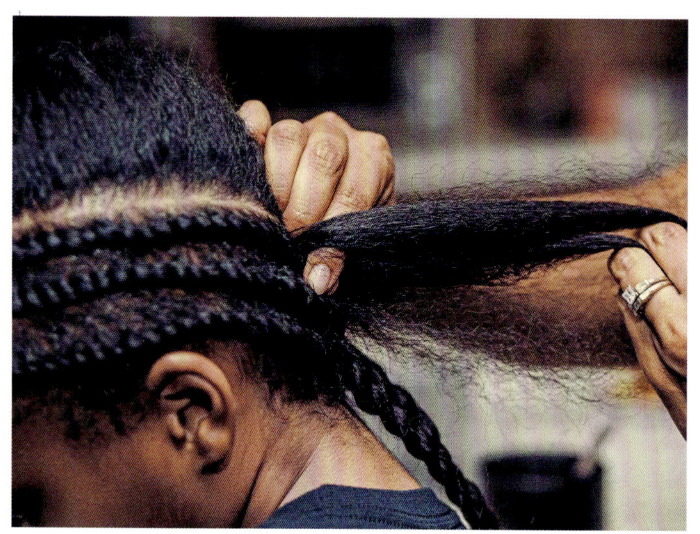 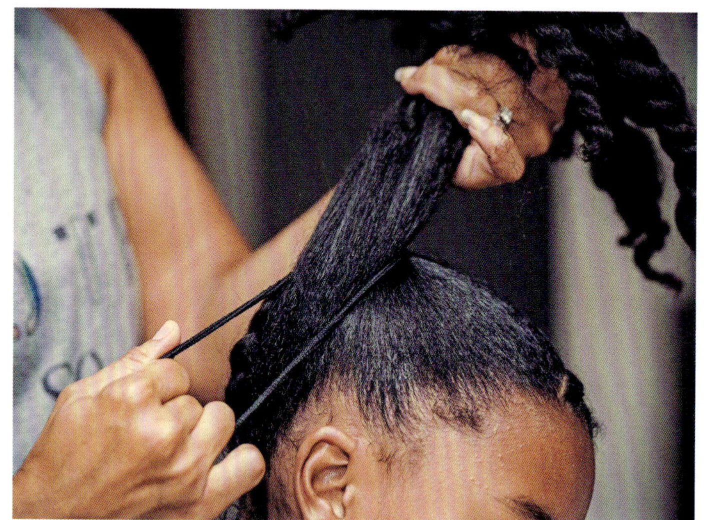

"I love that she loves her big hair and hope to help foster her growth and love for many years to come." —JEROLYN

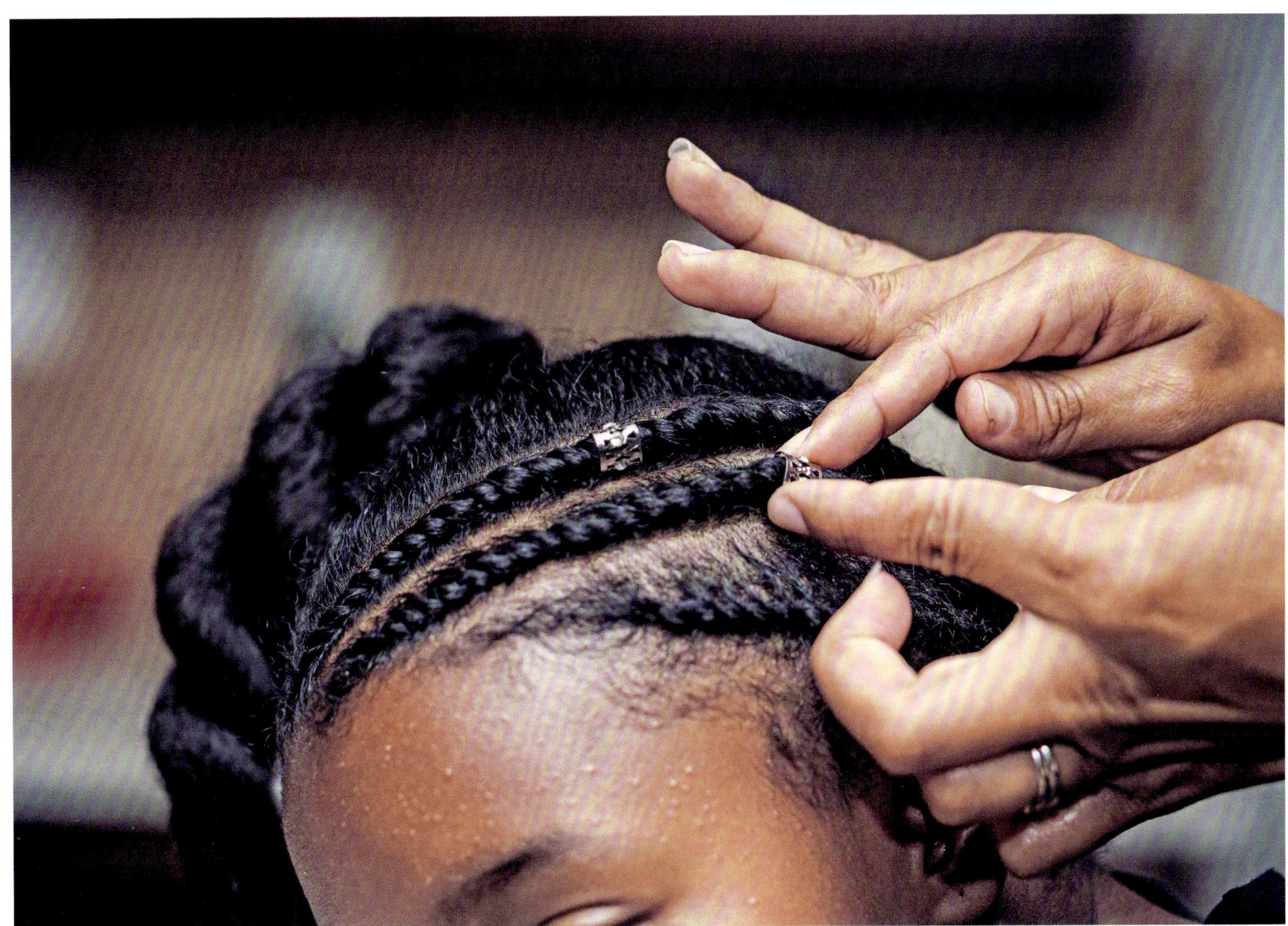

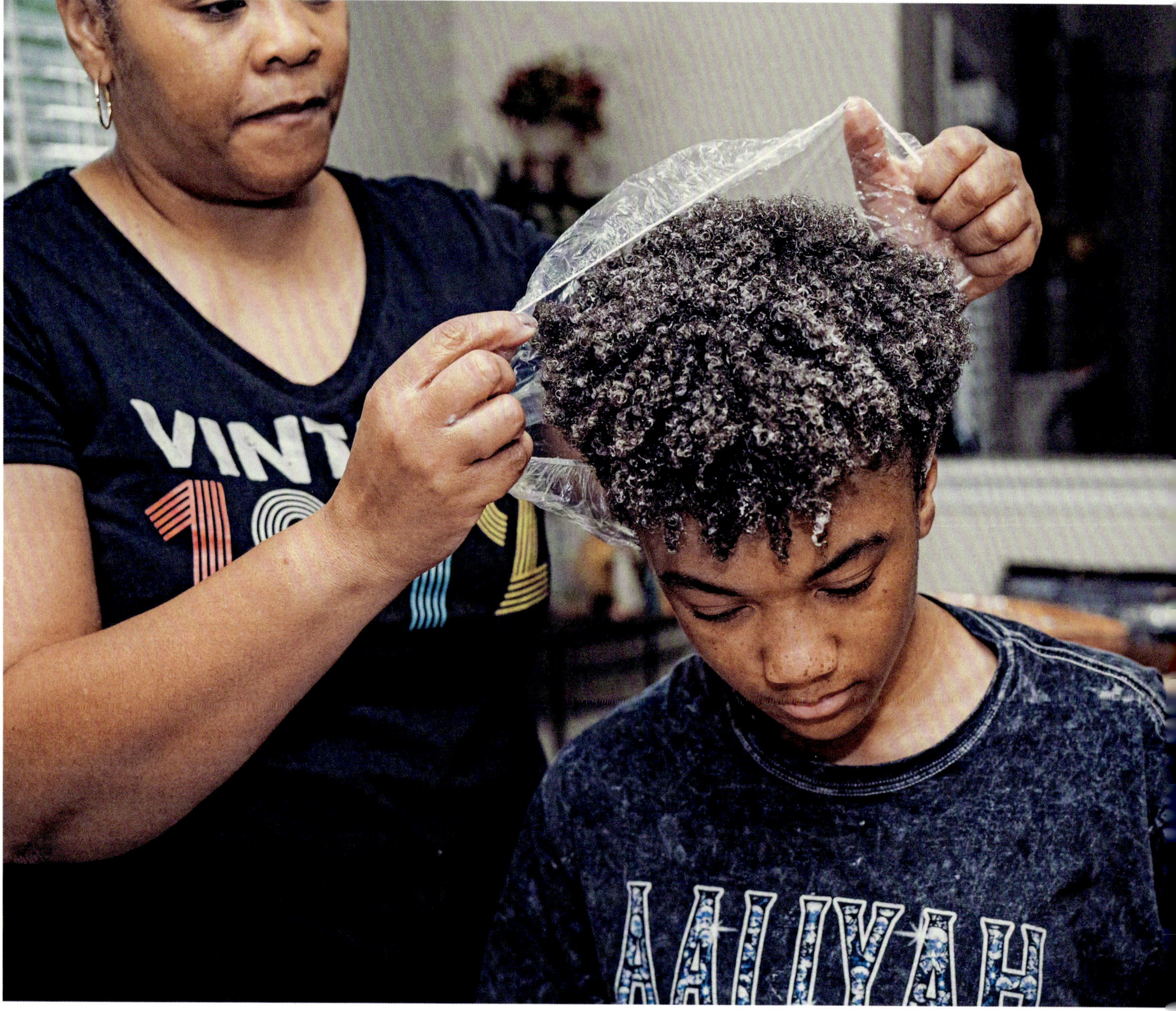

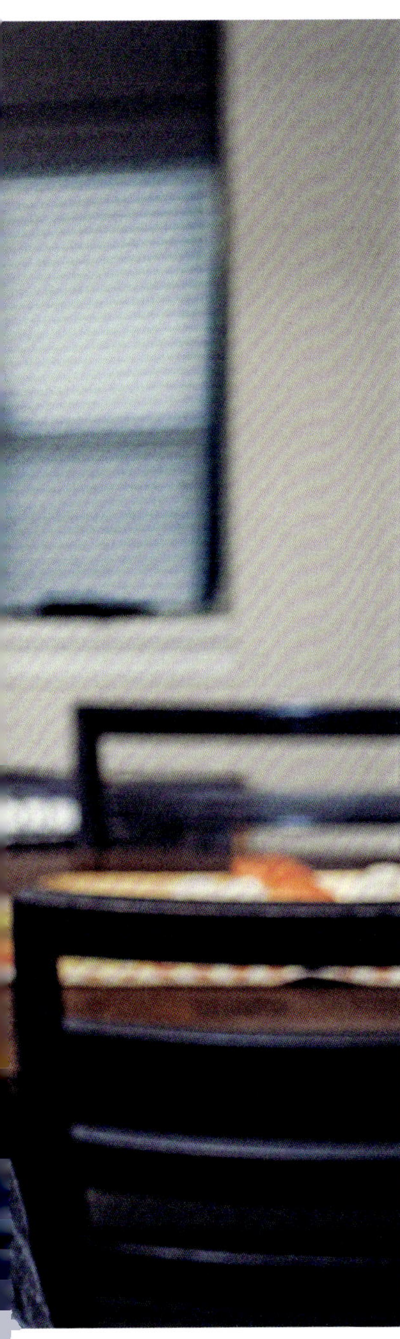

Trina & Zoē

WHILE every mother featured here desires to pass on natural hair pride to their children, this book would be incomplete if it only included children who are in love with their hair. Our world isn't there yet, so how can we expect them to be?

A significant number of the moms I've spoken to while creating this book reported that their daughters have struggled at some point with embracing their hair texture. Some of them began to question their hair texture as young as preschool. For my oldest daughter, Josie, it was kindergarten. She had only one White teacher, and she told me she wanted hair just like hers. Even though she had only ever seen me with natural hair, attended an all-Black school, and had several natural-haired aunties to look up to, it seemed as if this *one* White teacher and her flowing hair were enough to make her want something else. Of course, I understood then that it was more than just seeing this teacher's hair. It was also the countless other reminders in our world that straight hair is still favored over kinky hair.

When I asked moms if their daughters have ever expressed negative feelings toward their hair, I received the following responses:

"As she has gotten older, she has asked the question of why she can't have hair like Rapunzel's." —Vontressia

"She watches a lot of YouTube and a few years ago she wanted her hair straight like the girls she saw."—Montrell

"She sometimes wishes her hair was like the White girls." —Latricia

"Early in the school experience, she wanted her hair to be in a ponytail like others at her school." —Elisa

"At a very young age (maybe three years old) my older daughter went to a daycare where she was the only Black girl in her classroom. One day she came home and said she wanted yellow hair and flat bangs." —Dana

"Shrinkage gets to her a lot, and she expresses insecurity about her tight curls." —Cherise

"Growing up, both [of my] daughters wanted long, flowing, and fine hair—like their non-Black friends, especially when their exposure lacked diversity." —Tonya

"I believe that the extreme shrinkage bothers her because her hair appears shorter and it doesn't 'flow' like her peers. Additionally, we discovered through a Halloween costume that she loves wigs and sees that type of hair as beautiful." —Toni

"My daughters have mixed thoughts about their hair. There was [once a time when] one [of my daughters] shared that she wished her hair was straight and long." —Natolie

"Yes. Wanting it straight like [her] friends." —Jamia

At the end of the day, our children may still receive messages that contradict what we try to teach them about their hair. Movies, television, magazine covers, the kids at school, and for some, even elder family members, may provide alternate definitions of what "pretty" looks like. While children today are exposed to more positive images of natural hair in the media than older generations, completely removing problematic attitudes toward natural hair is going to take a bit more time.

While Trina has been natural since 1999, and loves her hair, her daughter, Zoē, is struggling to embrace hers. But Trina hopes to teach Zoē to love her hair texture and all that it is capable of, as well as to understand that she is beautiful no matter what her hair looks like.

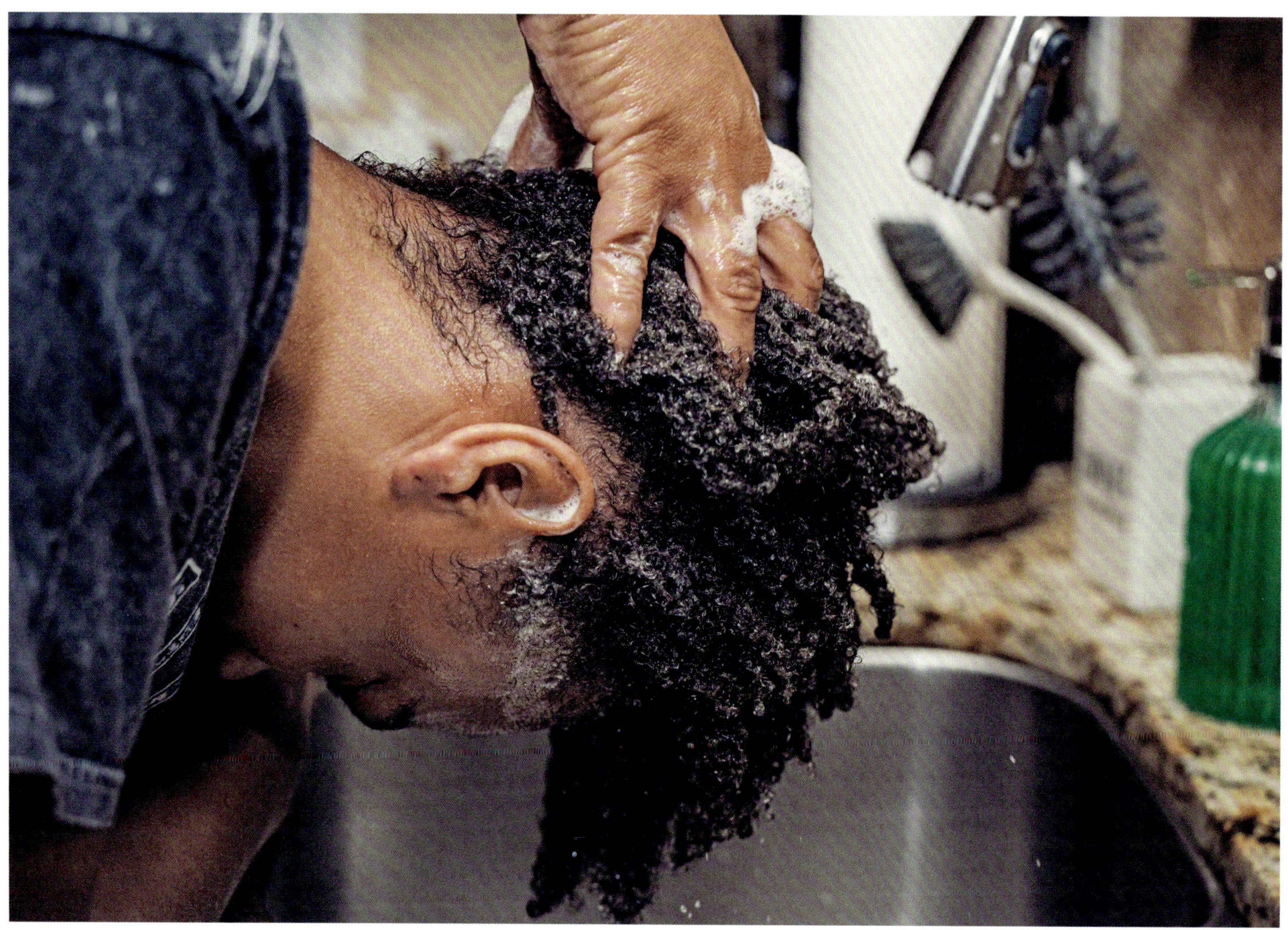

For Trina and Zoē, wash day takes places every two weeks and lasts about an hour and a half unless intricate styling is involved. *Page 194, top left:* After washing, Trina applies deep conditioner and a heating cap.

Page 194, bottom left and bottom right: After rinsing, Trina blow dries Zoē's hair. *Page 195:* Zoē enjoys wearing braids, so Trina has learned how to do them herself.

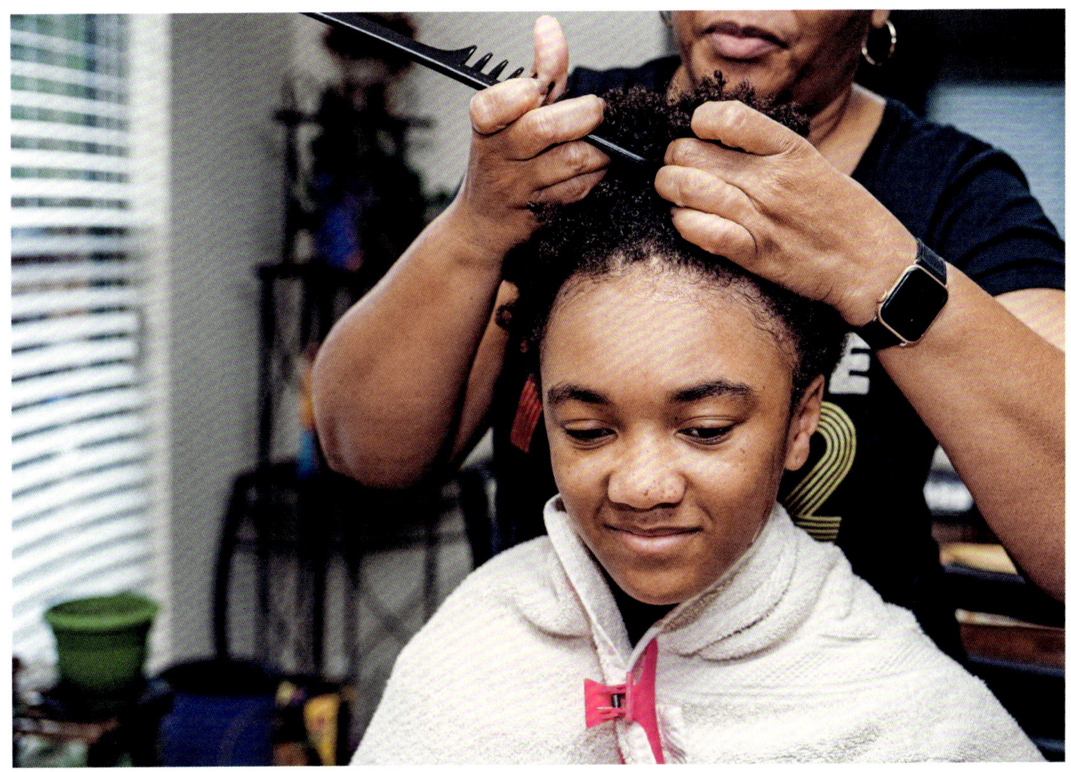

"Dear Zoē, I hope that when you open this book, you will feel nothing but pride. I hope that you will connect with at least one other beautiful girl pictured alongside of you. I hope the diversity of skin tones, textures, lengths, and styles will encourage you, and that you will see there is no one way your hair should be. Beauty exists in every single, kink, coil, and curl in this book, including yours." —TOMESHA

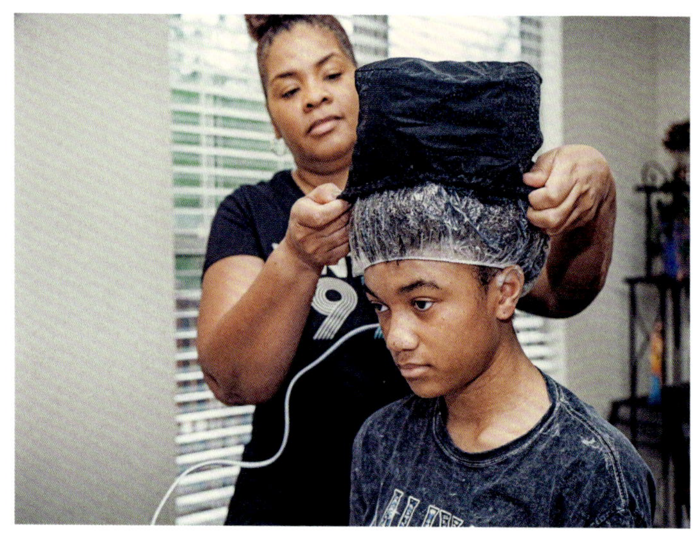
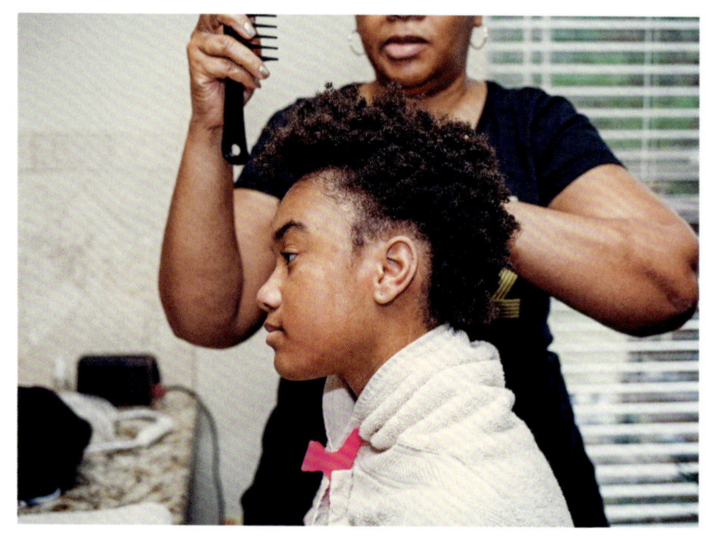
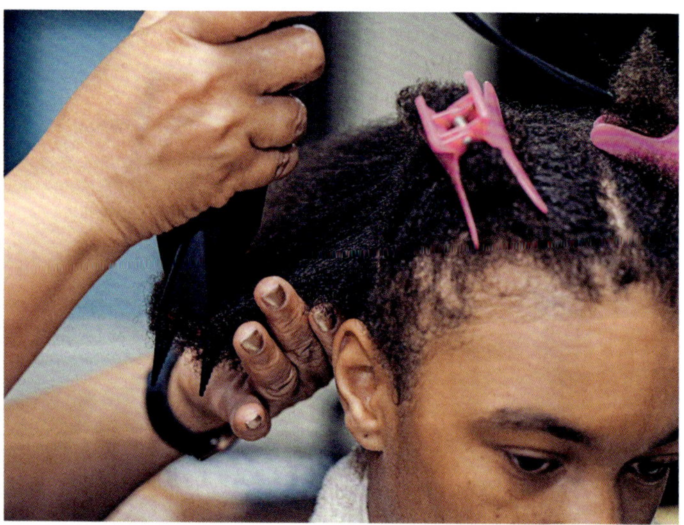
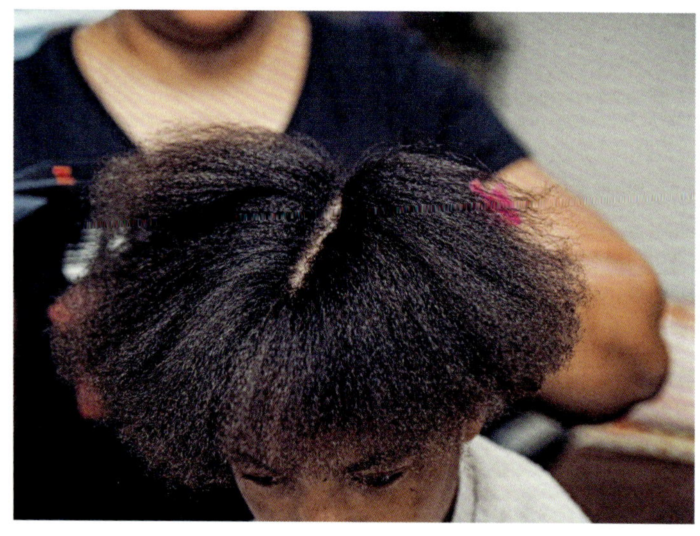

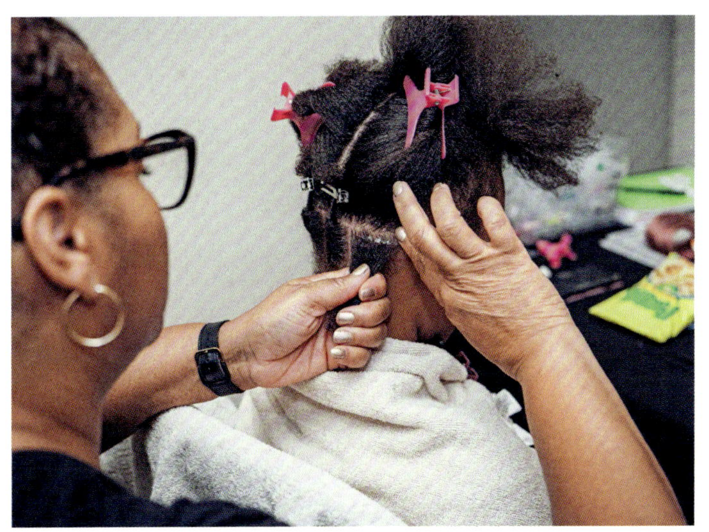
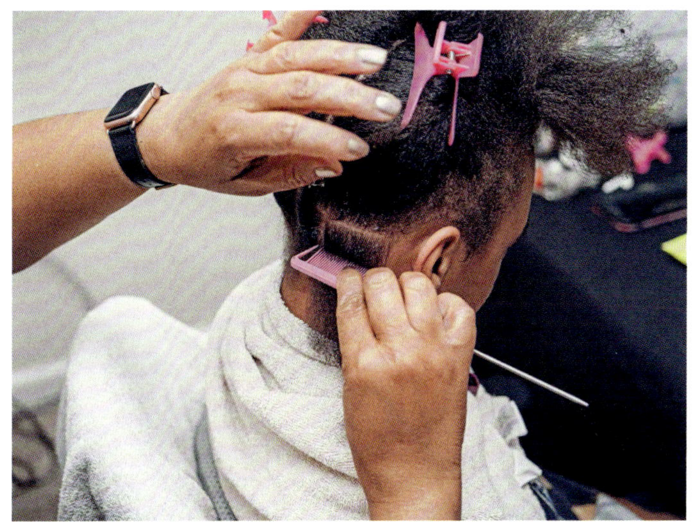
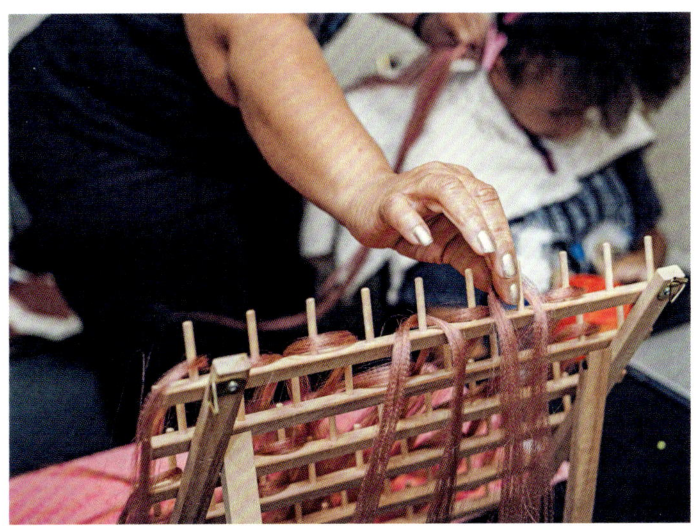
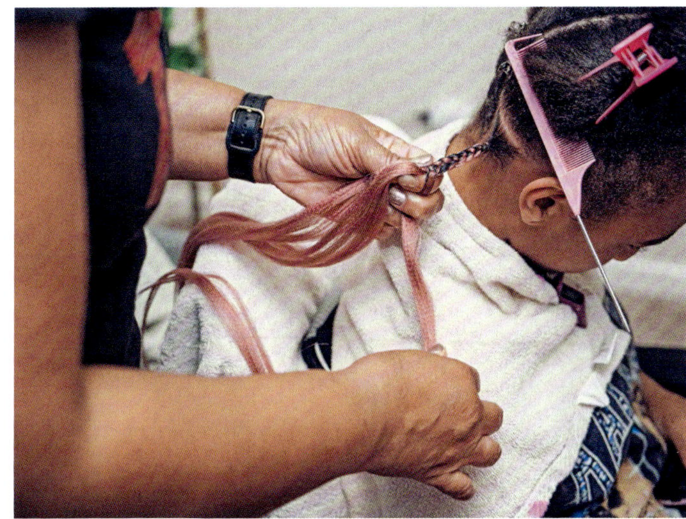

Darnita, Moriah & Maison

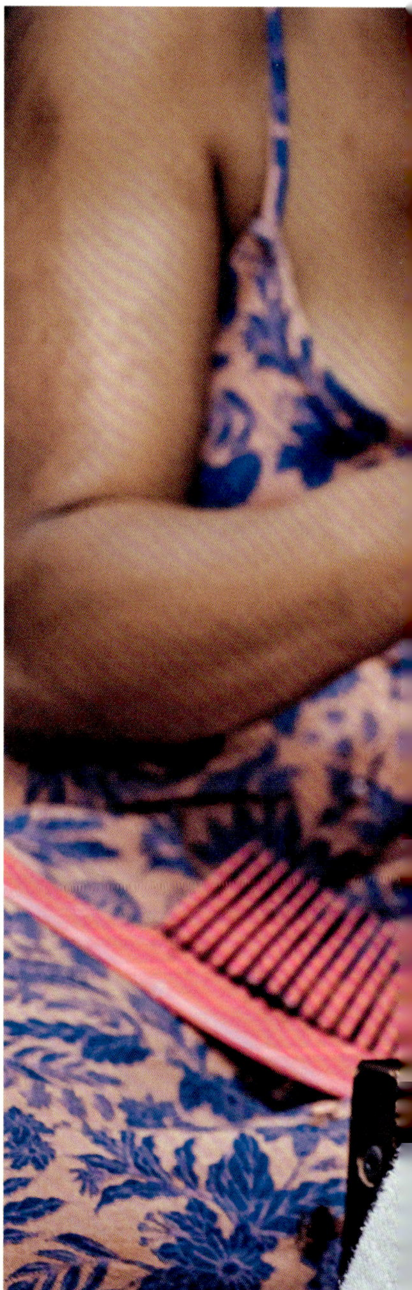

WHILE it may look staged, I promise I did not tell sweet little Moriah to read *Happy Hair*, by Mechal Renee Roe,[47] and *I Love My Hair!*, by Natasha Anastasia Tarpley, during her wash-day shoot.[48] She simply thought they were appropriate reading materials under the circumstances. In fact, according to Darnita, she routinely pulls these books out during wash day in order to find hairstyle inspiration. It was the absolute most adorable experience listening to her read her book while watching her mom care for her hair. After reading a line from *I Love My Hair!*, when the main character, Keyana, describes the discomfort that

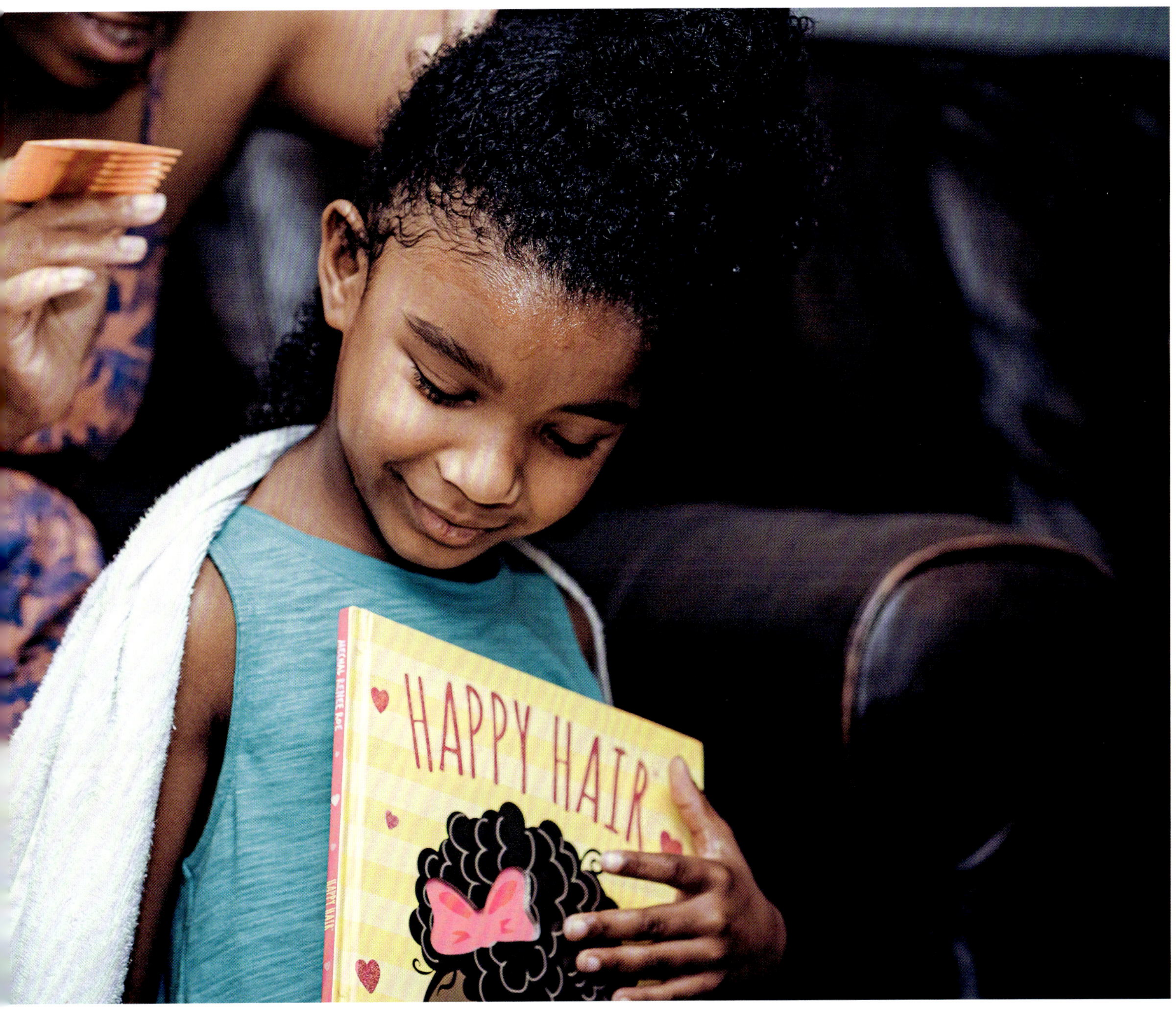
MEGHAN DEREK McE
HAPPY HAIR
HAPPY HAIR

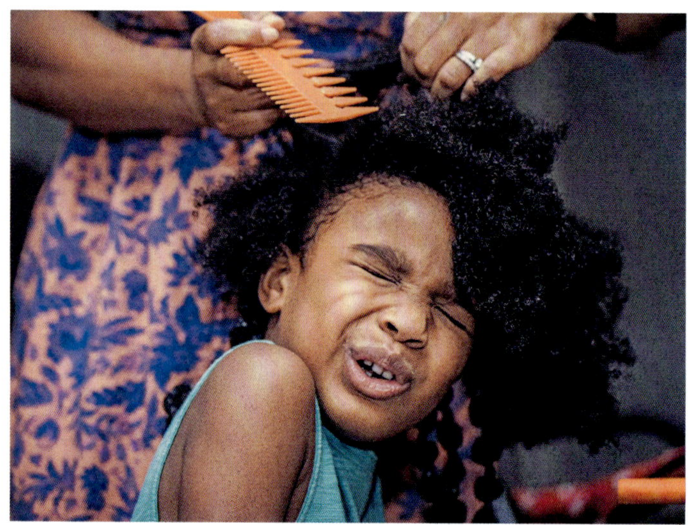

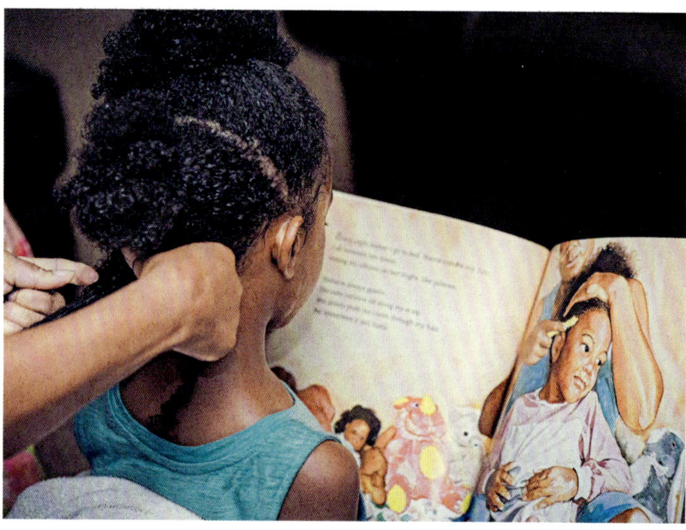

Moriah put on a brave face for our shoot, but according to Darnita, tears are customary on wash day. But Moriah isn't alone. Some aspects of wash day can be uncomfortable, no matter how hard we try to avoid it. Moriah has

found that being able to identify with the characters in her books helps her get through the process.

sometimes accompanies getting her hair detangled by her mother, Moriah stated, "Now that's me!"[49] This was a powerful example of what it's like for a Black girl to see herself represented. It really does matter.

Having experienced one too many negative comments about her natural hair, Darnita understands the importance of surrounding her children with positive imagery of natural hair. Darnita returned to natural in the mid-2000s; she was pregnant with her first child, Maison, and wanted to embrace a more holistic lifestyle. Currently, she even has her own natural supplement business. But the road to figuring out how to care for and style her natural hair was riddled with comments like, "What are you trying to do?" and "She just doesn't care how her hair looks." Rude. But Darnita understood that these comments came largely from people who were conditioned to believe Black women needed to have relaxed hair in order to be deemed acceptable. Sadly, too many of us have fit this description at one time or another. Oh, how we all could have benefited from Moriah's books while growing up.

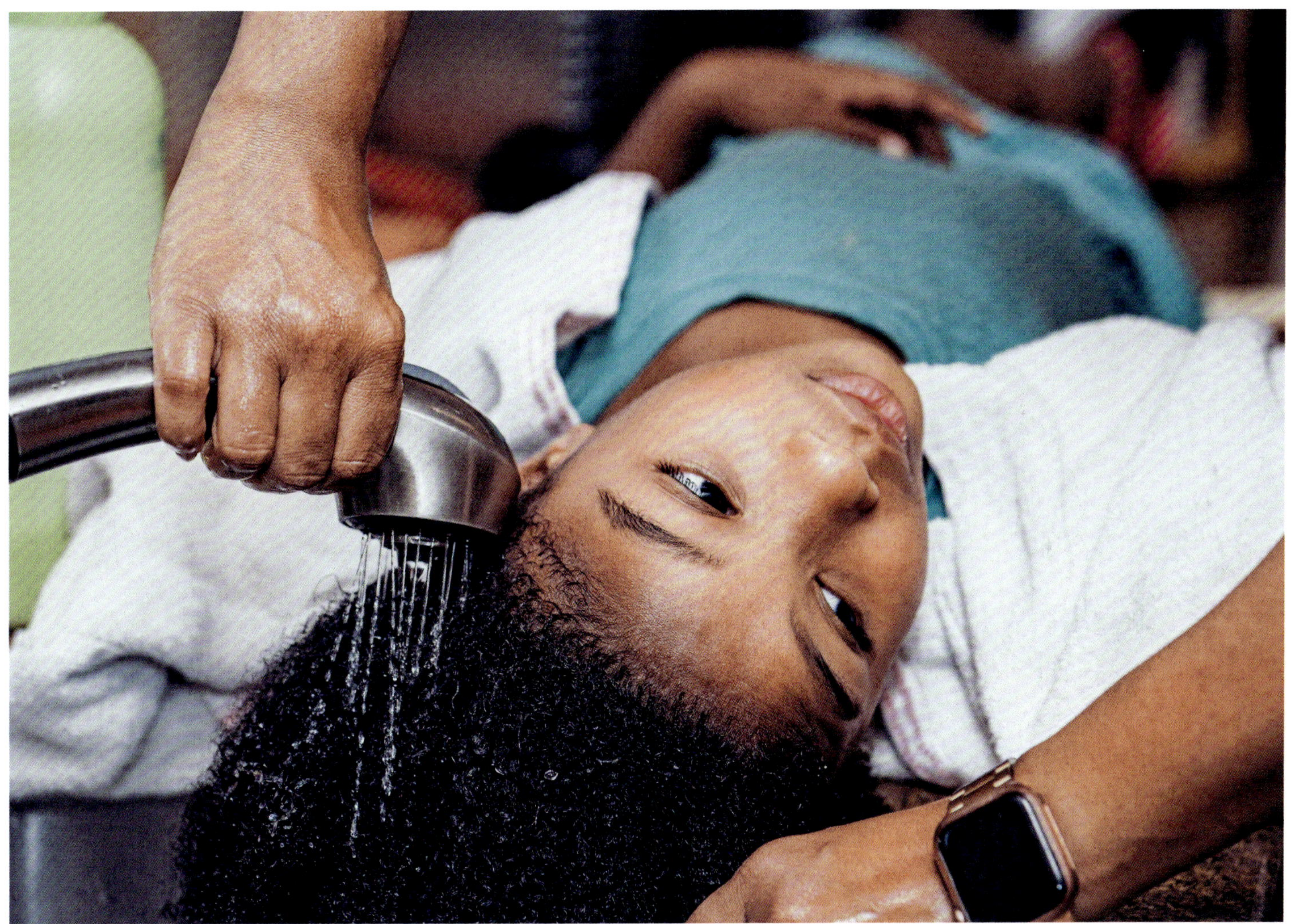

Darnita has wash day with Moriah about one to two times per month. The entire process takes about twenty-four hours because Darnita applies a pre-shampoo conditioner the night before.

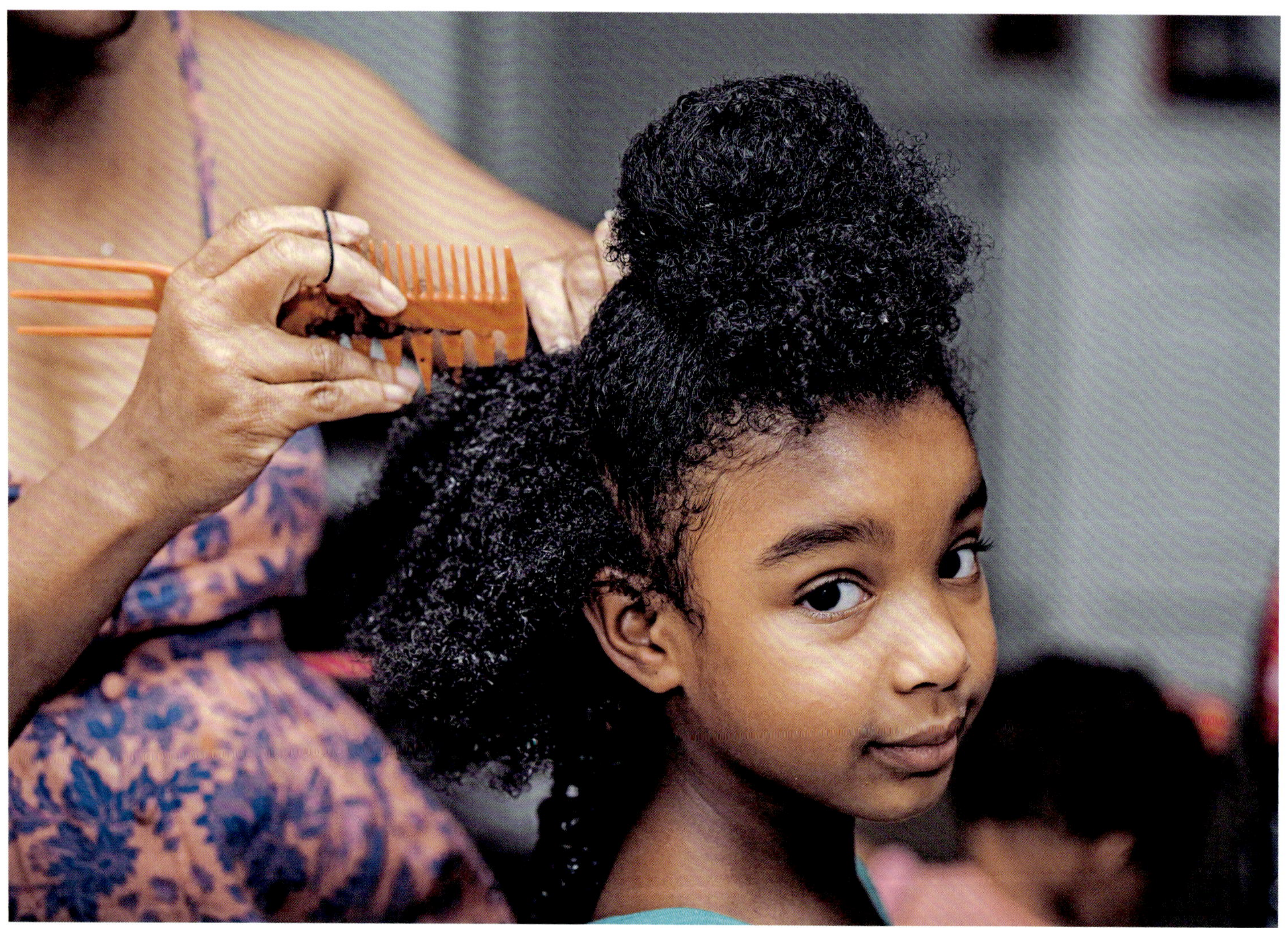

Opposite page, top right and bottom right: On the day of our shoot, Darnita's friend, Gabrielle, stopped by for a visit. Gabrielle's daughter, Lightning, and Moriah watch a show on Darnita's phone while Moriah gets her hair styled. *Opposite page, bottom left:* When the detangling gets intense, Darnita comforts Moriah.

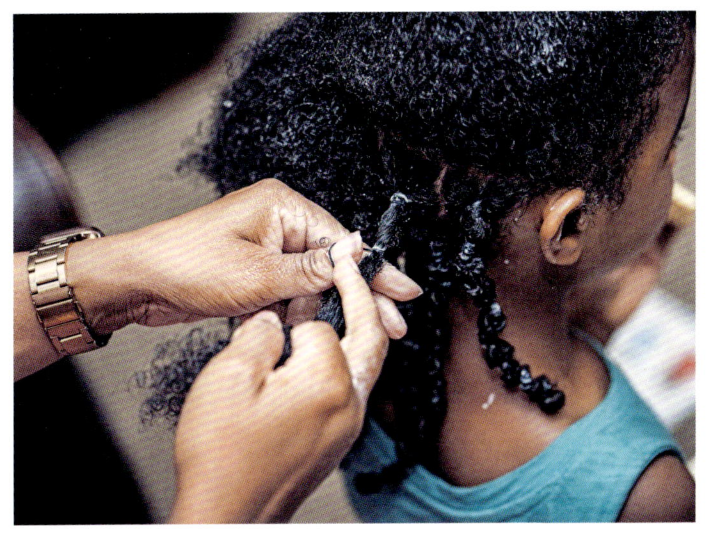 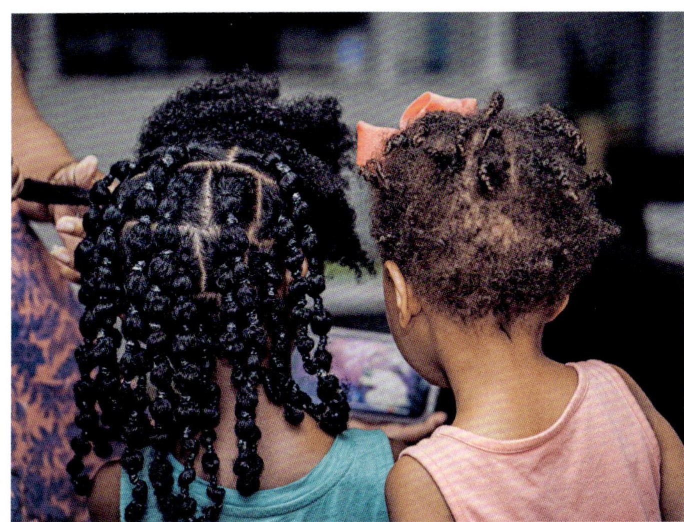
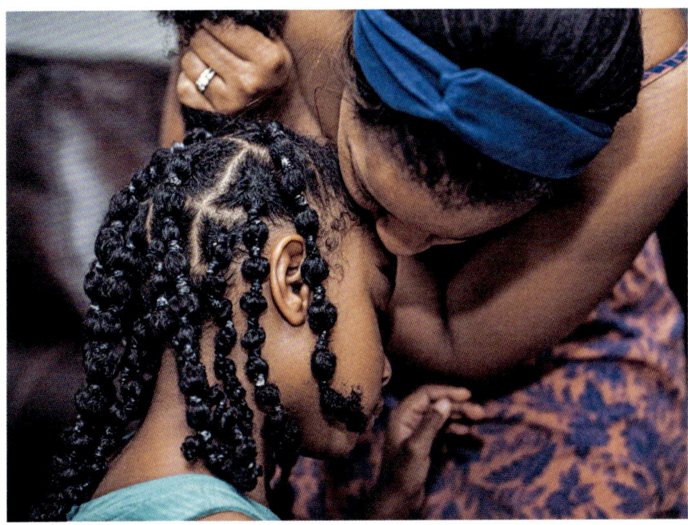 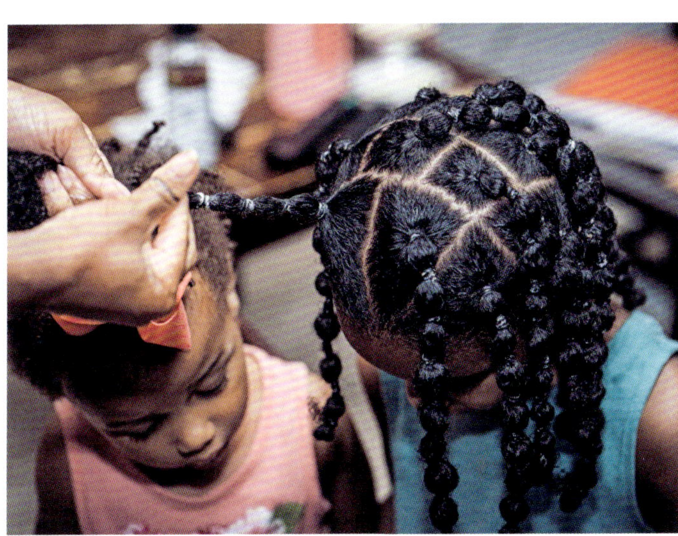

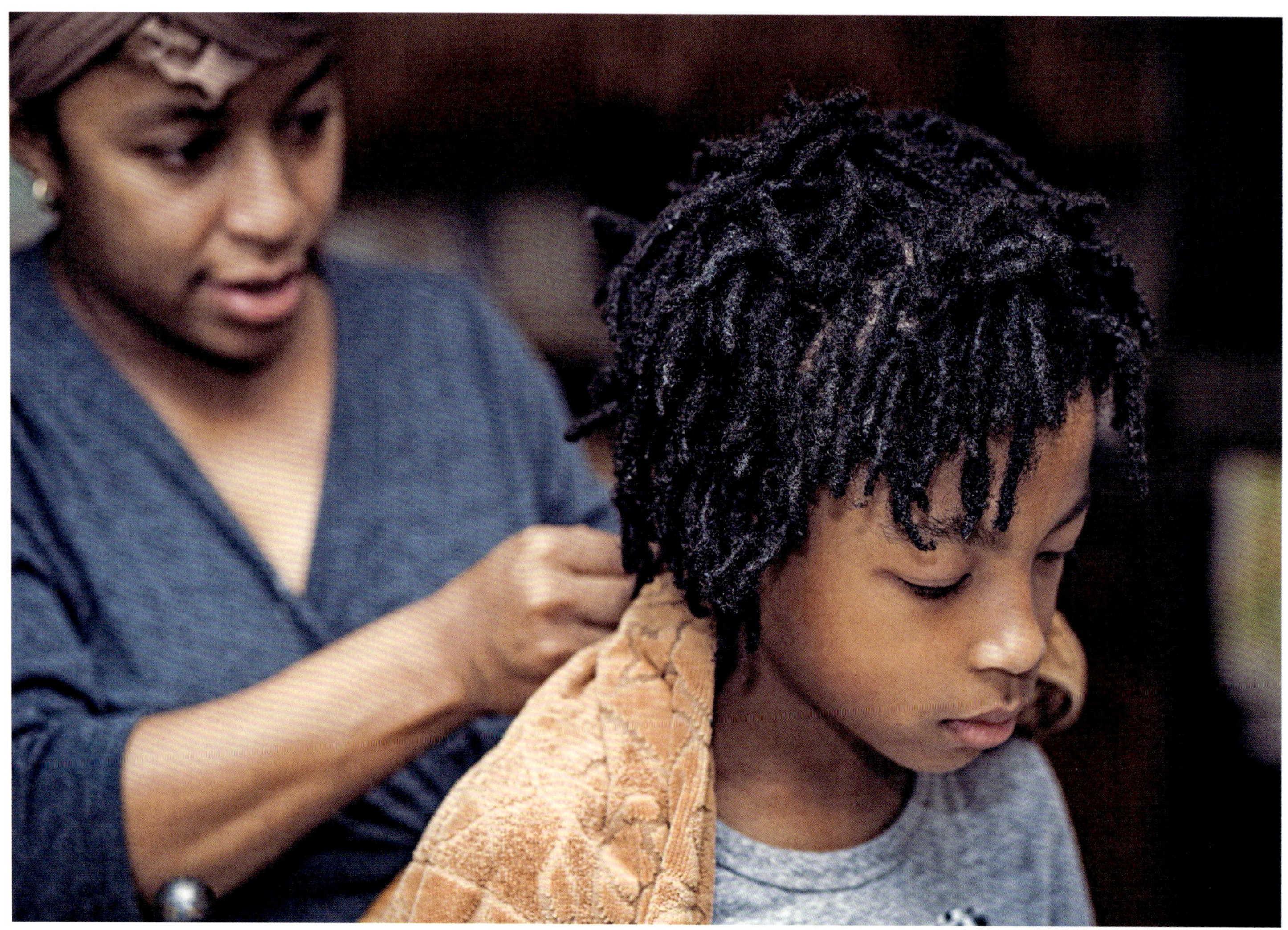

Darnita does not typically do Moriah's and Maison's hair on the same day, so I made two separate visits to capture both wash days. Wash day for Maison includes washing and palm rolling to maintain his locs.

Opposite page, bottom right: During a wash day break, Maison helps feed his baby brother.

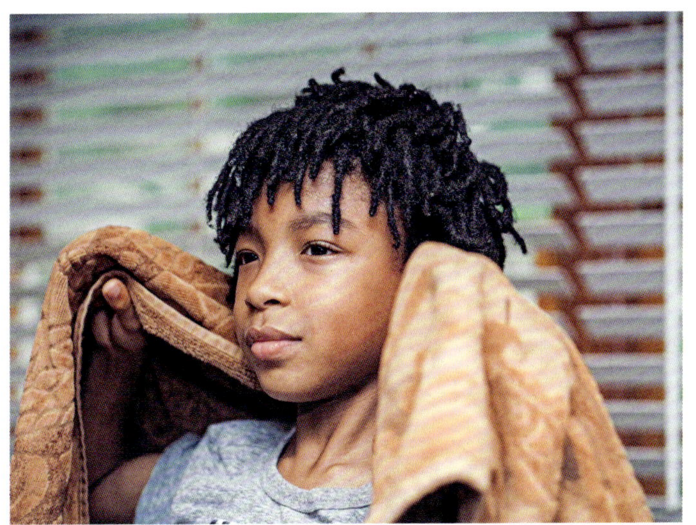
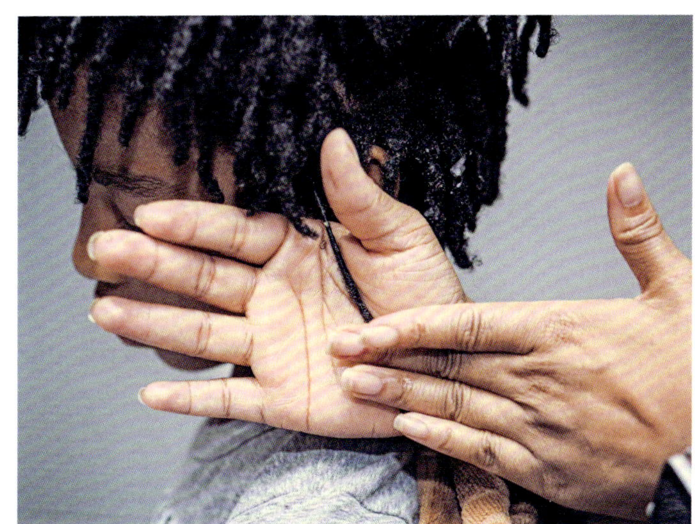
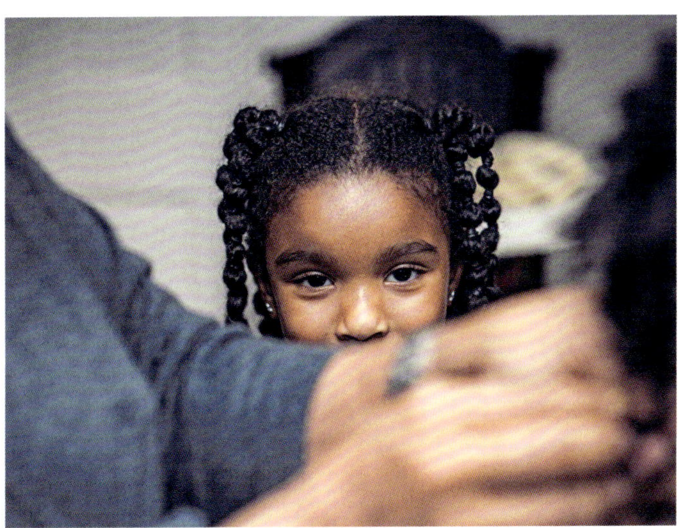
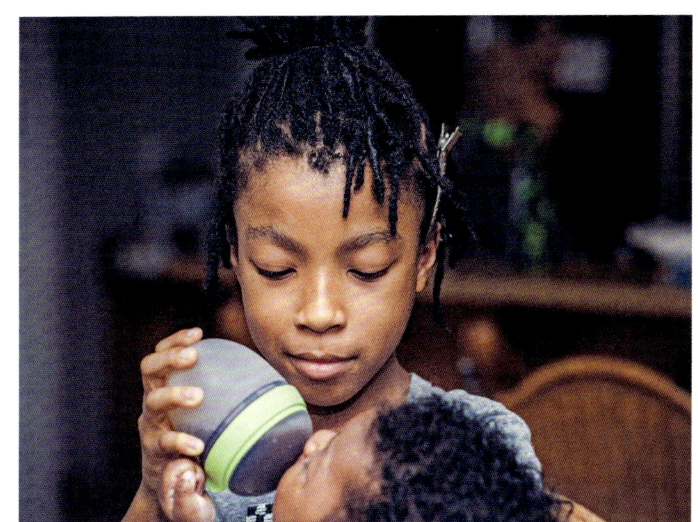

Jasmine & Sarai

". . . this journey has taught me to love myself
for who and how God created me."

GOING NATURAL isn't always hard. It is not always met
with resistance from family, friends, and coworkers. There is
not always an internal struggle with how the texture looks,
feels, or behaves. Sometimes, it's just easy.

Jasmine decided to go natural out of curiosity. When
she was seventeen years old, she realized she had no idea
what her real hair looked like. Perms were the norm. They
were all she knew. And like many of us, she assumed that all
little Black girls shared a common intimate knowledge of the
tingle of relaxers. It was just what Black girls did. Right? But
she wanted to know what life would be like without perms.

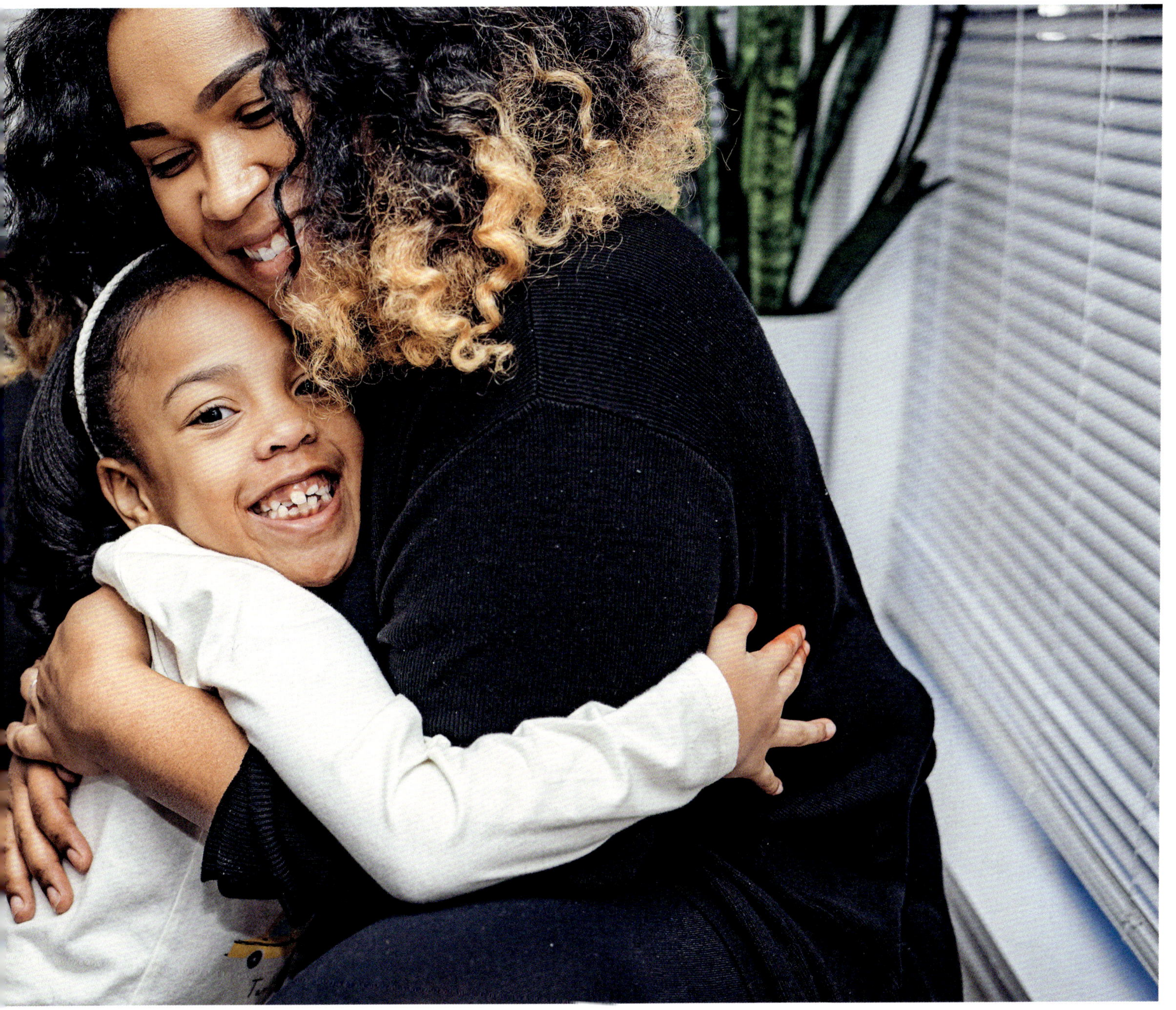

When Jasmine met her natural hair for the first time in 2007, it was love at first sight. She did the big chop and immediately fell in love with her curls. She grew more and more in love as her hair continued to grow and thrive. And given that many in her circle and family were already natural, or desired to go natural, she was met with positivity, acceptance, and encouragement.

I want to point out a few things about Jasmine's story. First and foremost, Jasmine loved her natural hair texture from the start. For many women, the toughest part is the internal struggle to love what we have been told is unlovable. Second, Jasmine had a natural hair–positive community that encouraged her on her journey. Unfortunately, too many women have the opposite experience. But thankfully, many of us are creating a natural hair–positive community for our children. Third, I think Jasmine's age, thirty-two, plays a role as well. Natural hair attitudes tend to differ from generation to generation. Indeed, the "Good Hair" study found that millennial naturalistas have more positive attitudes toward textured hair than women from other generations.[50] I'd guess that younger generations, especially those coming of age during the natural hair movement of the late 2000s, have grown up seeing more positive images of natural hair. Hopefully, it will only get better from here.

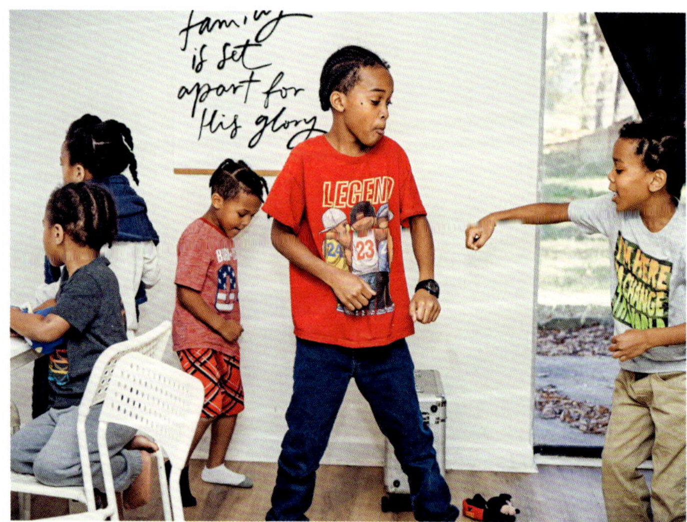

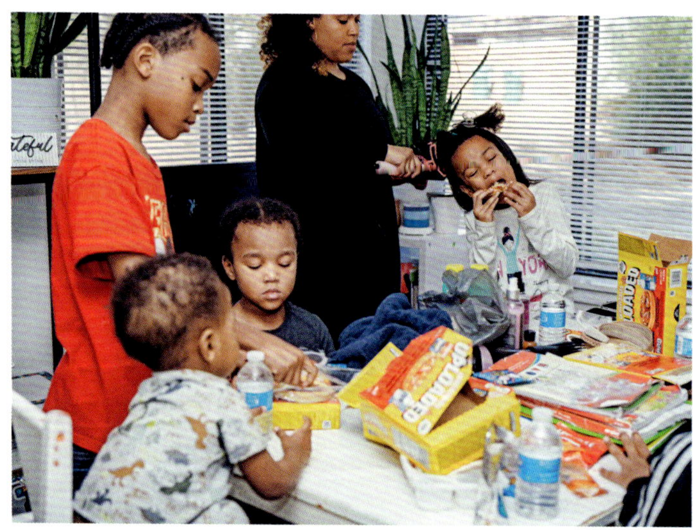

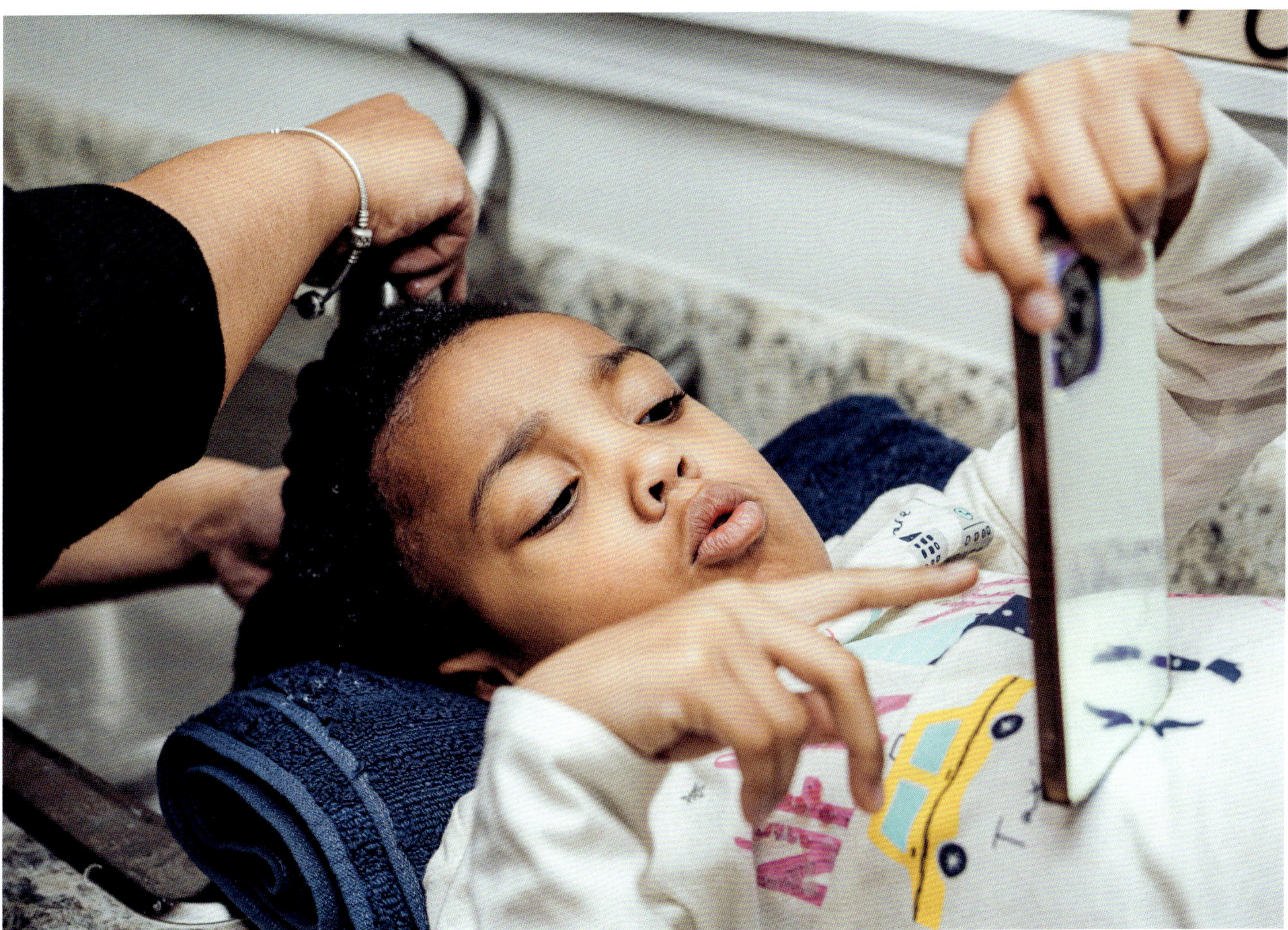

When I arrived at Jasmine's home on a Monday morning, she was in the middle of making breakfast for her six children while the five older children worked on homeschool lessons in the next room.

Opposite page, left: Later, Sarai's brothers took a dance break from their homeschool lessons. *Opposite page, right:* At lunchtime, the kids gathered to eat while Jasmine continued doing Sarai's hair.

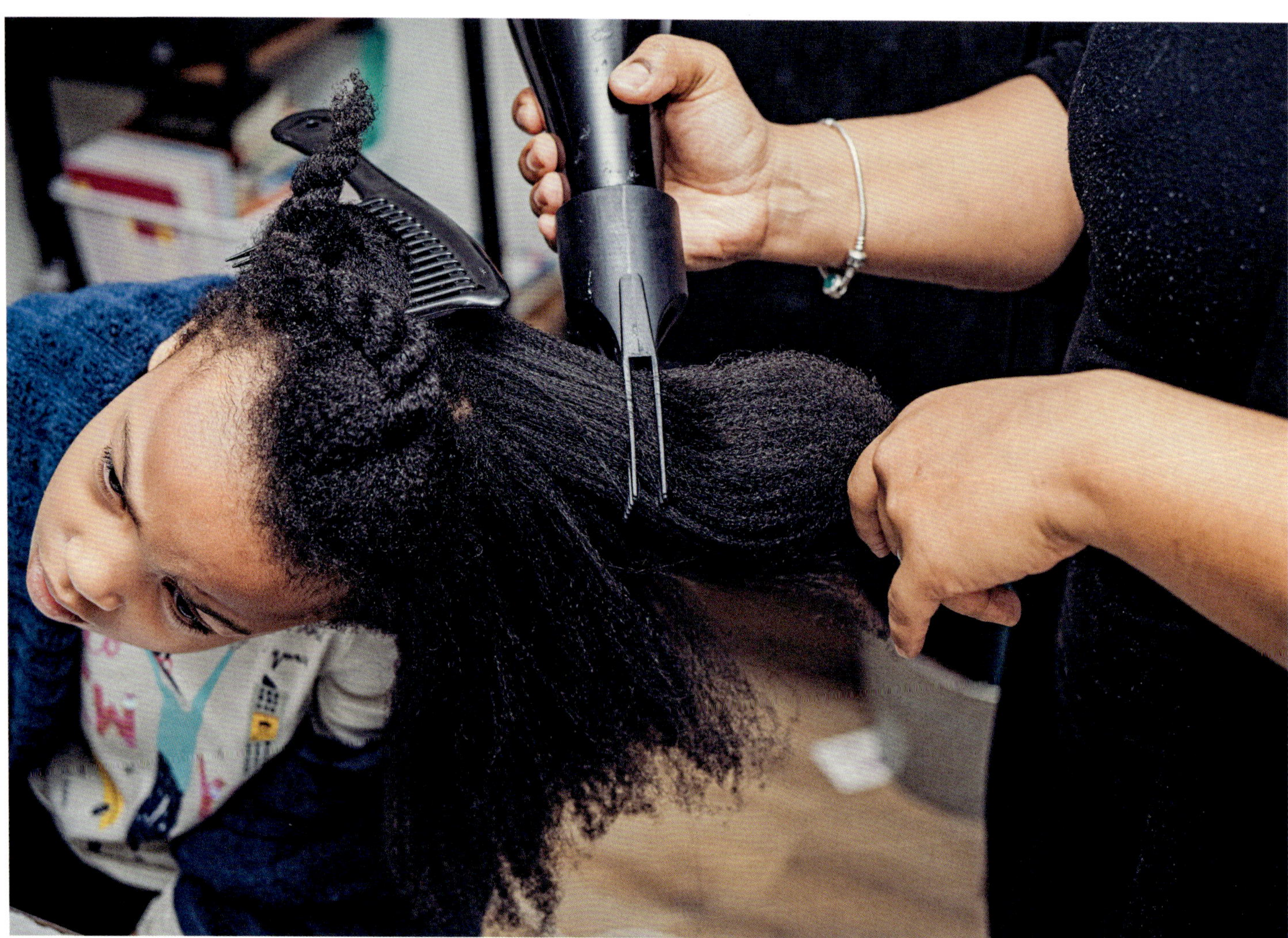

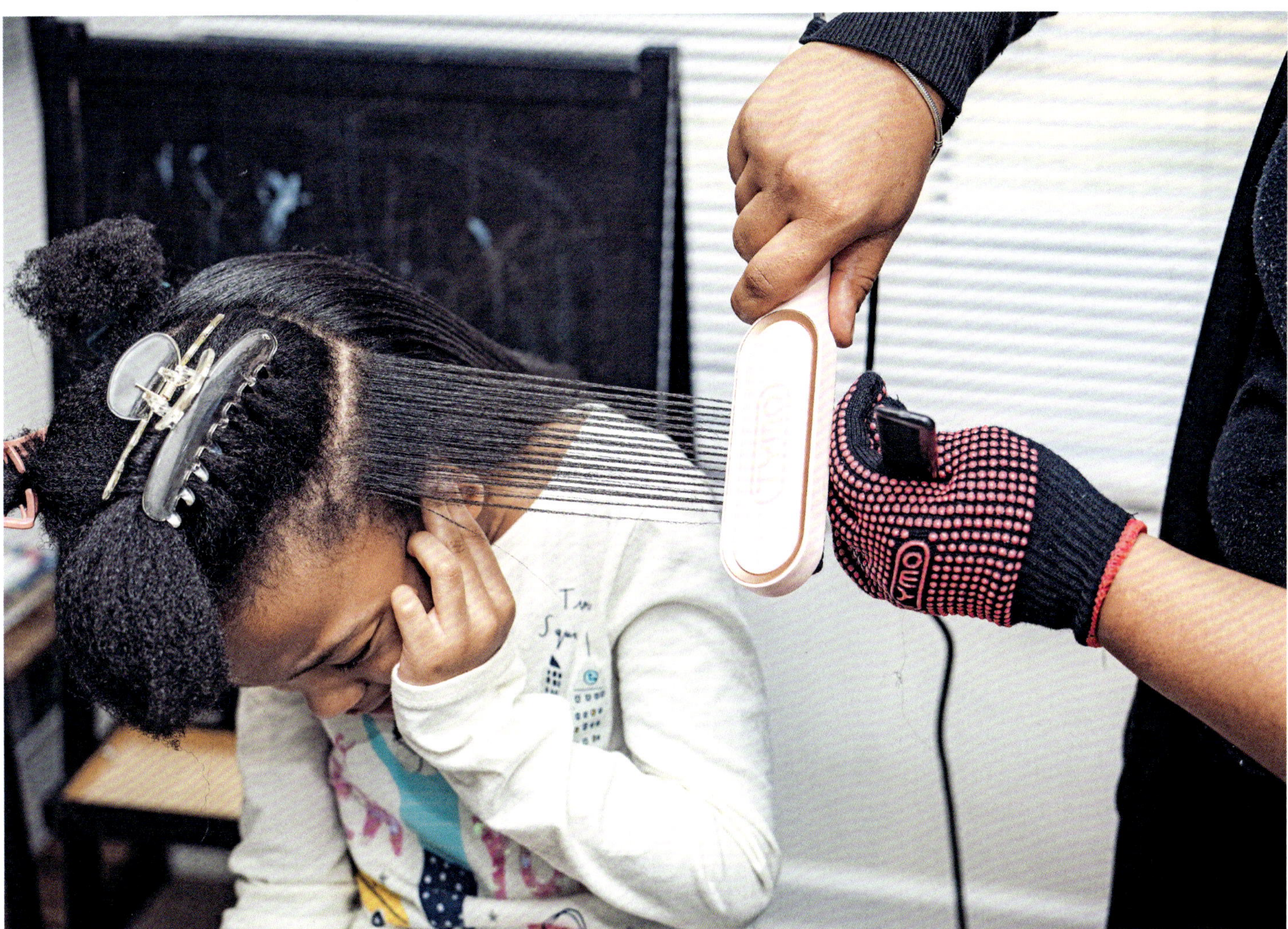

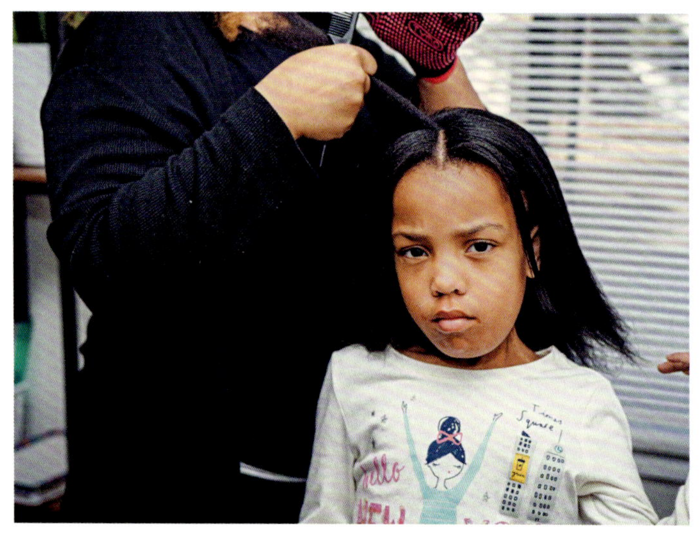
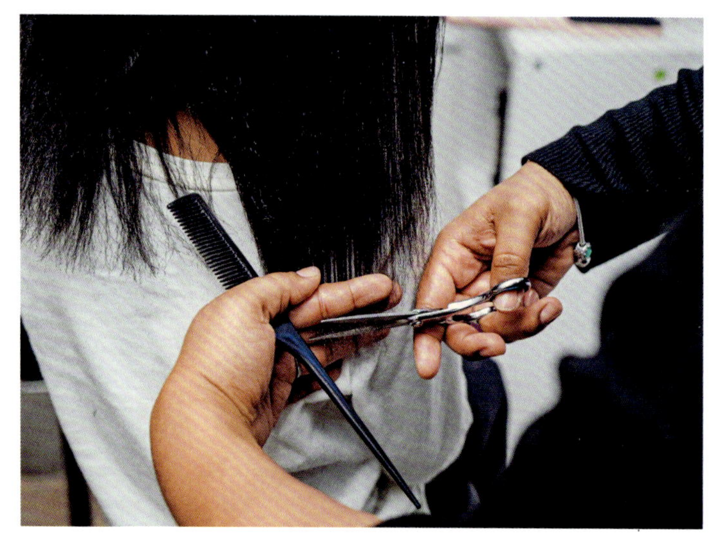
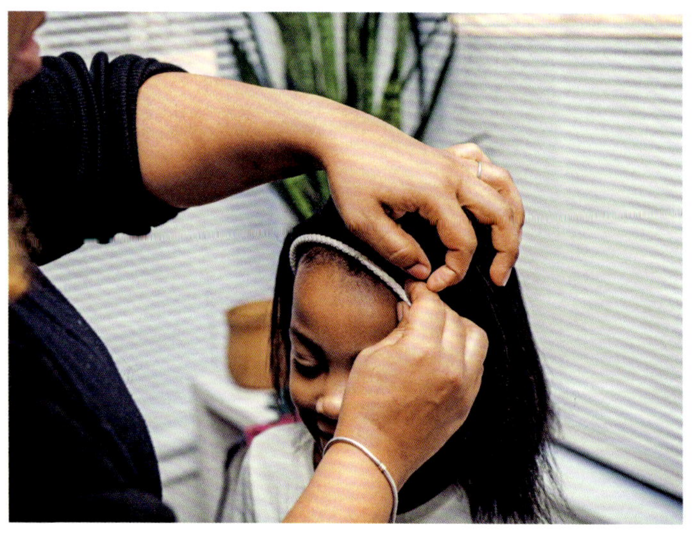
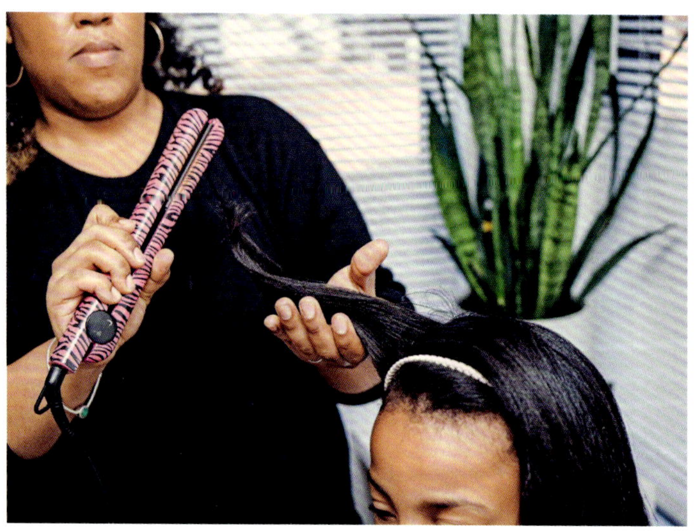

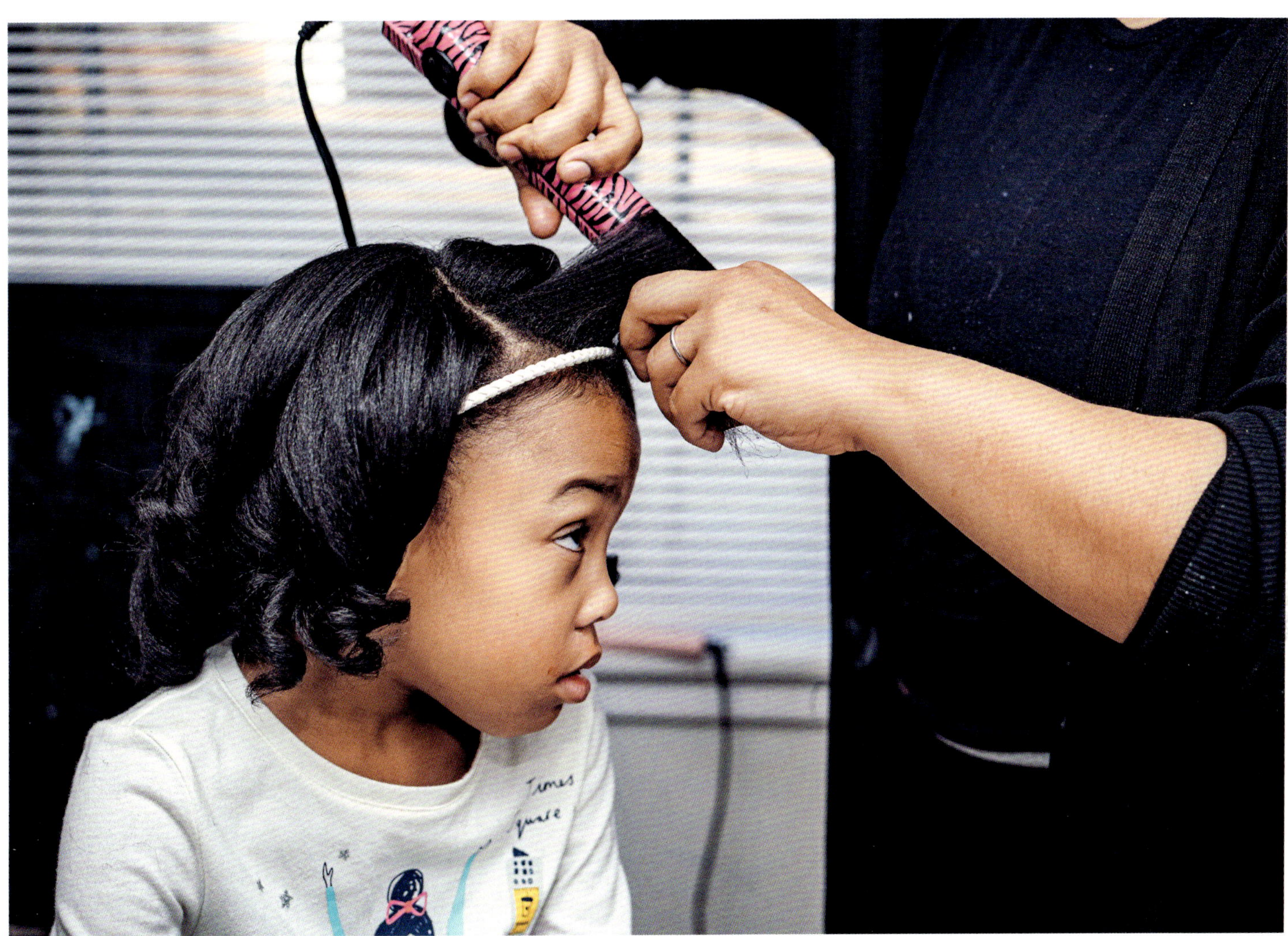

"My daughter loves her hair. I've given her the freedom to choose her hairstyles on wash day. She loves the versatility of wearing braids, puffs, twists, presses, and all types of new styles." —JASMINE

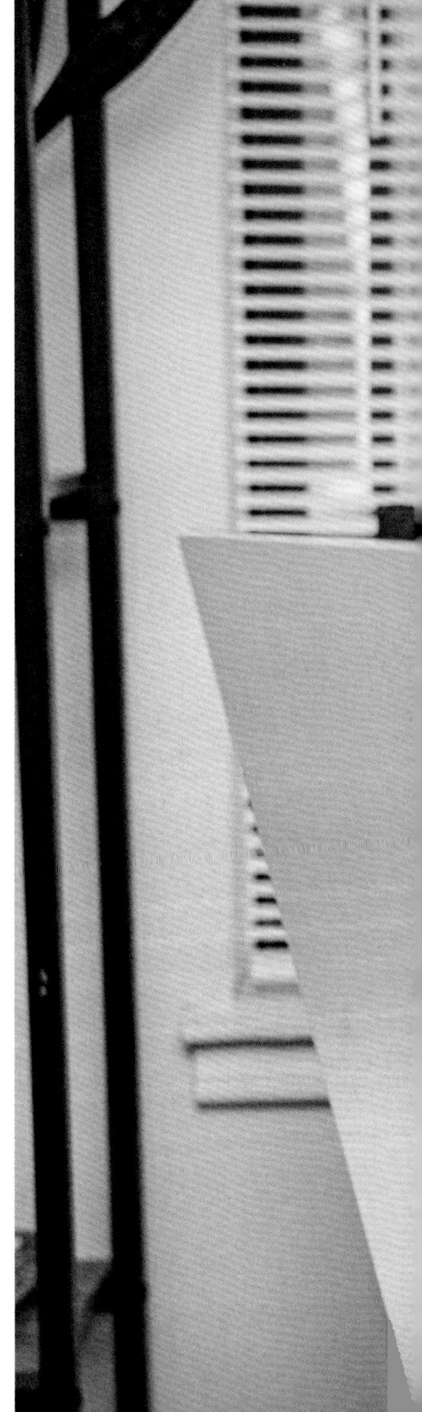

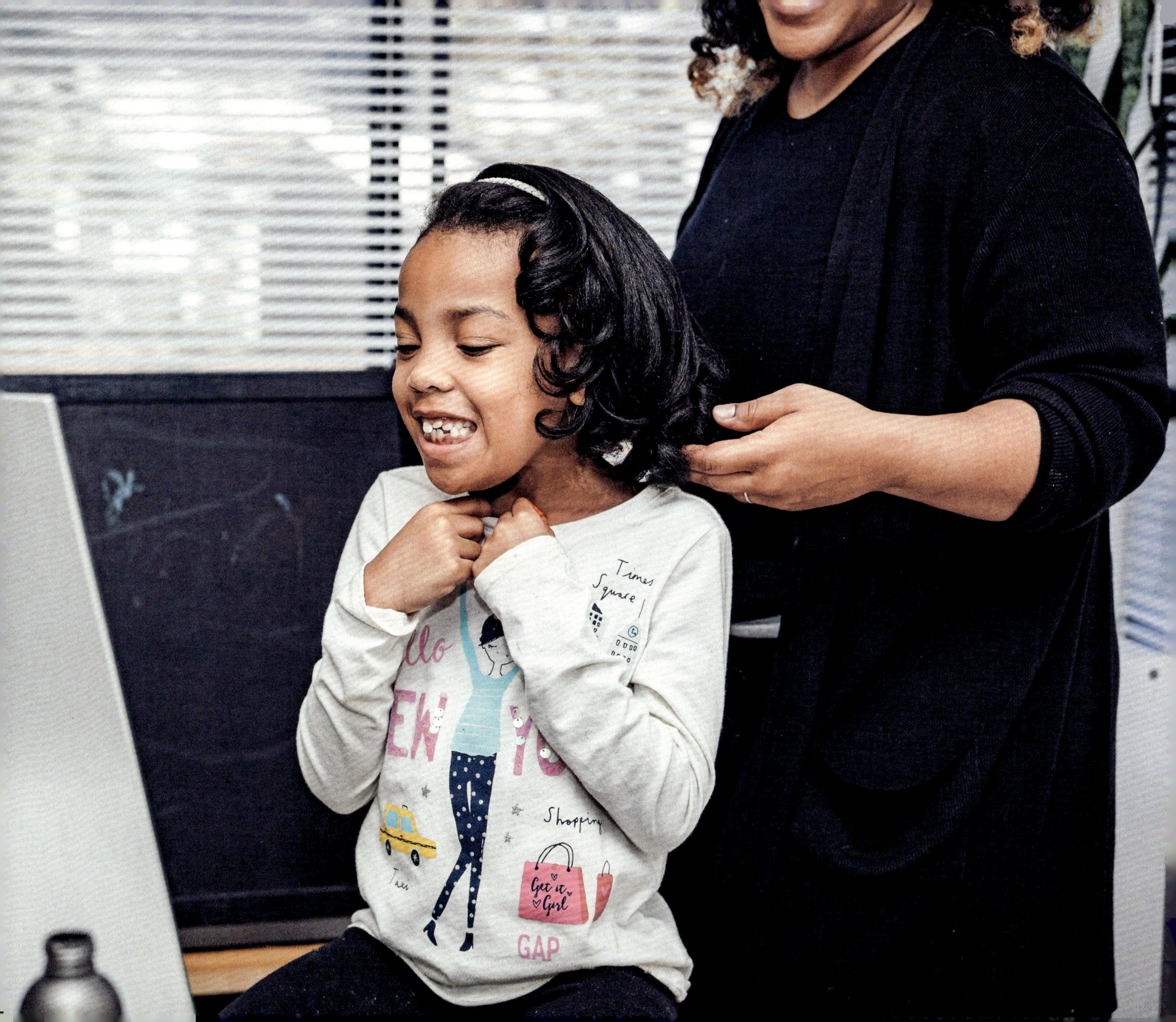

Times
Square
Shopping
GAP
Get it Girl
Taxi

Coretta & Rhiley

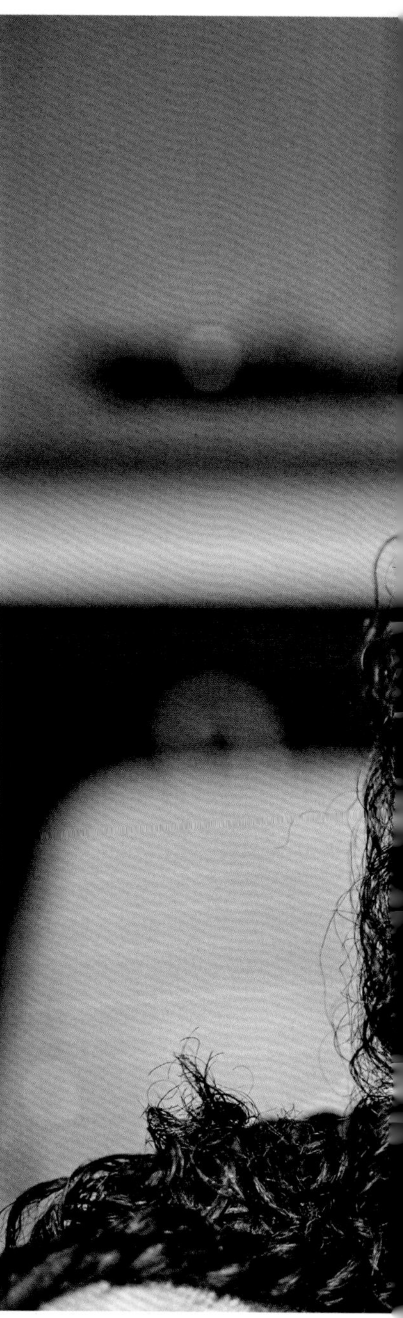

WHILE we are much further along than we have ever been in terms of normalizing natural hair, many of us still struggle. The mainstream beauty standard still isn't fully appreciative of all that natural hair has to offer. Undoing centuries of anti-Blackness and natural hair discrimination will take much more time, and many of us are still healing from past hair traumas and unlearning old attitudes. This book isn't just about those of us who have learned to love our hair. It's about *all* of us, no matter where we are on the journey.

Although Coretta has not had a relaxer since 1997, she often wears it pressed or in protective styles while she

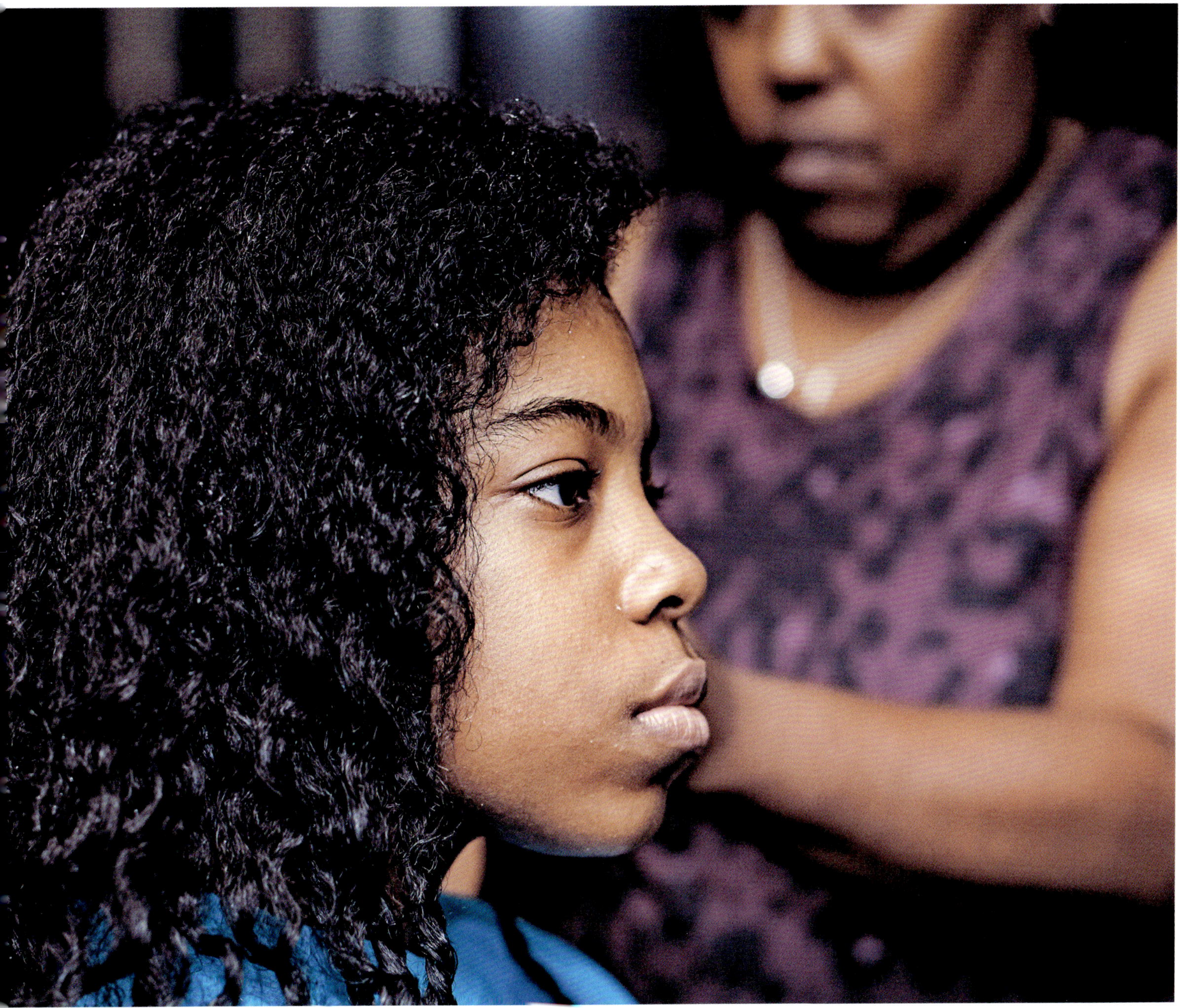

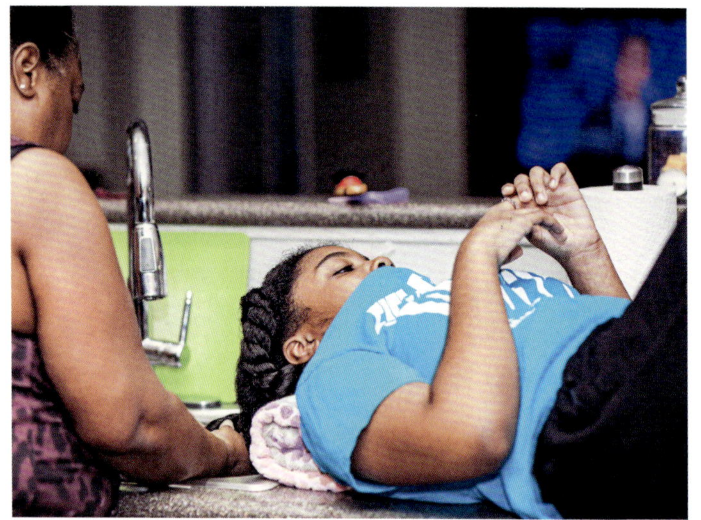

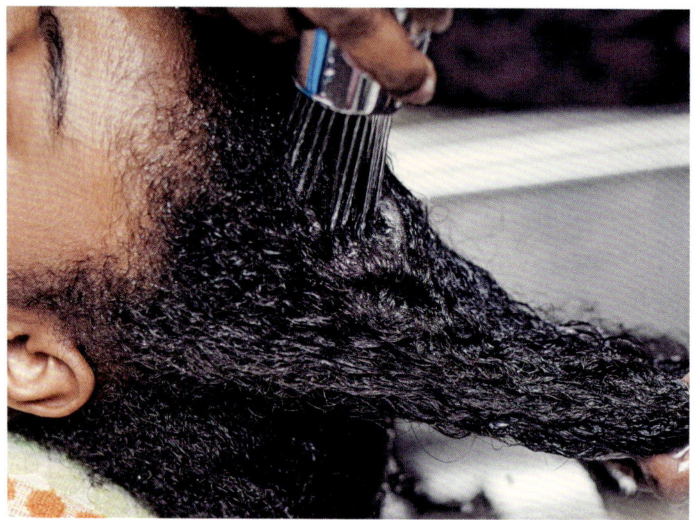

Rhiley has very long, thick hair, so wash day can last eight to twelve hours. Well actually, a bit longer; Coretta starts "getting [her] mind right" the night before. As many Black moms know, mental preparation is indeed a part of the wash-day process. Coretta washes Rhiley's hair in sections, a great technique that I also use from time to time, in order to manage the volume.

attempts to get more comfortable with her hair texture. The deeply rooted beliefs about natural hair being "messy," "wild," or "unkempt" have been difficult for Coretta to walk away from. But despite her own reservations, she has allowed her daughter, Rhiley, to celebrate her curls. Rhiley, loves her natural hair. For her, the bigger the better. And Coretta invests hours upon hours into Rhiley's long, thick, curly hair, ensuring that she is able to wear a variety of natural styles. In fact, Rhiley's freedom has had the unexpected consequence of helping Coretta pull further and further away from the mindset that "kept" hair needs to be straight. For Coretta, watching her daughter embrace and love her natural hair has been inspiring her to take more risks and embrace her own texture more fully.

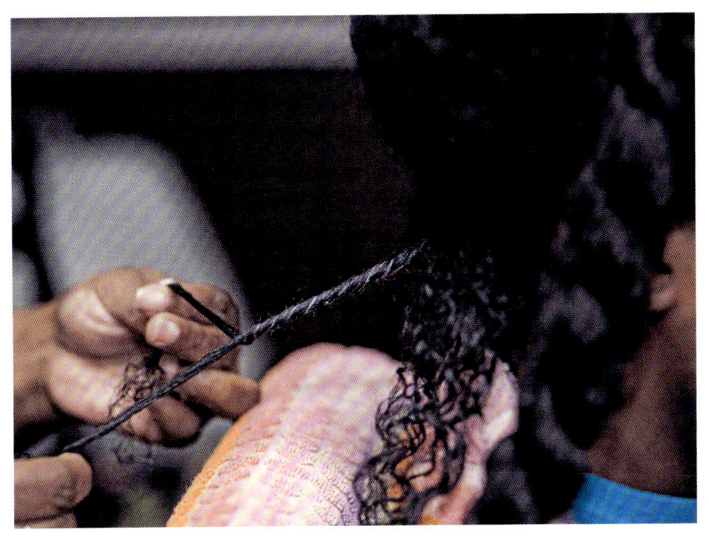
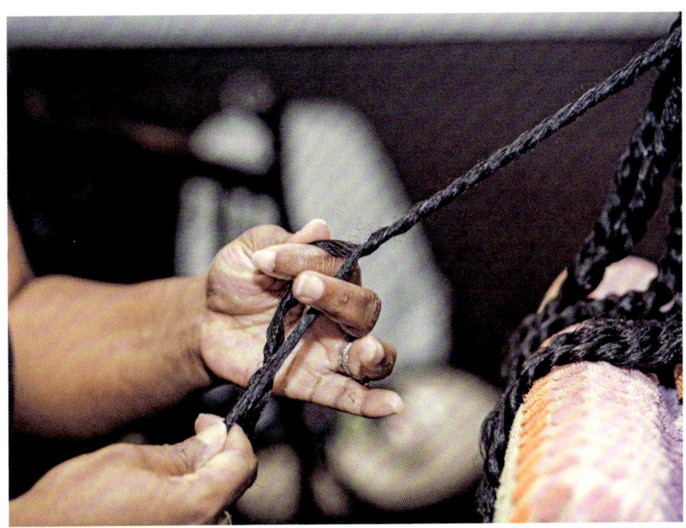
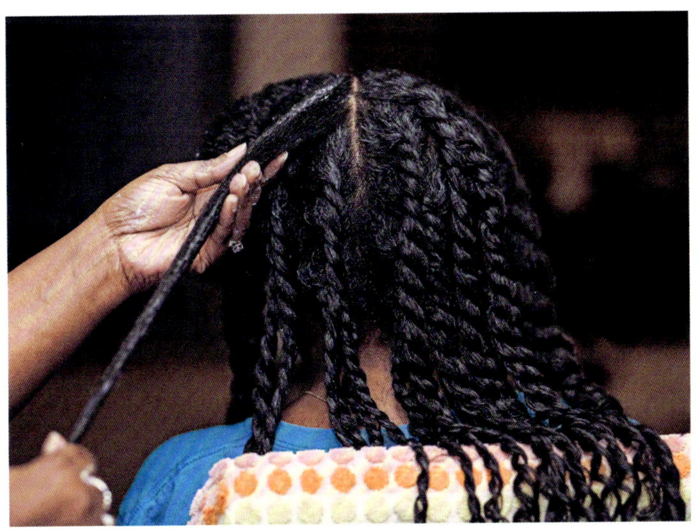
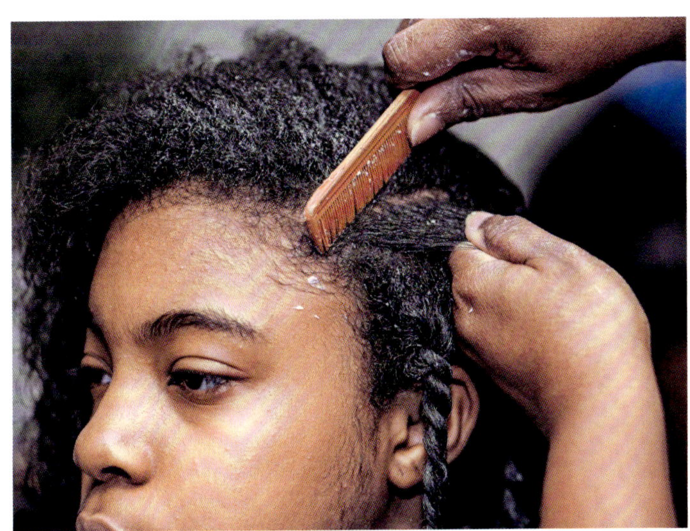

"I honestly feel [like] my child is teaching me. My generation is on the cusp of 'its ok to wear your hair natural' and 'it looks unkempt.' So, I struggle all the time. Seeing her embrace her natural hair has given me a little more courage to take risks with my hair naturally." —CORETTA

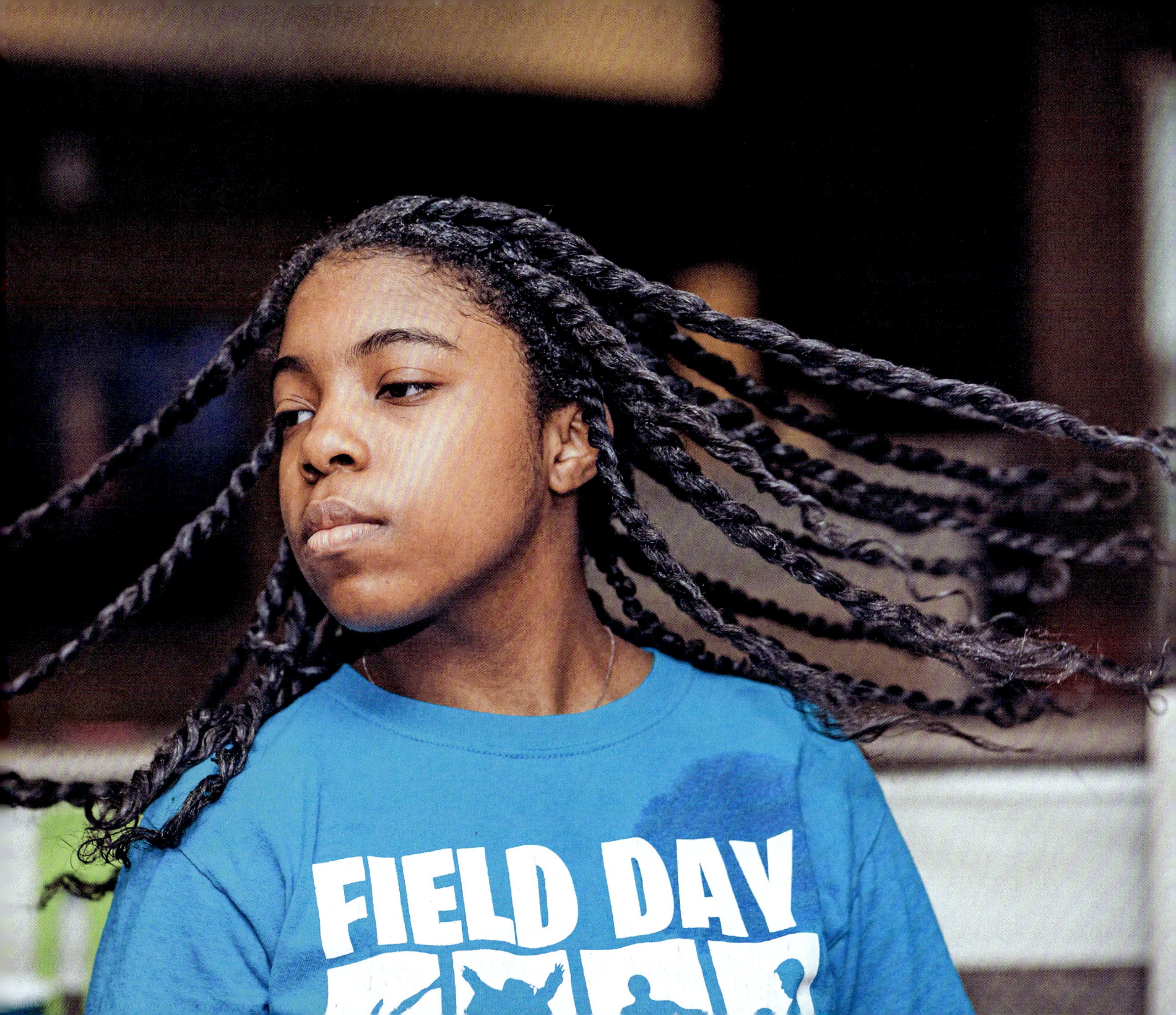

FIELD DAY

Natolie, Londyn & Hannah

"Honestly, I did not start my journey
on purpose."

NOT EVERYONE begins their natural hair journey for the purposes of self-discovery, healthier living, or rejection of White normative beauty standards. There is a plethora of reasons a Black woman may decide to go natural.

For Natolie, finances were the trigger. Natolie started her journey in 2010 when, due to financial difficulties, she could no longer afford to get her hair professionally relaxed. Her stylist explained that transitioning to natural (meaning, allowing her natural hair to grow while slowly cutting off the relaxed hair) would be easier with silk presses. Natolie soon discovered that she actually preferred the presses over

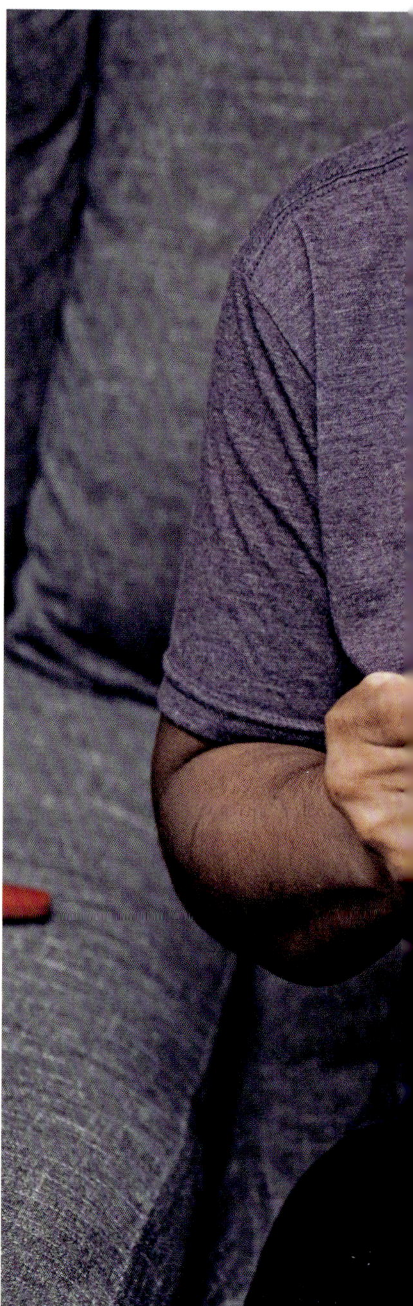

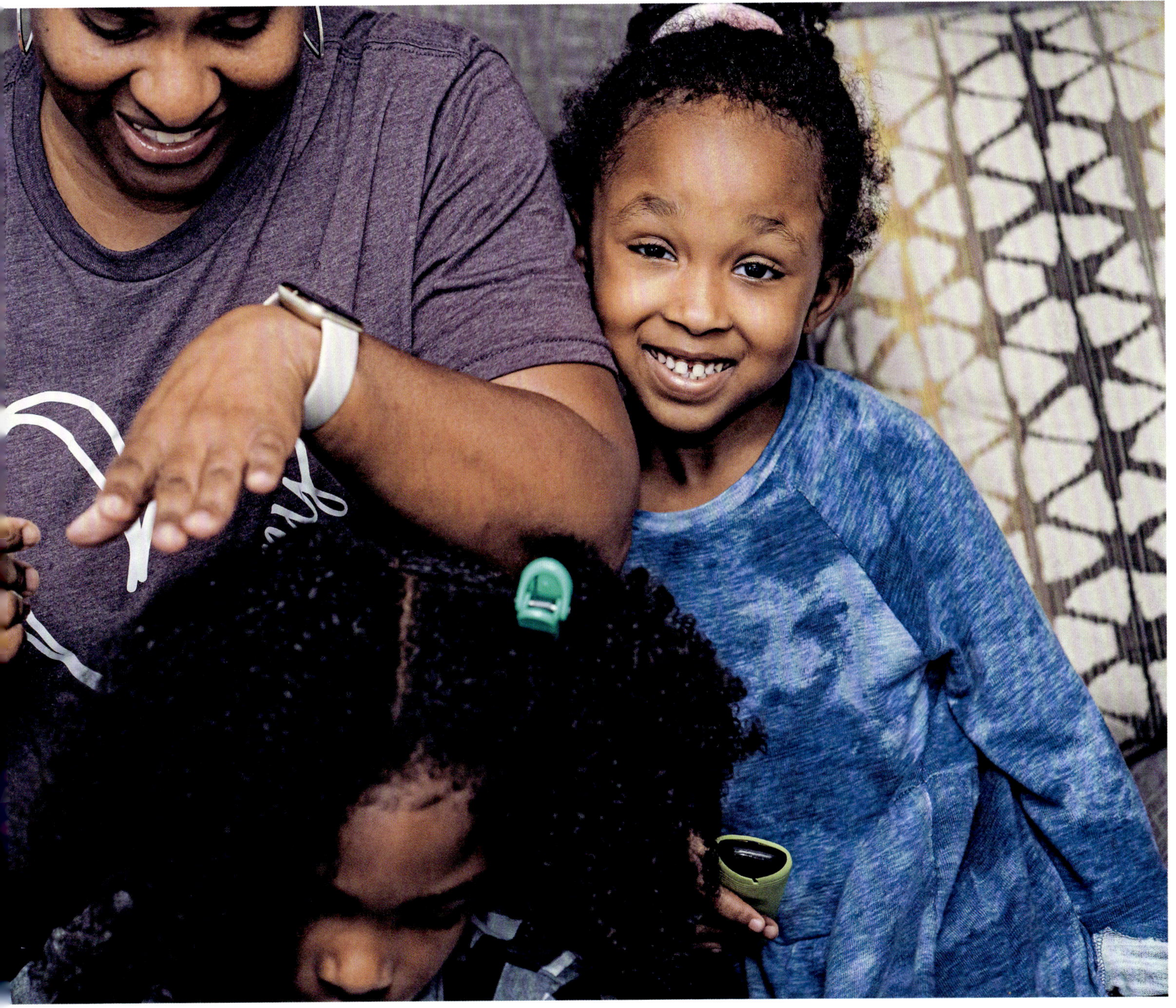

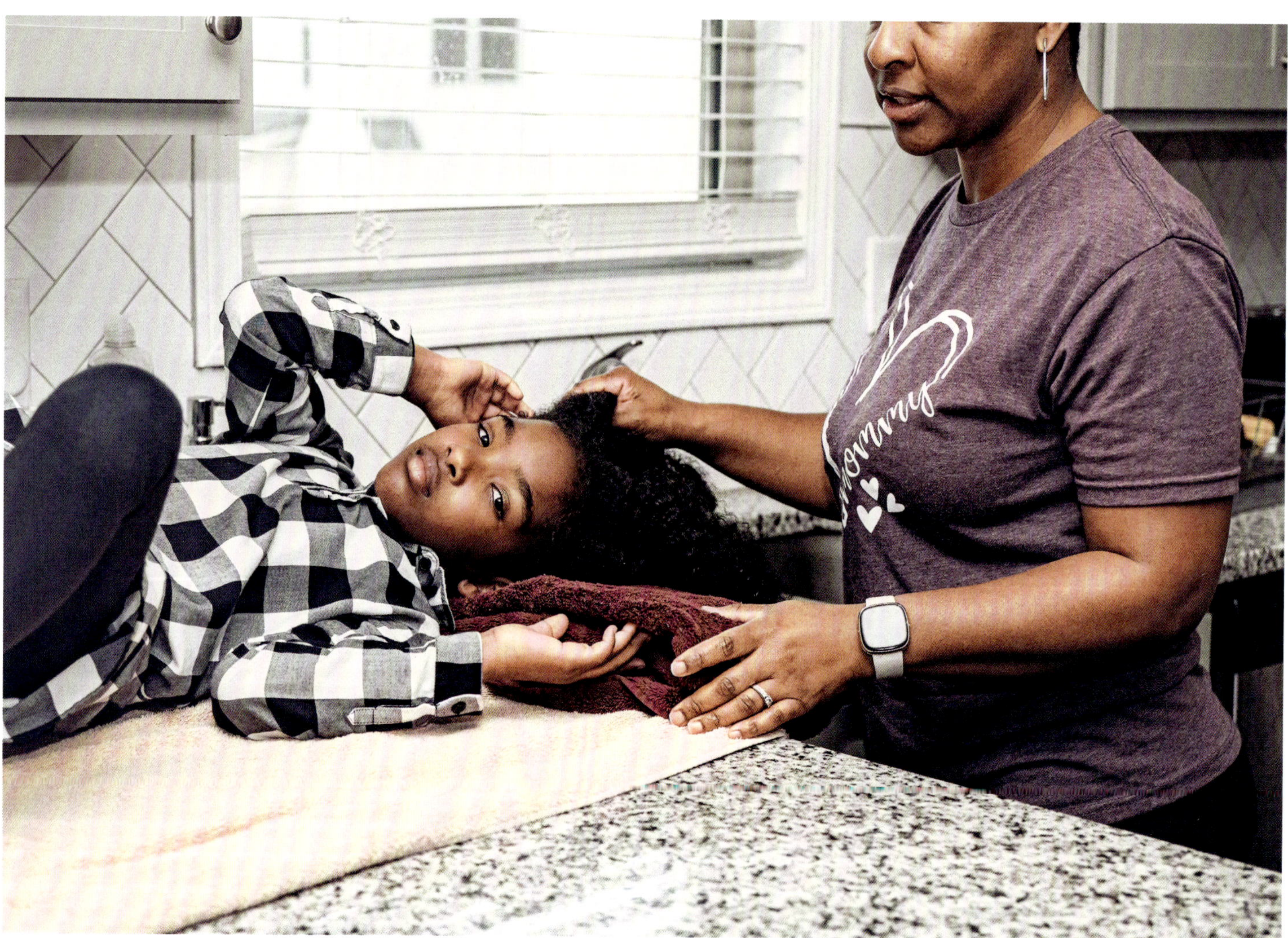

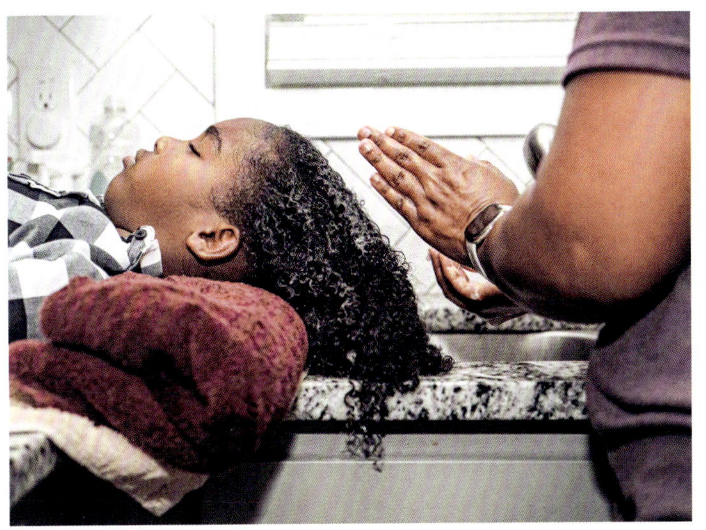

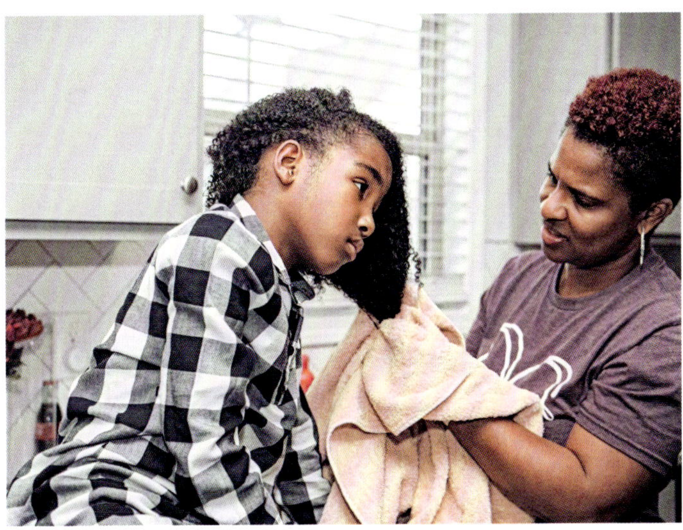

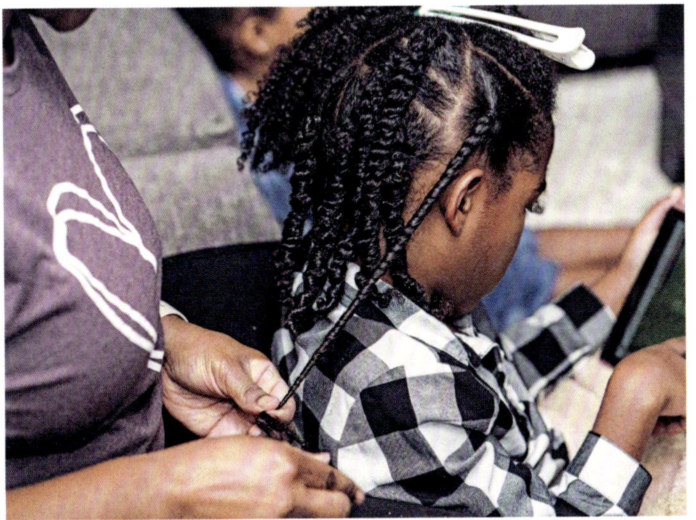

relaxers and questioned her mom's decision to relax her hair at the age of five.

As time went on, Natolie realized that she really loved wearing her hair short. She continued to press her short looks until the difficulty of keeping short natural hair straight all the time became burdensome. She decided to ditch the silk presses and embrace her natural texture. She soon discovered that not only do her short curls offer her more freedom, but they are also quite beautiful.

Natolie keeps wash day with her daughters relatively simple. Once a month for about an hour and a half, Natolie washes, conditions, detangles, and styles Londyn and Hannah's hair. This is on the quicker side, made possible by skipping the pre-wash, detangling, and deep conditioning steps. While I documented Natolie's wash-day process, Natolie's younger daughter, Hannah, said she did not want to get her hair washed that day. Natolie obliged. It was a Friday afternoon, and she was not about to add more work to her plate.

"My mom did not know how to do hair when I was a kid. . . . I started styling my own hair around second or third grade. I now want to pass on things to my daughters." —NATOLIE

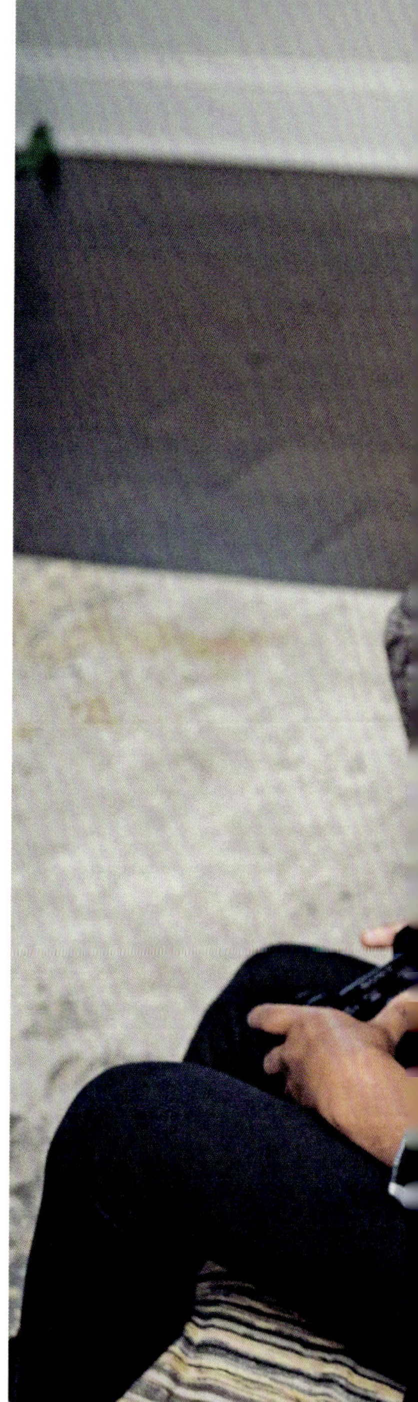

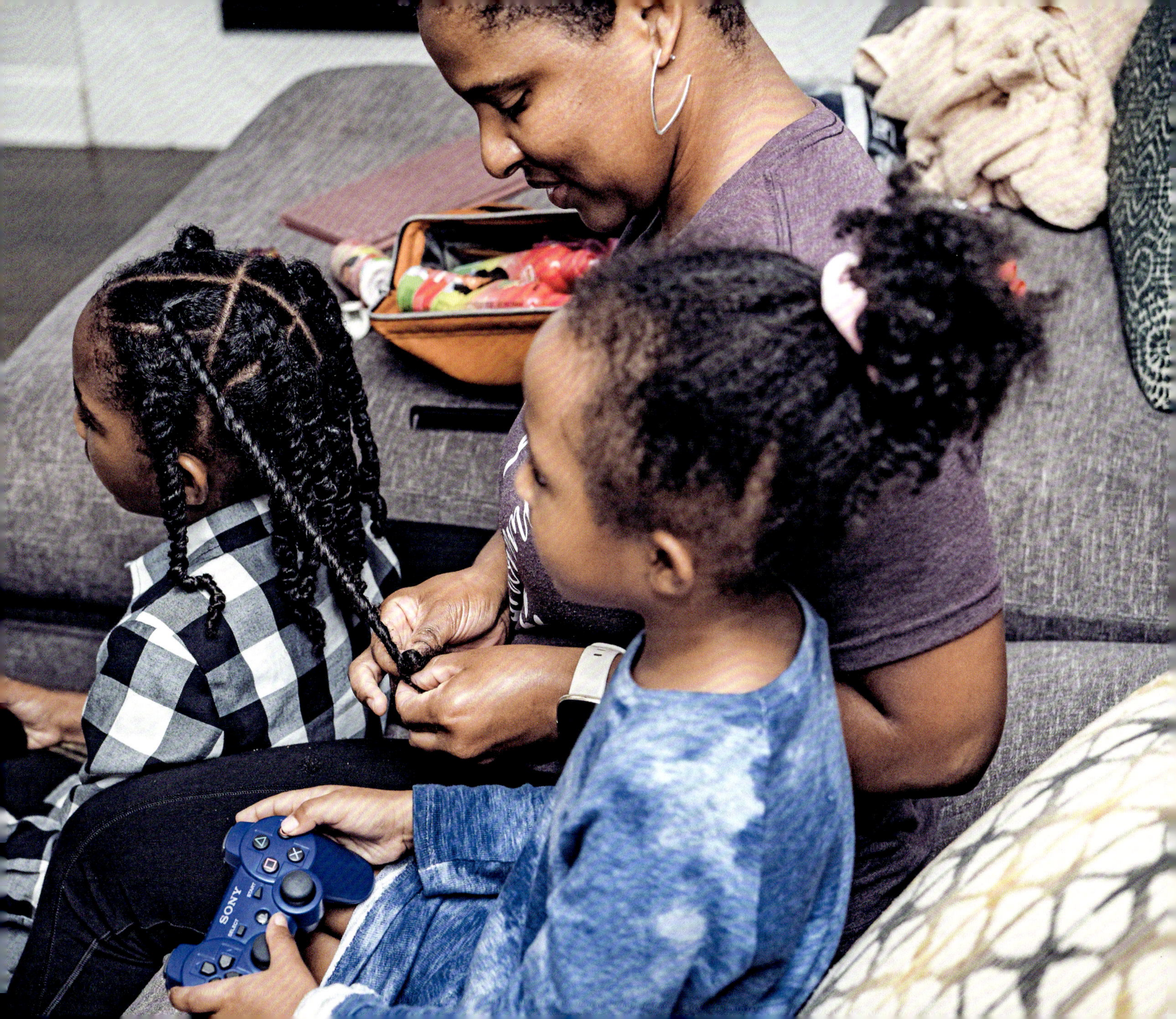

Montrell & Evalynn

". . . over the past seven years we've been
walking out this natural hair journey together.
How does that look? Finding products that
work for our texture, styling dos and don'ts,
YouTube fails and long wash days!"

REAL TALK. I haven't been to a hair salon in years. Mainly
because I've kept my hair short for so long that I've been
frequenting barbershops instead. While I have many good
salon memories, I do recall a time or two going to a salon
only to sit, and sit, and sit. And wait, and wait, and wait . . .
only to get a hairstyle that I just did not love.

It was an experience like this that propelled Montrell
onto her natural hair journey. She recalls:

I remember having an early Saturday morning ap-
pointment at a salon. The wait was ridiculous, and

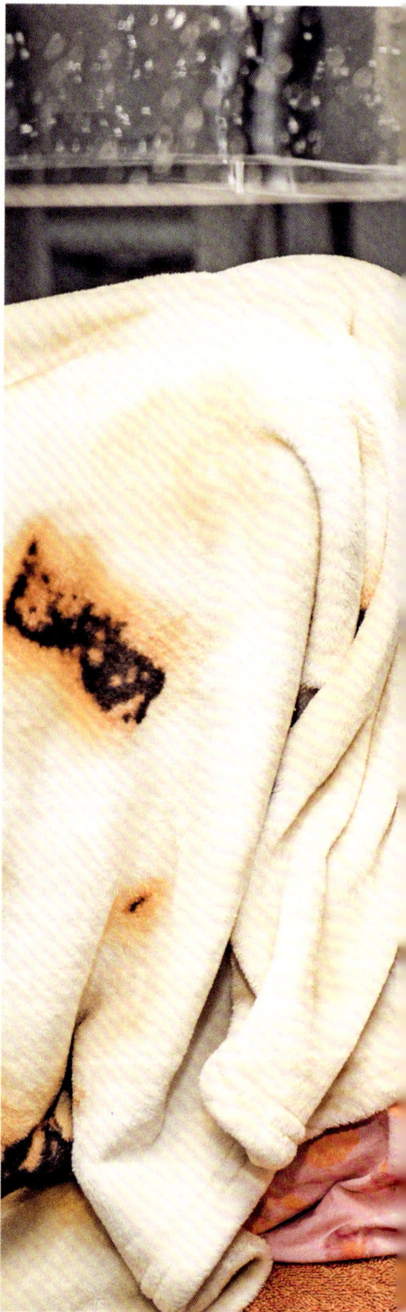

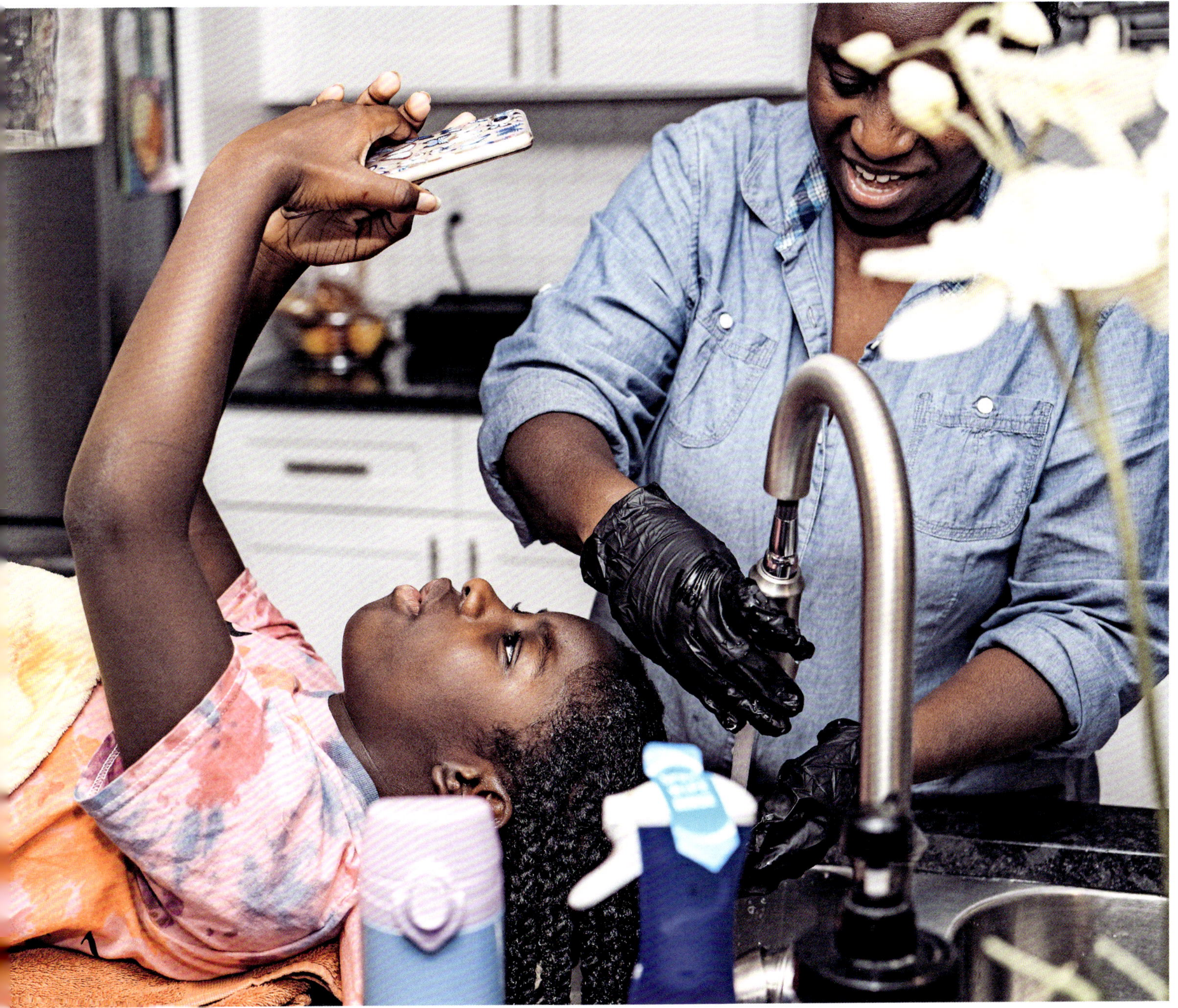

everyone walked out with the same style, a dooby wrap. That day I decided never again. I can't remember the date but the day itself is etched in my memory. From that point, I rocked cornrows, afros, and had my hair straightened a few times with the old-school straightening comb.

Montrell was over it. In September of 2001, she did the big chop and showed up to her now husband's sister's wedding with no hair. Now, you know that was a sight to see in 2001! First, the big chop was not yet popular *and* wearing short natural hair to a formal event is only recently being seen as an acceptable thing to do (thank you, Viola Davis). In December of 2001, Montrell was introduced to locs by a friend. She fell in love with the look and began loc'ing her hair right away.

In 2013, Montrell found out she was pregnant with a baby girl. She then realized she needed to purchase combs and brushes.

Say what, now?

Rewind. Montrell went straight from a big chop to locs. So, she had no need for the hair tools of loose naturals. But upon receiving the news of a quickly approaching baby girl, she knew she needed to do some shopping.

Montrell also realized that she needed to learn how to care for natural hair. She had very little time with her T.W.A. before starting her locs, so she never learned the tricks of the trade. Furthermore, a couple of years after her daughter, Evalynn, was born, she decided to cut off her locs. She quickly found herself simultaneously learning how to care for her daughter's hair as well as her own.

Talk about double duty.

For Montrell and Evalynn, wash day is part of their continuous journey of learning together. Wash day takes place every one to two weeks and lasts for about three hours. This time together allows them to test out different products and techniques in order to fine-tune their process. She has learned that washing Evalynn's hair in twists works best for managing both washing and post-wash detangling. She has also learned that the more the merrier when it comes to conditioner. "Mo product, mo product, mo product," is her mantra. She has also discovered the importance of applying moisturizer regularly, even when Evalynn's hair is in a protective style. As for products, she has found that African Pride and Melanin products work best for Evalynn's hair. I imagine this joint learning experience will serve to deepen Evalynn's knowledge and prepare her for the many solo wash days to come.

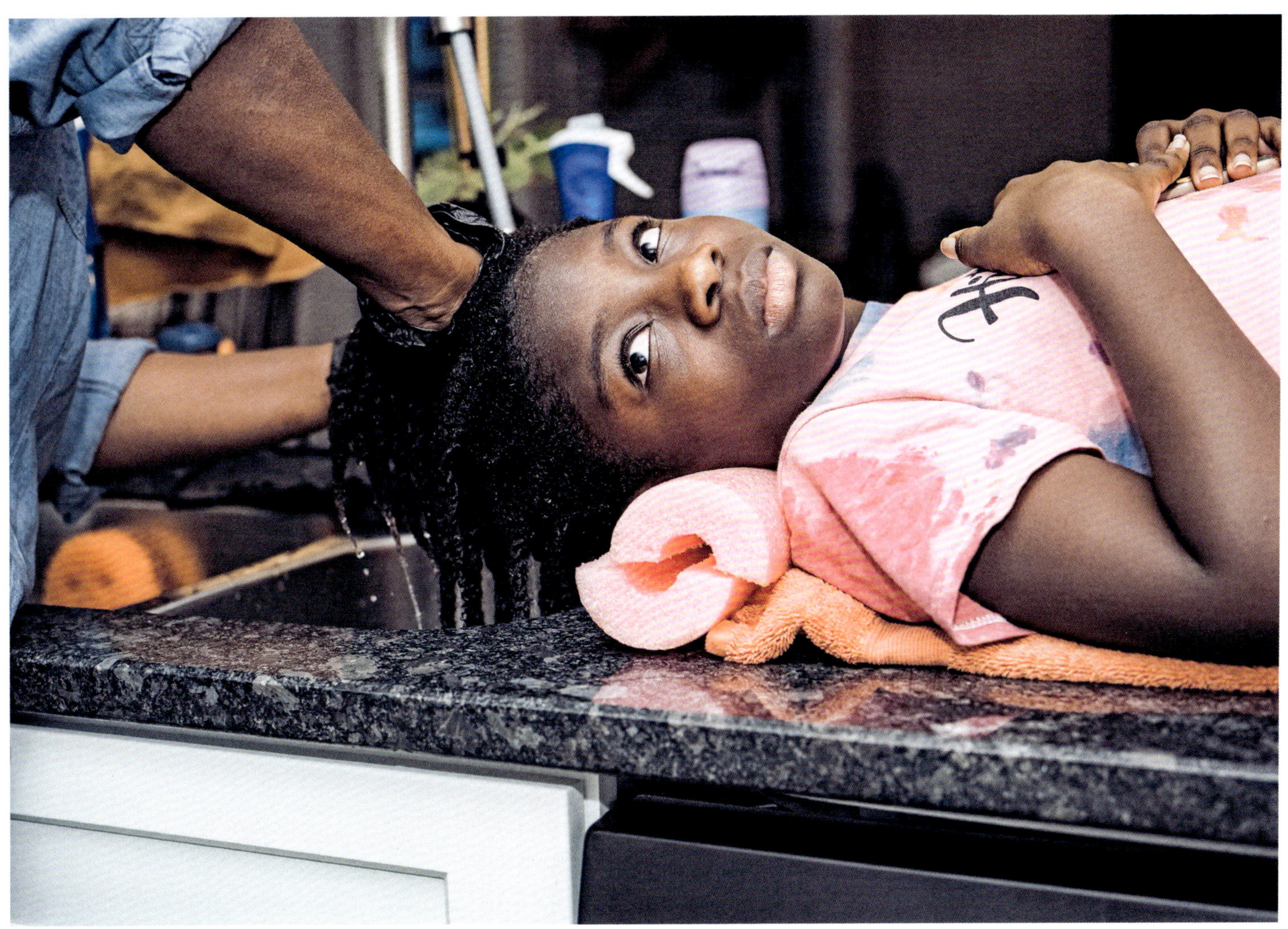

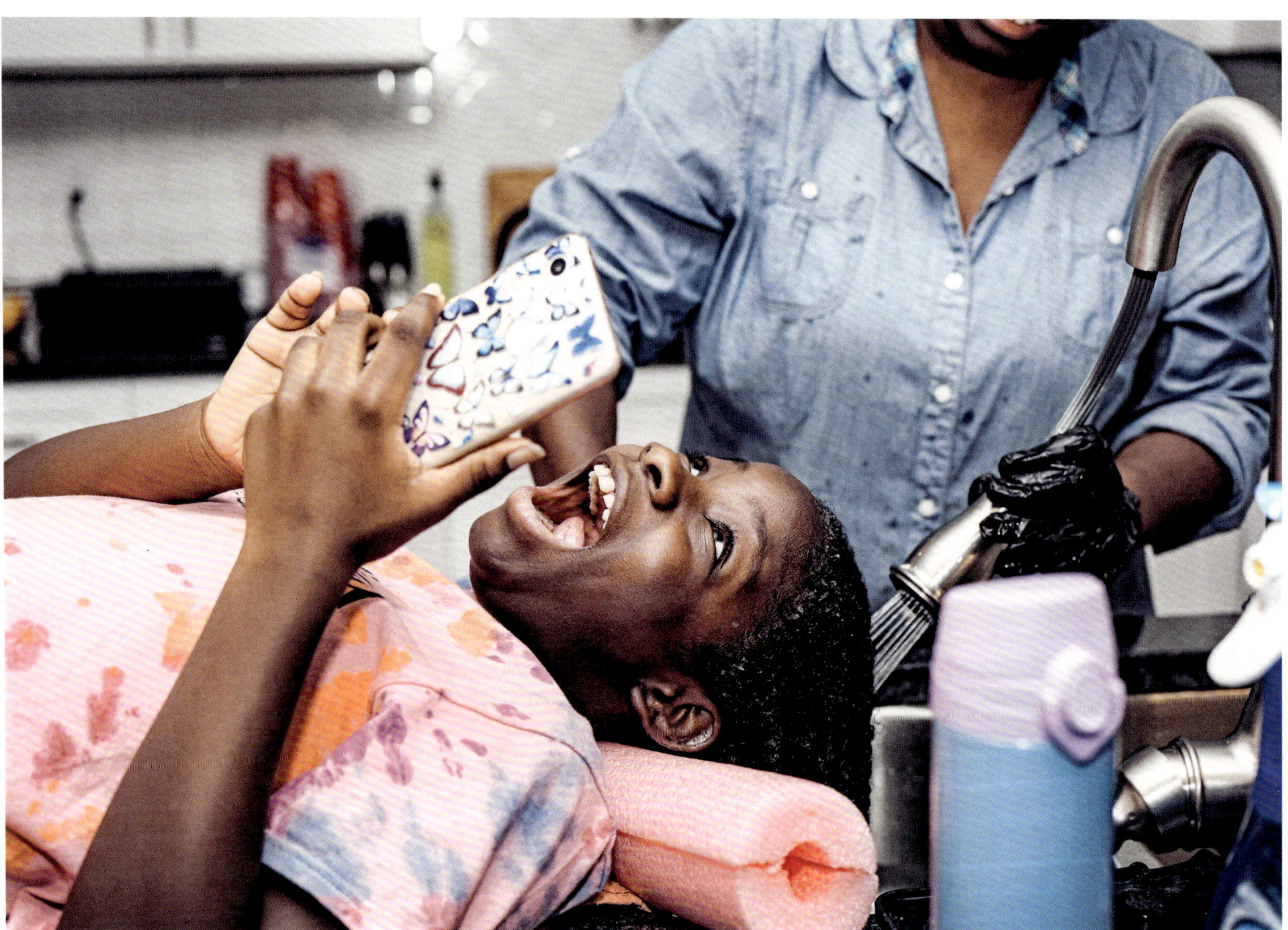

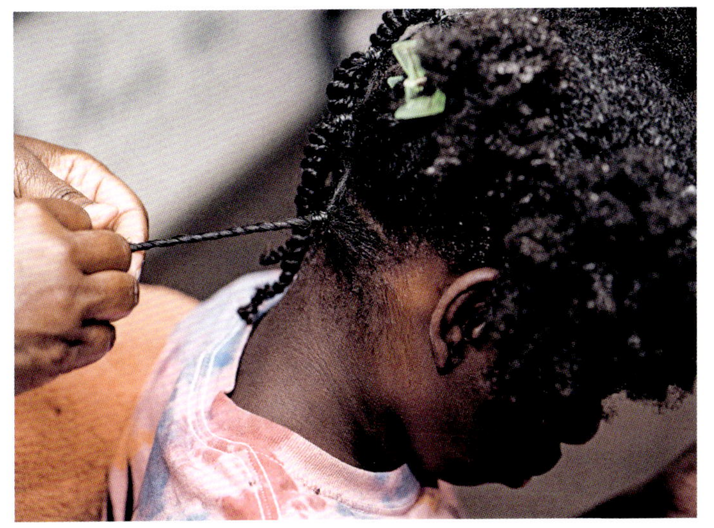
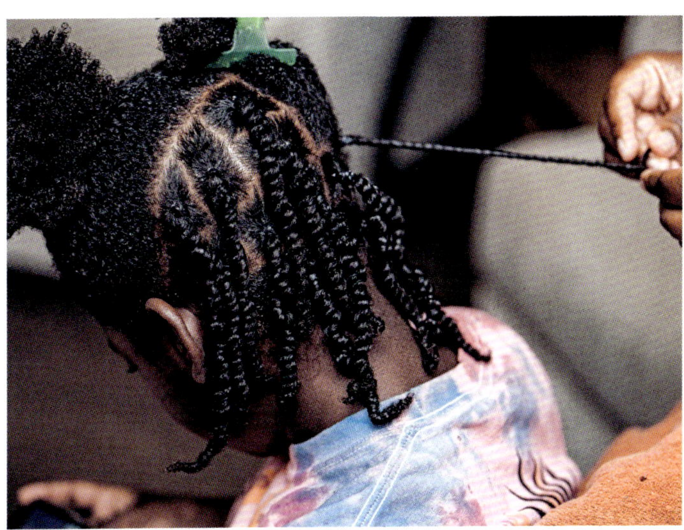
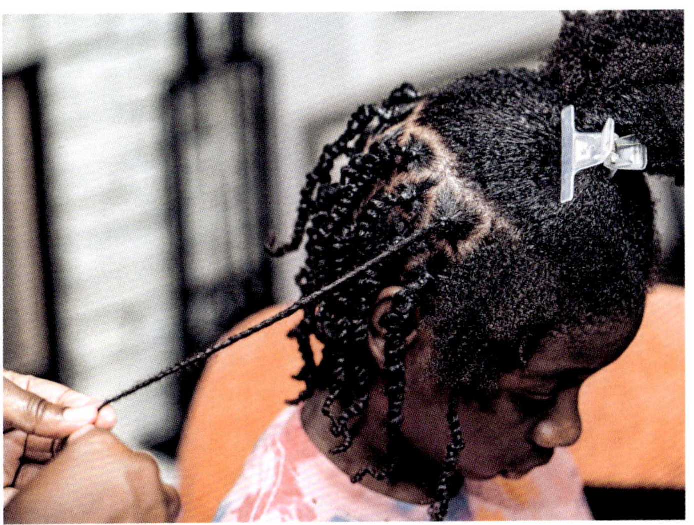
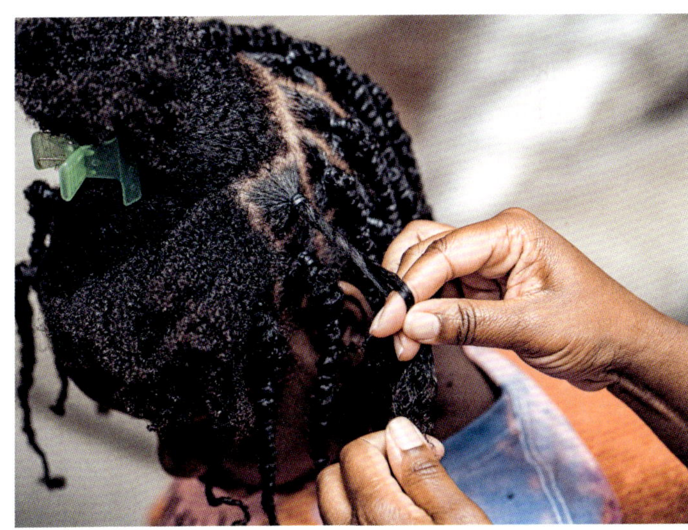

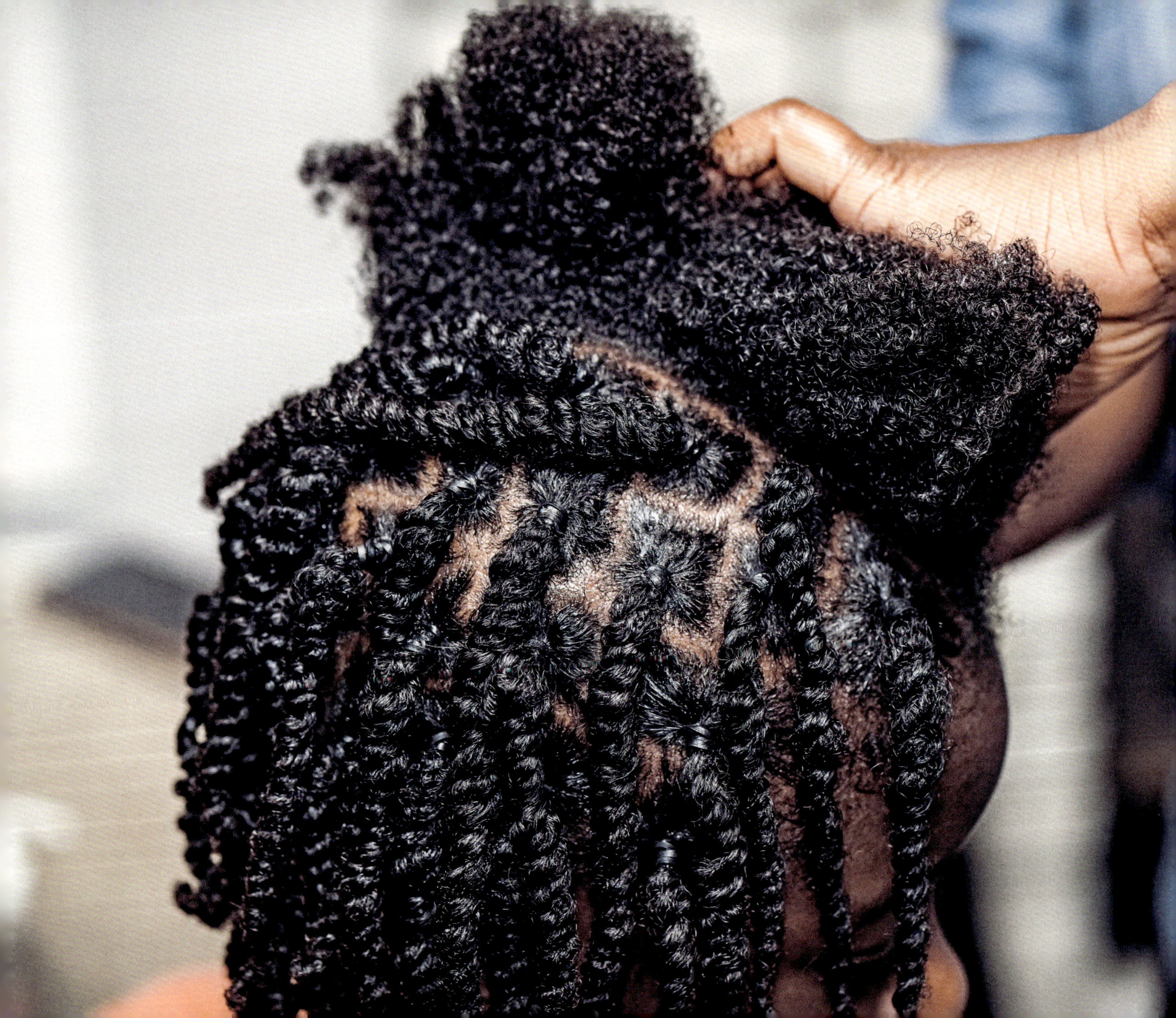

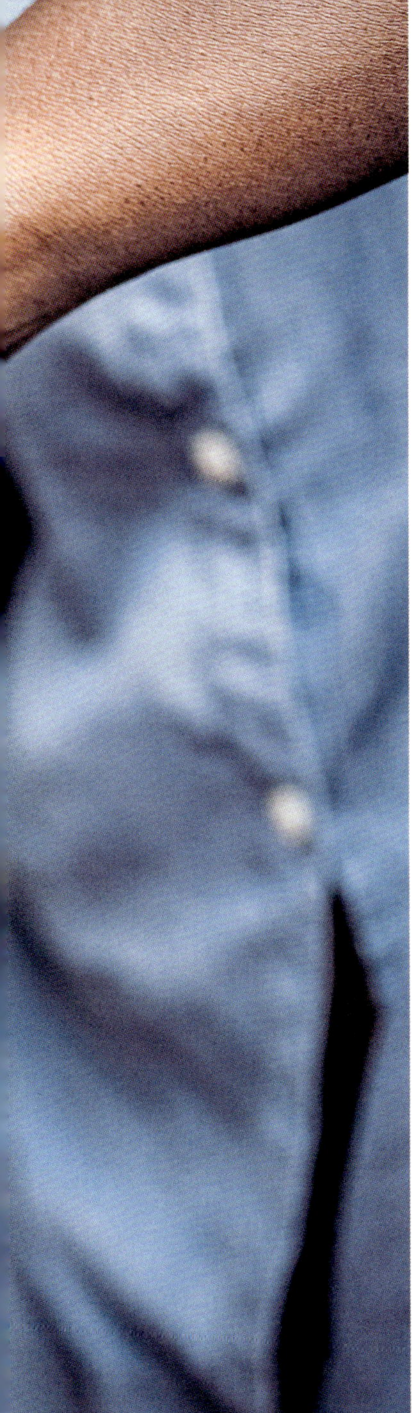

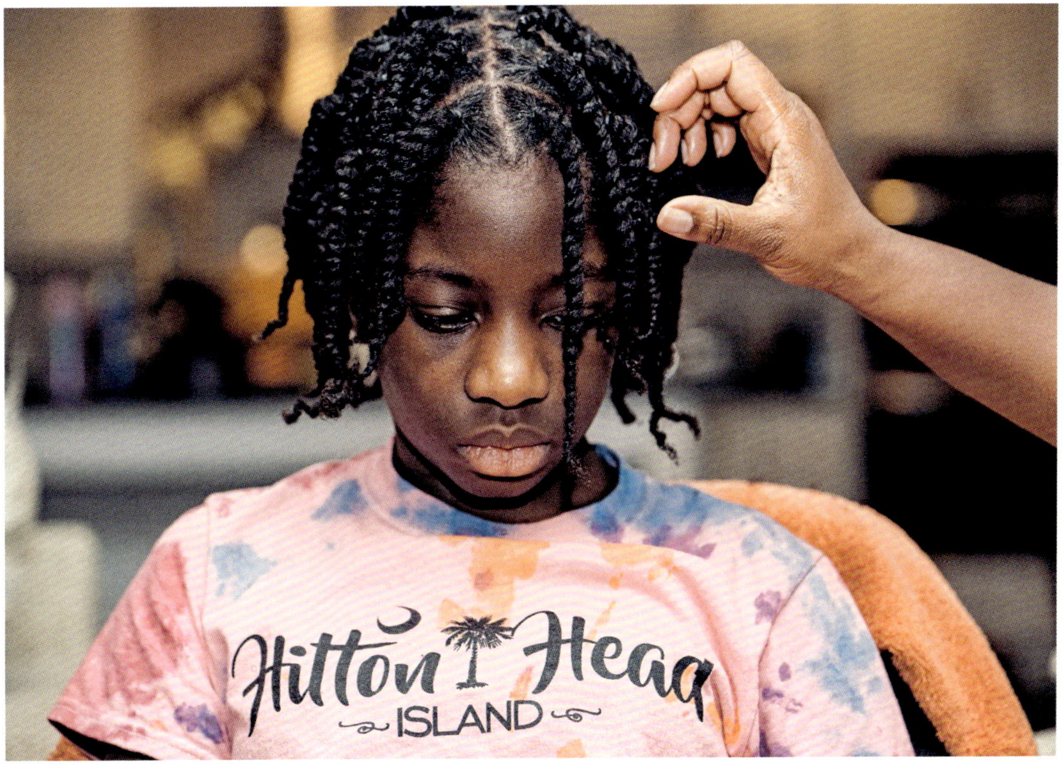

"It's a continuous journey. We never stop learning." —MONTRELL

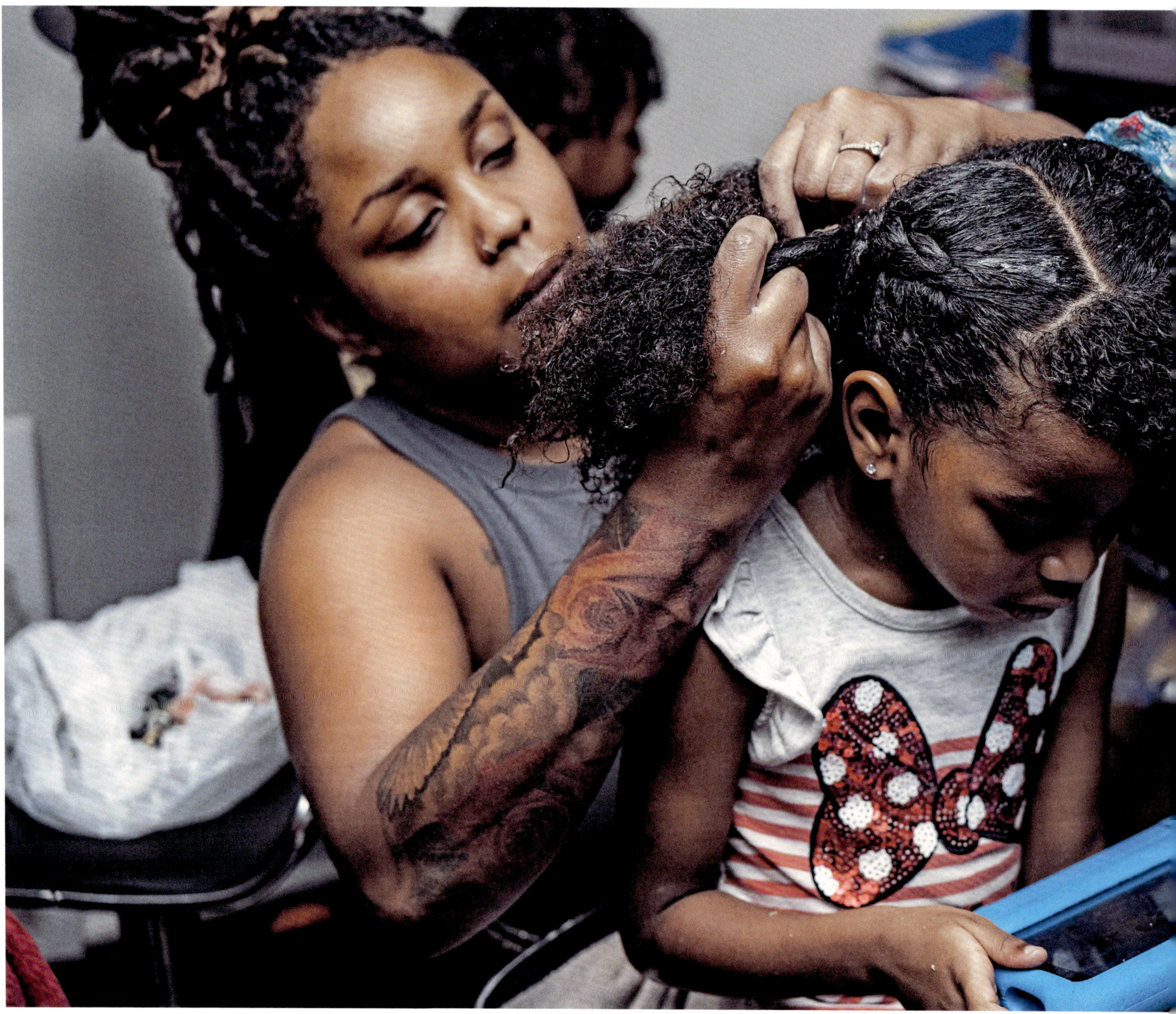

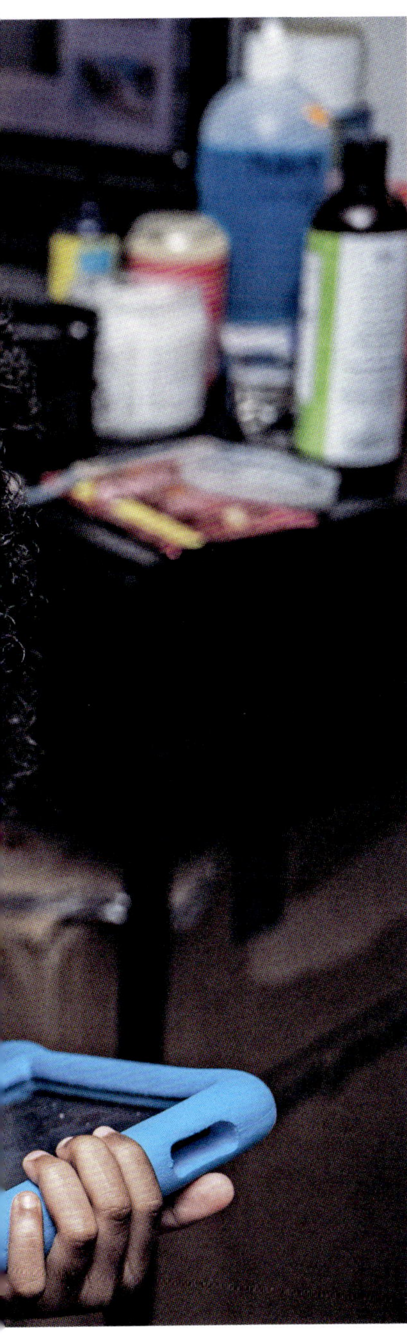

Alisha, Londyn, Lauryn & Kyrie

"My dad raised me. As a little girl he only had
a few different hairstyles [he] would do."

MOMS are certainly central to this book. But I want to give dads a shout-out as well. Some dads are instrumental during the wash-day process. More than one mom has mentioned to me that at times, the struggle is so real that dad will step in to help comfort the littles. Some dads entertain kiddos who are not getting their hair done so that mom can focus. And others are the primary hair stylists for their children.

Alisha experienced more dad involvement on wash day than most. Her father raised her alone and was solely responsible for hair care. Her dad was not the best hair stylist, so she recalls having very few hairstyle options. Desiring more versatility, she started learning how to do her own hair at a young age. By the fifth grade, she was styling her own hair. To make hair management a bit easier, her dad tried relaxers, as many parents did. However, Alisha realized that she much preferred her natural hair and stopped using relaxers in her senior year of high school. She continues to love her hair and has passed on this love to her three little ones.

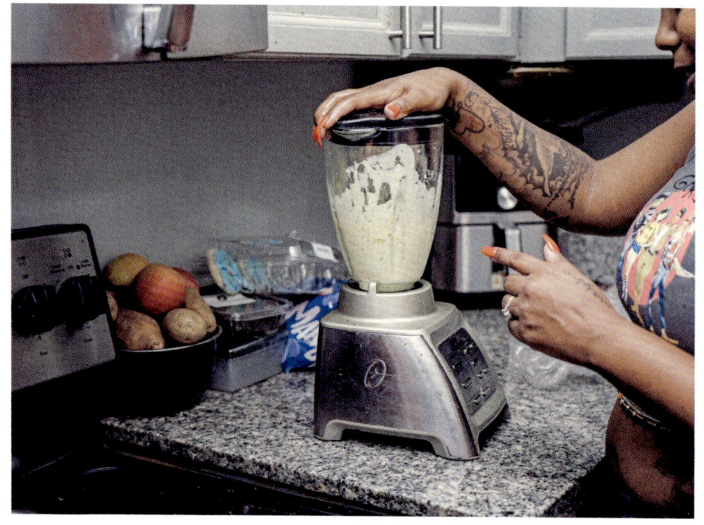

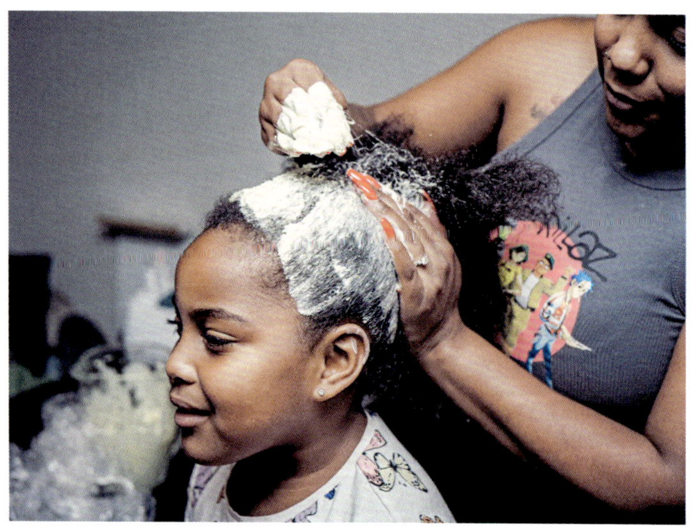

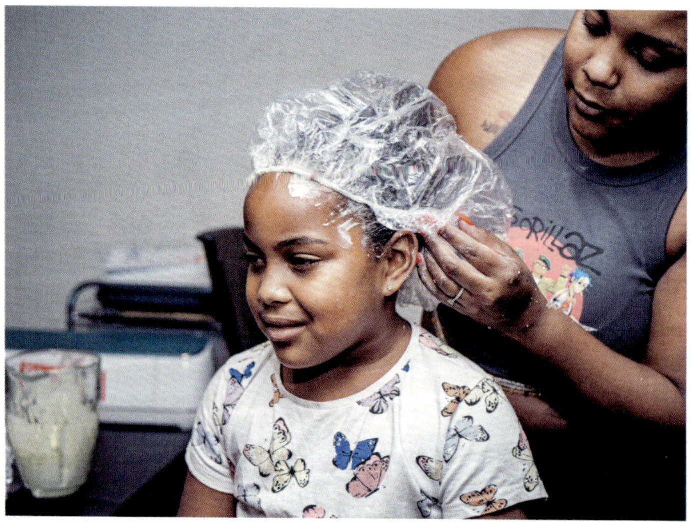

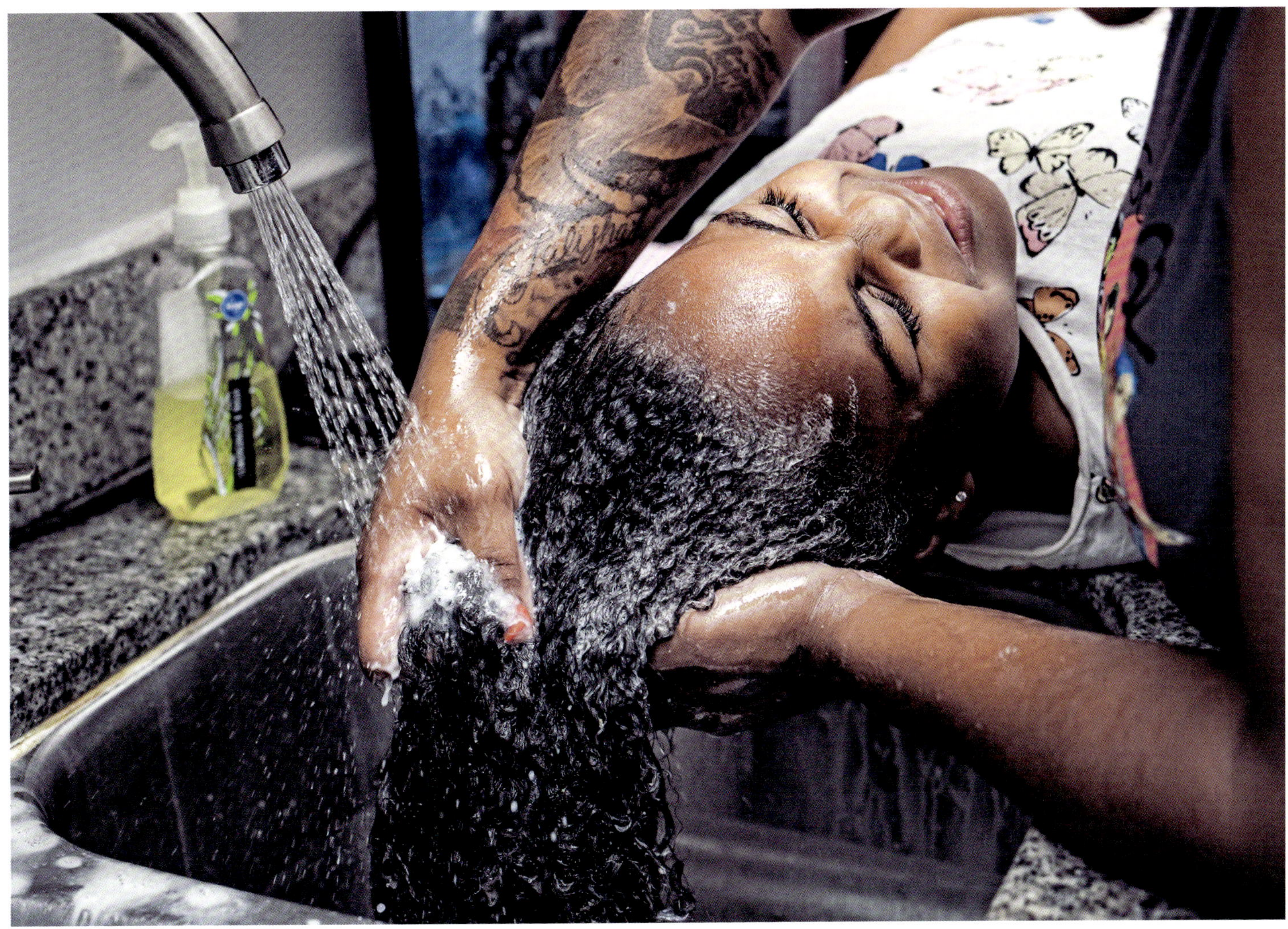

During each wash day, which takes place every two weeks, Alisha tackles three heads; London, Lauryn, and Kyrie, who are all under the age of eight. Whew! The entire process takes the whole day. Alisha usually makes her own pre-wash mask using natural items from her kitchen.

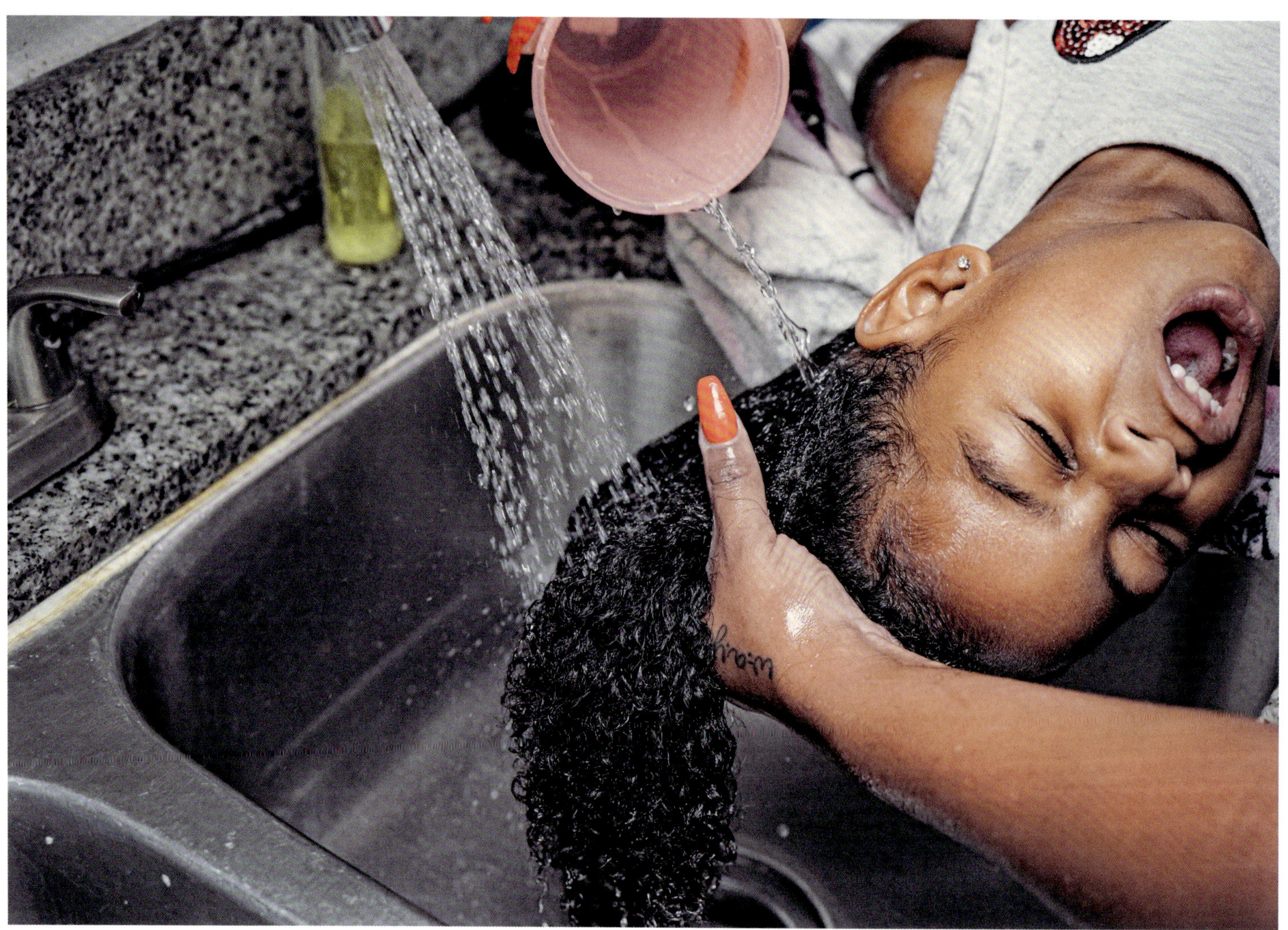

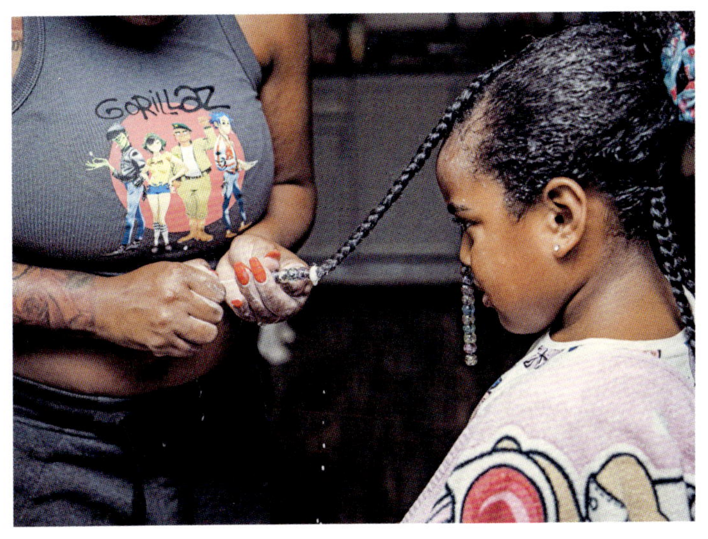
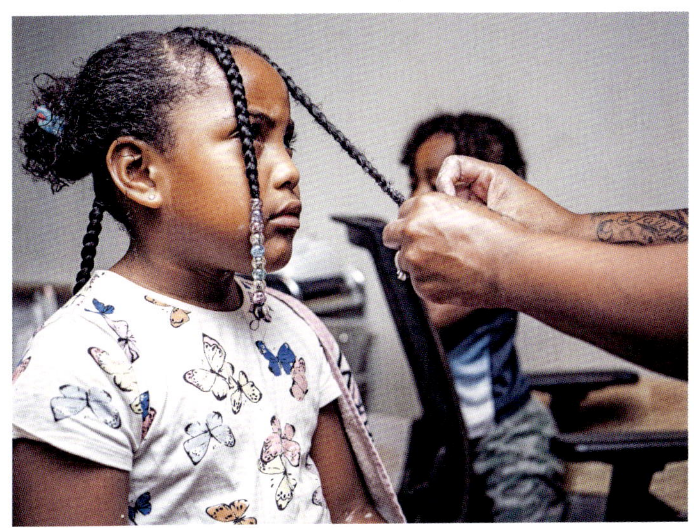
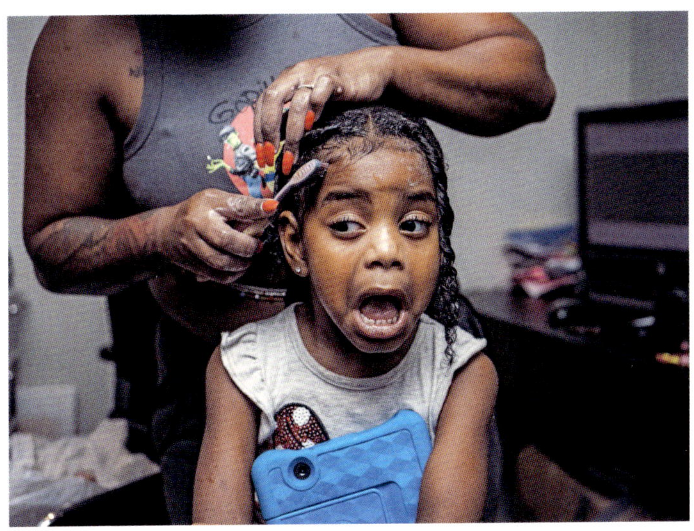
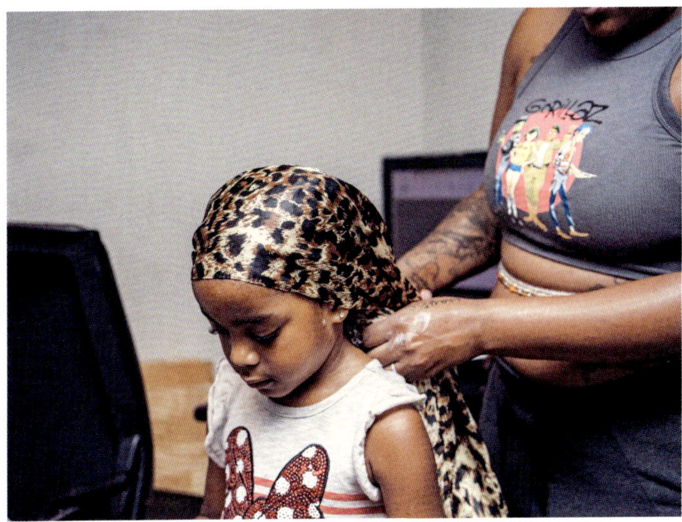

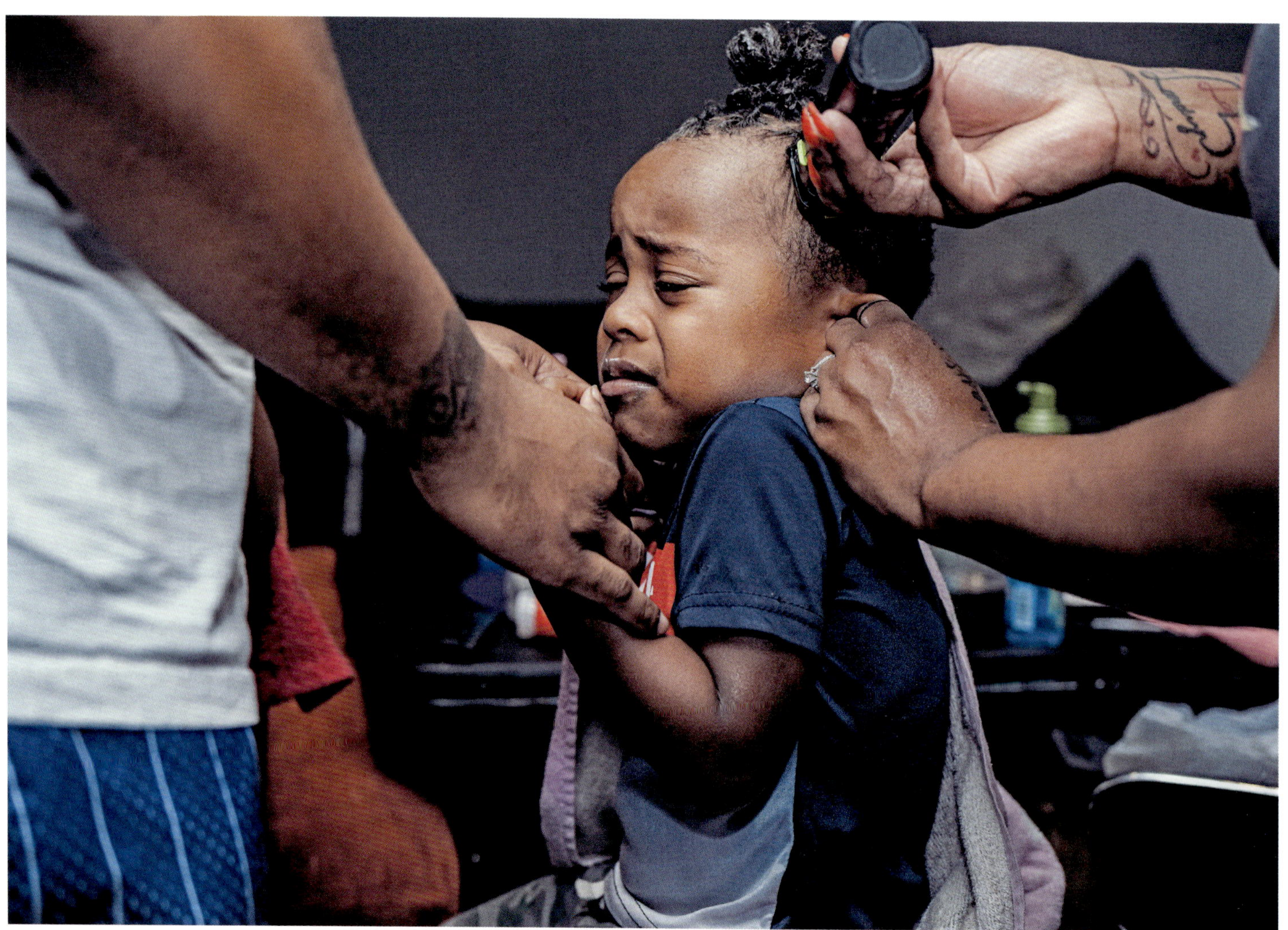

On wash days, Alisha's husband, Rodney, doesn't mind getting involved. One of the sweetest wash-day moments occurred when Alisha was cutting her son's hair. After washing and tightening his locs, she told him she would need to trim the sides. He immediately began to cry. Alisha called for her husband, who came in and held his hands to comfort him while Alisha finished up.

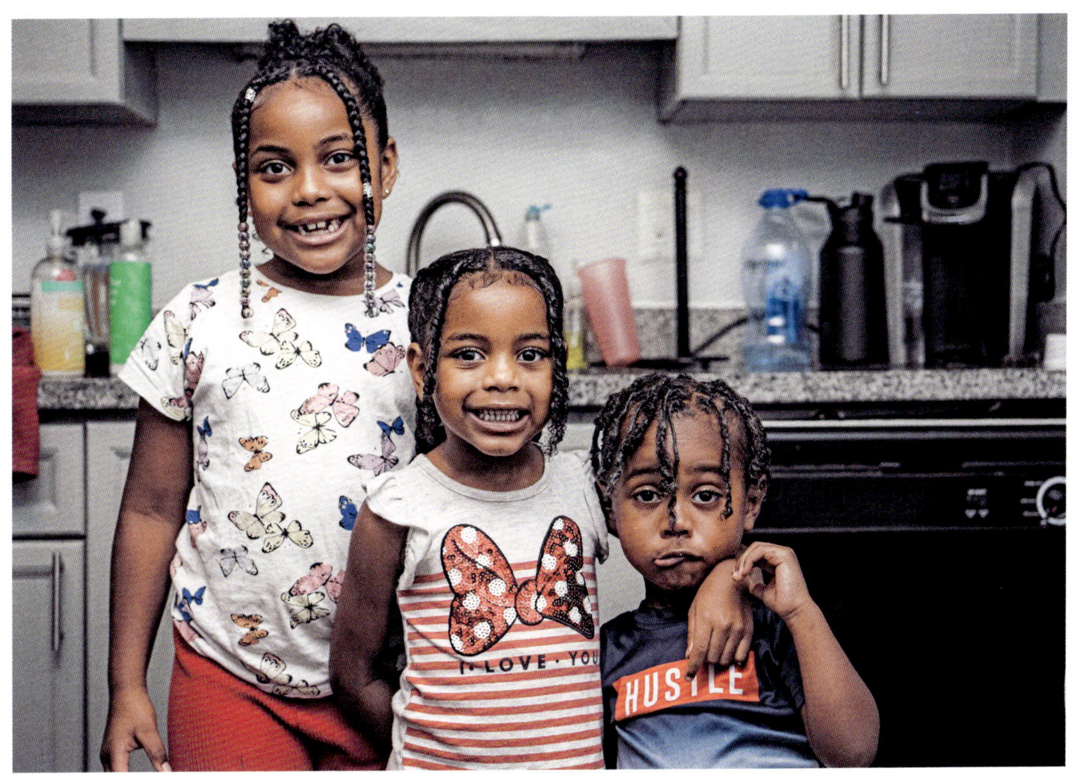

"[M]y kids love their hair. My son won't let me cut his, and my girls love to wear it out and curly." —ALISHA

Dana, Simone & Josie

AS I approach the end of this book, it seems like the perfect time to discuss how life-changing it has been to create it. I have been able to connect with new friends and reconnect with women I haven't seen or spoken to in years. We've talked about parenting, marriage, politics, religion, and of course . . . hair. Spending hours with these women, bonding over shared experiences, and sharing lessons learned about hair care has changed me. This is a testament to the relational nature of Black hair-care culture. Time invested into caring for each other's hair is truly a time of fellowship and community.

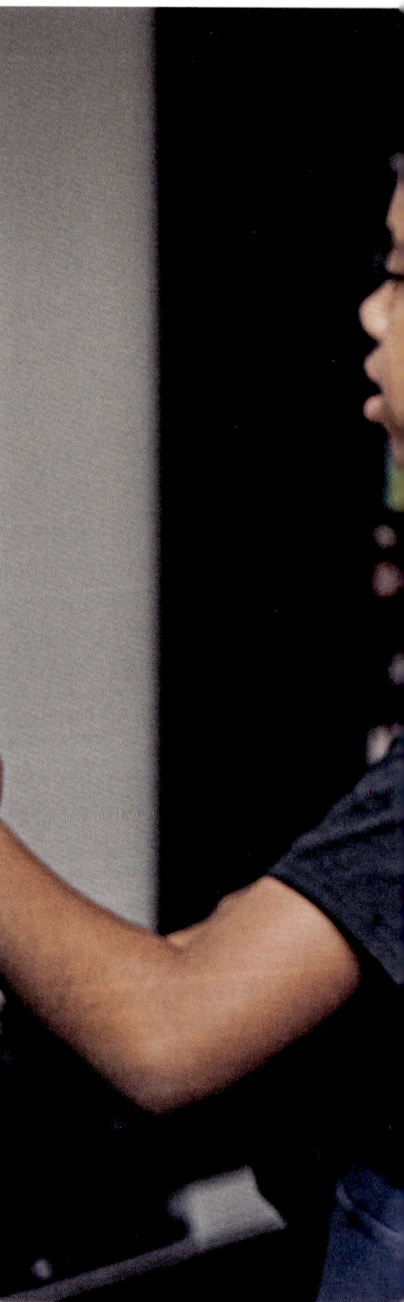

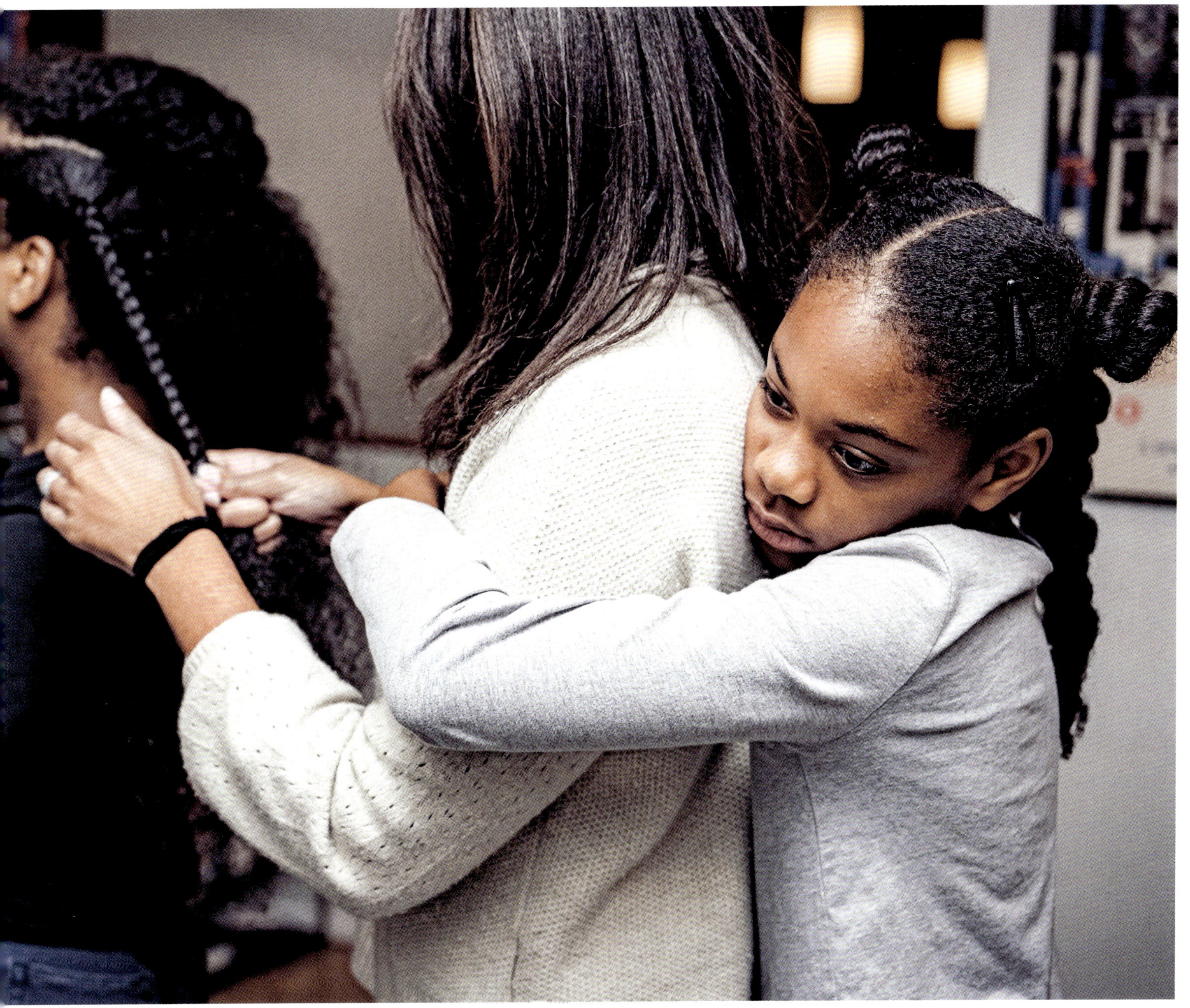

One of my most memorable shoots was probably also one of my most lengthy. I am thankful to have been able to spend the day with Dana and her two daughters, Simone and Josie, who are the same ages as my two daughters. I'll also note that I have a sister named Symone, and my oldest daughter's name is Josie. We had never met in person prior to this shoot, but by the end, we felt like old friends. I love the way Black hair has a way of building community.

There were so many memorable moments from that day. We discovered a shared love of the song "Master Blaster" as Dana started their Stevie Wonder playlist (funny, I'm actually listening to "Signed, Sealed, Delivered" as I write this). With Stevie playing in the background, we couldn't help but sing and dance. Throughout the day, Josie could be found playing in her big sister's hair. We watched some of the girls' favorite television shows, and I shared which of their beloved shows are also faves among my girls. After about an hour and a half, Josie walked up to me and said, "I'm ready for a hug now." It was like she was declaring I was no longer a stranger. It was such a sweet moment, and she reminded me so much of my daughter Abri (also a hugger). Later on, we erupted in laughter as I disclosed my absolute hatred of the word *tender*. Yuck. This prompted discussion of our shared hatred for the word *moist*. Double yuck. We laughed so hard, Dana's husband, Bobby, came into the living room where we were gathered and asked what could possibly be so funny. He was pretty underwhelmed by our answer, but the laughter was contagious.

We also shared stories that day. Dana shared how growing up, she was told she did not have "good hair" and needed a relaxer. Despite this, she remained natural all her life. When Josie asked, "Why don't you wear your hair curly, mom?" Dana responded that years of heat damage from pressing her natural hair has taken its toll. This is exactly why she doesn't use heat on their hair. She's still learning to love her texture, and she is intentional about ensuring that her girls love theirs.

By the end of the day, we were hugging and hoping to get our families together one day. Josie continued to hug me until Dana physically pried her little arms apart. I remain thankful to have been able to share this time with this sweet and beautiful family.

I'm thankful to have been able to spend time with so many families. To have earned their trust enough to be allowed into their homes to capture such intimate portraits. To have learned so much from each of them. And I'm thankful to be able to share the beauty of each of their wash-day rituals with the world.

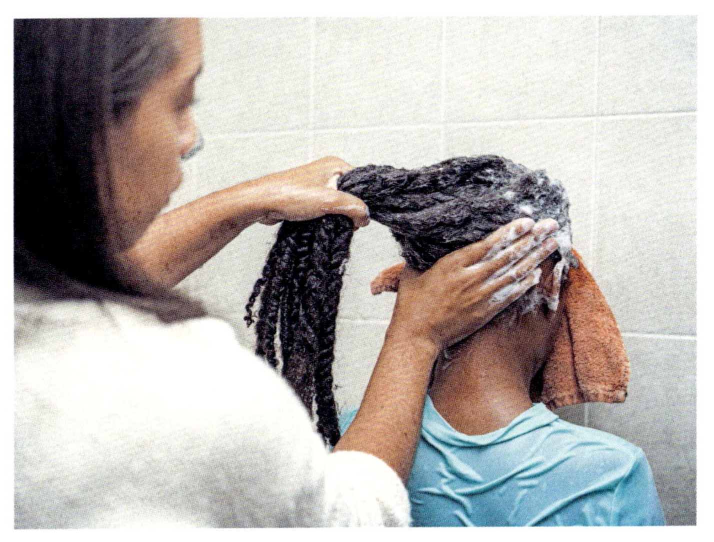
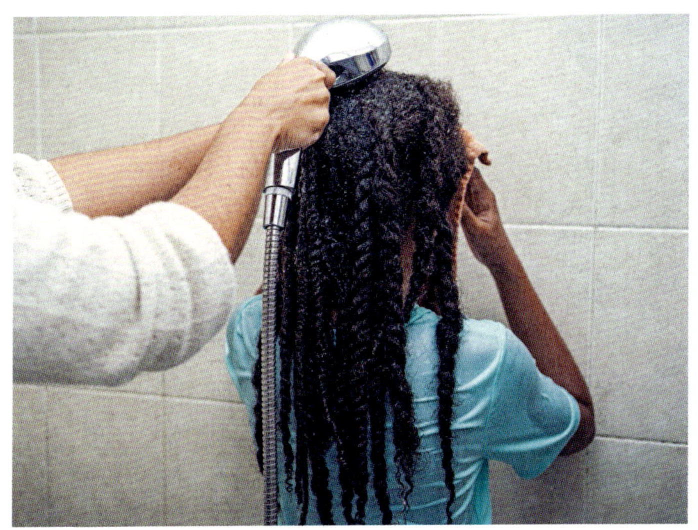
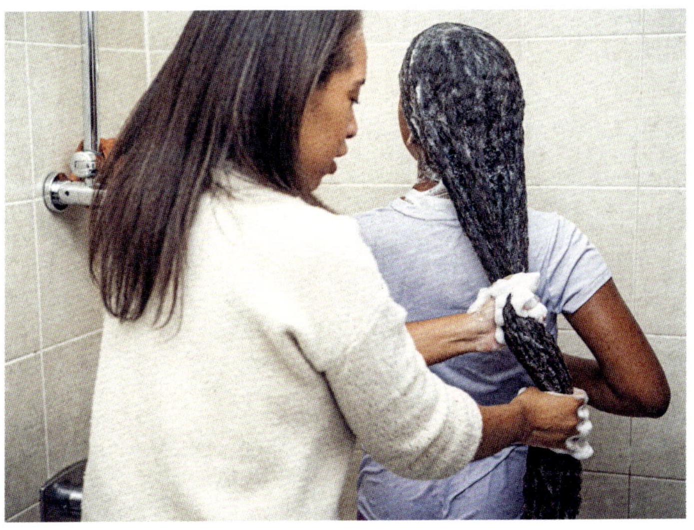
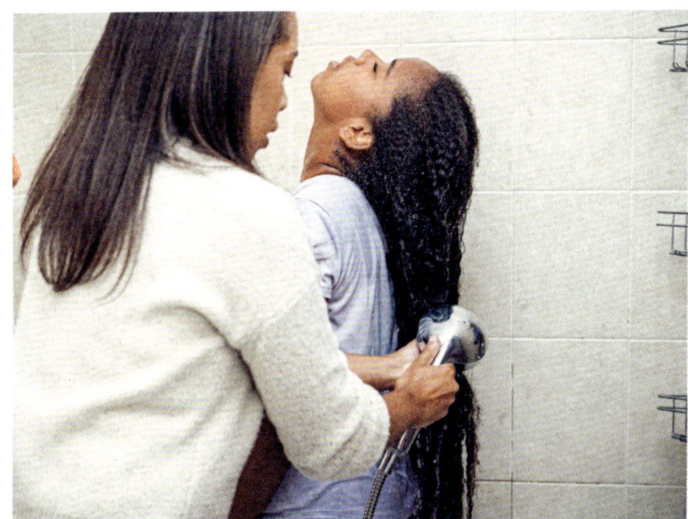

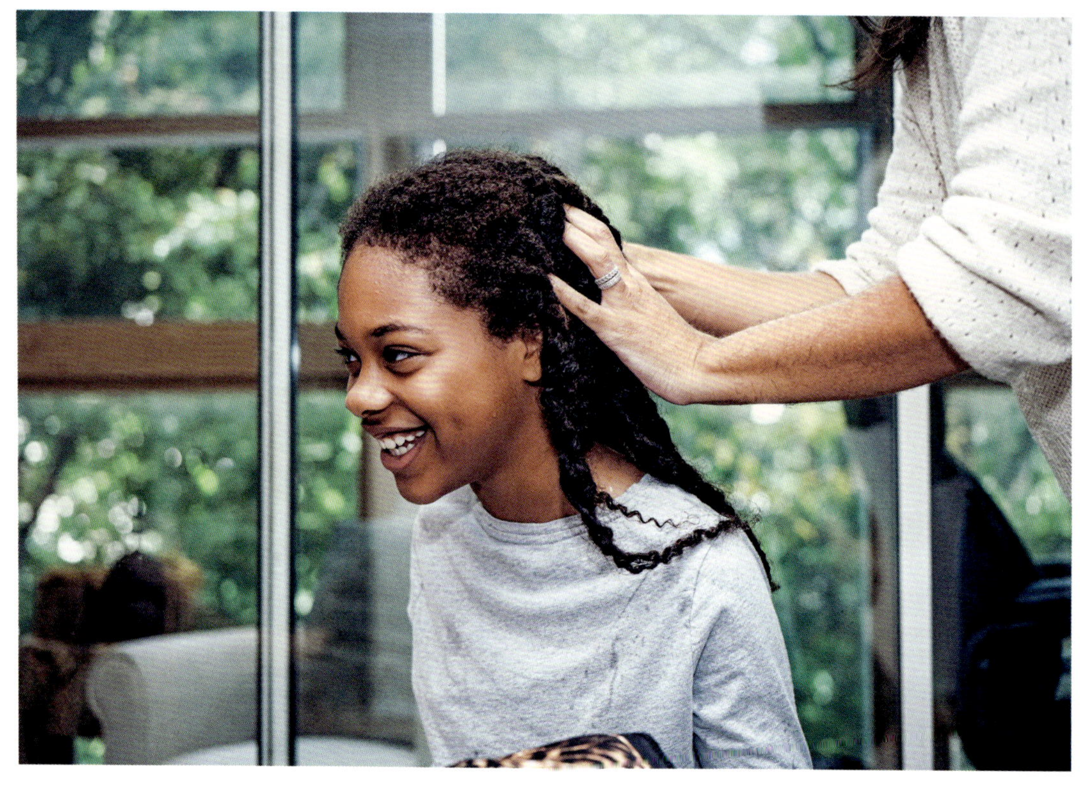

"I am happy with the hair I have.
My hair is luscious and curly." —JOSIE

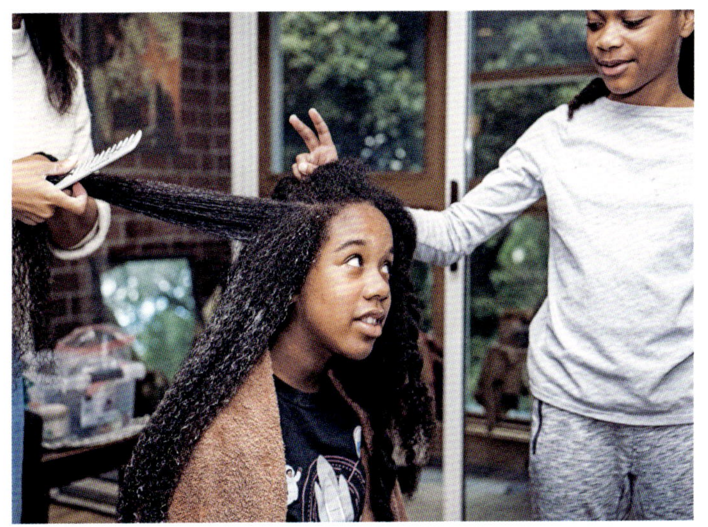
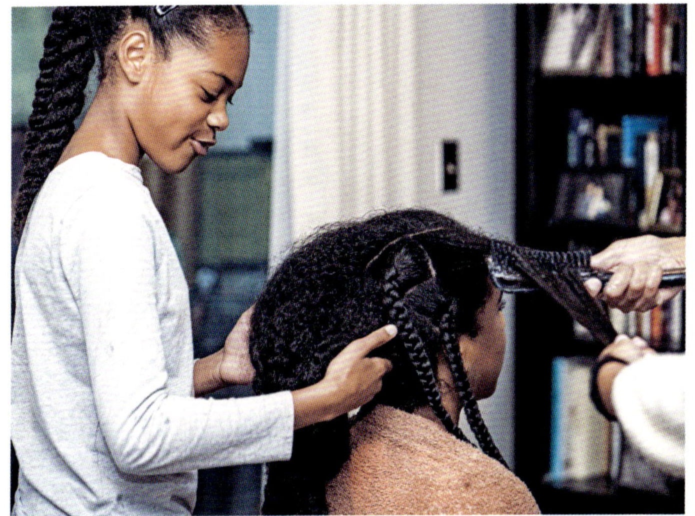
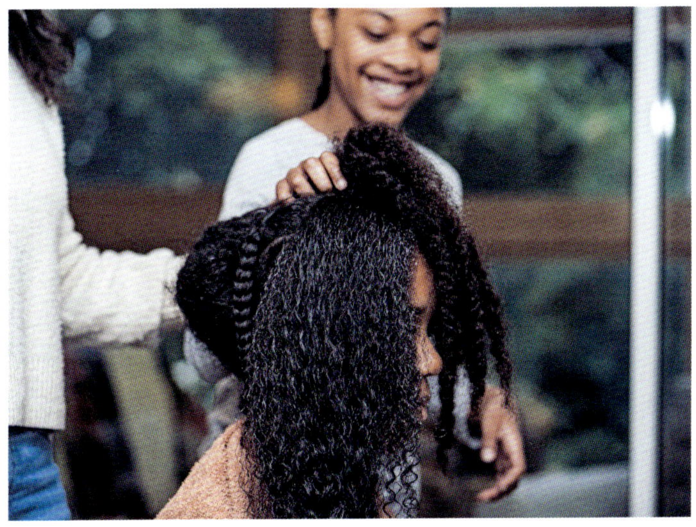
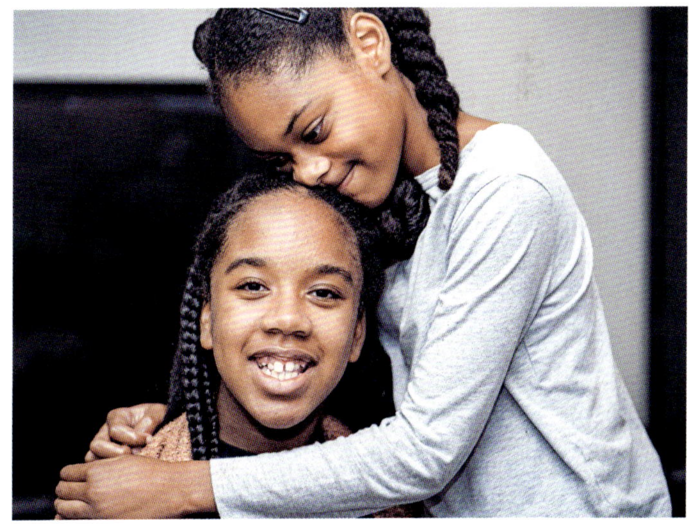

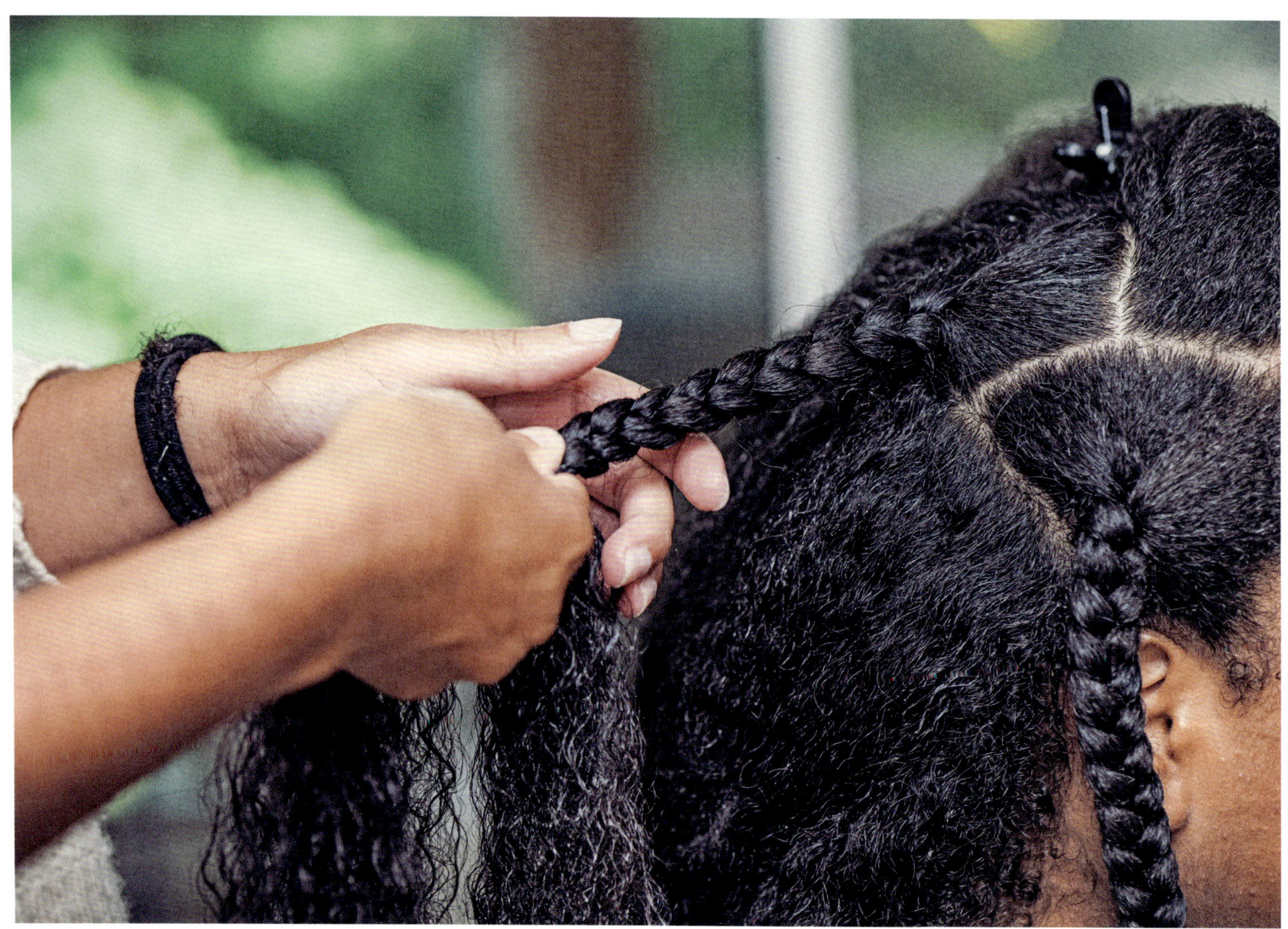

Wash day takes place every two weeks and lasts three to eight hours depending on whether Dana is washing both of their hair and what style she is doing. For small box braids, she breaks the process up over a couple of days.

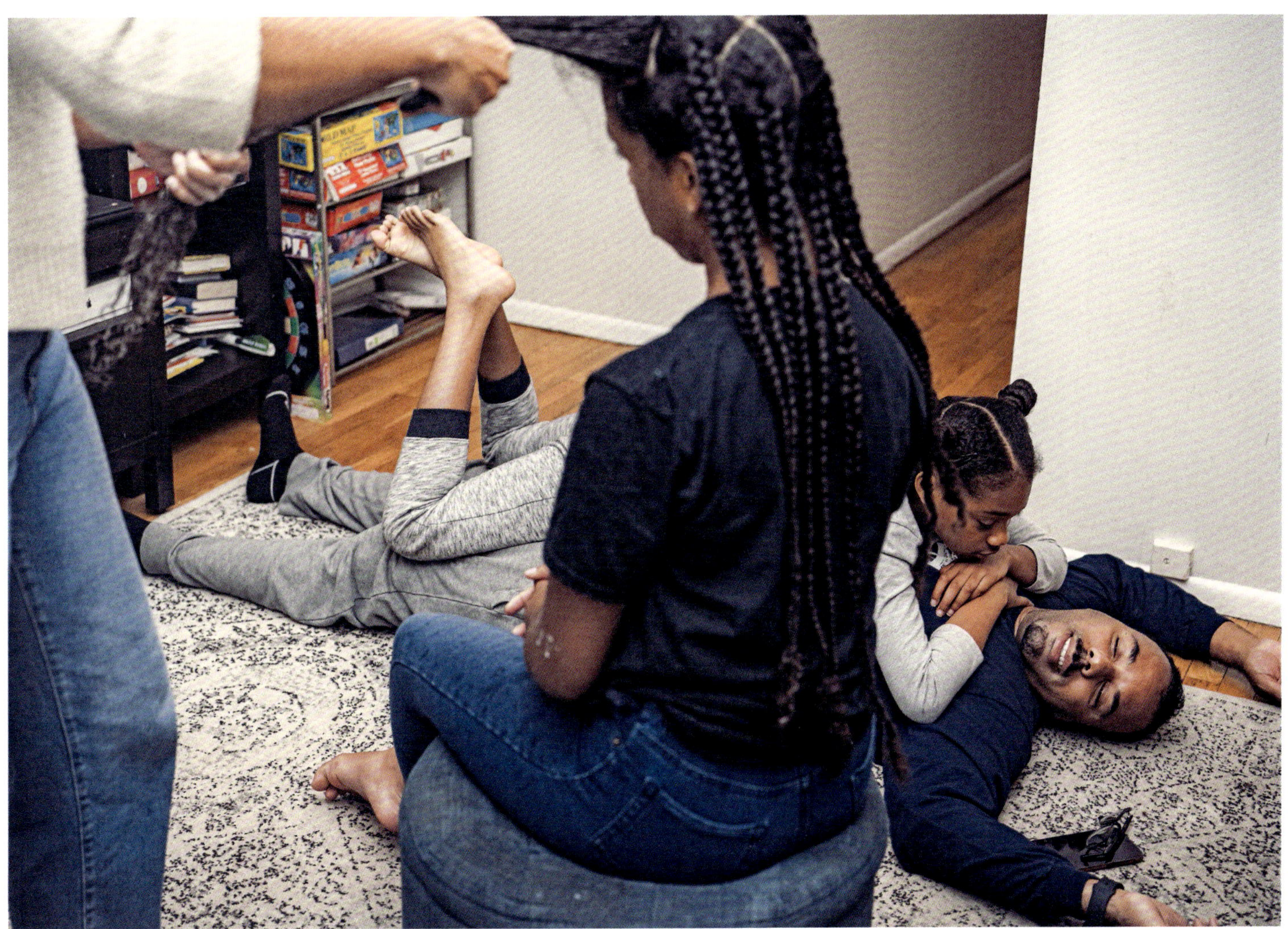

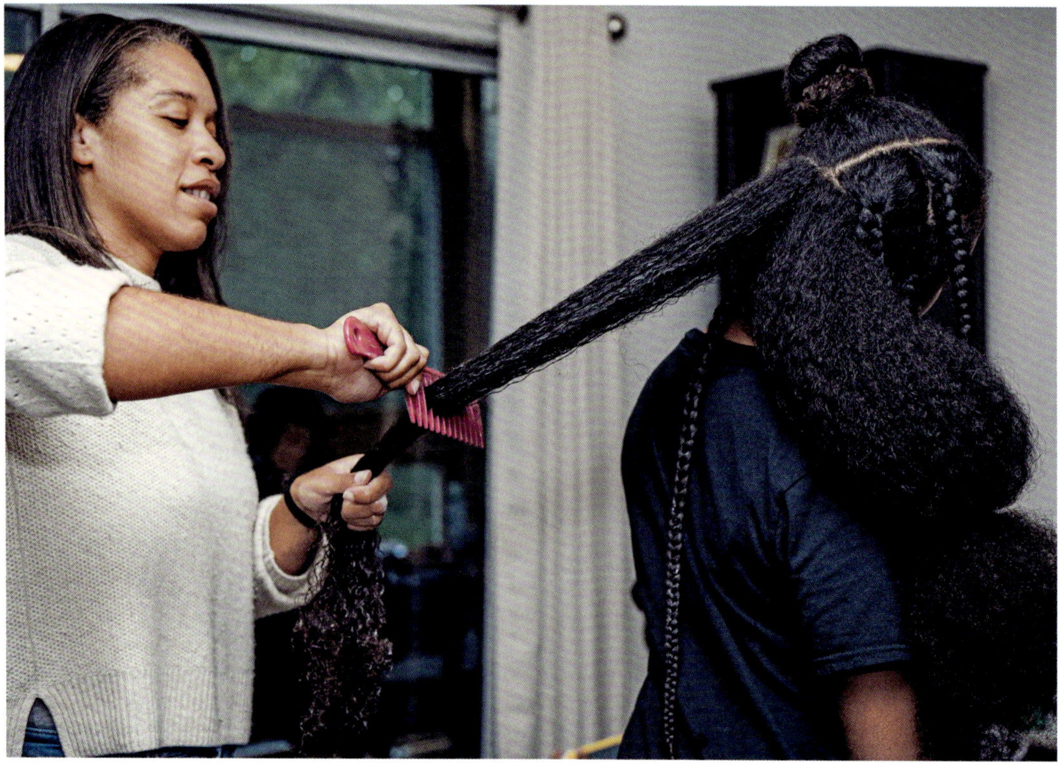

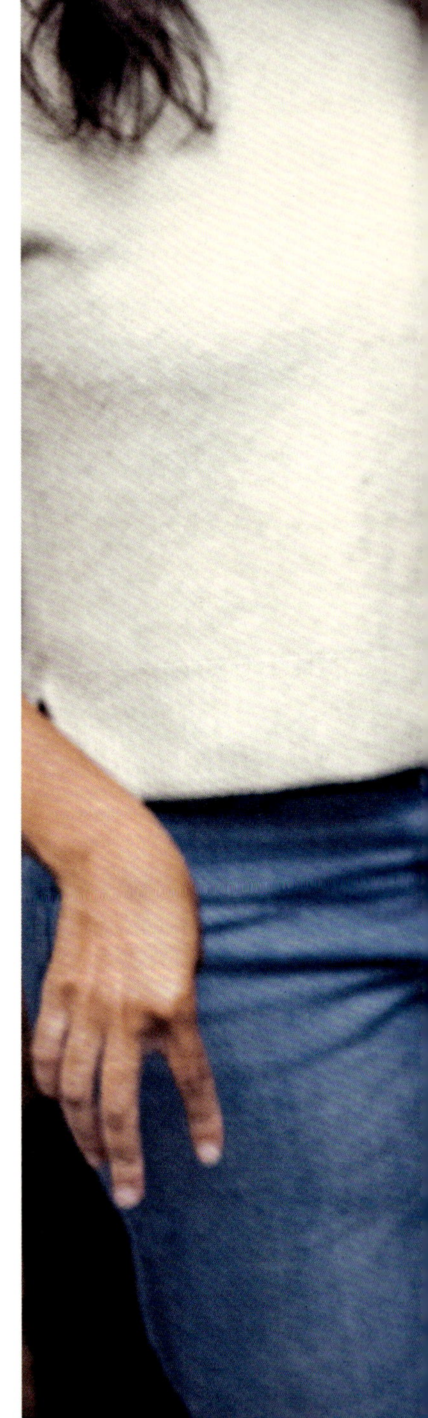

"I love my hair. It is a big part of who I am. I am glad that I am confident about my hair. I think it is really pretty." —SIMONE

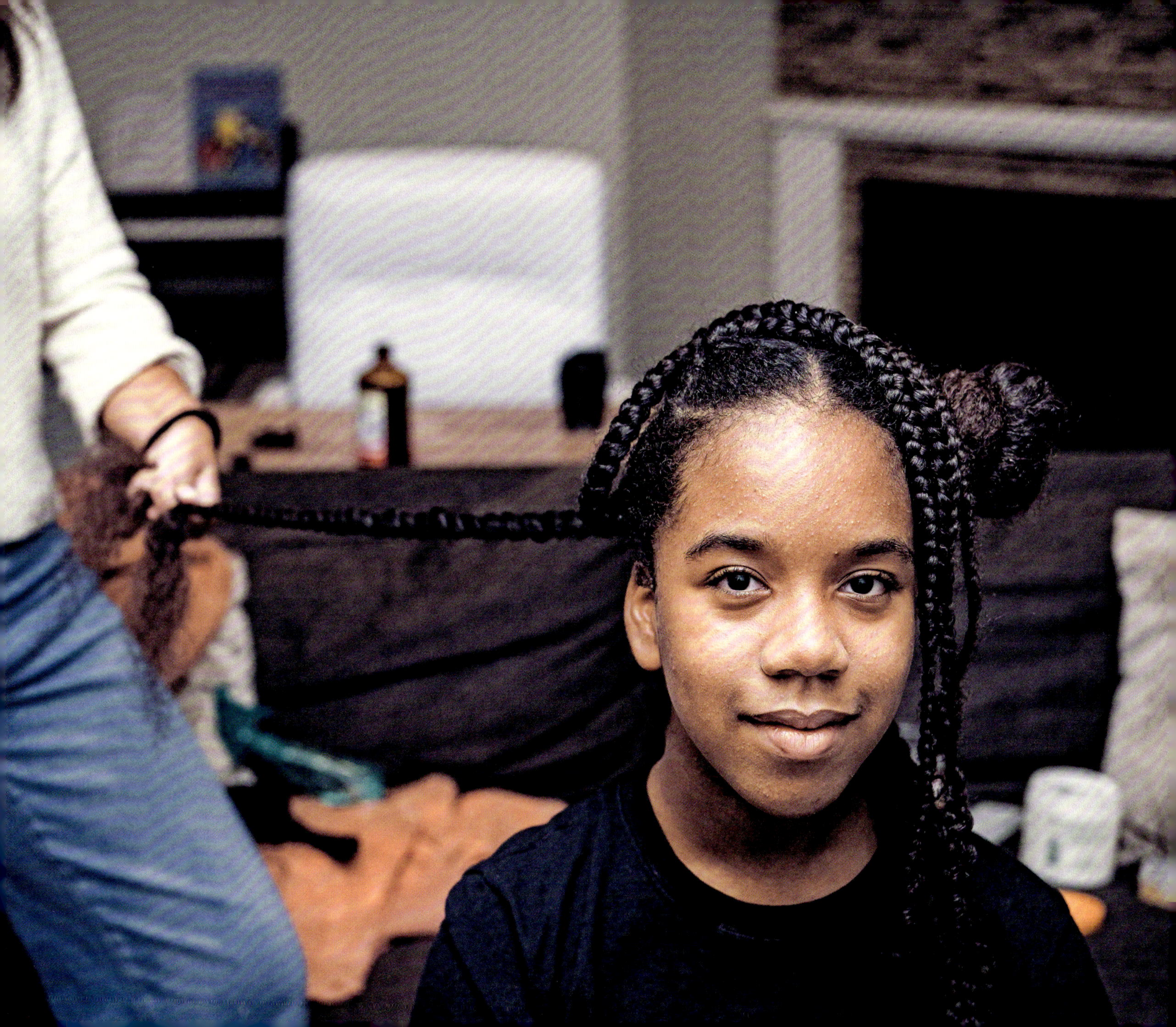

Notes

1. The definitions for the terms and processes came from multiple sources, including: "Curly Hair Glossary," Carol's Daughter, accessed February 21, 2023, https://www.carolsdaughter.com /curl-glossary.html. "Glossary," As I Am, accessed February 21, 2023, https://asiamnaturally.com/pages/glossary. "The Best Natural Hair Dictionary Online," Curl Centric, accessed February 21, 2023, https://www.curlcentric.com/natural-hair-dictionary/. Jenell Stewart, "The Essence Ultimate Natural Hair Dictionary," *Essence* (October 27, 2020), https://www.essence.com/hair/natural /essence-ultimate-natural-hair-dictionary/#339779.

2. Ayana D. Byrd and Lori L. Tharps, *Hair Story: Untangling the Roots of Black Hair in America* (New York: St. Martin's Griffin, 2014), 10.

3. Ibid.

4. Ibid, 2.

5. Ibid, 12–3.

6. Tameka N. Ellington and Joseph L. Underwood, *Textures: The History and Art of Black Hair* (Germany: Hirmer Publishers, 2020), 19.

7. Carrie Mae Weems. *The Kitchen Table Series.* 1990.

8. Ayana D. Byrd and Lori L. Tharps, *Hair Story: Untangling the Roots of Black Hair in America* (New York: St. Martin's Griffin, 2014), 56.

9. Ibid, 17.

10. Ibid, 17–8.

11. Ibid, 18.

12. Ibid, 18–9.

13. Ibid, 18–9.

14. Ibid, 19.

15. Ibid, 20.

16. Ibid, 21.

17. Emma Dabiri, *Twisted: The Tangled History of Black Hair Culture* (New York: Harper Perennial, 2020), 206.

18. Ayana D. Byrd and Lori L. Tharps, *Hair Story: Untangling the Roots of Black Hair in America* (New York: St. Martin's Griffin, 2014), 26.

19. "CROWN Act Research Studies," Dove and the CROWN Coalition, accessed February 21, 2023, https://www.thecrownact.com /research-studies.

20. Alexis McGill Johnson, Rachel D. Godsil, Jessica MacFarlane, Linda R. Tropp, and Phillip Atiba Goff, "The 'Good Hair' Study: Explicit and Implicit Attitudes Toward Black Women's Hair," *Perception Institute,* February 2017, www.goodhairstudy.com.

21. Ibid.

22. Sierra Leone Starks, "Stylists Across America Are (Finally) Getting Schooled in Black Hair." *Allure* (July 19, 2022), https://www.allure .com/story/hairstylists-curly-kinky-hair-training.

23. Britni Danielle, "Black Actors Call Out Hollywood For Lack Of Black Hairstylists." *Essence* (December 6, 2020), https://www.essence .com/entertainment/hollywood-needs-black-hairstylists/.

24. Ibid.

25. Priya Elan, "Black Actors Speak Out on Hair Mistreatment: 'I was told they didn't have the budget.' *The Guardian* (May 20, 2021), https://www.theguardian.com/fashion/2021/may/20 /black-actors-hair-mistreatment-hollywood.

26. Victoria W. Wolcott, "The Forgotten History of Segregated Swimming Pools and Amusement Parks," *The Conversation* (July 9, 2019), https://theconversation.com/the-forgotten-history-of -segregated-swimming-pools-and-amusement-parks-119586.

27. George Johnson, "Swimming's racist past makes Simone Manuel's win an even bigger deal," *Essence* (February 6, 2020), https://www .ebony.com/simone-manuel-racism/.

28. Emma Dabiri, *Twisted: The Tangled History of Black Hair Culture* (New York: Harper Perennial, 2020), 154–155.

29. Ayana D. Byrd and Lori L. Tharps, *Hair Story: Untangling the Roots of Black Hair in America* (New York: St. Martin's Griffin, 2014), 170.

30. "CROWN Act Research Studies," Dove and the CROWN Coalition, accessed February 21, 2023, https://www.thecrownact.com /research-studies.

31. Christy Zhou Koval and Ashleigh Shelby Rosette, "The Natural Hair

Bias in Job Recruitment," *Social Psychological and Personality Science* 12, No. 5 (July 2021): 741–50. https://doi.org/10.1177/1948550620937937.

32. "CROWN Act Research Studies," Dove and the CROWN Coalition, accessed February 21, 2023, https://www.thecrownact.com/research-studies.

33. The Official CROWN Act website, Dove and the CROWN Coalition, accessed September 21, 2023, https://www.thecrownact.com/.

34. Ayana D. Byrd and Lori L. Tharps, *Hair Story: Untangling the Roots of Black Hair in America* (New York: St. Martin's Griffin, 2014), 26.

35. Ibid, 28.

36. Ibid, 60.

37. Allison Samuels, "Gabby Douglas Takes Two Olympic Golds—And Hair Criticism." *Daily Beast* (August 2, 2012), https://www.thedailybeast.com/gabby-douglas-takes-two-olympic-goldsand-hair-criticism.

38. Malcolm X, *February 1965: The Final Speeches* (New York: Pathfinder Press, 1992), 157–8.

39. *The Color Purple,* directed by Steven Spielberg, story by Alice Walker, Warner Brothers, 1985.

40. "CROWN Act Research Studies," Dove and the CROWN Coalition, accessed February 21, 2023, https://www.thecrownact.com/research-studies.

41. Monnica T. Williams, "Microaggressions: Clarification, Evidence, and Impact," *Perspectives on Psychological Science* 15, No. 1 (January 2020): 3–26. https://doi.org/10.1177/1745691619827499.

42. Chester M. Pierce. "Psychiatric Problems of the Black Minority," *American Handbook of Psychiatry* 2 (1974): 512–23.

43. Sue, D. W., Capodilupo, C. M., Torino, G. C., Bucceri, J. M., Holder, A. M. B., Nadal, K. L., and Esquilin, M., "Racial Microaggressions in Everyday Life: Implications for clinical practice," *American Psychologist* 62, No.4 (2007): 271–86. https://doi.org/10.1037/0003-066X.62.4.271.

44. Monnica T. Williams, "Microaggressions: Clarification, Evidence, and Impact," *Perspectives on Psychological Science* 15, No. 1 (January 2020): 3–26. https://doi.org/10.1177/1745691619827499.

45. Ibid.

46. Che-Jung Chang, Katie M. O'Brien, Alexander P. Keil, Symielle A. Gaston, Chandra L. Jackson, Dale P. Sandler, and Alexandra J. White, "Use of Straighteners and Other Hair Products and Incident Uterine Cancer," *JNCI: Journal of the National Cancer Institute* 114, No. 12 (December 2022): 1636–45. https://doi.org/10.1093/jnci/djac165.

47. Mechal Renee Roe, *Happy Hair* (New York: Doubleday Books for Young Readers, 2020).

48. Natasha Anastasia Tarpley, *I Love My Hair!* (New York: Little, Brown Books for Young Readers; Reprint edition, 2001).

49. Ibid.

50. Alexis McGill Johnson, Rachel D. Godsil, Jessica MacFarlane, Linda R. Tropp, and Phillip Atiba Goff, "The 'Good Hair' Study: Explicit and Implicit Attitudes Toward Black Women's Hair," *Perception Institute,* February 2017, www.goodhairstudy.com.

51. Emma Dabiri, *Twisted: The Tangled History of Black Hair Culture* (New York: Harper Perennial, 2020), 50.

Acknowledgments

Whew. Here goes.

Thank you, Mama and Grandma, for teaching me what you could about hair.

Thank you, Dee and George, for giving me that camera.

Thank you, Joe, for being supportive when I decided to quit my job to pursue photography (twice).

Thank you to all of my former coworkers who told me I should quit my job and become a photographer.

Thank you, Dad, for never questioning my decision to change careers.

Thank you, Leslie, for urging me to get started.

Thank you, Titilayo, for sending me Kate's website.

Thank you, Kate, for believing in the vision.

Thank you, Sahara, for helping me write the vision.

Thank you, Jennifer, for helping me make the vision tangible.

Thank you, Clarkson Potter editing team, for ensuring semicolons are not misused in this book.

Thank you, Toni, for always asking how you can help—and actually helping.

Thank you to my day-ones who have supported, cheered, liked, shared, and followed.

Thank you to every Black woman who shared their story with me.

And of course, thank you to every family that allowed me to witness and photograph their wash day.

About the Author

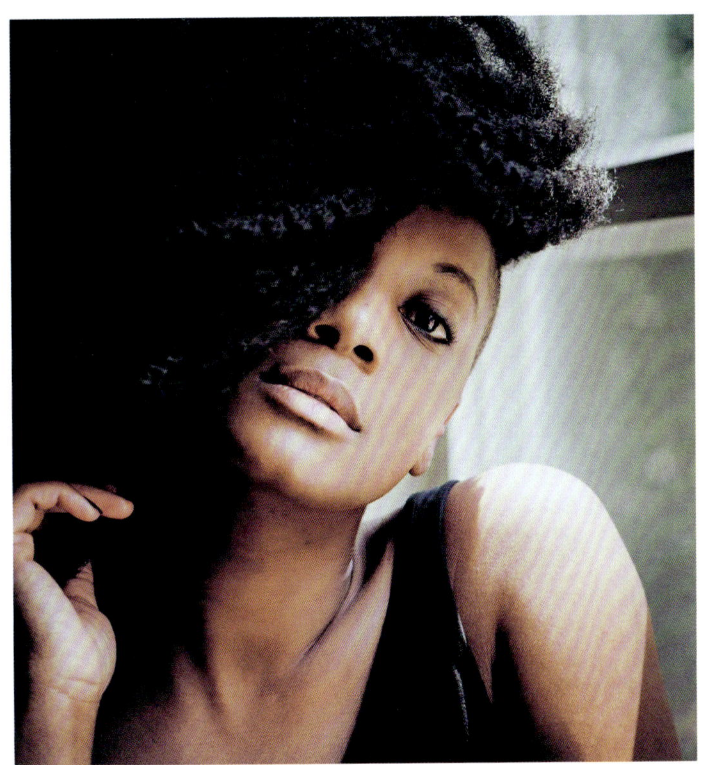

Tomesha Faxio is a self-taught documentary photographer dedicated to portraying and centering the Black experience. Tomesha strives to tell authentic stories that both inform and inspire. Before becoming a photographer, Tomesha was an intellectual property attorney. She is a graduate of Spelman College (BA, psychology) and Vanderbilt Law School (JD), and now lives with her husband and two daughters in Atlanta, Georgia.

Copyright © 2024 by Tomesha Faxio

All rights reserved.

Published in the United States by Clarkson Potter/Publishers, an imprint of the Crown Publishing Group, a division of Penguin Random House LLC, New York.
ClarksonPotter.com

CLARKSON POTTER is a trademark and POTTER with colophon is a registered trademark of Penguin Random House LLC.

Library of Congress Cataloging-in-Publication Data is on file with the publisher.

ISBN 978-0-593-57971-8
Ebook ISBN 978-0-593-57972-5

Printed in China

Editor: Sahara Clement
Designer: Jen Wang
Production editor: Sohayla Farman
Production manager: Kim Tyner
Compositors: Merri Ann Morrell and Hannah Hunt
Copyeditor: Janina Lawrence | Proofreader: Adaobi Obi Tulton
Publicist: Erica Gelbard | Marketer: Joey Lozada

10 9 8 7 6 5 4 3 2 1

First Edition